THE
BOOK OF
JEWISH
KNOWLEDGE

THE BOOK OF JEWISH KNOWLEDGE

613 Basic Facts about Judaism

Rabbi David E. Cahn-Lipman

JASON ARONSON INC.
Northvale, New Jersey
London

Production Editor and Interior Designer: Gloria Jordan
Editorial Director: Muriel Jorgensen
This book was set in 10 point Bernhard Modern by Books of Alabama.
It was printed and bound by Haddon Craftsmen of Pennsylvania.

First Jason Aronson Inc. Softcover Edition—1994

Library of Congress Cataloging-in-Publication Data

Cahn-Lipman, David E.
  The book of Jewish knowledge: 613 basic facts about Judaism / by
  David E. Cahn-Lipman.
    p.   cm.
  Includes index.
  ISBN 0-87668-575-0 (hardcover)
  ISBN 1-56821-182-1 (paperback)
    1. Judaism—Outlines, syllabi, etc.   2. Jews—History—Outlines,
  syllabi, etc.   3. Bible. O.T.—Outlines, syllabi, etc.   4. Israel—
  History—Outlines, syllabi, etc.   I. Title.
  BM51.C35   1991
  296'.02'02—dc20   91-10760

Manufactured in the United States of America. Jason Aronson Inc. offers books and cassettes. For information and catalog write to Jason Aronson Inc., 230 Livingston Street, Northvale, New Jersey 07647.

This book is dedicated to Eugene J. Lipman—
a scholar,
a rabbi,
a fiery prophetic voice,
a farmer,
a wonderful, supportive father—
with love

Contents

TaNaCH

Ritual Objects, Dress, and Prayer

History, Jewish Texts, and Tradition

Israel: The Geography and History of the Modern State

Jewish Thought and Values

Part III.   Two Self-tests

Index

Acknowledgment

The following people generously shared their time and knowledge in order to improve this book: Rabbi Lawrence Hoffman, Rabbi Leonard Kravitz, Rabbi Lisa Vernon, Rabbi Shaye Cohen, Rabbi Eugene Lipman, Rabbi Stephen Weisman, Dr. David Marcus, David Mallach, and Adele Rosenfeld. I am grateful to them for their help.

I also thank Kivie and Shira for their patience and understanding. For Kivie, this book represents hundreds of sacrificed computer game hours. For Shira, it represents hundreds of missed opportunities to play "house." Both accepted their losses graciously, and I appreciate it.

Introduction

One of my colleagues gave an Adult Education lecture on the Book of Genesis. He carefully described the different schools of scholarship that had analyzed its development, redaction, and emendation. He showed literary parallels to other works in the Middle East. His talk was a solidly presented piece of scholarship. When he asked for questions, one sweet lady stood up and said, "Rabbi, I loved your lecture. You are so knowledgeable, and it was a pleasure to listen to you. But tell me, Rabbi, please, what is a Genesis?"

We are living in an age of polarized extremes. On the one hand, our Jewish Adult Education and Judaic Studies programs are at a higher level of scholarship than they have been in over two thousand years. We know more details about Judaism and its development than in any other time of history. We are blessed with a plethora of superb lecturers and teachers who provide us with exciting presentations on every aspect of our tradition.

On the other hand, because few of us live a traditional Jewish life-style or have the time to study our texts, the vast majority of us don't recognize Jewish terms and names that used to be as familiar to the average Jew as Big Bird is to our children. We are often forced to ask "What is a Genesis?"

The purpose of this book is to help the reader become familiar with all those once-common names, objects, rituals, events, and Jewish concepts. There is irony in this. Although our tradition is a vast ocean of thoughts, stories, and laws, Judaism's basic terms are fairly few in number. It is possible to learn about them through a series of simple, one-sentence statements. That's the essence of this book.

If you can learn the 613 one-sentence building blocks in this book, you will be able to catch Jewish references in novels, understand lectures and discussions on every aspect of Judaism, and feel confident about your basic knowledge of our tradition.

That confidence is extremely important. The vast majority of us stopped studying Judaism when we were, at most, 13 years old. We haven't really lived our tradition. That makes Judaism foreign, arcane, mysterious to us. We are highly literate in our professions and our secular world, but Jewish knowledge has slipped past us. We don't know the basics, and that makes us uncomfortable and defensive. We tend to stay away from things that make us feel uncomfortable, and we therefore avoid Adult Education courses on Judaism.

If we do get brave and attend an Adult Education lecture, the details that assail us convince us that we just won't be able to get a real handle on the material. What is essential to know? What is extraneous detail? What is a Genesis? We remain overwhelmed.

This book will help you get rid of those defensive feelings. It will provide you with fact associations for every aspect of Judaism. It will help you focus on what is really important to know in our tradition. By pinpointing exactly what you need to know, this book makes it easy for you to assimilate basic Jewish knowledge. Once you feel that you are Jewishly literate, you will feel better about going to an Adult Education lecture to learn more about a given Jewish topic. This book can be the door to a new world of comfortable Jewish study.

This book began as a preparation program for Bar and Bat Mitzvah children. I wanted my 12-year-old students to develop fact associations in their minds that would stay with them for the rest of their lives. I made the facts into a game, a combination of Jeopardy® and Trivial Pursuit®. The only difference is that these data aren't trivial.

It quickly became clear that children learned most effectively when their parents participated in the process. This text, therefore, became a family education resource book. Part III of this book contains two self-tests with questions referring back to the facts and data. Some facts have more than one question (note numbering system). Some questions appear in both self-tests. Where there is a gap in the numbers, it means that the question has been answered elsewhere. If you create a game for learning these facts, you can succeed with your own Family Jewish Education Program. Use the self-test questions to make a set of flash cards for each fact. They will help you teach yourself and your children the basic building blocks.

Think of the Suzuki method for learning a musical instrument. Parent and child play together, and both succeed. By systematically flipping through your Fact flash cards, you can help your child achieve basic Jewish literacy simply and painlessly. And you will benefit as well.

One of the exciting aspects of Judaism is how beautifully our basic terms, events, and concepts intertwine. Each fact becomes a building block inextricably connected to other facts. In trying to help you retain the basic fact associations, I have cross-referenced each term used in the text to show those interconnections. By referring back to the cross-referenced one-sentence facts, you can reinforce your basic Jewish vocabulary of terms and events. As soon as you realize how much you really know and can retain, your willingness to delve further into these topics should increase.

It is not coincidental that I divided Judaism into 613 one-sentence facts. The number 613 is a significant one in our tradition. Almost two thousand years ago, a rabbi said that the Torah contained 613 mitzvot (commandments). These commandments became the starting point for Jewish law. Every letter in Hebrew has a numerical value. The Hebrew letters for 613 form the acronym *TaRYaG*. Therefore the commandments are frequently called *TaRYaG*, 613.

Over the centuries, thousands of rules were discussed and formulated based on *TaRYaG*. Jewish law and its discussions became a veritable ocean of words, as large as a modern lawyer's library.

In the twelfth century a great scholar, RaMBaM, reduced that ocean of laws into a fourteen-volume code. In his introduction he said, "You don't have to read any other text." Unlike RaMBaM's code, my book is not "all you need to know." It's only a beginning. It will provide you with the vocabulary and knowledge necessary for further Jewish learning. It will make the joy of Jewish study comfortably available to you. This text can serve as a bucket to begin collecting the rest of the ocean.

Hillel, a sage who lived two thousand years ago, was once challenged to reduce Judaism to its simplest essence. He answered, "What is hateful to you, do not do to anyone else. That is the whole of Torah. The rest is commentary. *Go and learn it.*" The facts in this book are the basics of Judaism. The rest is an exciting world of thought and detail. Go and learn it.

Part I

FACTS

Holidays

1. Rosh Chodesh is the celebration of the New Moon.
2. A "normal" Jewish year has 354 days.
3. During a Jewish leap year we add the month Adar II.
4. The Jewish day starts at sundown.
5. We light candles to begin most holidays.
6. We drink wine on every holiday to make the day holy, except on fast days.
7. On a number of holidays we read special Psalms called the Hallel.
8. Rosh HaShanah, Yom Kippur, Sukkot, and Simchat Torah all occur in the month of Tishri.
9. Rosh HaShanah and Yom Kippur are called the Yamim Nora'im.
10. On Rosh HaShanah we say "L'Shanah tovah tikatayvu."
11. The goal of the Yamim Nora'im is teshuvah, returning.
12. We prepare for the Yamim Nora'im throughout the whole Hebrew month of Elul.
13. We recite Selichot, prayers asking for forgiveness, on the Saturday night before Rosh HaShanah.
14. Rosh HaShanah celebrates the creation of the world.
15. On Rosh HaShanah we eat apples and honey.
16. Many Jews eat round challahs on Rosh HaShanah.
17. Tradition teaches that Isaac and Samuel were born on Rosh HaShanah.

18.   Rosh HaShanah is called Yom HaZikaron, the Day of Remembrance.

19.   Avinu Malkaynu means, "Our Father our King."

20.   On Rosh HaShanah traditionally we blow the shofar 100 times.

21.   Tashlich is the ritual of tossing our sins into a river on Rosh HaShanah.

22.   There are ten days between Rosh HaShanah and Yom Kippur.

23.   Shabbat Shuvah is the Shabbat between Rosh HaShanah and Yom Kippur.

24.   We fast on Yom Kippur.

25.   The best-known prayer on Yom Kippur is Kol Nidrei.

26.   On the Yamim Nora'im, we ask God to forgive us for all the wrongs we committed during the year.

27.   Sukkot, Pesach, and Shavuot are the three festivals on which Jews used to bring offerings to the Temple.

28.   Sukkot celebrates the fruit harvest.

29.   There are five days between Yom Kippur and Sukkot.

30.   The lulav is made of palm, myrtle, and willow.

31.   On Sukkot we wave the lulav and etrog.

32.   We build a sukkah on Sukkot.

33.   Special guests invited to the sukkah are called Ushpizin.

34.   On Sukkot we read the megillah (scroll) of Kohelet (Ecclesiastes).

35.   Atzeret is celebrated by many Reform Jews as Simchat Torah.

36.   Simchat Torah celebrates our finishing the reading of the Torah and immediately beginning to read it again.

37.   Hakafot are processions of congregants around the synagogue with the Torah scrolls.

38.   Chanukkah celebrates the time when King Antiochus tried to destroy Judaism but failed.

39.   The Jewish rebellion found its leadership in the priestly Hasmonean family.

40.   The Jewish priest Mattathias began the revolt against the Greek king Antiochus.

41.   The Jewish general leading the Hasmonean revolt was Judah the Maccabee.

42. Originally, Chanukkah lasted for eight days because it substituted for Sukkot.

43. Chanukkah begins on the 25th of the month of Kislev.

44. A Chanukkah legend says that oil enough for only one day burned in the Temple for eight days.

45. On Chanukkah we light a nine-branched candelabrum called a chanukkiyah.

46. The shamash (servant candle) lights the other eight candles in the chanukkiyah.

47. On Chanukkah we eat latkes.

48. On Chanukkah we play with a dreidl.

49. Tu BiShvat is the New Year of the Trees.

50. We plant trees in Israel and eat a variety of fruit on Tu BiShvat.

51. Adar is the last month in the Jewish calendar.

52. On Purim we read the Book of Esther from a scroll (megillah).

53. The name of God isn't mentioned in the Book of Esther.

54. The foolish king in the Purim story was Ahasuerus.

55. The first queen in the Purim story was Vashti.

56. The second queen in the Purim story was Esther.

57. Haman tossed purim (dice) to decide when to slaughter the Jews.

58. Purim occurs on the 14th day of the month of Adar.

59. Purim reminds us of how we were saved from Haman's plot to slaughter all Jews.

60. Adloyada is a Purim parade in Israel.

61. Before Purim, we read the commandment to wipe out the memory of Amalek.

62. We wipe out Haman's name on Purim by making noise with a gragger.

63. On Purim we eat hamentaschen.

64. Pesach begins on the 15th of Nisan.

65. Pesach lasts seven days.

66. On Pesach we don't eat anything that has leaven or yeast in it.

67. Shabbat HaGadol is the Sabbath before Pesach.

68. Pesach celebrates our escape from slavery in Egypt.

69. Pesach began the barley harvest in Israel.

70. On Pesach we eat matzah.

71. The lamb bone on Pesach reminds us of the Divine passing over the Hebrew homes in Egypt.

72. Maror are the bitter herbs we eat on Pesach.

73. The seder is a ritual meal we eat on Pesach.

74. On Pesach we eat charoset, which reminds us of the building mortar we used as slaves.

75. The afikoman is our Pesach dessert.

76. On Pesach we invite Elijah the prophet into our homes.

77. On Pesach we say, "Next year in Jerusalem."

78. On Pesach we read the megillah (scroll) of Song of Songs.

79. The Haggadah, the Telling, is the book we use at the seder on Pesach.

80. Shavuot began the wheat harvest in Israel.

81. There are seven weeks between Pesach and Shavuot.

82. The thirty-third day between Pesach and Shavuot is called Lag BaOmer.

83. Jews brought their first offerings to the Temple on Shavuot.

84. On Shavuot we received the Torah on Mount Sinai.

85. Many Jews stay up all night on Shavuot studying the Torah.

86. On Shavuot we read the Ten Commandments.

87. On Shavuot we read the megillah (scroll) of the Book of Ruth.

88. On Shavuot we eat blintzes and dairy foods.

89. Confirmation takes place on Shavuot.

90. Yom HaShoah reminds us of the Jews who died in the Holocaust.

91. Yom HaAtzmaut is Israel's Independence Day.

92. On Tisha B'Av we fast.

93. According to tradition, Tisha B'Av is the anniversary of the destruction of both the first and second Temples.

94. On Tisha B'Av we read the megillah (scroll) of Lamentations.

95. Shabbat reminds us of the Exodus from Egypt and God's finishing the creation of the world.

96. Traditionally, two challot are eaten on Shabbat to remind us of the double portion of manna in the desert.

97. On Shabbat we don't perform tasks we do the rest of the week.

98. An eruv is a special fence that enables traditional Jews to carry things out of their homes on Shabbat.

99. Kabbalat Shabbat is the ritual that welcomes Shabbat.

100. The Shabbat song "L'cha Dodi" welcomes Shabbat as a bride.

101. Cholent is a meat, bean, and potato stew traditionally eaten on Shabbat.

102. Havdalah ends Shabbat.

103. The three objects used for Havdalah are a glass of wine, a spice box, and a braided candle.

TaNaCH

104. The TaNaCH is divided into three parts: Torah, Prophets, and Writings.

105. The Torah consists of five books.

106. The first book of the Torah is Genesis.

107. Exodus tells how we were freed from Egypt.

108. Leviticus tells about our holidays and the sacrifices to God.

109. Numbers describes our wandering in the desert.

110. Deuteronomy is composed of three long speeches by Moses.

111. God created light on the first day of creation.

112. God created the world in six days.

113. God created Shabbat on the seventh day.

114. Adam was the first man.

115. Eve was the first woman.

116. Cain killed his brother Abel.

117. God commanded Noah to build an ark to save his family and him from the flood.

118. After the flood a dove found an olive branch, proof that there was dry land.

119. God made an agreement with Noah never to flood the world again.

120. The sign of God's agreement with Noah was a rainbow.

121. Because of the Tower of Babel, people were given many different languages and were dispersed around the world.

122.	Abraham was the first Hebrew.
123.	Sarah was Abraham's wife.
124.	Lot was Abraham's nephew.
125.	Hagar was the mother of Ishmael, Abraham's oldest son.
126.	As part of his convenant with God, Abraham was commanded to circumcise his sons.
127.	Abraham pleaded with God not to destroy Sodom and Gemorrah.
128.	Lot's wife turned into a pillar of salt.
129.	Sarah and Abraham's son was Isaac.
130.	The Akedah tells how Abraham sacrificed a ram instead of his son Isaac.
131.	Abraham bought a cave at Hebron, where he buried Sarah.
132.	Abraham's servant Eliezer found a wife for Isaac.
133.	Rebecca was Isaac's wife.
134.	Isaac and Rebecca had two sons: Jacob and Esau.
135.	Jacob cheated Esau out of his birthright.
136.	Jacob cheated Esau out of his special blessing.
137.	Jacob had a dream about a ladder and angels.
138.	Jacob married Leah and Rachel.
139.	Jacob had twelve sons and one daughter.
140.	Jacob's two youngest sons were Joseph and Benjamin.
141.	Jacob wrestled with an angel, and his name was changed to Israel.
142.	Jacob's twelve sons were the ancestors of the twelve tribes of Israel.
143.	Joseph had a special coat of many colors.
144.	Joseph's brothers sold him into slavery.
145.	Joseph became Pharaoh's second-in-command.
146.	Joseph had two children: Ephraim and Menasseh.
147.	Jacob and his family moved to Egypt because of Joseph.
148.	Moses lived *after* Abraham, Isaac, Jacob, Joseph, Sarah, Rebecca, Rachel, and Leah.
149.	The Hebrews became slaves in Egypt.
150.	Amram and Yocheved were Moses' parents.

151. Aaron was Moses' brother.

152. Miriam was Moses' sister.

153. Moses' wife was Tzipporah.

154. Moses saw a bush burning that wasn't consumed by the flames.

155. God's message to Pharaoh via Moses was, "Let My people go, so that they may serve Me."

156. God used the ten plagues to force the Egyptians to let the Hebrews go.

157. When God parted the Sea of Reeds, we sang, "Mi Chamocha?" "Who is like You, Adonai?"

158. Amalek attacked the Hebrews in the desert.

159. We received the Torah at Mount Sinai.

160. The Ten Commandments are found in Exodus 20 and in Deuteronomy 5.

161. The Ten Commandments are:

> I am Adonai, who brought you out of Egypt.
> Don't worship idols.
> Don't swear by God's name falsely.
> Keep the Sabbath.
> Honor your parents.
> Don't murder.
> Don't commit adultery.
> Don't steal.
> Don't lie as a witness.
> Don't covet what your neighbor has.

162. There are 613 mitzvot (commandments) in the Torah.

163. When Moses saw people worshiping the Golden Calf, he smashed the stones that held the commandments.

164. The Mishkan was the portable Temple in the desert.

165. The Temple menorah had seven branches.

166. Bezalel was the artist who made the Ark and Mishkan.

167. The priests were responsible for performing the rituals of the sacrificial cult.

168. The priests came from the tribe of Levi.

169. The Hebrew word for our priests was Kohanim.

170.   Aaron was the first High Priest.

171.   The High Priest wore a crown, a breastplate, a mantle, a sash, and bells.

172.   Leviticus 19 commands, "You shall be holy," because God is holy.

173.   Leviticus 19 commands, "Love your neighbor as yourself."

174.   Sh'mittah occurs every seventh year in Israel; the land must not be used for agriculture.

175.   Nadav and Avihu, two sons of Aaron, were struck by fire.

176.   Moses sent twelve scouts into Canaan to evaluate the land.

177.   Ten scouts gave the people frightening reports about Canaan, but Joshua ben Nun and Caleb ben Yefuneh told the people to trust in God.

178.   Korach attempted a revolution against Moses and Aaron.

179.   At Merribah Moses disobeyed God and struck a rock to get water.

180.   Zelophechad's daughters were allowed to own land in Canaan.

181.   If someone killed somebody accidentally, he or she could be protected at a City of Refuge.

182.   Moses died at the end of Deuteronomy.

183.   Joshua ben Nun led the people into the Land of Canaan.

184.   Charismatic fighting leaders were called judges.

185.   Deborah and Barak defeated Sisera's army at Mount Tabor.

186.   Deborah was a prophet and judge.

187.   Gideon defeated the Midianites.

188.   Samson's strength came from his hair.

189.   In the TaNaCH, the major enemies of the Hebrews were the Philistines.

190.   Delilah tricked Samson and had his hair cut.

191.   Hannah was the mother of Samuel.

192.   Saul was the first king of Israel.

193.   As a prophet, Samuel declared Saul king and, later, anointed David as king after Saul.

194.   David killed a Philistine giant named Goliath.

195.   David and Saul's son Jonathan were good friends.

196.	Saul and Jonathan were killed by Philistines on Mount Gilboah.
197.	David was the second king of Israel.
198.	David made Jerusalem the capital of Israel.
199.	David brought the Ark to Jerusalem.
200.	The Psalms are 150 poems attributed to King David.
201.	The mother of Solomon was Batsheva.
202.	According to tradition, King David came from the tribe of Judah.
203.	Solomon was David's son and the third king of Israel.
204.	Solomon built the Temple in Jerusalem.
205.	After Solomon, the Jewish kingdom split into two separate nations: Israel in the north and Judah in the south.
206.	During the period of the divided kingdom, the prophets thundered their demands for social justice.
207.	The prophets spoke the words of God.
208.	Elijah defeated the priests of Baal on Mount Carmel.
209.	Amos said, "Let justice well up as water and righteousness like a mighty stream."
210.	Hosea equated idolatry with adultery.
211.	Isaiah said, "They shall beat their swords into ploughshares and their spears into pruning hooks; nation shall not lift up sword against nation."
212.	Jeremiah was thrown into a pit for being a prophet.
213.	Jonah fled, only to be forced to prophesy.
214.	Jonah warned the people of Nineveh that they would be destroyed unless they changed their evil ways.
215.	Assyria conquered Israel.
216.	King Hezekiah built a water tunnel that saved Jersusalem.
217.	Nebuchadnezzar destroyed our Temple and Jerusalem on the Ninth of Av in 586 B.C.E.
218.	The Babylonian Exile followed our expulsion from the Land of Israel, when we were forced to live in Babylonia.
219.	Ezekiel had a vision of a field of dry bones that came to life and symbolized Israel; 2 Isaiah described God working through history.

220.   Nehemiah became governor of Judea after the exile.

221.   Ezra the scribe brought the Torah back from Babylonia.

222.   The Book of Proverbs praises the woman of valor.

223.   Job suffered greatly for no apparent reason.

224.   Daniel was thrown into a den of lions and survived.

225.   The Book of Esther tells the story of Purim.

226.   Ruth was the great-grandmother of King David.

227.   The Apocrypha are books that weren't accepted as part of the TaNaCH.

Ritual Objects, Dress, and Prayer

228.   Beautiful ritual objects fulfill a Mitzvah.

229.   Sephardic customs come from Spain and the Middle East, and Ashkenazic customs come from Northern Europe.

230.   The Aron HaKodesh is the ark where we keep the Torah.

231.   A sofer writes Torah scrolls on parchment with a quill pen.

232.   A Sephardic Torah has the same text as an Ashkenazic Torah, but it is kept in a vertical wooden case.

233.   The Torah is dressed to look like the High Priest.

234.   Atzei chayim are the wooden poles that hold the Torah scroll.

235.   A yad is a Torah pointer.

236.   Many synagogues contain a seven-branched menorah.

237.   The ner tamid is the eternal light.

238.   A mechitzah is a wall that separates men and women in an Orthodox synagogue.

239.   A mizrach is a wall hanging in a synagogue or home denoting the eastern wall.

240.   The sheliach tzibbur is the leader of the service.

241.   The bimah is the raised area where the sheliach tzibbur leads the service.

242.   A chazzan is a cantor.

243. The Septuagint is the Greek translation of the TaNaCH.

244. The Targum is the Aramaic translation of the TaNaCH.

245. A Chumash is a printed book that contains the Torah.

246. A Haftarah is a set portion from the Prophets read after the Torah portion on Shabbat and festivals.

247. Mezuzah means doorpost.

248. The mezuzah contains the Shema and V'ahavta written by a sofer on parchment.

249. Tefillin are leather boxes containing Torah passages written on parchment by a sofer, commanding us to bind the mitzvot on our hand and have them between our eyes.

250. Tzitzit are the fringes on the corners of a tallit.

251. A tallit is a shawl with tzitzit on the four corners.

252. Two words for a skullcap are kippah (Hebrew) and yarmulke (Yiddish).

253. A shtreimel is a round fur hat worn by male Chasidic Jews.

254. A kittel is a white robe worn on the Yamim Nora'im, on Pesach, and at a wedding.

255. Sha'atnez is the mixture of wool and linen.

256. Payot are side curls worn by traditional Jewish men.

257. The Magen David is a Jewish star.

258. A chamsa is a charm shaped like a hand.

259. The name of God is so precious that once it has been written, we don't ever want to erase or destroy it.

260. A genizah is a room where damaged scrolls and books containing the name of God are stored.

261. A mikvah is a ritual bath.

262. Kiddushin is the marriage ceremony.

263. A ketubah is a marriage contract.

264. A chuppah is a wedding canopy.

265. Sheva Brachot (seven blessings) are recited to celebrate a wedding.

266. A mamzer is the offspring of a forbidden sexual union.

267. Chalitzah is the ceremony that annuls a man's responsibility to marry his childless brother's widow.

268.   A get is a divorce document written by a sofer.

269.   A woman whose husband has left her without giving her a get is called an agunah.

270.   The ceremony of circumcision is called brit milah.

271.   A mohel performs the circumcision.

272.   The sandak is the person who holds the baby during the circumcision.

273.   According to the rabbis, a Jew is someone whose mother is Jewish.

274.   Since 1983 the Reform Movement has declared that a Jew is someone whose mother or father is Jewish, and who lives and acts like a Jew.

275.   In the Torah, a Hebrew was someone whose father was a Hebrew.

276.   A brit banot is one of the names of a covenant ceremony for a girl.

277.   A Bar/Bat Mitzvah is a Jew responsible for his or her actions.

278.   K'riyah is the ritual tearing of one's clothes as a sign of mourning.

279.   The Kaddish is a statement that God is all-powerful.

280.   Shivah is a seven-day period of deep mourning.

281.   It is a mitzvah to bring food and comfort to a house of mourning so that the family doesn't have to do any work.

282.   Sh'loshim is the first thirty days of mourning.

283.   A Yahrzeit candle is lit in memory on the anniversary of the death of a close relative.

284.   Yizkor is a memorial service.

285.   A traditional Jew says 100 blessings each day.

286.   Birkat HaMazon is the blessing said after eating.

287.   We say a blessing before we do a mitzvah.

288.   Kavannah is focusing on our prayers and their meaning.

289.   A minyan is a quorum of ten Jews, traditionally needed to recite specific communal prayers.

290.   A Siddur is a daily and/or Shabbat prayerbook.

291.   Piyyutim are liturgical poems that have become part of our prayer service.

292.   A Machzor is a festival prayerbook.

293.   Davvening is traditional praying.

294.   Shuckling is swaying rhythmically while praying.

295.   Traditionally, there are three daily prayer services.

296.   Shacharit is the morning service.

297.   Minchah is the afternoon service.

298.   Maariv is the evening service.

299.   Musaf is an additional service on Shabbat and festivals.

300.   The Shema and its blessings are recited twice a day.

301.   The Mi Chamocha reminds us of having been saved at the Sea of Reeds.

302.   The Amidah is the Standing Prayer, consisting of nineteen prayers on weekdays .

303.   The Kedushah quotes Isaiah quoting the angels: "Holy, holy, holy is Adonai."

304.   Duchenen is giving the Priestly Blessing.

305.   The Alaynu is a statement of God's majesty.

306.   The Torah is traditionally read on Shabbat, festivals, Mondays, and Thursdays.

307.   Trop are the cantillation notes for chanting Torah and Haftarah.

308.   The honor of being called to recite the blessings before and after the Torah reading is called an aliyah.

309.   The baal koray chants the Torah.

310.   Hagbahah is the honor of lifting the Torah, and Gelilah is the honor of rolling the Torah.

History, Jewish Texts, and Tradition

311.   Josephus was a Jewish historian who wrote about the Jews for the Romans during the Greek and Roman periods.

312.   After the Hasmoneans, Rome conquered Judea.

313.   Rome made Herod king of Judea.

314.   King Herod was responsible for an enormous number of building projects in the Land of Israel.

315. Herod enlarged the Temple Mount to make the Second Temple larger.

316. Herod used hundreds of thousands of Jews as slaves to build the structures and cities he wanted.

317. Herod built Masada overlooking the Dead Sea.

318. The Sadducees were the political party of the priests during Roman rule.

319. The Pharisees were the political party of the sages during Roman rule.

320. Olam HaBa is the Hebrew term for life after earthly life.

321. The Essenes were a group who dropped out of Jewish society.

322. The Dead Sea Scrolls were found in caves at Qumran.

323. When Herod died, some Jews wanted to rid Judea of the Romans.

324. Jesus lived during the Roman period.

325. The Holy Sepulchre in Jerusalem is the spot where many Christians believe Jesus was killed, buried, and rose on the third day.

326. Christians believe that Jesus was the Messiah; Jews believe that Jesus was neither the Messiah nor divine.

327. During the Roman period, the Jewish Supreme Court was called the Sanhedrin.

328. The Sanhedrin consisted of 71 rabbis.

329. We call our sages who lived during the Roman period Tanna'im.

330. For 200 years the Tanna'im made laws that were not officially written down.

331. Hillel said, "What is hateful to you, don't do to anyone else."

332. The two most famous law schools of the Pharisees were the School of Shammai and the School of Hillel.

333. Midrashim are TaNaCH-based stories written by the sages.

334. Aggadah includes rabbinic stories not based on the TaNaCH.

335. Philo was a Jewish philosopher during the Roman period.

336. The Roman general Titus destroyed the Second Temple in 70 C.E.

337. The Kotel is the Western Wall of the Temple Mount.

338. The Romans built a huge ramp up the side of Masada to conquer the Jewish rebels.

339. At Masada, more than 900 Jews chose to die rather than be made prisoners of the Romans.

340. Rabbi Yochanan ben Zakkai established a law school at Yavneh.

341. General (later Emperor) Vespasian gave Yochanan ben Zakkai permission to establish his law school at Yavneh.

342. Halachah is the Hebrew word for Jewish law.

343. When the Temple was destroyed in 70 c.e., there was a power shift in Judaism from the priests to the rabbis.

344. S'michah is the ceremony of ordaining a rabbi.

345. The first assumption of rabbinic Judaism is that all halachah was given at Mount Sinai and the rabbis have the authority to explain it.

346. The second assumption of rabbinic Judaism is that studying Torah and halachah serves as a substitute for the sacrificial offerings until another Temple is built.

347. According to tradition, Rabbi Akiva didn't begin studying until he was 40 years old.

348. Rabbi Akiva supported the Bar Kochba Revolt.

349. The Bar Kochba Revolt, an attempt to rebel against Rome, began successfully.

350. The Roman emperor Hadrian made Judaism illegal.

351. Following the Bar Kochba Revolt, the Romans executed ten rabbis including Rabbi Akiva.

352. Shimon bar Yochai said, "Kill the best of the non-Jews."

353. Tradition says that Shimon bar Yochai wrote the *Zohar*.

354. The *Zohar* is the central book of Kabbalah.

355. Kabbalah is Jewish mysticism.

356. Judah HaNasi edited the Mishnah.

357. The Mishnah is the written Oral Law.

358. Laws of the Tanna'im that didn't get into the Mishnah are called B'raitot.

359. *Pirkei Avot* (Ethics of the Fathers), provide rabbinic wisdom about how to live.

360. Rav took the Mishnah to Babylonia, where he established a Jewish law school.

361. Amora'im were Jewish law students who discussed and argued about the laws in the Mishnah.

362. The discussions about the Mishnah by the Amora'im are called the Gemara.

363. Mishnah + Gemara = the Talmud.

364. According to tradition, Rav Ashi in Babylonia wrote down the Gemara and the Mishnah in 500 c.e.

365. The Jewish law school in Tiberias also created a Talmud.

366. Most of the Gemara is written in Aramaic.

367. The Talmud is the beginning resource book for all Jewish law.

368. The exilarch represented the Babylonian Jews to the non-Jewish authorities.

369. From 200 to 1000 c.e. the greatest Jewish cultural centers were in Babylonia.

370. The Jews suffered under Byzantine rule.

371. In the seventh century, Muslims from Arabia conquered the Middle East, North Africa, and Spain.

372. The gaon was the head of the Babylonian law schools.

373. The gaon was responsible for making the Talmud available to world Jewry.

374. Answers to questions about halachah are called responsa.

375. The Gaon Amram wrote the first Siddur.

376. The responsa helped unify world Jewry for a while.

377. Saadia Gaon wrote the first medieval book of Jewish philosophy.

378. The Karaites were Jews who believed that the TaNaCH was divine but who didn't accept the authority of the rabbis.

379. Saadia Gaon opposed the Karaites.

380. The Golden Age of Spain lasted from 900 to 1300 c.e.

381. The Muslims who slaughtered Jews in Spain in the 1100s were the Almohads.

382. Thousands of Jews were slaughtered in Europe during the First Crusade.

383. Kiddush HaShem was Jewish martyrdom.

384. Rabbenu Gershom limited all Ashkenazic Jewish men to one wife at a time.

385. Samuel HaNagid was a Jewish general for the Muslims in Spain.

386. Rashi wrote the most important commentary for almost every verse in the TaNaCH.

387. Ibn Ezra was a great TaNaCH commentator.

388. On every page of a traditional TaNaCH, the commentaries of Rashi and Ibn Ezra surround the text.

389. Rashi wrote the most widely read commentary to the Talmud.

390. Surrounding the text on every page of the Talmud is Rashi's commentary on the inside and the Tosafot on the outside.

391. Meir of Rothenberg was one of the great Tosafists.

392. Judah HaLevi wrote poetry about Zion.

393. Judah HaLevi wrote *The Kuzari*.

394. Benjamin MiTudelo traveled around the world describing different Jewish communities.

395. Maimonides was the greatest medieval Jewish philosopher.

396. Maimonides is called RaMBaM in Hebrew.

397. RaMBaM wrote thirteen statements of Jewish faith.

398. RaMBaM wrote the *Mishneh Torah*.

399. The *Mishneh Torah* is a fourteen-volume law code.

400. RaMBaM described eight steps of tzedakah (giving to the needy).

401. RaMBaM wrote *Guide of the Perplexed*.

402. Nachmanides is called RaMBaN in Hebrew.

403. RaMBaN was a great TaNaCH commentator who established a synagogue in Jerusalem.

404. Blood Accusations falsely accused Jews of killing non-Jewish children for Jewish ritual.

405. England was the first country to expel all Jews.

406. Jews were forced to wear a "badge of shame" in all Christian countries.

407. Christians burned huge carts filled with handwritten Jewish texts and scrolls, especially the Talmud.

408. Jews were accused of causing the Black Plague.

409. Jews were expelled from France.

410. Spanish Christians called Jews who had been forced to convert to Christianity "Marranos" (pigs).

411. The Inquisition was an investigative court set up by the Catholic Church to try heretical Christians.

412. Torquemada, head of the Inquisition in Spain, caused the death of more than 13,000 people.

413. In 1492 Spain expelled all Jews from the country.

414. Ladino, a combination of Spanish and Hebrew, was the language of Sephardic Jews.

415. Yiddish is German mixed with Hebrew and Slavic words.

416. The first ghetto was in Venice.

417. Lurianic Kabbalah flourished in Tzfat in the 1500s.

418. Yehudah Loew of Prague was said to have built a golem.

419. Joseph Caro wrote the *Shulchan Aruch*.

420. The *Shulchan Aruch* is a code of Jewish law.

421. Moses Isserles wrote the *Mappah*, Ashkenazic additions to the *Shulchan Aruch*.

422. Chmielnitzky led Cossacks in riots against the Jews.

423. Shabbetai Tzvi was the false Messiah in the 1600s.

424. Pilpul was a skill to resolve all apparent contradictions in the Talmud.

425. A beit din is a court of three rabbis.

426. A posek is recognized as a Jewish legal authority.

427. The Baal Shem Tov founded the Chasidic Movement.

428. Chasidic Jews believe that they can best connect with the Divine through joy.

429. Chasidic Jews believe their leader, a Rebbe, has a special relationship with God.

430. Mitnagdim were Jews opposed to the Chasidic Movement.

431. The first Jews in North America sailed from South America to New Amsterdam in 1654.

432. The first Jews in North America were Sephardic Jews.

433. Spinoza was excommunicated because of his beliefs.

434. The richest Jewish bankers in Europe were the Rothschilds.

435. Moses Mendelssohn introduced European culture into the ghetto.

436. The Haskalah was the Enlightenment Movement for Jews.

437. The Pale of Settlement was the area of Russia where Jews were forced to live.

438. A shtetl was a little village where Jews lived.

439. Sholom Aleichem wrote funny and sad stories in Yiddish about the shtetl.

440. Chappers were Jews who stole children to meet the Russian army quota.

441. Napoleon gave Jews full civil rights.

442. The Reform Movement began as an attempt to keep Jews in the modern world from converting to Christianity.

443. Rabbi Samson Raphael Hirsch showed Jews how they could be both Orthodox and modern.

444. In the 1840s large numbers of Jews fled from Germany to America.

445. B'nai B'rith was the first and largest Jewish service organization.

446. The Jewish Chautauqua Society was founded to create better understanding between Christians and Jews on college campuses.

447. Rabbi Isaac Mayer Wise was one of the great pioneers of Reform Judaism in the United States.

448. Hebrew Union College was the first rabbinical seminary in the United States.

449. Rabbi Solomon Schechter was one of the founders of the Conservative Movement.

450. Rabbi Mordechai Kaplan founded the Reconstructionist Movement.

451. Pogroms were government-organized riots against the Jews in Russia.

452. More than 2 million Jews came to United States between 1880 and 1920.

453. Emma Lazarus wrote the poem inscribed on the Statue of Liberty.

454. When Jews came to America, many settled on the Lower East Side of New York.

455. Jews were actively involved in creating the labor unions.

456. The National Federation of Temple Sisterhoods supports the Reform Jewish Movement, and the Women's League for Conservative Judaism supports the Conservative Movement.

457. Mendel Beilis was a Russian Jew victimized in 1911 by a Blood Accusation.

458.   The Holocaust lasted from 1933 to 1945.

459.   Kristallnacht was an enormous Nazi pogrom against the Jews.

460.   The Nazis planned to exterminate all Jews.

461.   More than 6 million Jews were slaughtered during the Holocaust.

462.   The Jews in the Warsaw Ghetto fought back with tremendous bravery.

463.   Until the Holocaust, the greatest yeshivot and Jewish cultural centers were in Poland.

464.   Jews have been prominent in the civil rights movement in the United States.

465.   Havurot are small groups of Jews who study and celebrate Judaism together.

466.   Sally Priesand, the first woman rabbi, was ordained in 1972.

467.   WUPJ is the World Union for Progressive Judaism.

468.   The Falashas are black Jews from Ethiopia.

469.   The Conference of Presidents of Major American Jewish Organizations is the umbrella organization for forty-six Jewish institutions.

Israel: The Geography and History of the Modern State

470.   Israel connects Africa and Asia Minor.

471.   Ancient merchants had to go through the Yizrael Valley to get from Mesopotamia to Egypt.

472.   Three ancient cities guarded the Yizrael Valley: Hatzor, Megiddo, and Beit Shean.

473.   A tel is a hill consisting of layers of old cities.

474.   Jaffa has been a port in Israel for more than 4,000 years.

475.   Haifa is the main port in Israel.

476.   Israel's coastal plain has been the site of numerous battles.

477.   The north of Israel is called the Galilee.

478. Tzfat is the city of Kabbalah, Jewish mysticism.

479. Lake Kinneret is the only fresh-water lake in Israel.

480. Tiberias was the Roman capital in the Galilee.

481. A beautiful mosaic floor was found in the ancient synagogue of Beit Alfa.

482. Nablus is the city of the Samaritans.

483. Bab El Wad is the mountain pass between Tel Aviv and Jerusalem.

484. The Cave of Machpelah in Hebron is holy to both Muslims and Jews.

485. The Jordan River is the largest river in Israel.

486. Jericho is the world's oldest city.

487. The Dead Sea is the furthest below-sea-level area on earth.

488. The Negev is a large desert in the south of Israel.

489. Be'er Sheva, in the middle of the Negev, is a thriving modern city.

490. Bedouin still live in the Negev near Be'er Sheva.

491. Kibbutz Yahel and kibbutz Lotan are two Reform kibbutzim in the Aravah.

492. The southernmost city in Israel is Eilat.

493. The Crusaders built more than 250 forts in the Land of Israel.

494. Jerusalem is holy to Christians, Muslims, and Jews.

495. The Dome of the Rock stands on the Temple Mount.

496. The Mosque of al-Aqsa,   lims, also stands on the Temple Mount.

497. The Mount of Olives, opposite the Temple Mount, has a huge Jewish cemetery.

498. Zion became another name for the whole country of Israel.

499. The Ottoman Turks ruled Palestine from 1520 to 1920.

500. The Old City of Jerusalem is surrounded by a wall.

501. Sir Moses Montefiore built the first set of houses and a windmill outside the Old City of Jerusalem.

502. The First Aliyah began in 1882, led by the BILU.

503. The Jews returning to the Land of Israel were helped by Baron Edmund de Rothschild.

504. Eliezer Ben Yehuda created the modern language of Hebrew.

505. Alfred Dreyfus was a French captain framed by the army because he was a Jew.

506. In response to the Dreyfus trial, Theodor Herzl wrote "The Jewish State."

507. The First World Zionist Congress convened in 1897.

508. Theodor Herzl was the father of political Zionism.

509. The Jewish National Fund plants trees in Israel.

510. Young idealists hoping to create a new world in Palestine were involved in the Second Aliyah.

511. A. D. Gordon believed that making the Land of Israel green was the highest imperative for a Jew.

512. HaShomer was the first Jewish defense group in Palestine.

513. Degania, the first kibbutz, was founded by members of the Second Aliyah.

514. In 1909 Tel Aviv was founded on the sands just north of Jaffa.

515. The modern Jewish community in Palestine was called the Yishuv.

516. Jews joined the British in World War I to fight the Turks.

517. Josef Trumpeldor founded the Zion Mule Corps.

518. Zeev Jabotinsky helped found the Jewish Legion, which fought for the British.

519. The NILI were Jewish spies working for the British against the Turks in World War I.

520. The Balfour Declaration promised the Jews a homeland in Palestine.

521. Arabs destroyed the settlement of Tel Chai.

522. Trumpeldor's last words were, "No matter; it is good to die for our country."

523. The Haganah was originally founded by Zeev Jabotinsky.

524. The British were in charge of the Land of Israel from 1920 to 1948.

525. The chalutzim (pioneers) formed the Third Aliyah.

526. Henrietta Szold founded Hadassah.

527. The British prevented Jews from freely entering the Land of Israel.

528. Youth Aliyah saved thousands of children from the Nazis.

529. Aliyah Bet smuggled Jews into Palestine.

530. The Jews protected themselves from the Arabs by building tower and stockade settlements.

531. Zeev Jabotinsky founded the Irgun.

532. Jews joined the British in World War II to fight the Nazis.

533. Top Jewish troops, trained by the British, became the leaders of the Palmach.

534. Hannah (Szenes) Senesh wrote, "Blessed is the match."

535. Menachem Begin became the leader of the Irgun.

536. On November 29, 1947, the United Nations voted for the establishment a Jewish state and an Arab state in the Land of Israel.

537. On May 14, 1948, the State of Israel was born.

538. David Ben Gurion became the first prime minister of Israel.

539. On May 15, 1948, Israel was attacked by seven Arab armies.

540. Israel's parliament is called the Knesset.

541. Chaim Weizmann became the first president of Israel.

542. The Law of Return states that any Jew who comes to Israel can become a citizen.

543. In 1949 Operation Magic Carpet saved the Jews of Yemen.

544. El Al is Israel's national airline.

545. Israel's population doubled in size during her first three years of existence.

546. Israel created absorption cities to integrate immigrants.

547. Kiryat Shmoneh was built in memory of the settlers killed at Tel Chai.

548. Israel accepted reparations from Germany for the Holocaust atrocities.

549. Israel defeated Egypt in the Sinai Campaign.

550. Israel executed Adolf Eichmann for crimes against humanity.

551. The goal of the Palestine Liberation Organization (PLO) was to destroy Israel.

552. Israel took the Sinai Desert, the West Bank, and the Golan Heights in the Six Day War.

553. Jerusalem was united after the Six Day War.

554. Moshe Dayan was Israel's defense minister during the Six Day War.

555.   Golda Meir was the first woman prime minister of Israel.

556.   Egypt attacked Israel on Yom Kippur, 1973.

557.   On July 4, 1976, Israel freed hostages in the daring raid on Entebbe.

558.   The Good Fence allows Arabs to enter Israel for medical help.

559.   The Camp David Accord established peace between Israel and Egypt.

560.   In 1982 Israel initiated a war in Lebanon.

561.   Israel's capital is Jerusalem.

562.   Gush Emunim and Kach are right-wing Jewish groups.

563.   All buildings in Jerusalem must be faced with Jerusalem stone that looks golden in the sunlight.

564.   Hadassah Hospital's synagogue contains Chagall's magnificent stained-glass windows.

565.   Heichal Shlomo in Jerusalem is the office of Israel's Chief Rabbis.

566.   Hebrew Union College has a campus in Jerusalem, where all Reform rabbinical and cantorial students study for a year.

567.   Arza is the Reform Movement's Zionist Association.

568.   Operation Moses was Israel's airlift of Ethiopian Jews from the Sudan to Israel.

569.   In December 1987 the Arabs on the West Bank and in the Gaza Strip began the Intifada.

570.   When the Intifada began, Yitzchak Rabin was Israel's defense minister.

571.   When the Intifada began, Yitzchak Shamir was Israel's prime minister.

572.   Israel's army is called Tzahal.

573.   Operation Exodus provided for the mass immigration of Soviet Jews to Israel.

Jewish Thought and Values

574.   Hermann Cohen introduced the concept of "ethical monotheism" to describe Judaism.

575. Rabbi Leo Baeck wrote *The Essence of Judaism.*

576. Franz Rosenzweig wrote *The Star of Redemption.*

577. Martin Buber wrote *I and Thou.*

578. Abraham Joshua Heschel wrote evocative books encouraging traditional Jewish practice.

579. Tzedakah is the mitzvah of giving money to the needy.

580. Gemilut chasadim is the mitzvah of caring for others through special deeds.

581. Hachnasat orchim is the mitzvah of inviting strangers into our homes.

582. Bikkur cholim is the mitzvah of visiting and helping sick people.

583. Tza'ar baalei chayim is the mitzvah of not being cruel to animals.

584. Being a mensch means being a good, caring person.

585. Pikuach nefesh is the concept that preservation of human life transcends all other mitzvot.

586. A ger is a convert to Judaism.

587. The traditional way for a woman to convert to Judaism is to immerse in a mikveh.

588. The traditional way for a man to convert to Judaism is to undergo circumcision and to immerse in a mikveh.

589. Kashrut is the discipline of Jewish dietary laws.

590. An animal is potentially kosher if it both chews its cud and has completely split hooves.

591. A sea creature is kosher if it has both fins and scales.

592. Halachah forbids mixing milk and meat products.

593. Parve refers to any food that contains neither milk nor meat.

594. Halachah forbids the consumption of blood.

595. A shochet is a ritual slaughterer.

596. Traif is the Yiddish term to indicate that a food is not permitted to be consumed.

597. A mashgiach makes sure that the laws of kashrut are maintained.

598. Middah k'neged middah is the traditional belief that God provides specific consequences for our actions.

599. Zechut avot is the belief that because our ancestors were worthy, we get credit with God.

600. Musar is Jewish ethics.

601. Mazal tov means literally "good planet."

602. Judaism emphasizes that humans have free will.

603. "Bis hundert und tzvantzig" is the appropriate greeting on someone's birthday.

604. Gematriya is Hebrew numerology.

605. Traditional Judaism has always considered male homosexuality to be an abomination.

606. Tikkun olam means repairing the world.

607. Techiyat hamaytim is belief in the resurrection of the dead.

608. Intermarriage is forbidden in halachah.

609. Our rabbis struggled against gambling.

610. The Reform Movement maintains that abortion should be the personal choice of the pregnant woman.

611. Klal Yisrael is the unity of all Jews.

612. Emet is the Hebrew word for truth.

613. Shalom means hello, goodbye, and peace.

Part II

DATA

Holidays

Jewish Time

1. Rosh Chodesh is the celebration of the New Moon.

We determine our Jewish calendar according to both the lunar and the solar cycles. Months are determined by the lunar cycle. Rosh Chodesh, the New Moon, is a monthly holiday which celebrates the beginning of a new month. Traditionally, parts of the Hallel (see fact 7) are recited as part of the celebration.

According to our tradition, when we still had a Sanhedrin (see facts 327, 328), Rosh Chodesh was a major event because the declaration of that special day depended on eye witnesses who viewed the new moon. It was a great honor to be such a witness, and many people participated in the monthly ritual. Jews living outside the Land of Israel depended on the Sanhedrin to declare the New Moon. Bonfires would be lit on the tops of mountains to carry the message to far-off communities, and riders would spread the word. Because this confirmation took more than a day to reach them, Jews living outside of Israel celebrated the New Moon for two days. They also celebrated the first and last days of festivals (see data to facts 27, 43, 52, and 84) for two days each.

Today, traditional Jews outside the Land of Israel continue to celebrate the New Moon for two days if the new month contains thirty days. They also celebrate the first and last days of festivals for two days. Now that we have set calendars, many Reform Jews no longer add the second day of celebration at the beginning and end of festivals.

Moreover, we are less aware of the natural lunar cycle, and Rosh Chodesh has lost much of its specialness. This decrease in importance is a loss, because it removes us from the natural rhythm of time.

The Jewish months in order are Nisan (see fact 64), Iyar (see data to fact 91), Sivan (see data to fact 84), Tammuz, Av (see facts 92, 93), Elul (see fact 12), Tishri (see fact 8), Cheshvan, Tevet, Kislev (see fact 43), Shvat (see fact 49), and Adar (see facts 3, 58).

2. A "normal" Jewish year has 354 days.

A lunar month is 29½ days. Since it is impossible to celebrate half a day, some months are counted as having 29 days and others as having 30 days. Thus, a purely lunar year would consist of 354 days, eleven days fewer than a solar year of 365 days.

This disparity created a potential problem. Our major festivals, Pesach (see facts 64–79), Shavuot (see facts 80–89), and Sukkot (see facts 28–34), are all agriculturally oriented, so they are dependent upon the solar calendar. Even our minor holidays, such as Chanukkah (see facts 38–48) and Purim (see facts 51–63), are seasonally oriented. Over the year our holidays are a carefully orchestrated celebration of seasonal high points and dips. Rosh HaShanah (see facts 9–20), Yom Kippur (see facts 9, 11, 12, and 22–26), and Sukkot take place in the fall. Pesach celebrates the spring barley harvest. Shavuot takes place in early summer at the wheat harvest. If we maintained only a lunar calendar, we would lose eleven days each year. After six years Sukkot would be in the summer and Pesach would appear in the winter. We would lose the seasonal exclamation points of our holidays.

3. During a Jewish leap year we add the month Adar II.

In order to adjust our lunar calendar with the solar year, our sages added an extra month of 29 days on a careful schedule, seven times every nineteen years. This leap-year month, Adar II, was added at the end of the Hebrew year, immediately before the month of Nisan (see fact 64). Doing so guaranteed that the agricultural holidays remained in their proper seasons. The Jewish leap year takes place in the third, sixth, eighth, eleventh, fourteenth, seventeenth, and nineteenth years of the nineteen-year cycle.

Because of this leap year, the Jewish holidays appear on the secular calendar at a different time every year, either "early" or "late." No one ever thinks of the holidays as being on time.

4. The Jewish day starts at sundown.

The Jewish day consists of 24 hours, but it begins at sundown and lasts until the next sundown. When the Book of Genesis (see fact 106) describes the Divine's creative process, it concludes with the statement,

"It was evening, and it was morning: one day." Our sages understood these words to define a day as lasting from sundown to sundown.

Festival Rituals

5. We light candles to begin most holidays.

One of our obligations as Jews is to participate in the process of recognizing sacred time. Each holiday brings special holiness into the world, but only if we ritually acknowledge it. Our sages associated certain rituals with every holiday as our way of making those days holy.

The first ritual is candle lighting. Every important Jewish holiday begins with lighting candles and noting that this action is a mitzvah, a Jewish imperative. God's first creation was light (see fact 111). We respond to this ongoing miracle by bringing light into our homes, acknowledging the birth of a special day, a holiday.

In Western Europe hanging oil lamps were used. They became so common that they were called Judenstern (Jewish Stars), but they were unrelated to the Magen David (see fact 257). After the eighteenth century, most Jews used candlesticks with wax candles. These offered Jewish artisans an opportunity to create magnificent works of art.

Originally candle lighting was only a home ritual. However, as Reform congregations became concerned that many Jews were not lighting candles at home, the ritual was performed as part of Shabbat and festival services.

The ritual of lighting Shabbat and festival candles is called in Yiddish to *bench licht* (bless light) (see fact 415).

6. We drink wine on every holiday to make the day holy, except on fast days.

Jews have always viewed wine as a source of joy. With few exceptions, we have encouraged the use of wine as a medium for recognizing the holiness of our festivals.

The blessing over wine is called Kiddush, Sanctification. It is recited at every festival mentioned in the Torah except for Yom Kippur, which is a fast day (see fact 24). It is not recited on the minor holidays,

Chanukkah (see facts 38–48), Purim (see facts 51–63), and Tu BiShvat (see facts 49, 50); those holidays are not mentioned in the Torah because they began later. Kiddush is not recited on the other yearly fast days.

We recite a paragraph along with the Kiddush to note the special holiness and importance of the particular day being sanctified.

Although the Kiddush was originally a home ritual, during the Middle Ages it became the custom to recite it in the synagogue. In that way the poor and the strangers who gathered and stayed in the synagogue on Shabbat and festivals were able to participate in the sanctification of the day.

7. On a number of holidays we read special psalms called the Hallel.

Psalms 113–118 are read on the festivals (see facts 27 and 200), on Chanukkah (see facts 38–48), and on Rosh Chodesh (see fact 1). These psalms as a group are called the Hallel, the Praising. They are not read on the Yamim Nora'im (see fact 9) or on Purim (see facts 51–63). According to our tradition, these special joyous poems were recited by the Levites as part of the Temple worship on the festivals (see data to facts 167, 168).

Holidays in Tishri

8. Rosh HaShanah and Yom Kippur, Sukkot, and Simchat Torah all occur in the month of Tishri.

Tishri, the seventh month, is considered the holiest month of the Jewish year. The first of Tishri is Rosh HaShanah, the New Year (see facts 9–23). The 10th of the month is Yom Kippur, the Day of Atonement (see facts 9, 11, 12, 22–26). The 15th of the month begins Sukkot (see facts 28–34), and the 22nd of Tishri is Simchat Torah (see facts 35–37)—although traditional Jews celebrate it on the 23rd, except in Israel (see data to fact 1). For traditional Jews, Tishri also contains Hoshanna Rabba and Shmini Atzeret (see data to facts 30 and 35). It is a ritually busy thirty days.

Rosh HaShanah

9. Rosh HaShanah and Yom Kippur are called the Yamim Nora'im.

Yamim Nora'im means Days of Awe. For the past 2,000 years, the primary theme of the Yamim Nora'im has been judgment. Our sages taught that on Rosh HaShanah the Creator of Everything judges all creation, especially us, and decrees our fate for the coming year. For our sages, Yom Kippur marked the day of sentencing. The theme of judgment fits into the fundamental belief that Jews have free will (see fact 602) and are therefore rewarded and punished for their actions.

10. On Rosh HaShanah we say "L'shanah tovah tikatayvu."

"L'shanah tovah tikatayvu" means, "May you be written for a good year." This phrase refers to the traditional image of the Divine writing our fate into the Book of Life based on our actions during the year.

This theme is emphasized in the Yamim Nora'im prayer, the Un'taneh Tokef, ascribed to Rabbi Amnon of Mainz in the eleventh century. It starkly declares: "This time is awesome and full of dread . . . even the angels, gripped by fear and trembling, declare, 'This is the Day of Judgment. On Rosh HaShanah it is written and on Yom Kippur it is sealed, who will live and who will die'. . . ."

Although our tradition attributes the Un'taneh Tokef to Rabbi Amnon of Mainz, martyred because he refused to convert to Christianity, most scholars agree that it was probably written at least four hundred years before the time he supposedly lived. By enrobing the words with a story about a rabbi tortured for his beliefs, our tradition created an image all too familiar to us, one that unites the theme of judgment and awe with our history of suffering and persecution.

11. The goal of the Yamim Nora'im is teshuvah, returning.

While a sense of awe pervades both Rosh HaShanah and Yom Kippur, our sages added another much more important theme: God's desire and willingness to forgive us if we achieve teshuvah, repentance.

Teshuvah actually means *returning*. If we return to a life of wholeness, caring, and mitzvot, we become integrated again as Jews. The word *atonement* has this same root. Atonement also means "At-one-ment." Our sages assured us that teshuvah, real personal returning, results in divine forgiveness. Thus, the Un'taneh Tokef concludes with the statement, "Teshuvah, prayer, and tzedakah (see fact 579) temper the severity of the decree."

12. We prepare for the Yamim Nora'im throughout the whole Hebrew month of Elul.

The teshuvah process is a long one. It begins thirty days before Rosh HaShanah on the first day of the Hebrew month of Elul. Every day of Elul, the shofar (see fact 20) is blown in the synagogue in an attempt to awaken our souls to the difficult task of repentance, teshuvah, returning.

By spending the month of Elul in introspection, searching our souls for our past mistakes, we prepare for the Yamim Nora'im, the Days of Awe. For almost a thousand years this self-examination was done publicly in the synagogue. Jews would stand and ritually go through the act of confessing the mistakes and transgressions to which people are prone and would openly ask for forgiveness. In Poland there are even stories of Jews who would stand and confess their personal transgressions, asking for forgiveness. In some communities, Jews would spend the day before Rosh HaShanah going around to their neighbors' homes to ask for forgiveness.

We shudder at that level of vulnerability and loss of privacy, but it had a powerful influence on the individuals and their ability to achieve real teshuvah, real returning.

13. We recite Selichot, prayers asking for forgiveness, on the Saturday night before Rosh HaShanah.

On the Saturday night before Rosh HaShanah, we meet at midnight to recite special prayers of penitence, called Selichot. Medieval rabbis saw midnight as the most propitious time to make requests of God. According to our tradition, King David would awaken at midnight to create the Psalms (see fact 200). If it worked for him, they reasoned, it should work for us.

14. Rosh HaShanah celebrates the creation of the world.

Teshuvah, returning, creates in us a sense of personal renewal. A midrash (see fact 333) connected that feeling to the Yamim Nora'im by making Rosh HaShanah the anniversary of the creation of humans, the sixth day of creation. Rosh HaShanah reaffirms the world's renewal as well as our own. The Jewish tallying of years since creation therefore changes each year at Rosh HaShanah, the seventh month of the Jewish year. In 1991, according to Jewish tradition, the world is 5,752 years old.

15. On Rosh HaShanah we eat apples and honey.

A number of gastronomical customs developed to emphasize Rosh HaShanah as the anniversary of creation. Some Sephardic Jews (see fact 228), taking the word "rosh," head, literally, eat fish heads as a special Rosh HaShanah dish. It became a custom for Jews to use honey in cooking so the year would be sweet. Many Jews eat apples and honey as a wish for a sweet year.

Traditionally, Jews do not eat nuts on Rosh HaShanah. The numerical value (see fact 604) of the Hebrew word for nut, egoz, is the same as the Hebrew word for sin, chet.

16. Many Jews eat a round challah on Rosh HaShanah.

In many communities, the Rosh HaShanah challah (see data to fact 96) is traditionally round to represent the yearly cycle of creation. Some communities bake the challah in the shape of a ladder to symbolize the rising fate of some Jews and the fall of others, decided on Rosh HaShanah. Many Jews dip the challah into honey.

17. Tradition teaches that Isaac and Samuel were born on Rosh HaShanah.

Carefully connected to the affirmation of the world's renewal is the Rosh HaShanah theme of God's remembering. According to our sages, on Rosh HaShanah God remembered the divine promise to Abraham (see data to facts 126, 129), and Isaac was born. On Rosh HaShanah God remembered the divine promise to Joseph (see data to fact 145), and Joseph was released from prison. On Rosh HaShanah God remembered the divine promise to the Jewish people, and the steps resulting in the Exodus were begun (see data to facts 154–157). On Rosh HaShanah God remembered the divine promise to Hannah (see fact 191), and Samuel was born. On Rosh HaShanah God ordered Abraham not to sacrifice his son, and the ram was sacrificed instead (see fact 130).

18. Rosh HaShanah is called Yom HaZikaron, the Day of Remembrance.

The theme of God remembering is developed throughout the Rosh HaShanah liturgy. God not only remembers, God takes note. The Divine noted on the sixth day of creation, "This is very good" (see fact 112), and we in turn view this creative process as continuing. We see the world renewed; we are renewed not just biologically, but spiritually as well.

Thus we find four themes repeated again and again through the Yamim Nora'im, the Days of Awe: God as King and Creator who continually renews physical and spiritual life; God as Judge, who notes and remembers our deeds and thoughts; our need to repent and be forgiven; and God's willingness to forgive.

19. Avinu Malkaynu means, "Our Father our King."

One of the most familiar reminders of the majesty of the Divine combines all of the High Holy Day themes. The prayer "Avinu Malkaynu, Our Father our King" confesses our failings, notes our utter dependence on God's forgiveness, and begs for that forgiveness despite our inadequacies. The tension between a loving parent and a just ruler is poignantly expressed in each repetition of the words *Avinu Malkaynu*.

The phrase is credited to Rabbi Akiva, who lived in the second century (see fact 347). The Talmud mentions that there had been a terrible drought. People were starving. Rabbi Akiva appealed to God with the words, "Avinu Malkaynu, we have no king but you. Avinu Malkaynu, have mercy on us for your sake," and the drought ended.

Over the following 1,500 years more petitions were added to that original plea until today, traditionally, there are more than forty verses.

20. On Rosh HaShanah traditionally we blow the shofar 100 times.

The main synagogue ritual unique to Rosh HaShanah is the blowing of the shofar, a ram's horn. We are commanded in the Torah, "On the first day of the seventh month sound blasts." One of the names of Rosh HaShanah is the Day of Blasts, Yom Teruah. Traditionally, we blow 100 separate shofar blasts on Rosh HaShanah.

Our Sages connect the shofar with the ram sacrificed by Abraham instead of Isaac, his son (see fact 130). According to our sages, one of the shofrot (plural of shofar) from that ram will be blown by Elijah to announce the arrival of the Messiah (see data to facts 208 and 326).

There are four separate shofar blasts: tekiyah, a straight, unbroken sound; shevarim, three sets of low-high notes; teruah, nine fast, staccato notes; and shevarim–teruah, a combination of the second and third blasts. The 100 blasts are created by repetitions of these four sets of calls. The shofar blowing service ends with one long blast, tekiyah gedolah, the great tekiyah.

21. Tashlich is the ritual of tossing our sins into a river on Rosh HaShanah.

It became a custom for Jews to go to a river after Rosh HaShanah services and empty out their pockets, symbolically tossing their sins into the water. Tradition connects this ritual with the verse from the prophet Micah: You (God) will toss all their sins into the depths of the sea." The Hebrew word for "will toss" is "tashlich." Hence the ritual of tossing our sins into running water is called tashlich, the tossing.

Yom Kippur

22. There are ten days between Rosh HaShanah and Yom Kippur.

These ten days are called the Ten Days of Repentence, Aseret Yemei Teshuvah. They represent our final opportunity before Yom Kippur to ask and receive forgiveness from relatives, friends, and neighbors for our chataim, our sins.

23. Shabbat Shuvah is the Shabbat between Rosh HaShanah and Yom Kippur.

Shabbat Shuvah includes a special Haftarah (see fact 246) from the Book of Hosea which urges Israel to return to the contract with the Divine, thus continuing the primary theme of the Yamim Nora'im, teshuvah. The first word of the Haftarah is *Shuvah*, "Return, (O Israel)," so the Shabbat is called Shabbat Shuvah.

24. We fast on Yom Kippur.

Yom Kippur is the Day of Atonement. We are commanded in the Torah to "afflict our souls." Our sages indicated that this means we are to fast from sundown to sundown. In addition, as a sign of contrition we do not wear leather, which requires an animal's death and was viewed as a luxury. We refrain from any jovial practices such as singing, dancing, and sexual relations. Traditional Jews wear a white robe called a kittel (see fact 254). It is their burial shroud, and should the Divine find them guilty on Yom Kippur, they will be ready for burial and not burden their community.

Before the Temple was destroyed in 70 C.E. (see fact 336), the Yom Kippur ritual focused on the High Priest (see fact 171). Resplendent in his sacral vestments, the High Priest made atonement for himself, his family, and the entire community of Israel. He then entered the Holy of Holies (see data to fact 204), the only time during the year when any human was permitted there. He pronounced the Ineffable Name of God, pronounced only that one time every year. It must have been an awesome moment for the people waiting anxiously outside in the courtyard for reassurance that the Divine had forgiven them.

Today our ritual includes prayers asking for forgiveness (see fact 26) and reminders of that special moment when the High Priest made atonement for the community and returned, unharmed, from the Holy of Holies.

25. The best-known prayer on Yom Kippur is Kol Nidrei.

Yom Kippur begins with the evocative musical power of Kol Nidrei. More than any other set of ritual words, Kol Nidrei has become the epitome of the Yamim Nora'im, the Days of Awe. The music strikes a chord deep within us, and we respond.

Ironically, the words of this legal petition are not of great significance to us; as a matter of fact, at a certain level they are somewhat repugnant. Kol Nidrei asks that all vows, promises, and sworn statements that we made during the past year and that we will make in the year to come be null, void, and without meaning.

Tradition has linked the creation of this petition to the secret Jews of Spain (see fact 410), but there is no historical merit to this claim. The Gaon Amram (see fact 375) already knew the Kol Nidrei in the ninth century and was violently opposed to it because of its content.

By the 1500s the melody we now have was associated with Kol Nidrei. Early Reform leaders tried getting rid of the formula because it didn't fit their rational theology (see data to fact 442).

However, even when it wasn't printed in the prayerbook, people continued to demand that Kol Nidrei be sung on Yom Kippur evening. Its haunting melody meant too much to them to be removed, and Kol Nidrei continues to resonate in our souls. It is so important to us emotionally that we sometimes call the Yom Kippur evening service the Kol Nidrei service.

26. On the Yamim Nora'im, we ask God to forgive us for all the wrongs we committed during the year.

The major additions to both the Yom Kippur evening and morning services are a series of community confessions of sins and pleas for forgiveness. They are meant to help us pinpoint our transgressions so we can achieve teshuvah, returning.

Our sages knew their Jews: the vast majority of the sins mentioned deal with unkind words and thoughts. Violence and criminal transgressions are barely mentioned. As a community, we transgress through small day-to-day failings which, over a year, erode our character until, like the Grand Canyon, our inner integrity has been deeply eroded. Yom Kippur and our teshuvah process restore our unity, helping us achieve At-one-ment again.

The final service on Yom Kippur is called Ne'ilah, the locking. According to our tradition, the end of Yom Kippur marks the moment when the Divine Court completes its judgment of every human and locks the gates of judgment. However, there is always time for a reprieve should a person truly return in contrition.

Sukkot

27. Sukkot, Pesach, and Shavuot are the three festivals on which Jews used to bring offerings to the Temple.

The Torah commands all Hebrew males to appear three times a year at the temple (see fact 204) with offerings: on Sukkot, the fruit harvest; on Pesach, the barley and lamb harvest; and on Shavuot, the wheat harvest. These three festivals are called the Shalosh Regalim, the Three Pilgrimage Festivals.

28. Sukkot celebrates the fruit harvest.

In ancient times, by far the most important of the Shalosh Regalim, the three Pilgrimage Festivals, was Sukkot. It was called The Festival *par excellence*. Some scholars believe that the Hebrews used to gather every year for a special celebration. They link that yearly gathering of the Hebrews with Sukkot.

29. There are five days between Yom Kippur and Sukkot.

Sukkot takes place five days after Yom Kippur (see facts 9, 11, 12, 22–26), on the 15th of Tishri. Sukkot eve always takes place, therefore, when there is a full moon (see fact 1), as do Tu BiShvat and Pesach (see facts 49, 64). As people connected to the lunar cycle, the Hebrews clearly viewed the full moon as an important, propitious time. Our sages compared the Jewish people to the moon. Just as the moon waxes and wanes, so too does our well-being as a people increase and decrease.

30. The lulav is made of palm, myrtle, and willow.

The Torah commands us to take "the fruit of a goodly tree," palm branches, leafy boughs, and willow branches, and "rejoice" (Leviticus 23:40). We call these four varieties of vegetation the Arba Minim, the Four Varieties.
Our sages decreed that the fruit was the etrog, a citron (related to

the lemon, but larger and more fragrant). The leafy bough was myrtle. By wrapping palm, myrtle, and willow branches together, they created the lulav. Our sages offered a variety of explanations for the use of these specific trees.

First, the different parts of the lulav remind us of different parts of the human body: the palm represents our spine, the myrtle reminds us of our eyes, the willow leaf looks like a mouth, and the etrog is a symbol for our hearts. We use all parts of our body to praise and serve God, and the lulav and etrog symbolize this fact.

Second, the lulav and etrog represent different kinds of Jews. The etrog has both taste and fragrance and represents Jews who both study and practice mitzvot (see fact 162). The willow has neither taste nor fragrance and represents Jews who neither study nor practice mitzvot. The myrtle has fragrance but no taste, representing Jews who study but don't practice mitzvot. The palm has taste (the date) but no fragrance, representing the Jew who practices mitzvot but doesn't study.

It is interesting to note in Chapter 8 of the Book of Nehemiah (see data to fact 220) that when Ezra the Scribe (see fact 221) read the Torah laws about Sukkot to the people, they went and brought "leafy branches of olive trees, pine trees, myrtle, palms, and leafy trees to make booths and they dwelt in booths." Apparently at that time the rabbinic definitions of the Torah terms were not yet set.

31. On Sukkot we wave the lulav and etrog.

The lulav and the etrog are shaken together in all directions on Sukkot: north, south, east, west, up, and down. Our sages maintained that this shaking ritual reminds us that God is everywhere, in all directions. Historically, shaking the lulav and etrog served a more specific function. The primary concern of the Hebrew farmer during this season was the coming of the fall rains. If it didn't rain during the fall season, the average Hebrew farmer would starve. Thus this holiday season was tinged with tension. All of the vegetation used in the lulav requires a great deal of water. By waving the lulav and etrog, our ancestors may have been working at an early form of rain creation.

The seventh day of Sukkot, called Hoshanah Rabbah, included special rituals with the lulav. When the Temple was still in existence (see facts 315, 336), the lulavim (plural of lulav) were carried in procession around the altar seven times and palm twigs were beaten on the ground. Traditional Jews continue the tradition of carrying lulavim around the synagogue on Hoshanah Rabbah, though this tradition is no longer practiced by most Reform congregations.

32. We build a sukkah on Sukkot.

During Sukkot it is traditional to build a booth, a sukkah, and both eat and sleep in it. The Torah tells us that doing this reminds us of our desert wanderings when we lived in booths, sukkot. In all likelihood, the custom of staying in booths is more closely linked to the pragmatic needs of harvesters to remain in the fields during the harvest. Temporary shelters were built for the workers so they didn't waste time returning to their homes.

The sukkah had to be a temporary structure built outside, and it was not permitted to be under a tree. The walls could be of any material, but they could not be fastened with metal. The major building regulations concerned the roof of the sukkah. It had to be covered with organic material which had been separated from its root source. The most ubiquitous substance was corn stalks, called s'chach. There had to be enough s'chach on the roof to provide more shade than sun.

In Europe people would decorate their sukkot (plural of sukkah) with tapestries, rugs, lights, and paintings, and they would live in the sukkah during the entire festival.

Although it is a mitzvah, a commandment, to eat and sleep in the sukkah, our rabbis emphasized that anyone who tried to be pious by eating or sleeping in the sukkah while it was pouring was a fool and a blasphemer.

Many Israeli apartments are built with special balconies which allow a sukkah to be built on them, open to the sky.

33. Special guests invited to the sukkah are called Ushpizin.

It is praiseworthy to invite guests to join us in the sukkah. Our sages included on their guest list some of our ancestors: Abraham (see facts 122–131), Isaac (see facts 129–134), Jacob (see facts 134–142), Joseph (see facts 142–147), Moses (see facts 148–154), Aaron (see facts 151, 170, 171), and David (see facts 197–202). These special Biblical guests are called Ushpizin. Many liberal Jewish families are offering new sets of Ushpizin that include as role models a variety of women from our tradition.

34. On Sukkot we read the megillah (scroll) of Kohelet (Ecclesiastes).

It has become a tradition to read Kohelet (Ecclesiastes) on Sukkot. Kohelet isn't really a book with Jewish content; however, because it states that it was written by King Solomon, the sages included it in the Ketuvim, the Writings, division of the TaNaCH (see data to fact 104). The book focuses on the basic futility of life. Our sages made the book Jewish by noting that the book really says that without Torah, life is futile. Some scholars believe that the reading of Kohelet was connected to Sukkot as a sobering influence on a holiday which the sages feared might get out of control. The grape harvest and anxiety about rain and survival sometimes led to uncontrolled behavior. Our sages hoped that raucous gaiety would be limited by reminders of our own finitude and the futility of our actions.

Like the Book of Ruth, Lamentations, the Song of Songs, and the Book of Esther, Kohelet is read from a megillah, a scroll (see data to fact 52).

Simchat Torah

35. Atzeret is celebrated by many Reform Jews as Simchat Torah.

The Torah adds another holiday at the end of Sukkot, an eighth day called Atzeret. Our sages emphasized that this holy day was separate from Sukkot. They likened it to a king's inviting his friends to a feast. At its conclusion he took some special friends aside and invited them to stay over another day so he could enjoy their company. That added day is Atzeret, and there is no known reason for it. Traditional Jews living outside of Israel add a ninth day, Simchat Torah, after Atzeret. Liberal Jews and Jews living in Israel celebrate Simchat Torah on the eighth day from the beginning of Sukkot. It is the only time during the Jewish calendar that Reform practice and traditional practice result in holidays being celebrated on completely different days.

36. Simchat Torah celebrates our finishing the reading of the Torah and immediately beginning to read it again.

Originally, our sages divided the Torah (see fact 105) into portions so that the entire Torah was read every three years or so. Each portion was read four times a week: on Mondays, Thursdays, and twice on Shabbat. Mondays and Thursdays were opportune times to read Torah because they were market days, and everyone would gather at those times.

During the medieval period the Babylonian communities switched to larger Torah portions, so they were able to finish reading the Torah every year. They then planned the portions so that the Torah would be completed each year at the end of Sukkot. The holiday celebrating the completion of the Torah reading and the immediate resumption of the cycle at Genesis (see fact 106) is Simchat Torah, the Joy of the Torah.

37. Hakafot are the processions of congregants around the synagogue with the Torah scrolls.

Simchat Torah is celebrated with much joy. The Torah scrolls (Sifrei Torah) are paraded (traditionally, seven times) around the synagogue with singing and dancing. These parades around the sanctuary are called Hakafot.

In the past hundred years the addition of children marching with flags was instituted. Many congregations now welcome new students into their Religious School at Simchat Torah with a ceremony called Consecration. Each new student is given a small Torah to carry at that time.

Traditionally, on Simchat Torah three scrolls are used for the Torah reading. One is turned to the end of Deuteronomy (see fact 110), and one is turned to the beginning of Genesis (see fact 106). (The third is used for the additional reading, the Maftir; see data to fact 246.) Doing this guarantees that there is no pause between our completion of the Torah and our immediate beginning again.

Some congregations have the custom of using only one scroll and visibly rewinding it back to the beginning so that everyone can see the physical process of beginning again.

In some congregations the children are invited to stand under a large tallit (see fact 251) while saying the blessings before and after the Torah.

The purpose of all of these customs is to get the children involved in the process of reading Torah and feeling that Simchat Torah is a special time.

Chanukkah

38. Chanukkah celebrates the time when King Antiochus tried to destroy Judaism but failed.

Chanukkah celebrates a historical event. In 165 B.C.E., a group of Jews successfully rebelled against the Seleucid King Antiochus.

Although the holiday focuses on the specific victory against King Antiochus's army, the story of Chanukkah begins long before that specific event.

In 334 B.C.E. Alexander the Great conquered Judea and brought to it Greek culture. He didn't force anyone to participate in that culture, but he lowered the taxes for any group willing to accept this way of life.

When Alexander died, his Middle Eastern kingdom divided into two groups: the eastern kingdom (including modern-day Syria, Iran, Iraq, and Lebanon) was called the Seleucid kingdom; the western kingdom (including Egypt) was the Ptolemaic kingdom. These two groups fought one another for political control, and Judea was caught between them.

The Jews of Judea didn't care which group ruled them. They had their Temple (see data to fact 220), their sacrifices (see fact 167), and their High Priest (see facts 169–171), who governed the country. It didn't matter to whom they had to pay vassal taxes; the taxes were always too high anyway.

The major political center of Greek life was the polis, the city, and the wealthier Jews succeeded in having Jerusalem recognized as a polis. They changed their dress, their names, and their life-style to those of the Greeks.

In 169 B.C.E. the Seleucid King Antiochus IV attacked the Ptolemies. He lost. Word got back to Jerusalem that Antiochus was dead. A former High Priest, Jason, saw this as an opportunity to wrench the priesthood from Antiochus's lackey, Menelaus. He set up a revolution in Jerusalem.

Antiochus, of course, was still alive. Furious, he slaughtered a large number of Jews, declared martial law, and banned certain practices of Judaism as capital crimes, specifically Shabbat (see facts 95–100) and circumcision (see facts 270–272). In addition, he profaned the Temple by introducing foreign worship. Antiochus was supported by some Jews.

39. The Jewish rebellion found its leadership in the priestly Hasmonean family.

The prohibitions established by King Antiochus were intolerable to a group of Jews called the Hasidim (not related to the modern-day Chasidim; see facts 427–429). They fought against these decrees, but they needed leadership. They found this leadership in a priestly family, the Hasmoneans.

40. The Jewish priest Mattathias began the revolt against the Greek king Antiochus.

The head of the Hasmonean clan was Mattathias. We don't know much about him personally. The First Book of Maccabees reveals that he was a priest who moved from Jerusalem more than thirty miles to Modi'in. Therefore, he was probably not part of the big-power priesthood.

When a Seleucid ordered Mattathias to participate in a foreign sacrifice in Modi'in, he refused and slew a Jew who came forward to obey the command. After slaying a Greek officer as well, Mattathias and his followers fled to the hills, and thus began the Hasmonean revolt. He successfully united the people under his authority.

41. The Jewish general leading the Hasmonean revolt was Judah the Maccabee.

Judah, called Maccabee, the Hammer, was one of Mattathias's five sons. There is a tradition stating that Judah inscribed on his shield the Hebrew letters M,CH,B,Y, which are the first letters of the words, "Who is like you among the gods, Adonai" (see facts 157, 301). By themselves, they form the word *Maccabee*.

Antiochus sent down an army to wipe out the revolt. Judah and his revolutionaries defeated that army in the mountains surrounding Jerusalem by using guerrilla tactics.

Antiochus sent another, larger army under the famous general Nicanor, but Judah and the revolutionaries defeated his army as well and entered Jerusalem.

42. Originally, Chanukkah lasted for eight days because it substituted for Sukkot.

After defeating Antiochus's army, the Jews systematically cleaned the defiled Temple in Jerusalem; it apparently took almost a year. Judah declared a great holiday to celebrate the fact that the Temple was again in Jewish hands. In order to make this dedication a big event, the Hasmoneans declared that the ceremony should serve as a reminder of Sukkot, which lasts eight days (see data to fact 35). The Jews had been unable to celebrate Sukkot for three years because of their guerrilla fighting, so they celebrated Sukkot at the time of the Temple dedication.

43. Chanukkah begins on the 25th of the month of Kislev.

The dedication of the Temple took place on the 25th of Kislev and, like Sukkot, lasted for eight days. The Hebrew word for dedication is Chanukkah.

Neither the Seleucids (the Greek power in Damascus) nor many Jews accepted the Hasmonean family as the governing priesthood. As a matter of fact, civil war continued in Judea for twenty years after the first Chanukkah. Judah's family was finally victorious. Simeon, Judah's brother, was made High Priest, and Chanukkah became a yearly celebration of the Hasmonean victory. The Hasmonean family ruled for a hundred years. During that time, there was a great deal of tension between the Hasmoneans and the sages (see facts 318–319). As a result, the sages were not particularly interested in maintaining a holiday that commemorated the dedication declared by the Hasmonean family. We find evidence of this power struggle in the traditional legend concerning the eight days of Chanukkah (see data to fact 44).

44. A Chanukkah legend says that oil enough for only one day burned in the Temple for eight days.

We find in the Talmud (see facts 360–367), compiled 700 years after the event, a legend which explained the eight-day holiday as a time when the Temple had been desecrated and there was no sacred oil. Only one small jar marked with the High Priest's seal was found. This oil, enough to burn one day, burned eight days. This miracle (said the sages) resulted in the eight-day celebration of Chanukkah.

If you think about the miracle story carefully, you will see that it is a subtle put-down of the Hasmonean family. If the Hasmoneans had been recognized as the true priesthood, they could have simply provided more oil. Instead, the story implies, there had to be a waiting period to get more oil. Moreover, by not mentioning the Hasmoneans at all, the sages tried to downplay their religious/political victory.

At any rate, Chanukkah remained a minor holiday until the modern period. Because of its juxtaposition with Christmas, it gained popularity in the United States. Because of its nationalist flavor, it gained popularity in Israel.

45. On Chanukkah we light a nine-branched candelabrum called a chanukkiyah.

Each night of Chanukkah we light a special candelabrum called a chanukkiyah. Unlike the seven-branched menorah found in the Temple (see fact 165), the chanukkiyah has nine candles. It is lit only on Chanukkah. Although Israelis distinguish between the terms chanukkiyah and menorah, most Jews still call the chanukkiyah a menorah.

46. The shamash (servant candle) lights the other eight candles in the chanukkiyah.

The word shamash means *servant*. It is the candle that is lit first and then lights the other candles, each candle corresponding to one night of Chanukkah. The number of candles increases by one each night, from right to left, until by the eighth night all nine candles are lit. Each night the candles are lit from left to right; thus the new candle is always lit first.

In addition to lighting the other candles, the shamash serves another purpose. According to the sages, the Chanukkah candles may not serve any function other than to publicize the miracle of the oil; their light may not be used. By including the shamash with the other candles, it is possible to claim that the light thus produced is from the shamash and not the other candles; therefore a person may read by the light of the chanukkiyah.

A special prayer, Al HaNissim (For the Miracles), is recited on Chanukkah reminding us of the Divine Providence involved in saving us from the Seleucids.

47. On Chanukkah we eat latkes.

The Chanukkah custom of eating foods fried in oil was another reminder of the miracle of the oil cruse. Sufganiyot (doughnuts), originally a Sephardic confection (see fact 228), are now eaten by Israelis on Chanukkah. Latkes (fried potato pancakes), originally an Ashkenazic dish (see fact 229), are eaten by most American Jews.

48. On Chanukkah we play with a dreidl.

It became a tradition to play with a four-sided top, a dreidl, on Chanukkah. Originally, the dreidl was made of lead. On each side of it was a Hebrew letter: nun, gimmel, hay, and shin. In the early Middle Ages the Germans had dice with those four letters on them, and we applied the same game rules to the dreidl. However, we made the game Jewish by creating a new meaning for the letters. We said that the letters stood for the words, "A great miracle happened there." In Israel, the *shin*, the first letter of the Hebrew word for *there*, was replaced by a *pay*, the first letter of the Hebrew word for *here*. This created the phrase, "A great miracle happened here."

Tu BiShvat

49. Tu BiShvat is the New Year of the Trees.

Leviticus 19:23-25 contains the following laws concerning fruit trees: You may not eat any fruit of a tree for the first three years of its growth. Then, in the fourth year, you must give all of the fruit to the priests. In the fifth year you may eat the fruit yourself.

The fifteenth of the month of Shvat, Tu BiShvat, is the New Year of Trees. Any tree planted during the year before Tu BiShvat became a year old on Tu BiShvat (even if it was planted the day before).

Equally important, Tu BiShvat was the first day for tax collectors to count buds on a tree to determine what the tithe for an orchard would be. Every year, one tenth of the crop went to the Temple.

In ancient Israel the days before Tu BiShvat were the busiest time of the year for planting trees. Farmers tried to beat the Tu BiShvat deadline, just as some people give to more charities in December, trying to beat the New Year tax deadline.

When Jews were exiled from the Land of Israel, we celebrated Tu BiShvat by eating fruit grown in the Land of Israel. In the sixteenth century, kabbalists living in Tzfat (see facts 417, 478) created a special ritual meal, a mystical Seder for Tu BiShvat connecting the land's yearly cycle of growth and rest with our own. This was important to them because one of the mystical images of God was "The Tree of Life." The New Year of Trees thus became an opportunity for *imitatio Dei*, imitating the Divine.

Many synagogues and communities have revived the custom of conducting a Tu Bishvat Seder.

50. We plant trees in Israel and eat a variety of fruit on Tu BiShvat.

After the Jewish National Fund was created in 1901 (see fact 509), it became a tradition to buy trees in the Land of Israel on Tu BiShvat.

Today, many families have special Tu BiShvat meals where different fruits are tasted, a reminder of the New Year of Trees in Israel. It became a tradition especially to taste fruit native to the Land of Israel.

Purim

51. Adar is the last month in the Jewish calendar.

Purim takes place on the 14th of Adar, the last Hebrew month, at the end of winter. It is the last holiday of the Jewish year, and its raucous spirit is the result of people, having gone stir-crazy in their homes during the cold months, finally finding relief. In Babylonia the people held a huge festival, got drunk, and had orgies in the early spring. Purim is the Jewish format of this early holiday, complete with a suitable story which emphasizes drinking, parties, foolish non-Jews, and victorious Jews.

52. On Purim we read the Book of Esther from a scroll (megillah).

The story of Purim is found in the Book of Esther, part of the Ketuvim, the Writings, division of the TaNaCH (see fact 104). It is traditionally read from a scroll, a megillah, which means "rolled." There are five books in the Division of Ketuvim which are called scrolls: Ruth (see facts 87, 226), Lamentations (see fact 94), Ecclesiastes (see fact 34), Song of Songs (see fact 78), and Esther. Each of these scrolls is read on a specific holiday.

The Book of Esther became the most popular in our tradition, and it is called "The Megillah."

53. The name of God isn't mentioned in the Book of Esther.

Because the story does not mention God (the only book in the Bible that doesn't), Jewish artists were willing to decorate the Megillah with pictures. At Qumran, by the Dead Sea, hundreds of pieces of parchment have been found, called the Dead Sea Scrolls (see facts 321, 322). Scholars believe it is significant that they have found pieces from every book in the TaNaCH except the Book of Esther. Some suggest that this is a strong indication that there were groups of Jews two thousand years ago who did not view the Book of Esther as part of the TaNaCH. Others disagree.

The writers of both the Septuagint (see fact 242) and the Targum (see fact 243) provide additions to this book which include God within them.

54. The foolish king in the Purim story is Ahasuerus.

The Purim story is simple. A powerful Persian king, Ahasuerus, ruled over 127 provinces. Some scholars believing that the Purim story is based on actual historical events, have tried to associate him with the Persian king Artaxerxes. Ahasuerus invited nobles from every province for a six-month drinking party. At the end of that time he invited all residents of Shushan, his capital, to a seven-day drinking party.

55. The first queen in the Purim story was Vashti.

At the end of seven days, Ahasuerus ordered his wife Vashti to appear at his drinking party. Having a drinking party of her own for all the women, she refused, and the king got rid of her.

One of the interesting modern developments concerning the Book of Esther is the role of Vashti. Feminists view her response as being praiseworthy and consider her an excellent role model for modern women. According to the Megillah, Vashti was involved with her own party and, when ordered to appear before her drunken husband, she refused, maintaining her own integrity and dignity.

Esther, on the other hand, obediently remained silent about being Jewish and acted only when pushed to do so by Mordechai (see data to facts 56, 57). It's interesting how Jews in different time periods can view biblical characters differently.

56. The second queen in the Purim story was Esther.

King Ahasuerus, needing a new wife, rounded up all the virgins so he could pick a new queen. One of these maidens was a Jewish orphan named Hadassah. The text shows that she was clearly assimilated into the Persian culture, because her official name was Esther (from the Persian goddess Ishtar). King Ahasuerus selected Esther to be his queen. Her cousin Mordechai (from the Persian god Marduk) ordered her never to reveal her Jewish background, and she acquiesced.

57. Haman tossed purim (dice) to decide when to slaughter the Jews.

The king's second-in-command, Haman, was said to be a descendant of Amalek (see fact 158). He ordered everyone to bow down to him, but Mordechai refused. When Haman learned that Mordechai was a Jew, he plotted to kill all Jews in retaliation. He cast dice, *purim* in Hebrew, to determine when to slaughter the Jews, and the date was the 13th of Adar. Haman got the king's permission to kill all the Jews.

Mordechai notified Queen Esther of the impending disaster. Taking her life into her own hands, she approached the king. After several drinking parties and some clever humiliations of Haman, she finally begged the king for her life. Haman was impaled instead of Mordechai. The Jews joyfully slaughtered 75,000 of their enemies.

58. Purim occurs on the 14th day of the month of Adar.

To commemorate the great victory and salvation of the Jews, Mordechai decreed that the 14th of Adar would be a day of joyous celebration every year. He commanded that the Megillah of Esther was to be read at that time to celebrate the defeat of Haman. In addition, everyone was commanded to send *mishloach manot*, gifts to the poor.

59. Purim reminds us of how we were saved from Haman's plot to slaughter all Jews.

There is no historical evidence that such an event ever took place in Persia. However, it has been our reality for the past 2,000 years that tyrants like Haman have tried to wipe us out. Whenever a community was threatened with disaster but was miraculously saved, the community celebrated that day by declaring a new community-wide Purim in addition to the traditional one. There are more than 127 separate communal Purims celebrated by specific cities each year to commemorate community salvations.

It is fitting that the 1991 war in the Persian Gulf ended on Purim. Israelis removed their gas masks and donned Purim masks (see data to facts 60, 514).

60. Adloyada is a Purim parade in Israel.

The celebration of Purim is a bit zany. In the fourth century Rava declared, "One must drink until one does not know the difference between 'Cursed be Haman' and 'Blessed be Mordechai.'" In gematriya (see fact 604) "Cursed be Haman" and "Blessed be Mordechai" have the same numerical value. Despite the fact that the rabbis frequently tried to curb excessive drinking, Rava's statement became a Purim custom, although today it is losing popularity. The Hebrew words for "until one does not know" are "ad lo yada." Each year Israel has a well-organized Purim parade, called the Adloyada, complete with floats and marching bands.

Beginning in the 1500s, Jews copied the Christian custom of Fastnachtshpiel and created Purim Shpiels, costumed plays. Originally these plays were only slightly related to Purim. The rabbis tried to limit them and again failed.

Today it is customary to dress up in costume on Purim; the plays created now tend to follow some aspect of the Purim story. Costumed children sing and prance through the synagogue, excitedly retelling the story of Purim.

The primary mitzvah connected with Purim is still the reading of the Megillah, the Scroll of Esther.

61. Before Purim, we read the commandment to wipe out the memory of Amalek.

On the Shabbat before Purim we read an additional Torah portion, Deuteronomy 25:17–19. Beginning with the word *zachor*, (remember), this portion commands us to remember what Amalek did to us in the desert and orders us to blot out his memory (see fact 158). According to our tradition, Haman was a direct descendant of Amalek, so it is a mitzvah to wipe out the memory of Haman. After the Holocaust (see facts 458–462), Hitler was also viewed as being a direct descendant of Amalek. The Shabbat before Purim is called Shabbat Zachor, after the first word of the additional reading.

62. We wipe out Haman's name on Purim by making noise with a gragger.

Following the custom of wiping out the name of Amalek, Haman's ancestor, people make huge amounts of noise whenever Haman's name is mentioned during the reading of the Megillah. Originally this was done with horns and percussion instruments. In the 1400s someone created a special noisemaker called a gragger, and it is now used in most communities to wipe out Haman's name. In France in the 1600s, Jews used to write Haman's name on the bottom of their shoes and literally wipe out his name by shuffling their feet.

63. On Purim we eat hamentaschen.

In Ashkenazic countries it became the custom to eat three-cornered pastries filled with poppyseeds. These pastries were originally called *mun taschen*, (poppyseed pockets). Someone made the obvious word play on their name and called them hamentaschen.

Elsewhere these pastries were called Haman's ears. Some illustrators showed Haman wearing a tri-cornered hat, and the hamentaschen became associated with Haman's hat. During Purim, costumed children bring plates of hamentaschen to friends and the needy. These gifts of food are called mishloach manot (see data to fact 58).

Pesach

64. Pesach begins on the 15th of Nisan.

Nisan is the first month of the Jewish year, marking the advent of spring. The Torah also calls this month Aviv, spring. It is a special month because on the 15th of Nisan begins Pesach, or Passover.

65. Pesach lasts seven days.

According to Leviticus 23:6, Pesach, or Passover, lasts seven days. In order to make sure that they celebrated the holiday at the correct time, Jews living outside the Land of Israel added an extra day at the beginning of the festival (see fact 1), thereby making Passover eight days. Today Jews living in Israel and most Reform Jews celebrate Passover for seven days. Even though we don't live in the Land of Israel, our calendar is now fixed. We don't rely on the Sanhedrin (see fact 327) to announce the New Moon of Nisan (see fact 1), so rationally there is no reason to add the extra day of Passover, but traditional Jews living outside the Land of Israel continue to celebrate the festival for eight days. Like Sukkot, Pesach is one of the few times when Reform Jews and traditional Jews have different calendars for holidays.

66. On Pesach we don't eat anything that has leaven or yeast in it.

The primary mitzvah associated with Pesach, or Passover, is the prohibition against owning or eating anything containing leaven or yeast during the holiday. Our sages took this commandment one step further and ordained that during Passover there should be no eating of any grain that might have risen (except previously prepared matzah). In Ashkenazic communities that included rice and legumes, since both could be used as a fermenting agent. Potatoes, however, were permitted because they were the primary food staple. In Sephardic communities, rice was permitted for the same reason.

The preparations for Passover are, traditionally, very rigorous. We thoroughly clean our houses to remove all vestiges of chametz (leaven and grain products). Many Jews use separate dishes and pans, which are not used during the rest of the year. All matzah for the holiday has to be specially prepared. To ensure that no person accidentally has leaven or yeast, it became the custom to sell all foods to a gentile for a symbolic price of a dollar, thus guaranteeing that we no longer own any leaven.

67. Shabbat HaGadol is the Sabbath before Pesach.

The laws concerning Passover were so complex that it became a tradition for the rabbi to lecture the congregation about all of the Passover details on the Shabbat preceding it. This Shabbat became known as Shabbat HaGadol, the Great Shabbat. Some scholars associate the name "the Great Shabbat" with its ritual importance. Some note that the Haftarah portion for that Shabbat (see fact 246) contains the phrase "the great day of Adonai," thus providing the day with its title.

The sages instituted a ritual for the night before Passover, whereby, using a candle and a feather (as a broom), the family makes a final search for leaven. Traditionally, a parent has hidden some pieces of bread wrapped in small bags so that the search is successful. The next morning these packets, along with all leftover chametz (see fact 66), are burned.

68. Pesach celebrates our escape from slavery in Egypt.

Passover is the classic example of how we creatively took foods and customs from surrounding peoples and made them special, Jewish symbols. Our primary association with Passover is the Exodus from Egypt. We had been slaves, cruelly oppressed by the Egyptians (see fact 149). God, striking Egypt with the Ten Plagues, forced Pharaoh to release us (see fact 156). After letting us go, Pharaoh changed his mind again and pursued us. At the Sea of Reeds, Pharaoh and his army were drowned while we were saved. We were commanded to relive this redemption every year, through the festival of Passover (see fact 157).

69. Pesach began the barley harvest in Israel.

Originally, Passover was an agricultural holiday celebrating the barley harvest and the lambing season. The ancient Canaanites had a festival at this season which included eating flat barley cakes, a year-old lamb, and special, sharp herbs. They offered a year-old lamb as a sign of trust that the gods would provide more lambs during the next year. By offering a year-old lamb, they hoped to get more lambs back.

We took those same agricultural foods and imbued them with special historical meaning for our people. The original foods became particularistic symbols of our redemption from slavery.

70. On Pesach we eat matzah.

The Torah tells us that the flat barley cakes, now called matzah, remind us of the bread our Hebrew ancestors baked hurriedly when they left Egypt. We are told that the dough, not given time to rise, baked flat. In all likelihood the Torah took a food from the Canaanites and made it into a reminder of our own history.

During the Seder, three pieces of matzah are used. We use two pieces as a reminder of the double portion of manna we received in the desert on Shabbat and holidays (see fact 96). The third piece is used to identify the "bread of affliction" and to serve as the afikoman (see fact 75). A tradition identifies the three pieces of matzah with the three groups of Jews: Kohanim (see fact 169), Levites (see fact 168), and Israel, the rest of us. Another tradition identifies the three pieces of matzah with Aaron (see fact 151), Miriam (see fact 152), and Moses (see fact 148).

71. The lamb bone on Pesach reminds us of the Divine passing over the Hebrew homes in Egypt.

In all likelihood, our tradition took the Canaanite custom of offering a lamb at this season and made it Jewish. The Torah tells us that prior to the last plague, God commanded all the Hebrews to sacrifice and eat a lamb. We were then commanded to dip hyssop (a sweet-smelling, leafy green plant) into the blood and splash it on the doors of our dwellings, so that the Divine would pass over our houses. When the first born of Egypt were struck dead, the blood on the doors of the Hebrews saved us.

We are told that the lamb which we ritually ate each year served as a reminder of the blood we put on our doors in Egypt so God would pass over our homes. No mention is made of the lambing season or the earlier Canaanite festival. The agricultural food became historical symbols.

When the Temple was destroyed (see facts 336, 343, 346), our rabbis ordained that we could not eat roasted lamb on Pesach. We've kept the lamb bone as a symbol of the first lamb eaten in Egypt and of the traditional seder meal eaten in the Temple precincts. Some traditional Jews are so cautious about the prohibition against eating lamb on Pesach that they place a roasted chicken neck on the seder plate instead of a lamb shank. When the Temple still existed, there used to be an additional sacrifice on Pesach, called the chagigah. Since we no longer have sacrificial worship, we roast an egg as a reminder of that offering.

72. Maror are the bitter herbs we eat on Pesach.

The sharp herbs called maror remind us of how bitter our lives were in Egypt. We usually use horseradish as maror.

The Torah commands us to take the three major symbolic foods, lamb, matzah, and maror, and eat them together as physical reminders of our Exodus from Egypt. We thus took the three foods that were consumed by the Canaanites in their yearly spring festival and made them Jewish.

73. The seder is a ritual meal we eat on Pesach.

We are commanded to tell our children the story of our escape from Egypt every year and to relive that redemptive experience. Our sages provided us with the method for reliving redemption: a ritual meal, a seder.

The Hebrew word *seder* means order. It is not a service; it is a meal with a purpose. Our sages organized the seder into fourteen specific steps, thus creating an *ordered meal*. On the seder table is a plate containing the foods that symbolize our slavery and our redemption. The purpose of the seder is to use those foods to tell the story of our redemption and relive that experience. The first four ritual symbols have already been explained: matzah (see fact 70), a roasted lamb bone (see fact 71), maror (see fact 72), and a roasted egg (see data to fact 71). There are a number of other symbols on the seder plate: charoset (see fact 74), salt water, and parsley.

Our sages created the seder in the style of a Roman feast, and the three additional seder plate foods originated with Roman customs. At Roman meals everyone lounged on couches while they ate; the sages ordered that on Pesach everyone should lounge. At Roman feasts guests were given greens dipped in a sharp dip, usually vinegar, sometimes salt water. Our sages took that appetizer and made it Jewish. The greens (now usually parsley) became a reminder of spring, the season of redemption. The salt water became a symbol of the tears we shed in Egypt.

74. On Pesach we eat charoset, which reminds us of the building mortar we used as slaves.

At feasts, Roman guests were frequently offered a sweet dip made of either ground dates and wine or apples, nuts, and honey. This was eaten before the main meal. Our sages used the same food, charoset, and made it into a historical symbol. According to the Torah, the Hebrew slaves built garrison cities. Charoset reminds us of the mortar they used. The charoset contains wine, and traditionally we dip maror, bitter herbs, into this mixture. It has been suggested that this dipping of greens into red wine might serve as a subtle reminder of splashing red blood on our doorposts with the green hyssop (see data to fact 71).

75. The afikoman is our Pesach dessert.

Roman feasts tended to end with orgiastic entertainment, called the epicomios. Our sages were against this immoral behavior, so they ordered that the afikoman, the final entertainment, be a piece of matzah. The ritual must end with that piece of matzah.

The Romans were famous for getting drunk at feasts and parties. The sages wanted to show that we were free on Pesach, so they insisted that every Jew drink four glasses of wine. In Exodus 6, God promises that the Divine will do five things for the Hebrews. Four of them are: I will bring you out, I will save you, I will redeem you, I will take you to be My people. Our sages ordained one glass of wine for each of these fulfilled promises. Thus wine, instead of being the Roman way of getting drunk, became a symbol of God's promises and redemption.

It is probably not coincidental that the number four appears frequently in the seder: we drink four glasses of wine, we ask four questions, and there are descriptions of four kinds of children.

76. On Pesach we invite Elijah the prophet into our homes.

Since Pesach celebrated our redemption from Egypt, our sages viewed the Pesach season as a good time for the final redemption, the arrival of the Messiah (see fact 157). According to our tradition, the Messiah would be announced by Elijah the prophet (see fact 208). Therefore Jews invite Elijah to our Passover meal, hoping that he will join us and, finally, fulfill the fifth promise made by God in Exodus 6: I will bring you into the land. We therefore leave a full glass of wine on the table for Elijah. At times when Jews believed that the Messiah had arrived or was about to arrive, they would drink this fifth glass, Elijah's cup.

77. On Pesach we say, "Next year in Jerusalem."

The seder ends with the words, "Next year in Jerusalem." Our sages emphasized that this does not refer to the physical Jerusalem in Israel; rather, it refers to the Final Jerusalem created by the coming of the Messiah. Therefore, even Jews living in Israel say either, "Next year in Jerusalem," or "Next year in the rebuilt Jerusalem."

78. On Pesach we read the megillah (scroll) of Song of Songs.

Since Pesach is connected with spring, it was natural that the added megillah (scroll) to be read on Pesach would involve spring. That scroll, found in the Ketuvim, Writings, section of the TaNaCH, is the Song of Songs.

The Song of Songs is a sensual love poem. It emphasizes how at the beginning of spring things come back to life, including passions. These passions are described in wonderful detail and poetic metaphor. The really exciting part of Song of Songs is that it attributes passions to both the man and the woman. The Middle East always recognized woman's sexuality, putting Western cultures to shame.

The Song of Songs had a very difficult time making it into the TaNaCH (see fact 104). Rabbi Akiva (see fact 347) saved the day. He pointed out that the book wasn't sexual at all. It wasn't even about a man and a woman. It was about the relationship between Israel and God. That relationship, stated Akiva, was a true love affair, and the images found in the Song of Songs were pure, metaphorical descriptions of that spiritual love. The book got in the TaNaCH, and, traditionally, we read it every Pesach.

79. The Haggadah, the Telling, is the book we use at the seder on Pesach.

Since the major Pesach commandment is to tell our children about our Exodus from Egypt, the book used at the seder, the ritual meal, is called the Telling, the Haggadah. During the Middle Ages the Rabbis began writing down the Telling. This provided an opportunity for Jewish artists to use their creativity and create beautiful Haggadot (plural of Haggadah). The written Haggadah also ensured that the order of the seder became somewhat standardized. Although many traditional Jews concentrate on simply reading the Haggadah as it is written, it was intended to serve as a springboard for discussions, lessons, and additional learning among the guests. We encourage people to ask questions and dig further into the text and its meanings for us today. We are told in the Haggadah that it is praiseworthy to lengthen the Telling until all present understand the complete meaning of Pesach and redemption.

Shavuot

80. Shavuot began the wheat harvest in Israel.

Both Pesach and Shavuot were originally agricultural festivals. Pesach marked the barley harvest, the cutting of the omer (barley sheaf), and Shavuot marked the wheat harvest.

81. There are seven weeks between Pesach and Shavuot.

The correct time to cut wheat is 50 days after the barley is ripe. Therefore, it was natural to count seven weeks of seven days, 49 days from the time of the barley harvest to the wheat harvest. We call this tradition the Counting of the Omer. Shavuot means Weeks.

In the Middle East the omer period between barley and wheat was an anxious time. Ripening wheat needs rain to survive. However, too much rain rots the kernels. Therefore, those seven weeks were a tense season.

Our tradition reflects that tension. Traditionally, except for the two New Moons (see fact 1) and Yom HaAtzmaut (see fact 91), it is forbidden to have celebrations during that time, including marriages. Traditional Jews don't cut their hair. Music and dancing are considered inappropriate. Because there are six Sabbaths between Passover and Shavuot, and the Mishnah tractate *Pirkei Avot* has six chapters (see facts 357 and 359), it became a tradition to read a chapter each week during that season.

82. The thirty-third day between Pesach and Shavuot is called Lag BaOmer.

There is one exception to the tense period between the barley and wheat harvests. The thirty-third day of the omer counting is a day of celebration. The Hebrew letters equalling 33 are LG. The thirty-third day of the omer is therefore called Lag BaOmer, the thirty-third of the omer.

Marriages are permitted on Lag BaOmer. There are many traditional reasons offered, but none of them is really satisfactory.

Our sages tell us that during the time of Rabbi Akiva (see fact 347), there was a plague which killed his students. The plague ceased on the thirty-third day of the Counting of the Omer, so it became a day of rejoicing.

Another legend associates Lag BaOmer with the Bar Kochba Revolt against the Romans in 133 c.e. (see fact 349). The Jewish revolutionaries apparently won a victory on Lag BaOmer, thus making it a day of festivities. This led to the custom of having picnics with bows and arrows on that day.

Another legend makes Lag BaOmer the Yahrzeit (the anniversary of the death) of Rabbi Shimon Bar Yochai (see fact 352). According to tradition, Rabbi Shimon Bar Yochai was the author of the *Zohar*, the major book of Kabbalah, Jewish mysticism. (The *Zohar* was actually written almost a thousand years later, see facts 353, 354). Kabbalah-oriented Jews gather at his grave on Mount Meiron (near Tzfat) on Lag BaOmer. They give their 3-year old sons their first haircuts and toss the hair into bonfires on the mountain (see fact 353).

Modern liberal Jews tend not to feel the anxiety and tension associated with the period between Pesach and Shavuot since most of us are not farmers. Many Jews no longer acknowledge the traditional prohibition against getting married during this season. Lag BaOmer has become a very minor celebration, usually involving, at most, a picnic.

83. Jews brought their first offerings to the Temple on Shavuot.

The Torah refers to Shavuot only as the wheat harvest and the time for bringing the choicest produce, the bikkurim, to the Temple. The Torah does not provide a specific date for the wheat harvest, simply noting that it takes place 50 days after Pesach. Like Sukkot and Pesach, Shavuot was one of the Shalosh Regalim, the Three Pilgrimage Festivals (see fact 27).

84. On Shavuot we received the Torah on Mount Sinai.

After the destruction of the Temple in 70 c.e. (see fact 336), our sages infused new meaning into the holiday of Shavuot by making it the anniversary of our acceptance of the Torah at Mount Sinai. From Chag HaBikkurim (the Festival of Choice Produce), Shavuot became Zeman Matan Torah, the Season of Giving the Torah. Our sages declared that Shavuot was to be celebrated on the 6th of Sivan. Traditional Jews living outside the Land of Israel celebrate Shavuot on both the 6th and 7th of Sivan (see data to fact 1).

85. Many Jews stay up all night on Shavuot studying the Torah.

As a reliving of our experience at Mount Sinai, many Jews stay up all night on Shavuot studying the Torah. According to our tradition, the Hebrews at Mount Sinai also didn't sleep the night after they received the Torah. Moreover, since we personally relive the acceptance of Torah each year on Shavuot, it is necessary for us to review the contract.

86. On Shavuot we read the Ten Commandments.

We read the Ten Commandments, found in Exodus 20 and Deuteronomy 5, as the Torah portion for Shavuot because that describes our acceptance of Torah (see facts 160, 161). Akdamut, a long poem praising God and thanking the Divine for giving us the Torah, is also traditionally read.

87. On Shavuot we read the megillah (scroll) of the Book of Ruth.

We read the Book of Ruth (see fact 226) on Shavuot for three reasons. First, it describes the barley harvest, which takes place between Pesach and Shavuot. Second, it describes Ruth's insistence that she stay with Naomi: "Wherever you go, I will go; where you lodge, I will lodge; your people will be my people; and your God, my God."

Since Shavuot recreates our acceptance of the Torah at Mount Sinai, our sages connected Ruth's acceptance of the Jewish people to that holiday as well.

Finally, Shavuot is the traditional anniversary of King David's death. Since David was the great-grandson of Ruth, our sages felt it was appropriate to read her story on his Yahrzeit.

88. On Shavuot we eat blintzes and dairy foods.

It has become a custom to eat only dairy products on Shavuot. Ashkenazic Jews specifically eat blintzes. A variety of reasons are offered for this custom. The most frequently quoted reason is based on the verse in Song of Songs 4:11: "Honey and milk shall be under your tongue." Our sages assumed that this referred to Torah; thus milk products became a symbol of Torah.

Another explanation notes that the Torah contains the laws dealing with the eating of meat (see facts 590, 595, 596). Until Torah was received, the Hebrews didn't know what meat products were permitted and the rules weren't yet binding upon them. From the moment they received the Torah, however, the laws contained therein became obligatory. Since they were going to eat on the day they received Torah, they had to eat foods that they were sure met the new contract. Therefore, they stayed away from meat products and ate only dairy foods.

Historically, during the wheat harvest it was unlikely that people would take the time to prepare heavy meals. Therefore, during Shavuot the workers probably ate light meals, relying on dairy products.

89. Confirmation takes place on Shavuot.

In the nineteenth century the Reform Movement added a new Shavuot tradition. The Reform leaders had always been concerned about Bar Mitzvah (see fact 277). They didn't believe that a 13-year old was really old enough to accept the adult religion of Judaism. They therefore discouraged the ceremony celebrating Bar Mitzvah and instituted a new ceremony originally for ninth graders and later, tenth graders. They imported it from the Protestant Church and called it Confirmation.

The ceremony focused on the teenagers' acceptance of the covenant enacted at Mount Sinai, and the obvious time for Confirmation was Shavuot. Confirmation also encouraged students to continue studying Judaism for several years after the age of 13, thus providing more education for Jewish teenagers.

The ceremony has been very popular for almost a century. Many Conservative congregations have also instituted Confirmation. Besides its solemn initiation of Jewish teenagers into Jewish adulthood, Confirmation also serves the beneficial function of bringing large numbers of people into the synagogue for Shavuot services.

Yom HaShoah

90. Yom HaShoah reminds us of the Jews who died in the Holocaust.

Two new commemorative holidays have been created because of twentieth-century events. The first of these, Yom HaShoah, is the yearly Memorial of the Holocaust (see facts 458–463). It was instituted by Israel's Knesset (see fact 540) in 1951 and has been recently recognized by the Reform Movement as an official Jewish holiday. It takes place on the 27th of Nisan, a week and a day after Pesach.

The ceremonial practices for remembering the Holocaust have not yet been formalized. Many congregations light six candles, one for each million Jews slaughtered. Holocaust survivors are invited to speak, and powerful readings and liturgical dramas are presented. The recitation of the Mourners' Kaddish (see fact 279) and the El Malei Rachamim (see data to fact 284) has become almost traditional.

Yom HaAtzmaut

91. Yom HaAtzmaut is Israel's Independence Day.

On the 5th of Iyar, corresponding to May 14, 1948, the State of Israel proclaimed its creation (see facts 536–539). We celebrate that miracle with the holiday of Yom HaAtzmaut, Israel's Independence Day.

In Israel, Yom HaAtzmaut follows a day of deep mourning: Yom HaZikaron, the Day of Remembrance. That day honors all those who died fighting for Israel's survival. A horn blows at 10 A.M. on that day, and the entire nation stops for a minute of silence.

Yom HaAtzmaut is a day of parades, dancing, hikes, contests, and picnics. In the United States, Yom HaAtzmaut usually includes a major rally demonstrating Jewish solidarity with Israel.

In 1951 the Reform Movement declared Yom HaAtzmaut to be an official Jewish holiday. Liturgy and rituals are being created to celebrate this miraculous time in Jewish history.

Tisha B'Av

92. On Tisha B'Av we fast.

Fasting has always been a Jewish way of showing contrition and mourning. Both the sages and the prophets sought to limit fasting, but there are five public fast days in the Jewish year. The most important fast day is Yom Kippur. The second most important is one of the saddest days in the Jewish Year, Tisha B'Av, the Ninth of Av.

93. According to tradition, Tisha B'Av is the anniversary of the destruction of both the First and Second Temples.

According to tradition, on Tisha B'Av in 586 B.C.E. Nebuchadnezzar and the Babylonians destroyed Solomon's Temple (see fact 217).

On that date in 70 C.E. Titus and the Romans destroyed the Second Temple (see fact 336).

On that date in 1290 England banished all Jews (see fact 405).

On that date in 1492 Spain expelled all Jews (see fact 413).

The Ninth of Av symbolizes all of the horrors we have suffered as a people over the past three thousand years. According to our sages, the precedent for the Ninth of Av being our day of misery was an incident in the desert. It was on the Ninth of Av that the people heard the negative report of the ten scouts and rebelled against Moses, refusing to go forward into the Land of Canaan (see facts 176, 177). Historically, there is no evidence that any of our moments of horror actually occurred on the ninth of Av.

94. On Tisha B'Av we read the megillah (scroll) of Lamentations.

Tisha B'Av is commemorated by reading the Book of Lamentations, found in the Ketuvim, the Writings section of the TaNaCH. According to our tradition, Lamentations was written by the prophet Jeremiah (see fact 212) when he viewed the destruction of the First Temple. It is a paean of grief and loss.

It is customary not to wear leather on Tisha B'Av because leather was viewed as a luxury. The fast on Tisha B'Av lasts from sundown to sundown.

Shabbat

95. Shabbat reminds us of the Exodus from Egypt and God's finishing the creation of the world.

While all other holidays mark special agricultural or historical events in our year, Shabbat provides us with the weekly opportunity to reevaluate our goals and our values, to change the perspective on our otherwise complicated, hurried lives.

For the past three thousand years Shabbat has been carefully observed. It is a day totally separate from the rest of the week, a day of holiness, sacred time. Our rabbis instituted a number of rituals celebrating Shabbat. It is welcomed each week with the lighting of Shabbat candles (see fact 5). Kiddush is said (see fact 6). However, there is no Hallel (see fact 7); a different set of psalms, Psalms 95–99 and Psalm 29 are read instead.

The Torah calls Shabbat the eternal sign of our covenant with the Divine, the reminder of creation, and a reminder of our Exodus from Egypt (see fact 156).

It is easy to see the connection between Shabbat and creation because the Torah states specifically that on the seventh day God ceased the creative sequence (see fact 113). By changing our actions on Shabbat we identify with that original Shabbat and note the perfection in the world around us. We allow the world to sweep over us rather than trying to control our environment.

The connection of Shabbat to the Exodus from Egypt is a little more complicated. At an existential level, slaves cannot feel complete; they are not treated as humans. They do not control their use of time. Only free people can be complete and use their time creatively. Thus Shabbat, the time when we feel complete and free, reminds us of our redemption from Egypt.

96. Traditionally, two challot are eaten on Shabbat to remind us of the double portion of manna in the desert.

God's first command to us in the desert after redemption concerned Shabbat. When we first entered the desert, we had no food. God provided us with manna, a special food which we scooped off the ground every day.

God commanded the Hebrews on the sixth day to collect enough manna for two days because the manna would not appear on Shabbat. Thus, our first Shabbat observance took place in the desert after our Exodus from Egypt.

As a reminder of the double portion of manna in the desert, we traditionally eat two challot (plural of challah) on Shabbat and the festivals.

Originally, challah was a loaf of bread offered as part of the afternoon sacrifice at the Temple (see data to fact 295). With the destruction of the Temple, our rabbis ordained that every home should become a mini-altar (see facts 346, 589). They therefore ordered all households to take a small piece of raw dough and throw it into the fire before making loaves of bread, as a reminder of the challah offering. This small piece of burnt dough was called the challah. We eventually called the loaves baked after this dough had been burned "challot" (plural of challah). This custom became especially important for loaves prepared for Shabbat and the festivals. Traditionally, challah is baked as a braided loaf.

97. On Shabbat we don't perform the same tasks we do the rest of the week.

Exodus 20 commands us to "do no manner of labor on Shabbat." Our sages spent a great deal of time trying to determine what the phrase "Do no manner of labor" meant. They decided that it referred to 39 specific categories of work, which they derived from the Torah text. Exodus 31:12–18 includes a prohibition against doing any labor on Shabbat. It is preceded by a description of all of the work needed to make the Mishkan, the portable Temple and its furnishings (see fact 166). Our rabbis connected the Shabbat prohibition with the actions needed to build the Mishkan, and those labors became the 39 forbidden categories of work.

98. An eruv is a special fence that enables traditional Jews to carry things out of their homes on Shabbat.

One of the activities forbidden by the rabbis was carrying anything from one domain to another. It was possible, however, to make a town or a city into a single private domain by surrounding the area with either a wall or a continuous wire. By enclosing the entire area, our sages declared that it was permissible to carry within that enclosure because all of the private domains were thus mixed into one. Today many towns and cities are creating these enlarged "mixed private domains." The process is called "building an eruv, a mixture (of private domains)."

99. Kabbalat Shabbat is the ritual that welcomes Shabbat.

Jews have always prepared for Shabbat with eagerness and joy. In the sixteenth century the kabbalists (see fact 417) created a special welcoming ceremony for Shabbat called Kabbalat Shabbat, Greeting the Sabbath. This ceremony included Psalms 95–99 and Psalm 29, plus additional songs and readings which they used as a prelude to their Shabbat service.

100. The Shabbat song "L'cha Dodi" welcomes Shabbat as a bride.

The prime image of Shabbat is as a bride. Israel, the groom, eagerly awaits Shabbat. This imagery was beautifully expressed in a poem, "L'cha Dodi," created by Shlomo Alkabetz, a sixteenth-century Kabbalist (see fact 417).

Shabbat is not observed merely through a set of prohibitions. It is meant to be a day of joy, study, prayer, and recuperation. Our sages instituted some required acts of joy: It is a mitzvah to engage in sexual intercourse with your spouse on Shabbat. It is a mitzvah to drink wine. It is a mitzvah to have three full meals on Shabbat.

This last mitzvah resulted in a number of specific Shabbat customs. One of the 39 forbidden categories of work is to cook on Shabbat. The evening Shabbat meal was no problem; the meal was prepared before Shabbat and could be served hot when the family came home from Kabbalat Shabbat. To fulfill the mitzvah of eating a hot meal during Shabbat day, a special food, cholent, was made (see fact 101). In keeping with the theme of Shabbat joy, it became the custom to sing zemirot (songs) during the meal.

101. Cholent is a meat, bean, and potato stew traditionally eaten on Shabbat.

The meal for Shabbat day required some creativity. Our sages ordained that, although it was forbidden to cook on Shabbat, it was permitted to put foods on a fire before Shabbat and leave them there throughout the day. Jews therefore created long-cooking stews to eat on Shabbat day. These were made from beans, potatoes, and meat and were called cholent. They fulfilled the mitzvah of providing a special meal at Shabbat midday.

In order to fit a third meal into the period of Shabbat, it became the custom to have a meal at the synagogue between Minchah (see fact 297) and Maariv (see fact 298). This meal was usually accompanied by zemirot (songs) and Torah study. This third meal was called Seudah Sh'lishit, the Third Meal.

One of the challenges of modern Judaism is to find ways of observing Shabbat that enhance and enrich our lives. The Central Conference of American Rabbis (see data to fact 448) has recently published a new Shabbat Manual which offers some excellent guidelines. The bottom-line purpose of any act on Shabbat, however, should be to make our sacred time different, separate from secular, weekday time.

Havdalah

102. Havdalah ends Shabbat.

The theme of separateness is emphasized in the ritual that ends Shabbat, Havdalah, the Separating. We acknowledge the difference between sacred time and secular time, and we welcome the new week with the words, "Shavua tov, " "A good week."

Unlike the beginning of Shabbat, which begins at sundown, Havdalah does not take place until we can see three stars in the sky (about 45 minutes after sundown). In this way we show our reluctance to part with the Shabbat bride.

Since one of the possible times for the arrival of the Messiah (see fact 326) is the end of Shabbat, part of the Havdalah ceremony is to invite Elijah the Prophet into our homes (see fact 208). However, we do not offer him a cup of wine as we do on Pesach.

103. The three objects used for Havdalah are a glass of wine, a spice box, and a braided candle.

Havdalah is one of our loveliest ceremonies. Traditionally, it takes place at home and does not require a minyan, a quorum of ten Jews (see fact 289). It uses three ritual objects. In a darkened room, we light a multi-wicked candle. The candle has to have more than one wick because the accompanying blessing includes the words, "Who creates the lights of fire," with "lights" in the plural.

The Havdalah ceremony begins with a blessing over wine, the symbol of our joy (see fact 6). Just as Shabbat begins with wine (see data to fact 95), it ends with wine.

During the Havdalah ceremony we smell sweet spices. According to our tradition, Jews receive an added Shabbat soul during the Sabbath. The pain of saying goodbye to that extra spark of the Divine needs comfort, and smelling sweet spices serves that purpose. Originally, myrtle (hadas) was used as the spice. For the past thousand years artisans have worked at making beautiful Havdalah spice boxes. Many were created in the shape of a fortress with a flag on top decorated with filigree work, imitations of the ritual containers of the Catholic Church (called monstrances and thuribles). Although no longer containing myrtle, the spice boxes were called *hadas*. Today they are called *besamim*, spice boxes.

As part of the Havdalah ritual, we use the light of the multi-wicked candle to examine our nails, thus emphasizing that the Shabbat is over and light can again be used pragmatically. Some rabbis noted that such an examination also made a shadow on our hands, separating light from darkness, emphasizing the theme of Separation, Havdalah.

The final blessing of Havdalah notes a number of separations: between sacred and secular; between light and darkness; between Israel and the other nations; between Shabbat and the six days of creation.

TaNaCH

TaNaCH/Torah Overview

104. The TaNaCH is divided into three parts: Torah, Prophets, and Writings.

TaNaCH is the Hebrew word for Bible. It is divided into three parts. The first, Torah, consists of the first five books of the TaNaCH (see facts 105–110).

The second division is the Prophets, Nevi'im, dealing mostly with the lives and words of the prophets (see facts 205–214). Nevi'im also includes the historical books of Joshua (see fact 183), Judges (see facts 184–190), Samuel (see facts 191–202), and Kings.

The third division is the Writings, Ketuvim. This includes the five scrolls (see facts 34, 52, 78, 87, 94), the book of Psalms (see fact 200),

Proverbs (see fact 222), Ezra (see fact 221), Nehemiah (see fact 220), Chronicles, Job (see fact 223), and Daniel (see fact 224). By taking the first letter of each of these three divisions—T N CH—our sages created the acronym TaNaCH, the Hebrew word for Bible.

105. The Torah consists of five books.

The Torah is the first five books of the TaNaCH. Since Moses is credited with writing the Torah text, receiving the dictation from God, it is also called the Five Books of Moses. In Greek it is called the Pentateuch (Five Books). According to our tradition, it contains 613 mitzvot, commandments (see fact 162), our beginning contract with the Divine. It is our most important text, the constitution of the Jewish people.

Orthodox Jews believe that the Torah is eternal, was divinely created, contains all truth, and is unchanging. Kabbalah, Jewish mysticism (see facts 355, 417), describes the Torah as being written before creation; God utilized the text as the blueprint for the universe.

Torah study is one of the most important Jewish activities, and it entails an entire lifetime of loving labor. According to our tradition, Torah can be studied at four different levels:

1. Peshat is the actual literal meaning of the Torah text. When you pick up the Torah and read a sentence, you are studying the peshat.
2. Remez is the finding of hints within the text which allude to different meanings than what the literal meaning implies. For example, finding numerical relationships between words (see fact 604) in the text would be studying remez.
3. Derash is the interpretation of the text provided by the rabbis through midrash (see fact 333). Studying derash provides rich overlays to the literal text.
4. Sod is the studying of the hidden mysteries in the Torah, available only to those who immerse themselves in Kabbalah, Jewish mysticism (see facts 355, 417).

The first letters of these four study disciplines form the acronym PaRDeS, orchard. It is the source of our word *Paradise*.

106. The first book of the Torah is Genesis.

Genesis tells the story of our people from creation to the death of Joseph. It is almost entirely narrative. According to our sages, it contains three mitzvot: to be fruitful and multiply, to circumcise your sons (see facts 126, 270), and to avoid eating the sciatic nerve in animals (see data to facts 141, 590). The book is called Bereishit in Hebrew, after the first word in the text. Facts 111–147 refer to events told in the book of Genesis.

107. Exodus tells how we were freed from Egypt.

The second book, Exodus, tells of our redemption from Egypt; our acceptance of the Torah at Mount Sinai; and the building of the Mishkan, the portable sanctuary, in the desert. The book is called Shemot in Hebrew, after the first important word of its text. Facts 148–166 and fact 171 refer to events and laws found in the book of Exodus.

108. Leviticus tells about our holidays and the sacrifices to God.

The third book of the Torah, Leviticus, contains laws concerning the sacrifices, ritual purity, sexual relations, the holidays, and the Holiness Code. With the exception of a few brief incidents, the entire book is made up of specific laws and regulations. It ends with the short Tochacha, the Rebuke, a description of all of the horrible things that will happen to the Jewish people if we break the divine contract and don't follow the mitzvot. The book is called Vayikra in Hebrew, after the first word of its text. Facts 167–175 refer to events and laws found in the book of Leviticus.

109. Numbers describes our wandering in the desert.

The fourth book of the Torah, Numbers, tells of our forty years of desert wanderings. It also contains laws dealing with the Nazirite (see data to fact 188), the suspected adulteress (see data to fact 266), the Cities of Refuge (see fact 181), tzitzit (see fact 250), and the sacrifices connected with the festivals. The book is called Bamidbar in Hebrew, after the first important word of its text. Facts 176–181 refer to events and laws found in the book of Numbers.

110. Deuteronomy is composed of three long speeches by Moses.

The fifth book, Deuteronomy, consists of three long sermons by Moses which include repetitions of many laws found elsewhere in the Torah. It contains a community covenant-renewal ceremony which assumes total conquest of the land. Many scholars believe that the book of Deuteronomy was created during the reign of King Josiah and was read to the people in 622 B.C.E. (as described in II Kings 22). King Josiah lived during a period when many Hebrews were following Canaanite cultic practices forbidden by the Torah. By reading the Teaching of Moses (Deuteronomy) to the people, Josiah was able to destroy the idolatrous cultic altars and return the people to correct Hebrew worship (with the help of his army).

Orthodox Jews believe that Deuteronomy, like the other books of the Torah, was written on Mount Sinai (see data to fact 159), except for the last verses. According to tradition, those verses, praising Moses after his death, were written by Joshua, Moses' successor. Deuteronomy is called Devarim in Hebrew, after the first important word of its text.

Creation and the Garden of Eden

111. God created light on the first day of creation.

According to our tradition, the light created on the first day was different from the light we are accustomed to today. Our sages noted that the sun and the moon, our sources of natural light, were not created until the fourth day of creation. Therefore this first light was extraordinary. Some writings in Kabbalah, Jewish mysticism (see facts 355, 417), refer to this original light as being black fire. Just as it illumined the world through darkness, it is possible for mystics to read not only the written words in the Torah, but the spaces around the letters.

One of the major prayers said each morning, the Yotzer, praises God for creating light (see data to fact 300). Significantly, the prayer notes this process as being in the present tense. God is continuously in the process of creating. Each day offers us the opportunity to view the world as a new wonder, a series of miracles which require our awe.

112. God created the world in six days.

According to the Book of Genesis, God created the whole world and all its creatures within a six-day period. In the first chapter of Genesis, the mode of creation was speech. "And God said, 'Let there be light,' and there was light." In the second chapter of Genesis, God appears more like an artisan, making a man from clay and blowing life into him. These two different forms of creation have led modern scholars to suggest that Genesis offers two separate creation stories. This idea is unacceptable to Orthodox Jews, who believe that God dictated the Torah text in its entirety. There continues to be tension between Jews who believe that the Torah's description of creation is exactly what happened and those who, believing in evolution, view the stories as human attempts to describe the unity and goodness of the world.

According to the Torah text, God created all animals and humans on the sixth day. According to some of the sages, however, the sixth day was even more hectic. On that day, God created all animals, man, and woman; Eve was tempted by the serpent; Eve convinced Adam to eat the forbidden fruit; and both were evicted from the Garden of Eden. What a day!

With the completion of the creative process, God is quoted as saying, "This is very good." Our tradition has understood this statement to refer both to the aesthetic quality of the world and to its ethical potential. The world and all its creatures are both beautiful and morally good.

113. God created Shabbat on the seventh day.

Genesis 2:1–3 describes God completing creation, resting, and "taking a breath" on the seventh day, thus creating Shabbat, the day of rest (see facts 95–101). Although some people today might have problems with the image of the Divine "resting," the important value concept for our sages was the image of the world being, for that moment, complete. There was nothing to add, nothing to take away. That moment made Shabbat sacred time.

Each week we try to imitate the Divine's world by attempting to recapture that same extraordinary moment when everything in our lives is complete, whole, set. Shabbat is a spiritual refueling stop on our train track of life.

114. Adam was the first man.

In Genesis 2:7 God creates the man from the dust of ground. The Hebrew word for ground is "adamah." Adam, derived from adamah, reminds us of our earth nature: dust to dust. On the other hand, we are told in Genesis 1:26 that we are created in the Divine image. This tension between trying to be holy, above the animals, while made of the same animal protoplasm, remains the primary human challenge.

115. Eve was the first woman.

Genesis 2:21–24 describes God creating woman from the rib of Adam. When Adam first sees this new creation, he calls her *Ishah*, woman, a word which the Torah derives from the Hebrew word *ish*, man. Ironically, the roots of the two words are actually unrelated.

The new creation, woman, isn't named Eve until after the forbidden fruit debacle. With encouragement from the serpent, Woman eats the forbidden fruit and gives it to Adam, who also eats it. God banishes them from the Garden of Eden. When God announces to Adam and Woman that they are to be mortal and finite, Adam names the woman Eve (Chavah), because she will be the mother of all living (chai).

According to the sages, Adam had a partner before Woman/Eve. When God first created Adam, the Divine created an equal creature named Lilith. Adam tried to order Lilith around and was rebuked because Lilith viewed herself as Adam's equal. Adam complained to God, who banished Lilith and created woman from Adam, thus making her biologically subordinate.

For the sages, Lilith became a she-devil threatening the lives of newly born children and causing nocturnal emissions in men. The rabbinic message about the proper attitude of women toward men thus became clear. In the 1970s a Jewish feminist magazine was created called *Lilith*. Its purpose was to restore Lilith to a place of honor in our consciousness. Rather than being viewed as evil, Lilith deserves to be viewed as our feminist prototype.

Cain and Abel

116. Cain killed his brother Abel.

The Torah describes how both Cain and Abel made offerings to God. God accepted the lamb of Abel, the shepherd, but rejected the vegetables of Cain, the gardener. From the wording of the text, our sages assume that Abel brought the best that he had while Cain offered mediocre goods.

Some scholars believe that the important element is that God enjoys meat more than vegetables since our Hebrew ancestors were shepherds, not farmers.

At any rate, Cain murders Abel in a field. The text does not specify why or how. When God confronts Cain about his missing brother, he replies: "I do not know. Am I my brother's keeper?" (Genesis 4:9).

The answer is immediate and thunderous: "The bloods of your brother cry to me from the ground." The Hebrew usage of the word *bloods* led our sages to note that "he who takes a life takes a world of lives," that is, all of the potential descendants of the dead person.

Noah

117. God commanded Noah to build an ark to save his family and him from the flood.

Many civilizations in the Near East have stories about terrible floods caused by the gods. The vast majority of these stories, however, hold the concept that the gods are whimsical in their decision to destroy the earth. In Genesis, God's decision is based on moral outrage. All living creatures had sinned, and God decided to wipe out creation and begin again.

We are told that Noah was a righteous man for his generation. Our sages discussed whether that meant that he was super-special, having remained righteous despite the iniquities of his entire generation, or that he was really mediocre—righteous only when compared with the wicked in his generation.

Since Noah was recognized as being pre-Abraham (see fact 122) and a representative of the non-Jewish world, it is not surprising that the sages decided that, had Noah lived in a less wicked generation, he would not have been considered righteous. Following God's command, Noah built an ark and placed into it seven pairs of every animal fit for sacrifice (see fact 590) and one pair of every other living creature. The Divine then flooded the earth, annihilating all other life. Our rabbis pointed out that the only living creatures who obviously hadn't sinned were the fish, since they weren't destroyed.

118. After the flood a dove found an olive branch, proof that there was dry land.

After the flood waters had begun to recede, Noah sent out a raven. It is not clear from the text what happened to it. According to the sages, the raven was a wicked bird and did not fulfill its errand honestly.

Noah then sent out a dove. It couldn't find any dry land. Seven days later, however, it went out again and returned with an olive leaf in its beak. The dove carrying an olive branch has become a symbol of peace, the end of destruction.

119. God made an agreement with Noah never to flood the world again.

According to Genesis 9, the terms of the covenant between God and Noah were as follows:

1. Noah was to be fruitful and multiply.
2. Noah was permitted to eat meat.
3. Noah was forbidden to commit the barbarism of eating a limb of an animal while it was still alive.
4. Noah was forbidden to take human life.

In return, God promised never to destroy the world by flood.

Noah was seen by the sages as being the paradigmatic non-Jew in the world. Thus the covenant between God and Noah was binding upon all humans.

According to the sages, Noah's side of the agreement included seven laws applicable to all humans:

1. There must be a court system among humans.
2. Humans must not commit blasphemy.
3. Humans must not commit incest or adultery.
4. Humans must not commit murder.
5. Humans must not commit theft or robbery.
6. Humans must not worship idols.
7. Humans must not cut the flesh from a living animal.

120. The sign of God's agreement with Noah was a rainbow.

Our sages disagree whether the rainbow, the sign of the covenant between Noah and God, was created solely to serve as the sign of the new agreement. Ibn Ezra (see fact 387) maintains that God changed the atmosphere after the flood, thus creating the rainbow for the first time as the sign of the covenant. Numerous other sages maintain that the rainbow had always been a natural phenomenon after a storm; God merely designated it as the sign of the ongoing contract between all life and the Divine. The purpose of the rainbow was to remind God of the newly created contract and hold the Divine to the promise never to destroy the world by flood.

The Tower of Babel

121. Because of the Tower of Babel, humans were given many different languages and were dispersed around the world.

Noah's sons did replenish the earth. At that time all people spoke one language. With unmitigated gall, they planned to build a city and tower that would reach into heaven. Angered by this project and threatened by the ability of humans when unified in their building efforts, God confused their speech, creating a babble of languages. Peoples were then dispersed around the world. The tower that caused all the trouble was called the Tower of Babel (Genesis 11:9).

Our sages offered a variety of reasons for the Divine's wrath. They maintained that the people built the tower for idolatrous purposes. Some suggested that the tower was built higher than the flood waters at the time of Noah, thus serving as a human attempt to escape Divine punishment a second time. This attempt would certainly have angered God because the Divine had just finished establishing a covenant with Noah promising never again to destroy the earth by flood (see fact 119). Such a tower therefore demonstrated lack of faith in the Divine's word.

Historically, towers as high as 300 feet constructed from baked bricks were central sites of worship in Mesopotamia. They were called ziqqurats in Akkadian. Scholars continue to argue over which ziqqurat was the prototype for the Tower of Babel in the Torah. Most agree that it was probably the tower of Esagila, built in the nineteenth century B.C.E. and rebuilt several times after that.

Abraham and Related Stories

122. Abraham was the first Hebrew.

Avram's father, Terach, lived in Ur. He moved to Haran, about halfway around the Fertile Crescent toward Canaan (see fact 470). Avram received a divine command to leave Haran and move his entire family to Canaan. There, Avram made a covenant, a brit, with God. The agreed terms were that Avram would accept the Divine as God, and God would give all of Canaan to Avram and his descendants, who would be as numerous as the stars and the sand. In establishing a subsequent covenant with God, Avram's name was changed to Abraham.

We frequently refer to Abraham as the "first Jew," because we are his direct descendants. However, the term *Jew*, coming from the word *Judah* (see fact 202), didn't refer to our people until the time of the Babylonian Exile (see fact 218). Before that time, we were called *Hebrews*. Scholars are not in agreement over that term's etymology.

123. Sarah was Abraham's wife.

Our Torah text doesn't tell us where Avram met Sarai or anything about her except that she was barren. When Avram and his wife Sarai went down to Egypt, Avram feared that the Egyptians would murder him in order to marry Sarai. He therefore said that she was his sister. According to the sages, Avram was justified in saying this because Avram's brother Haran was Sarai's father. That made Sarai Avram's niece, and we are permitted to call family members sister. At the time that God changed Avram's name to Abraham, the Divine changed Sarai's name to Sarah (see data to fact 126).

124. Lot was Abraham's nephew.

The Torah tells five stories about Lot. As Avram's nephew (and, according to some rabbis, Sarah's brother), Lot joined Avram's family when they left Haran and came into the Land of Canaan (Genesis 12:5). Lot gained wealth along with Avram in their journey down to Egypt (Genesis 13:5). Lot separated from Avram and set up residence in the wealthy, materialist cities by the Dead Sea (Genesis 13:7–11). Lot was captured during a war and subsequently freed by Abraham (Genesis 14:1–16). Lot showed hospitality to the angels who came to Sodom, even offering his two virgin daughters to the wicked city dwellers rather than allowing them to hurt his guests (Genesis 19:1–11).

125. Hagar was the mother of Ishmael, Abraham's oldest son.

Sarai was barren. After ten years, in order to provide Avram with an heir, she gave him her Egyptian maid servant, Hagar. Hagar conceived and gave birth to Ishmael. When Ishmael was 13, Sarai, now Sarah, gave birth to Isaac. She begged Abraham to send Hagar and Ishmael away, and he did so. Alone in the wilderness, Hagar and Ishmael were saved by an angel and, according to tradition, Ishmael became the progenitor of the Arabian nations.

There has been at least one famous rabbi named Ishmael. The name lost its popularity with Jews after the rise of Mohammed (see fact 371), because the Muslims viewed Ishmael, and not Isaac, as the main inheritor of Abraham. This tension can be seen today in Hebron, where both Muslims and Jews consider the grave of Abraham to be a holy shrine (see fact 484).

126. As part of his covenant with God, Abraham was commanded to circumcise his sons.

In Genesis 17, God made a covenant with Abraham. According to our tradition, this covenant marks the beginning of our existence as a chosen people. The covenant included the following terms:

1. Abraham was to circumcise all males in his household (including himself at 99 years of age).
2. Abraham accepted the Divine as God.
3. God guaranteed a son to Abraham through Sarah (who, according to tradition, was 89 at the time).
4. God promised to make Abraham's descendants into a great nation.

It was at this point that Avram's name became Abraham and Sarai's name became Sarah.

127. Abraham pleaded with God not to destroy Sodom and Gemorrah.

God informed Abraham that the Divine was going to destroy the cities of Sodom and Gemorrah because of their wickedness. Abraham pleaded for justice, maintaining that if there were ten righteous people living in the cities, they must not be destroyed with the wicked. The thought that such an action by the Divine would be possible was unthinkable to Abraham, who asked, "Could the judge of the whole world possibly do something unjust?!"

God assured Abraham that if ten righteous people could be found, the cities would be saved.

Our sages point to this incident as proof that Abraham was much greater than Noah. When God notified Noah that the world was going to be destroyed, Noah obeyed God's command and built an ark, but he said nothing. When Abraham heard that destruction was imminent, he pleaded with God to show mercy and not destroy the cities.

128. Lot's wife turned into a pillar of salt.

During the destruction of Sodom, Lot's wife (whose name was not recorded) looked back at the city and was turned into a pillar of salt. There are numerous salt pillars by the Dead Sea, and tour guides still point to "Lot's wife."

After the destruction of Sodom, Lot's daughters, fearing that they were the last humans on earth, seduced him. Each became pregnant and thus began the nations of Moab and Ammon. This is the Torah's not-very-subtle way of calling the enemy Moabites and Ammonites illegitimate.

129. Sarah and Abraham's son was Isaac.

After Abraham was circumcised, Sarah conceived and, at the age of 90, gave birth to Isaac. Our sages make a direct connection between the covenant of circumcision and Sarah's ability to conceive. Until Abraham had the sign of the contract in his flesh, Sarah's body was not able to be fertile. The Torah offers three separate etymologies of Isaac's name: when God informs Abraham that he and Sarah will have a son, Abraham laughs. God assures Abraham that it will happen and orders him to name the child Yitzchak, Isaac, from the Hebrew root *to laugh* (Genesis 17:17–19). When God's messenger informs Abraham and Sarah that she is going to become pregnant, the text tells us that Sarah laughed, again utilizing Isaac's name (Genesis 18:12–15). After Isaac is born and Abraham names him Yitzchak, Sarah notes that God brought her laughter, again explaining her son's name (Genesis 21:6).

130. The Akedah tells how Abraham sacrificed a ram instead of his son Isaac.

God ordered Abraham to take his son Isaac and sacrifice him on a mountain. Abraham started to obey God's command but, just before he slaughtered his son, God stopped him and ordered him to release Isaac.

The Binding of Isaac for the sacrifice, called the Akedah, is tradition's most powerful image of Abraham's obedience to God.

We moderns have problems with the story. Such a test seems, at best, cruel on the part of the Divine and inhuman on the part of Abraham. A nice modern interpretation changes the focus of the story. God's test is not whether Abraham will sacrifice his son; rather, it is whether Abraham will listen when told not to sacrifice his son, since child sacrifice was part of the culture of the time. By not sacrificing Isaac, Abraham reaffirmed his faith in the Divine and led the world into a gentler, kinder society. Scholars are not in agreement, however, whether human sacrifice was ever a common ritual in the Near East.

When Abraham obeyed God and put down the knife, he offered, instead of his son, a ram that was caught in the thicket by its horns. We remember the story of the Akedah by blowing a ram's horn, a shofar, on the traditional anniversary of the event, Rosh HaShanah (see facts 18, 20).

According to the sages, Mount Moriah, the locale of the Akedah, is the site in Jerusalem where the First and Second Temples were built. The rock on which Abraham built his altar was believed to be the stone within the Holy of Holies.

Muslims have the same tradition of Abraham's near-sacrifice of his son, but according to their story, the son was Ishmael, not Isaac. On the Temple Mount today stands the Muslim shrine, the Dome of the Rock (see fact 495). Inside is said to be the rock on which Isaac (or Ishmael) was not sacrificed.

In response to early Christian theology that Jesus died to save the souls of the world through his suffering, some sages added the midrash that Abraham really did sacrifice Isaac. Isaac's death thus saved the Jewish world, making Jesus superfluous; God then miraculously brought Isaac back from death. This story, meeting specific needs in the second century, never became a significant part of Jewish belief.

131. Abraham bought a cave at Hebron, where he buried Sarah.

When Sarah died, Abraham negotiated the purchase of the Cave of Machpelah as a burial site for her. The cave, located in Hebron, became the ancestral burial cave for our Patriarchs and Matriarchs. Abraham, Sarah, Isaac, Rebecca, Jacob, and Leah are all buried there. According to our sages, Adam and Eve are interred there as well.

The Cave of Machpelah has become a site of controversy in our time. Since Abraham is also the ancestor of Ishmael, important to the Muslim world, the cave is sacred to Muslims as well as to Jews (see fact 484).

Isaac and Related Stories

132. Abraham's servant Eliezer found a wife for Isaac.

After Sarah's death, Abraham sent his servant back to Mesopotamia to find a wife for Isaac. Although the servant is never named, our sages maintained that he was Eliezer, mentioned in Genesis 15:2.

Abraham gave his servant (henceforth known as Eliezer) two

admonitions: first, the girl could not be a Canaanite, and second, Isaac was not to travel to Mesopotamia.

When Eliezer reached Mesopotamia, he asked God for a way to find the right girl. Any girl who offered to water his ten camels would be the right one. At the well where the townspeople drew their water, Rebecca immediately offered to water Eliezer's camels. When he discovered that she was the daughter of Abraham's nephew, Eliezer knew that his mission had been successfully fulfilled.

133. Rebecca was Isaac's wife.

Rebecca received permission from her brother Laban to return to Canaan with Eliezer to become Isaac's wife. We are told that when Isaac took Rebecca as his wife, "he found comfort after his mother's death" (Genesis 24:67). Some rabbis view this as the paradigmatic relationship of husband and wife: a wife can relieve her husband's pain at the loss of his mother. Some modern thinkers have suggested that Rebecca's relationship with Isaac was not particularly healthy since a wife isn't supposed to substitute for a mother. In either case, the Torah's description of Rebecca and Isaac is an excellent example of how we can make the relationships described in the Torah text relevent and important for us today as we struggle with our own understanding of intimacy.

Jacob and Esau

134. Isaac and Rebecca had two sons: Jacob and Esau.

Early in their marriage Rebecca was barren. After much difficulty, she finally gave birth to twin boys. The first to be born was Esau, covered with red hair. The second son was Jacob, whose name means *heel*. According to the Torah, Jacob emerged from the womb holding onto Esau's heel. Esau was a hunter, whereas Jacob preferred to stay around the tents. Isaac loved Esau; Rebecca preferred Jacob. According to our tradition, Esau represented Rome and was therefore portrayed by the rabbis as being wicked, even threatening to kill Jacob while still *in utero*. Jacob represented Israel and was therefore portrayed in the midrash (see fact 333) as righteous, pious, and a great scholar of Jewish law.

135. Jacob cheated Esau out of his birthright.

Esau returned hungry from hunting, and Jacob traded a bowl of lentil stew for Esau's birthright. According to our rabbis, Jacob was saving Esau's life because the major responsibility connected to the birthright was offering sacrifices to God. Our tradition maintains that while out hunting, Esau had raped a virgin, killed a king, and committed armed robbery. Moreover, the reason Jacob was preparing lentil stew was because his grandfather Abraham had just died and he was preparing the Meal of Comfort after the burial (see data to fact 281). If Esau had offered a sacrifice to God in his horribly impure state, he would have been struck dead. By taking Esau's birthright, Jacob was protecting his brother.

This is an excellent example of the difference between the peshat of the Torah text and the derash of the text (see data to fact 105).

136. Jacob cheated Esau out of his special blessing.

Not only did Jacob obtain Esau's birthright, but later, urged and helped by Rebecca, he lied, telling his now-blind father that he was Esau. He succeeded in fooling his father by covering his hands and neck with woolly skins to feel like Esau. Isaac remarked, "The voice is the voice of Jacob, but the hands are the hands of Esau" (Genesis 27:22). Jacob fed Isaac a stew prepared by Rebecca, also to fool his father. After eating, Isaac gave Jacob his final blessing, thus cheating Esau of it.

Our rabbis emphasized that all of Rebecca's actions were committed out of piety. She knew through Divine revelation that Jacob, not Esau, was destined to be the patriarch of the Hebrews. She therefore took the necessary steps to ensure that the divine plan was fulfilled. According to some of our sages, Isaac realized the deceit and followed Rebecca's lead since he trusted her. According to others, angels helped Rebecca in her plan; how else could she make goat taste like venison?

The Jacob and Esau midrashim (plural of midrash) are among the most fascinating rabbinic overlays in our tradition (see fact 333). In them our rabbis represent the Torah characters as diametrically opposite of what the actual text suggests.

Jacob and Family

137. Jacob had a dream about a ladder and angels.

When Esau realized that Jacob had cheated him of his birthright and his special blessing (see facts 135, 136), he plotted revenge against his brother. Rebecca urged Jacob to flee to her brother in Mesopotamia. During his flight from Esau, Jacob slept and dreamed of a ladder with angels going up and down. When he awoke, he said, "God is in this place and I did not know it" (Genesis 28:16). He named that site Bethel, the House of God. Jacob then made a fairly infantile contract with God: if God would protect him, clothe him, feed him, and make sure he returned safely, then Jacob would accept the Divine as his God.

138. Jacob married Leah and Rachel.

When Jacob arrived in Mesopotamia, he proceeded to work for his uncle Laban (Rebecca's brother). He fell in love with Laban's daughter Rachel and agreed to work for seven years in order to marry her. On the wedding night, Laban exchanged Leah, his oldest daughter, for Rachel. On discovering the switch (in the morning), Jacob agreed to work another seven years if he could marry Rachel the following week. It was agreed, and Jacob had two wives. Because of this story, it has become a Jewish custom at a wedding for the groom always to double-check that his bride is the correct woman (see data to fact 263).

139. Jacob had twelve sons and one daughter.

Genesis 29:31–30:24 describes a fertility contest between Leah and Rachel. Leah began by providing Jacob with four sons. Reuben was the eldest, followed by Simeon, Levi, and Judah. When the Talmud discusses a legal case and needs two parties to serve as examples, the two parties are always named Reuben and Simeon.

Rachel remained barren. Envious of her sister, she gave Jacob her maid Bilhah as a concubine. Bilhah conceived twice, giving birth to Dan and Naphtali.

Leah, entering into the contest full force, gave Jacob her concubine Zilpah. Zilpah conceived twice and gave birth to Gad and Asher.

In exchange for some mandrakes that Reuben picked (a plant believed capable of inducing pregnancy), Rachel gave her conjugal turn with Jacob to Leah. Leah conceived and gave birth to her fifth son, Issachar. She then gave birth to her sixth son, Zebulun, and a daughter, Dinah.

140. Jacob's two youngest sons were Joseph and Benjamin.

After years of being barren, Rachel finally became pregnant and gave birth to Joseph. Pregnant again, she died in childbirth while delivering Benjamin (Genesis 35:18).

Our sages, trying to make Jacob's twelve sons basically equal, maintained that Zilpah and Bilhah, the two maids/concubines (see fact 139), were really sisters of Leah and Rachel, thus raising them to the status of real wives.

In order to keep the religion in the family, our sages added the midrash that a twin daughter was born at the same time as each son. These daughters became the wives of their half-brothers (never their twin) to enable their lineage to continue without getting involved with Canaanite or Egyptian women.

141. Jacob wrestled with an angel, and his name was changed to Israel.

When Jacob returned to the Land of Canaan with his two wives, two concubines, twelve sons, and daughter Dinah, he learned that he was going to encounter his brother Esau. Fearing reprisal for his earlier dishonest behavior (see facts 135, 136), Jacob attempted to appease his brother by sending him gifts. The night before their meeting, a mysterious man wrestled with Jacob. The man injured Jacob's hip, but Jacob hung on. Finally the man blessed Jacob by announcing that his name would be changed from Jacob, (heel) to Israel, "one who strives with God and wins." Our tradition assumes that the man was, in fact, an angel. Our goal, God-wrestling, comes from this tradition of struggling with ourselves and our world.

Because of Jacob's hip injury, Genesis 32:33 prohibits Jews from eating the meat from the place of his injury, the *gid hanasheh*, the sciatic nerve (see data to fact 590).

142. Jacob's twelve sons were the ancestors of the twelve tribes of Israel.

While enslaved in Egypt, the twelve sons of Jacob reproduced in fairly startling numbers. According Exodus 1:5, when they went down to Egypt, there were 70 Hebrews. When they came out of Egypt (according to our sages, 210 years later), they numbered 603,550 (Numbers 2:32). Each of the sons of Jacob became the head of a tribe of Hebrews, thus creating the twelve tribes of Israel.

Joseph

143. Joseph had a special coat of many colors.

Because they were the children of his beloved Rachel, Jacob established special relationships with Joseph and Benjamin. Jacob demonstrated this love by giving Joseph a multicolored tunic, traditionally translated "a coat of many colors." Joseph's brothers were jealous because of their father's special love for him. Joseph did not help matters when he told them of his dream that they all would one day bow down to him. And so they plotted to kill him.

144. Joseph's brothers sold him into slavery.

Reuben, the eldest of Jacob's sons, determined to save Joseph from his brothers, who wanted to kill him (see fact 143), and recommended that his brothers throw Joseph into a pit, from which Reuben could later save him.

At the same time, Judah convinced his brothers not to kill Joseph, but rather to sell him as a slave. His brothers agreed, and Joseph was ultimately taken to Egypt in chains.

Jacob, heartbroken over the loss of his son Joseph, then turned his love toward his youngest, Benjamin, also the son of his beloved Rachel. Years later, when Joseph's brothers had the opportunity to get rid of Benjamin in Egypt, they responded differently. Judah offered to become a slave in place of his brother Benjamin, thus showing that the brothers had truly repented and had changed their ways.

145. Joseph became Pharaoh's second-in-command.

As a slave in Egypt, Joseph worked for Potifar, one of Pharaoh's ministers. Falsely accused by Potifar's wife, Joseph landed in an Egyptian prison. There, Joseph correctly interpreted the dreams of the Pharaoh's baker and cupbearer. When Pharaoh had difficulty interpreting his dreams concerning seven fat cows being consumed by seven lean cows, and seven healthy ears of corn being consumed by seven diseased ears of corn, the cupbearer remembered Joseph.

Joseph was able to explain the dreams to Pharaoh and recommended that he prepare his land for the seven years of famine which would follow seven years of bumper crops. Pharaoh raised Joseph to second-in-command to supervise the process. According to our sages, Joseph was released from prison on Rosh HaShanah (see data to fact 18).

146. Joseph had two children: Ephraim and Menasseh.

Joseph married Asenat, the daughter of the priest Potifera. From this union came two children, Menasseh and Ephraim.

Years later, after Jacob was reunited with Joseph, Jacob adopted and blessed Joseph's two children. His words of blessing were, "By you shall Israel bless, saying, 'may God make you like Ephraim and Menasseh'" (Genesis 48:20). In so doing, Jacob reversed the order of the two sons, blessing the younger Ephraim before the firstborn Menasseh. Traditionally, we bless our sons on Shabbat with this same inverted order blessing. (We bless our daughters by saying, "May God make you like Sarah, Rebecca, Leah, and Rachel.")

Some of our sages had problems with Joseph marrying the daughter of an Egyptian priest (see fact 608). They therefore maintained that Asenat was really Joseph's half sister Dinah, who had run away after being raped by Shechem. She supposedly hid under a bush (sneh), so her name became Asenat.

147. Jacob and his family moved to Egypt because of Joseph.

Just as Joseph had predicted to the Pharaoh, after seven years of plenty came seven years of famine. There was no food anywhere except in Egypt, where Joseph had stored it during the years of plenty, so Jacob sent his sons there to buy grain.

Joseph recognized his brothers, but they didn't recognize him. He tested them and then revealed who he was. Jacob was notified that his long-lost son was alive and brought his entire family to Egypt. Jacob died in Egypt, and his sons carried his body back to Canaan, where he was buried in the Cave of Machpelah with the other Patriarchs (see facts 131, 484).

Joseph died in Egypt, and the tribes promised to carry his body back to Canaan when they returned there.

Moses and Enslavement in Egypt

148. Moses lived *after* Abraham, Isaac, Jacob, Joseph, Sarah, Rebecca, Rachel, and Leah.

The stories in Genesis, the tales of Abraham, Sarah, Isaac, Rebecca, Jacob, Rachel, and Leah, all lead to our enslavement in Egypt. This enslavement led to divine redemption when God destroyed Egypt's might and brought us out of slavery. The leader of this Exodus was Moses. He lived long after the Patriarchs. However, because we focus so much on Moses and his life, we sometimes forget the chronology and think that Moses came first.

Although we view Moses as our greatest prophet, the man who communicated "face to face" with God (Deuteronomy 34:10), it is important to note that our tradition never made him into a cult figure. There are no special prayers to, about, or for Moses.

149. The Hebrews became slaves in Egypt.

Our slavery in Egypt became our tradition's symbol of our worst experience as a people. Pharaoh incited his people against the Hebrews; they placed upon us bitter bondage and tried wiping us out by slaughtering all male children.

Historically, there is no Egyptian record of such an enslavement. The Egyptians systematically conscripted all foreigners to work on civic projects. We Hebrews took this conscription personally.

Our rabbis emphasized that despite pain and suffering, the Hebrews never lost their identity. They didn't assimilate into the Egyptian culture. They didn't take Egyptian names, and their women insisted that they continue to procreate despite their anguish. Later generations of Jews, suffering in Europe, Spain, and Africa, found, from the story of our slavery in Egypt, the courage and strength to keep their tradition.

150. Amram and Yocheved were Moses' parents.

Although the Torah text tells us little beyond the names of Moses' parents, our rabbis provided us with many stories about them. Moses' father was Amram of the tribe of Levi. (Jewish poetry frequently refers to Moses as Ben Amram the son of Amram.) According to our rabbis (who frequently retrojected later Jewish institutions back into the time of the Torah), Amram was a great Jewish scholar and head of the Sanhedrin (see fact 327). He was a very pious and righteous Jew. Moses' mother was Yocheved. Our rabbis maintained that she was one of the midwives who saved Hebrew baby boys from Pharaoh's decree of death. Because of her piety, Yocheved was spared pain during the birth of Moses. She was so righteous that she outlived her children and entered the Land of Israel with Joshua.

151. Aaron was Moses' brother.

Moses had an older brother, Aaron, who later became the High Priest and head of the cult. Because Aaron was connected with the Golden Calf debacle (see fact 163), our rabbis went to great lengths to make him righteous enough to deserve the priesthood. They claimed that he was the leader of the Hebrews while they were slaves. When God ordered Moses to bring the Hebrews out of Egypt, Aaron was overjoyed that his brother had been selected.

The primary trait connected with Aaron was his love and desire for peace. According to tradition, Aaron would go to great lengths to achieve peace between spouses and among quarreling friends. It was this desire to maintain peace, they claimed, that led to his mistake with the Golden Calf.

152. Miriam was Moses' sister.

Miriam was responsible for creating the liaison between Pharaoh's daughter and Moses' mother after Moses was rescued from the bulrushes. It was Miriam who danced at the Sea of Reeds when the Egyptians drowned, and the Hebrews were saved (see fact 157). Our sages credited her with providing a miraculous well for our people while we were wandering in the desert: Because she was so righteous, the Divine made sure that all the Hebrews had enough water; it was only with her death that there was no water in the desert (see data to fact 179). Our rabbis also maintained that Miriam was a prophet.

153. Moses' wife was Tzipporah.

After killing an Egyptian who was beating a Hebrew, Moses had to flee Egypt. He found refuge in the tent of Jethro, a priest of Midian. Moses married Jethro's daughter Tzipporah. Our tradition emphasized that Tzipporah was a pious woman who systematically removed from her father's tent all signs of any form of idolatry.

Exodus from Egypt

154. Moses saw a bush burning that wasn't consumed by the flames.

The incident of the burning bush was of great importance to the sages. One group maintained that God waited for Moses to come along and then created the miracle of the burning bush. Others believed that the bush had been burning, but unconsumed, for generations and only Moses was perceptive enough to see the miracle.

According to the first tradition, God selected Moses without his showing any special characteristic. Moses had no special merit but was God's arbitrary choice.

According to the second tradition, it was a special quality in Moses, his ability to note the bush burning unconsumed, that led to his being selected for the task of saving the Hebrews from bondage.

155. God's message to Pharaoh via Moses was, "Let My people go, so that they may serve Me."

Moses never wanted the job of leading the Hebrews out of Egypt. Like many of the Hebrew prophets, he was pushed into it. Moses served as God's mouthpiece, demanding of Pharaoh, "Let My people go that they may serve Me." The Hebrew word for "Let go," is "Shelach." It usually has the meaning of "send away." According to a midrash (see fact 333), the Hebrews, having been passive slaves for so long, weren't prepared to leave Egypt on their own. In order to achieve redemption, the Hebrews had to be pushed out of Egypt by Pharaoh.

156. God used the ten plagues to force the Egyptians to let the Hebrews go.

When God hardened Pharaoh's heart and he refused to release the Hebrews, God brought ten plagues upon Egypt to emphasize that the Egyptian idols had no real power at all.

1. The Nile River turned to blood.
2. Frogs overwhelmed the land. When they died, they rotted in enormous piles, causing all of Egypt to stink.
3. Lice crawled over the Egyptians and their animals.
4. Swarms of insects (or, according to one tradition, wild beasts) attacked the homes of the Egyptians.
5. All Egyptian livestock were struck with disease.
6. All Egyptians and their animals were afflicted with painful boils.
7. All of Egypt was struck by huge hail which destroyed the crops.
8. Locusts attacked the land, eating everything that the hail hadn't destroyed.
9. The Egyptians suffered total darkness.
10. The Destroyer killed the firstborn of every Egyptian home and barn.

While each plague was afflicting Egypt, Pharaoh considered relenting and allowing the Hebrews to go free. However, when the plague ended, Pharaoh changed his mind and refused to release the Hebrews.

The Torah text emphasizes that none of the plagues struck the

Hebrews. While the Egyptians suffered, the Hebrews miraculously were spared.

Because of God's power, Pharaoh, who believed that he was God, was humiliated, broken, and, at the Sea of Reeds, totally defeated.

Although there is no mention of such an exodus in any Egyptian document, Pharaoh Merneptah in 1274 B.C.E. bragged on a stele that he had wiped Israel out completely. That is pretty good evidence that the Hebrews by that date were already known as Israel.

Theologically, the Exodus is the most important event in Jewish history. Through that redemption, God established a special relationship with the Jewish people. As a result of that redemption, we responded to the Divine and accepted the terms or our special contract with God. The Torah regularly identifies the Divine as "Adonai, who brought you out of Egypt," and our redemption from Egypt is the *raison d'être* for our doing mitzvot, commandments.

157. When God parted the Sea of Reeds, we sang, "Mi Chamocha?' "Who is like You, Adonai?"

The final moment of that first redemption was at the Sea of Reeds, where the Egyptians were drowned in the waters, thus guaranteeing the escape of the Hebrews.

According to Exodus 15, when the Hebrews saw that they were saved, they sang a song of thanksgiving and victory. In the middle of this "Song of the Sea" are the words, "Who is like You among the gods, Adonai, who is like You, wonderful in holiness, awesome in praise, doing wonders?" Traditional Jews remember the redemption at every morning and evening service by quoting the Song of the Sea. The preliminary prayers of the morning service include the entire poem.

Some rabbis were concerned about the joy we expressed at the death of our enemies. They introduced a midrash in which the angels joined the Hebrews in their song of rejoicing. God rebuked them and said, "How can you sing when my creatures are drowning?" This touch of universal humanism appealed to many modern liberal Jews, and we included the midrash in our Haggadah (see fact 79).

So great was the moment of redemption from Egypt for us, that we relive it every year as the Festival of Pesach, hoping for the final redemption, the Messianic Age. Getting out of Egypt began the redemption process which continues in every generation until the entire world is finally redeemed (see fact 606).

158. Amalek attacked the Hebrews in the desert.

The Hebrews had several adventures between the Sea of Reeds and Mount Sinai. The most momentous was their encounter with Amalek.

According to Exodus 17:8-16, Amalek, the leader of a desert tribe, was related to the Hebrews. He was a descendant of Esau (see facts 134-136).

In the desert, Amalek attacked the Hebrews. According to Deuteronomy 25:17-19, he went after the old and frail. In the Book of Exodus there was a major battle between the Amalekites and the Hebrews. Joshua ben Nun was the commander of the Hebrews (see fact 183).

Whenever Moses raised his hands, the Hebrews would prevail. When he lowered his hands, Amalek would prevail. Moses' arms became heavy trying to keep them raised, so Aaron and Hur sat him down on a stone and each supported one of his arms, thus allowing Joshua and the Hebrews to overwhelm Amalek.

Our tradition treats Amalek as a prime enemy. We are commanded to utterly blot out the memory of Amalek from under heaven.

Haman, the tyrant in the Book of Esther, was a descendant of Amalek. Since we are commanded to wipe out the memory of Amalek, we wipe out Haman's name whenever it is mentioned by making a huge noise (see fact 62).

Revelation at Sinai

159. We received the Torah at Mount Sinai.

At Mount Sinai we established our contract with the Divine. Belief about what happened at Sinai defines the different streams of Judaism. Orthodox Jews believe that God gave all of Torah, Revelation, to the Hebrews at Mount Sinai: the written Torah and the orally transmitted Torah (see fact 345). For Orthodox Jews, God's law is unchanging, eternal, and therefore binding for every Jew.

Conservative Judaism maintains that the Torah, the first five books of the Bible, was given directly and infallibly at Mount Sinai, but that the interpretation of these 613 mitzvot developed in each generation by the great rabbinic minds. This developmental process is still in progress, and change is possible within the confines of the defined Torah law.

Reform Jews believe a wide variety of things. Basically, however, the assumption is that Torah, both written and oral, was created and developed by humans in a quest for holiness under Divine command. Jews are in contract with God, but the details are defined by each Jew in his or her own way. Every Reform Jew has to acknowledge his or her own mitzvot (commandments) in this ongoing, fluid relationship with the Divine.

Reconstructionist Jews believe that each Jew is in covenant with the Jewish People. Judaism is a civilization, and the mitzvot are folkways defining the peoplehood.

For all four streams of Judaism, the moment at Sinai was of supreme importance. It was there that we became a covenanted people with the Divine.

Our sages had two differing views of our covenant acceptance. In one story, God held Mount Sinai over our heads and said, "Here is my Torah; accept it or I drop the mountain." And Israel accepted the Torah.

In the other story, God offered Torah to every nation on earth, but only Israel responded affirmatively.

There are clearly two different understandings about the nature of our covenant relationship with God. In the first, God chose us long before we chose God and the Torah. In the second, we became a covenanted people by freely choosing to accept Torah.

160. The Ten Commandments are found in Exodus 20 and Deuteronomy 5.

The term *Ten Commandments* (literally, the Ten Words) appears in the Torah three times. Twice in Deuteronomy (4:13, 10:4) it refers to the commandments found in Exodus 20. In Exodus itself, however, the term *Ten Commandments* is found only in Exodus 34:28. Ironically, there it refers to a set of commandments different from the set we call the Ten Commandments.

The sages already called the laws found in Exodus 20 and Deuteronomy 5 the Ten Commandments. These laws have acquired an importance in the Western world greater than the other 603 mitzvot.

Although the basic intent of the Ten Commandments in Exodus and Deuteronomy is identical, the language is not. The two versions of the tenth commandment, "You shall not covet," switch the order and content of the different sources of envy.

Exodus cites creation as the primary reason for the commandment to keep Shabbat. Deuteronomy says we are commanded to keep Shabbat because we were slaves in Egypt.

The two versions begin the fourth commandment with different words. Exodus says, "Remember the Sabbath day and keep it holy." Deuteronomy says, "Observe the Sabbath day and keep it holy."

According to Exodus 19, God spoke the Ten Commandments directly to the people. Because of the differences in the Deuteronomy and Exodus versions, our sages emphasized that the transmission of these laws was a miracle. God delivered both versions at the same time; the Hebrews heard and understood both sets of laws simultaneously.

As a reminder of the words *Remember* and *Observe,* found in the two versions of the fourth commandment, the sages instituted the tradition of lighting at least two candles to begin Shabbat (see fact 5).

161. The Ten Commandments are: I am Adonai who brought you out of Egypt; don't worship idols; don't swear by God's name falsely; keep the Sabbath; honor your parents; don't murder; don't commit adultery; don't steal; don't lie as a witness; don't covet what your neighbor has.

One of the ironies of the Ten Commandments is that if you didn't know you were looking for ten mitzvot, you could actually find fourteen or fifteen commandments in the set. Our tradition held so strongly to the fact that there were ten commandments, however, that we now have them listed the way we know them. Both the Protestant and Catholic traditions number the Ten Commandments differently.

According to our rabbis, the Ten Commandments were recited as part of the daily liturgy in the Temple. However, when sectarian groups began insisting that the Ten Commandments were the only important ones, we removed the reading of the Ten Commandments from our service. Today they are read only when the Torah portions in which they appear are read, as well as on Shavuot (see fact 86). We also created a midrash that on the tablets, between the lines of the Ten Commandments, were written the 603 other mitzvot, thereby emphasizing that they were of equal importance to us.

Our tradition provides many insights into the Ten Commandments. One group of sages viewed the first five commandments as emphasizing the relationship between Jews and God, and the second five as concentrating on the relationship between Jews and Jews.

The fifth commandment, Honor your father and your mother, was therefore in the section of God-Jew relationship. This placement made sense to our sages, who viewed the relationship of child to parent as being equally important to the Jew-God relationship.

The sages also suggested that the commandments are listed in order of importance. Duties to the Divine come first; avoiding idolatry precedes misusing the Divine Name. Both are more important than keeping the Shabbat or honoring our parents.

The ethical injunctions follow a similar hierarchy: life, then the family, then personal possessions, then personal integrity in public. The final commandment, against coveting, serves as a safeguard against breaking any of the other ethical imperatives.

Our rabbis noted that only the commandments dealing with our particularistic relationship with the Divine (the first five) contain words beyond the direct prohibition.

Our traditional image of the Ten Commandments on the two tablets has the first five dealing with our relationship with the Divine on one tablet, and the five dealing with our relationship with fellow humans on the second tablet. Therefore, the first commandment would be on the same line as the sixth, the second would be on the same line as the seventh, and so on. A midrash notes the relationship between these commandments situated on the same line:

1. Since humans were created in the image of the Divine, murder is an injury to Adonai, who brought us out of Egypt.
2. Idolatry is infidelity to God, just as adultery is infidelity to spouse.
3. Stealing will lead to taking a false oath, thus misusing the Divine name
4. One who breaks the Shabbat is swearing falsely that God did not create the world in six days and rest on the seventh.
5. One who covets his fellow's wife will end by fathering a child who will not honor his true parents.

162. There are 613 mitzvot (commandments) in the Torah.

The Torah never mentions how many mitzvot (commandments) there are. As a matter of fact, the Torah regularly uses three separate words to describe the laws that make up the Jewish contract with God: mishpatim (judgments), chukkim (ordinances), and mitzvot (commandments). According to our rabbis, mishpatim are commandments that are obvious to all civilizations: prohibitions against murder, theft, adultery, and the like. Chukkim are particularistic commandments given specifically to the Jewish people without any explanation: the dietary laws, clothing regulations, and others. Our tradition had always viewed these as being of equal importance.

It was the tradition of the tanna'im (see fact 329) that the Torah contains 613 commandments. Our rabbis maintained that there are 365 prohibitions (one for each day of the year) and 248 positive precepts (one for each bone in the body). However, until the time of the geonim (plural of *gaon*; see fact 372), no one had systematically listed the 613 mitzvot. The number 613 can be written in Hebrew letters as TRYG, which is pronounced TaRYaG.

With the rise of the rabbis and the Oral Law (see facts 327-334, 342-347), the mitzvot became the building blocks for rabbinic legislation. Our tradition thus divided mitzvot into two categories: commandments from Torah directly, and commandments of the rabbis. In this way was created the ocean of Jewish law which now makes up our tradition.

Finally, our rabbis also divided mitzvot into separate functional categories: mitzvot dealing with relations between human beings, and mitzvot dealing with the relationship of a Jew with God.

In its presentation of mitzvot, the Torah makes no distinction between what we would call ethical commandments and cultic commandments. Our rabbis recognized this fact and concluded that, unlike Greek and modern secular culture, which separated these practices into different categories, Torah held ritual practices to be ethical, and ethical practices to be ritual, all responses to divine command.

The Golden Calf

163. When Moses saw people worshiping the Golden Calf, he smashed the stones that held the commandments.

While Moses was up on Mount Sinai receiving the Torah, the people, frightened and leaderless, convinced Aaron to build an idol, a Golden Calf. They declared that this was their God who had brought them out of Egypt. Moses returned and, seeing the revelry and orgy, smashed the Torah tablets he was carrying.

Our sages had different explanations for why Moses broke the tablets, which, after all, had been written by God. Some sages believed it was an attempt to protect Israel. One of the commandments is "Don't commit idolatry." By smashing the tablets, Moses hoped to avoid confronting Israel directly with the broken commandment at the time of their sin.

Other sages see Moses responding in uncontrollable anger to the sin of Israel. In fury, he smashed the tablets.

Another explanation takes the responsibility away from Moses entirely. The tablets weighed hundreds of pounds. Only the miracle of God's writing made them light as a feather. When the letters saw the Hebrews sinning, they flew back to the Divine. This returned the tablets to their natural heavy state and Moses couldn't hold them. Their own weight caused them to smash.

The sin of the Golden Calf has remained the major sin of the Hebrews in the desert. It serves as a sobering reminder that, even in the face of miracles, at the moment when we experience divine revelation, the best of us still fall on our faces.

Mishkan and Furnishings

164. The Mishkan was the portable Temple in the desert.

The only form of institutional worship described in the Torah was the sacrificial cult. The offerings required a site of holiness, a designated divine mailing address. The Book of Exodus describes in detail God's architectural plans and the actual building of the Mishkan, the portable sanctuary. Scholars believe that the description of the Mishkan with all of its equipment was based on the Temple built by King Solomon (see fact 204). The Torah author retrojected Solomon's Temple in portable form back to the Sinai wilderness experience. Orthodox Jews believe that the Mishkan was an actual sanctuary.

According to the Book of Exodus, the Mishkan, a rectangular tent with a wooden frame, was divided into two rooms. It was covered with goat skins and dyed ram skins, and, according to the text, the wooden frame was overlaid with gold.

165. The Temple menorah had seven branches.

The main part of the Mishkan contained a seven-branched menorah, a table containing twelve loaves of bread (one for each tribe), and a small altar for burning incense. An inner room contained the Ark, a wooden box overlaid with gold, which contained the tablets of the covenant. The two rooms were separated by a tapestry, a parochet. Many of these ritual objects are used in our synagogue today as a reminder of the Temple and its equipment (see facts 230, 236, 237).

Outside the Mishkan in the courtyard, the sacrifices were offered.

There are two traditions in the Torah concerning the Mishkan, which is also called the Tent of Meeting. In one tradition, the Mishkan stood in the center of the camp and the priests served there. In the second tradition, the Mishkan was outside the camp and was the site where Moses and the Divine communicated. When God's Presence entered the Tent of Meeting, smoke covered the Mishkan, and only Moses could approach.

166. Bezalel was the artist who made the Ark and the Mishkan.

According to Exodus 31, the artist for the Ark and the Mishkan (see fact 164) and all of its furnishings was Bezalel. Our sages disagreed about Bezalel's skills. One group of rabbis maintained that Bezalel was an extraordinary artisan capable of making the furnishings designed by the Eternal. Another group maintained that Bezalel had no skills whatsoever, but he was a righteous man. When God selected him to build the Mishkan with all its furnishings, the Divine miraculously placed within Bezalel the necessary skills.

The Art Academy now in Jerusalem is called, not coincidentally, the Bezalel School.

Priests and the Sacrificial Cult

167. The priests were responsible for performing the rituals of the sacrificial cult.

The primary form of worship described in Leviticus 1-8 was the offering of sacrifices. The Book of Leviticus describes the different kinds of offerings. These sacrifices could be performed only by the correct priestly group. The Hebrews understood that the priests served as functionaries between them and the Divine. Any undesignated person who approached either the Mishkan or the sacrificial area itself would die.

168. The priests came from the tribe of Levi.

Of the twelve tribes of Israel, only one tribe was designated to perform the sacrificial cult practices: the tribe of Levi.

There was a revolution in the desert against this. Representatives of the tribe of Reuben (the eldest son of Jacob) challenged the authority of the tribe of Levi to be the priests. Through a miracle (Aaron's staff sprouted almond blossoms overnight), God indicated that the tribe of Levi was indeed the designated tribe to serve in the Mishkan. As the tribe of priests, Levi received no land in Canaan. They depended on their portions of the sacrifices offered in the Temple. According to the Torah, the Levites were given 48 towns throughout Canaan. There is no proof that this actually happened.

169. The Hebrew word for our priests was Kohanim.

The tribe of Levi subdivided into different functioning groups, with the Kohanim, the priests, taking over primary jobs. They were direct descendants of Aaron, who served as the first High Priest. It was their duty actually to make the sacrificial offerings.

The other members of the tribe of Levi, the Levites, were involved in the cultic practices but were responsible for less auspicious functions: they cut and carried the wood for the sacrifices and provided the water needed for maintaining the sacred areas. According to our sages, the Levites also provided music during the sacrificial worship: they chanted psalms (see fact 200), including the Hallel (see fact 7). They also played a variety of instruments, probably including the harp, the lyre, the lute, pipes, horns, and cymbals.

Today, even without sacrificial offerings, traditional Jews maintain distinctions between Kohanim, the Levites, and everyone else (called simply Israel). They still honor Kohanim by giving them the first aliyah at the Torah reading (see data to fact 308). The Levites are given the second aliyah. The custom of duchenun, the Priestly Blessing, also still takes place (see fact 304).

Since the founders of Reform Judaism viewed the sacrificial cult as primitive and obsolete, they systematically removed the distinctions between Kohanim, Levites, and Israel. However, in many congregations we still note families that are Kohanim (notably those with the family name Cohen, Kohn, Kahn, Cahn, etc.), families that are Levites (Levi, Levy, etc.), and families that are Israel (the rest of us).

It is interesting to note that the lineage of Kohayn (singular of Kohanim), Levi, and Israel was patrilineal. If the father was a Kohayn, the children were Kohanim.

170. Aaron was the first High Priest.

Ironically, although Aaron was responsible for creating the Golden Calf, that idolatrous debacle in the wilderness at Mount Sinai, he was designated to be the High Priest. After his death, his sons also held this august office.

171. The High Priest wore a crown, a breastplate, a mantle, a sash, and bells.

The High Priest wore special sacral clothes consisting of a miter, a tunic, a breastplate, and a special apron garment with epaulets at the shoulder called the ephod (Exodus 28).

Aaron, the High Priest, was in charge of all sacrifices. Only the High Priest could pronounce the Ineffable Name of God, YHVH, and live. He did so once a year on Yom Kippur (see data to fact 24).

By the time of the Second Temple the High Priest, for all intents and purposes, was the ruler of a theocratic Jewish Commonwealth (see data to facts 38, 43, 221, 319). Since all taxes went into the Temple treasury, the head of the sacrificial cult was the power in the kingdom.

The Holiness Code

172. Leviticus 19 commands, "You shall be holy," because God is holy.

The Torah contains various sets of laws, called codes. Leviticus 17-26 is called the Holiness Code because it contains a dozen times the imperative (in several formulations) that we are to be holy. Leviticus 19 is the most-quoted section of the Holiness Code because it begins specifically with the words, "You shall be holy, because I, Adonai, your God, am holy." This command to attempt to imitate the Divine is followed by a list of laws that concentrate on both ritual matters and the relationships between people. Among the latter are commandments about leaving part of our harvest for the poor, dealing fairly in business, and not oppressing the stranger. It is the Torah's clearest declaration that the way to holiness includes ethical behavior in both business and our personal lives.

While ritual has always been an important element in our contract with the Divine, the primary route to holiness is through ethical behavior. Our tradition has always emphasized that holiness is not achieved through asceticism or denial.

173. Leviticus 19 commands, "Love your neighbor as yourself."

One of the commandments found in the Holiness Code states, "Love your neighbor as yourself. I am Adonai." Our tradition has always viewed this as one of the most important mitzvot in the Torah. However, obviously, it is a difficult commandment to fulfill. Our sages pointed out that the commandment has two parts. It is possible to fulfill the mitzvah to "love your neighbor as yourself" only if you are aware of the second part: "I am Adonai." Without feeling the Divine Presence in both ourselves and in others, it is impossible to love another as much as we do ourselves. The bridge over the chasm of our own selfishness is awareness of the divine spark in each of us. Leviticus 19 calls us to meet that imperative.

Sh'mittah

174. Sh'mittah occurs every seventh year in Israel; the land must not be used for agriculture.

Leviticus 25 includes the following law: every seventh year, the Land of Israel is to remain unplanted. This year of noncultivation is called the Sh'mittah, the Sabbatical year. Traditional Jews continue this law today, buying food from the Arabs in Gaza rather than eating produce grown in the Land of Israel during the Sh'mittah year.

In addition, during the Sabbatical year all loans and debts are cancelled. Hillel (see fact 331), fearing that people would refuse to lend money during the fifth and sixth years of the cycle, created the prozbul, a document that guaranteed their loans would be repaid even after the Sh'mittah year.

All food that grows naturally during the Sabbatical year belongs to the poor, the stranger, and undomesticated animals; it is a concrete reminder that people don't own land: the earth and all its fullness are Adonai's. We are simply stewards.

This principle is further emphasized by a law found in Deuteronomy 20:19. Fruit trees are under divine protection even in times of war and may not be cut down around a besieged city. They are part of God's creation, and they are not at war. It is a simple commandment, but its nuances about the role of humans in a world created by the Divine are powerful. The earth belongs to Adonai, the creator of everything. Fruit trees are there to provide food for future generations and may not be destroyed to meet the immediate needs of a warring group.

Nadav and Avihu

175. Nadav and Avihu, two sons of Aaron, were struck by fire.

Aaron's two oldest sons were Nadav and Avihu. They would have inherited the priesthood from their father. However, at the time of the first offerings at the new Mishkan (see fact 164), they brought "foreign fire," obviously some form of incense. God, infuriated, annihilated them. Their father Aaron, already anointed and serving as priest, was forbidden to mourn. He had to serve as the cultic liaison between the people and the Divine, and that responsibility transcended his own personal grief.

Immediately following this incident, the commandment appears that the priests should not make an offering while drunk (Leviticus 10:8). Therefore our sages link the death of Nadav and Avihu to their being intoxicated. This makes the story a little more acceptable, but not much.

Scouting the Land of Canaan

176. Moses sent twelve scouts into Canaan to evaluate the land.

In the second year after the Exodus from Egypt, Moses sent twelve scouts to evaluate the Land of Israel. They came back with a mixed report.

All agreed that the land was wonderfully fruitful. In fact, it took two men to carry a single bunch of grapes on a pole (the symbol now of both a tour guide company in Israel and a company of vintners). However, ten of the scouts also had serious reservations about the Land of Canaan, and this had radical consequences for the Hebrews.

177. Ten scouts gave the people frightening reports about Canaan, but Joshua ben Nun and Caleb ben Yefuneh told the people to trust in God.

Along with their positive description of the land's fertility, ten scouts reported that the land, filled with giants and huge cities, would be impossible to conquer, and they frightened the people.

Two of the scouts, Joshua ben Nun and Caleb ben Yefuneh, insisted that with God's help they could do anything including take the land of Israel. The people, however, insisted on returning to Egypt.

God was furious at the lack of faith shown by the Hebrews and decided that the entire generation would die in the wilderness with the exception of Joshua and Caleb.

Because of the people's lack of faith, the Hebrews remained in the wilderness for another 38 years. According to our sages, this incident took place on the Ninth of Av. For that reason, God decreed that the Ninth of Av would be a day of mourning forever for the Jewish people (see facts 92, 93).

Korach

178. Korach attempted a revolution against Moses and Aaron.

Korach, a member of the tribe of Levi, along with 250 supporters, challenged the authority of Moses and Aaron, also of the tribe of Levi.

He maintained that Moses and Aaron had no right to assume leadership of the Hebrews since the entire people was holy. Moses accused Korach of being ambitious for personal aggrandizement. Korach and his followers were swallowed up by the earth, never to return, a clear sign that God preferred Moses and Aaron over Korach.

According to the rabbis, Korach represented all seditious Jews who attempted to mock the religious leaders by making Jewish law appear silly, meaningless, or unfair. Korach became the symbol of anyone who was consumed with jealousy or personal ambition. He is the prime example of what happens to someone who challenges legitimate authority.

Waters of Merribah

179. At Merribah Moses disobeyed God and struck a rock to get water.

During their desert wanderings, the Hebrews sometimes lacked water. At Merribah, this happened immediately after Miriam's death. Our rabbis assumed that Miriam's righteousness had provided the Hebrews with sufficient water. They introduced the image of a well that followed Miriam through the desert. With her death, the well disappeared, and there ceased to be an adequate water supply.

The Hebrews once again threatened to turn against Moses. God commanded Moses to take his staff and speak to a rock. Instead, Moses struck the rock, and enough water flowed for the community. However, God informed Moses that he had desecrated God's name by not talking to the rock. To be fair, one must consider that Moses had been under a lot of pressure: his family was in crisis. Miriam, his sister, had recently died, and Aaron, his brother, was ill (the story of Aaron's death follows closely upon this one). Moreover, on a previous occasion God had commanded Moses to *strike* a rock to provide water for the Hebrews (Exodus 17:5–7).

In this case, however, Moses disobeyed God by striking the rock instead of speaking to it, and his punishment was that he would not be allowed to enter the land of Canaan.

Zelophechad's Daughters

180. Zelophechad's daughters were allowed to own land in Canaan.

Zelophechad died while the Hebrews were wandering in the desert. He had no sons, and his five daughters asked Moses what would happen to his inheritance in the Land of Israel. Moses checked with God and was told that daughters could inherit land. Zelophechad's land therefore went to his daughters.

This situation created a problem: when Zelophechad's daughters married, did the land then go to their husbands' tribes or did it stay within their tribe? The answer was pragmatic: Zelophechad's daughters could marry only men from their own tribe, thus guaranteeing that the land remain within the clan.

The story of Zelophechad's daughters is significant because it is an excellent example of Moses not knowing the answer to a question and having to ask God directly. There are a number of such examples:

Moses didn't know what to do about a man who gathered sticks on Shabbat. He checked directly with God (Numbers 15:32–36).

Moses didn't know what to do about the half-Hebrew who blasphemed. Again he checked with God (Leviticus 24:10–14).

It is also important to note that in our tradition women may inherit land.

Cities of Refuge

181. If someone killed somebody accidentally, he or she could be protected at a City of Refuge.

Although it is never described in detail, it appears that the Hebrews had a tradition of blood vengeance. If a relative was killed, the family had the responsibility to track down the killer and avenge the death.

Numbers 35:16 notes that if a person killed someone intentionally, then the murderer deserves death. However, accidents do happen. In the case of an involuntary manslaughter, Numbers 35 provides protection against blood vengeance. The accidental killer had to flee to designated Cities of Refuge or to the Temple altar. If the person arrived safely and the subsequent investigation proved that the homicide was accidental, he or she was protected within the walls of the city from all avenging relatives of the deceased.

The accidental killer had to stay there until the death of the presiding High Priest. After that, he or she was permitted to return home in safety.

Varying numbers of cities are designated in different places in the Torah. In one place, three are provided within the Land of Israel and three are created on the east side of the Jordan. For this reason, the sages assumed that the tribes of Reuben, Gad, and half of Menasseh, all located on the east side of the Jordan, must have been an unruly, wild group to need so many refuge cities.

We have no cases described in the Bible of anyone fleeing to one of the designated cities of refuge. However, Joab, who had sided with Adonijah, the brother of Solomon (see fact 203), grabbed the horns of the altar at the "Tent of Adonai." Solomon ordered him slaughtered there, and he was killed, an example where altar-grabbing didn't help.

Moses' Death

182. Moses dies at the end of Deuteronomy.

At the end of Deuteronomy, God shows Moses the entire Land of Israel which the Divine promised to our ancestors. Then "by the mouth of Adonai," Moses dies (Deuteronomy 34:5). Our rabbis noted this strange wording describing Moses' death. They explained that Moses' righteousness defeated the Angel of Death, who could not kill him. Finally, the Divine had to come and personally take Moses' life with a kiss. Thus Moses died by the mouth of Adonai.

We are not told where Moses was buried, and our tradition never developed any shrines for him. The Muslims, who also honor Moses, built a shrine near the Dead Sea called Nebi Musa, the Prophet Moses. They believe that it marks the site of Moses' grave. According to the Torah, Nebi Musa is on the wrong side of the Jordan.

Since Moses is one of the people honored by both Muslims and Jews, it is ironic that Nebi Musa was the starting site for many Muslim riots against the Jewish community while the British were in power (see data to fact 523).

When Moses died, the people mourned thirty days and then, under the leadership of Joshua ben Nun, proceeded to cross the Jordan River to begin the conquest of the Land of Canaan. This practical continuation even after the death of our greatest prophet has always been one of the important principles of Judaism. The living have the obligation to continue living despite painful losses.

Joshua

183. Joshua ben Nun led the people into the Land of Canaan.

Before Moses died, God told him to appoint Joshua ben Nun to be his successor. Joshua was one of the two scouts who had come back with a positive report 38 years earlier (see fact 177).

Joshua was primarily a general; the book bearing his name is the first in the division of Nevi'im, Prophets, in the TaNaCH (see fact 104). It describes the military campaigns that were necessary to take the Land of Israel from the Canaanite tribes. The most famous battle was at Jericho, where, after the priests blew shofrot (plural of shofar; see fact 20), the walls came tumbling down.

At Shechem, Joshua officiated at a covenantal ceremony that included all of the Hebrews. Described in Joshua 24, this ceremony appears to have been the beginning of an ongoing tradition of reaffirming the covenant every year, possibly at the time of Sukkot (see fact 28).

The land of Canaan was divided among the twelve tribes of Israel. The tribe of Levi received no land but received part of every sacrifice offered. In addition, they received special monies because they were the Temple functionaries. Joseph's two children, Ephraim and Menasseh, received Joseph's land inheritance, thus becoming two separate tribes. This division brought the number of tribes possessing land to twelve again.

These twelve tribes split naturally into two confederations. The North consisted of ten tribes, and the South consisted of two tribes.

Judges

184. Charismatic fighting leaders were called judges.

After the Hebrews had settled in the land of Canaan, they were persecuted by the better-organized Canaanite tribes who lived there. Historically, the Hebrews did not conquer all of the Land of Israel until the time of King David. Until King David, they had failed to unite as a single people. Each tribe was independent, and there were frequent intertribal conflicts.

On occasion, however, when some of the tribes were in trouble, a leader would arise capable of uniting them against a common foe. These charismatic leaders were called Judges, and there is a book in the Bible about them. The book, which is filled with gore, sex, and violence, is found in the second division of the TaNaCH, Nevi'im (see fact 104).

185. Deborah and Barak defeated Sisera's army at Mount Tabor.

One of the first judges was Deborah. She succeeded in uniting some of the northern tribes on top of Mount Tabor against the king of Hazor. With the help of her general, Barak, Deborah was able to defeat Sisera and his chariots. Sisera fled but was pegged through the brain by a woman named Yael.

186. Deborah was a prophet and judge.

The Book of Judges 4 describes Deborah's ability to unite the tribes, qualifying her as a judge, and calls her a prophet, a spokeswoman for God (see fact 207). Judges 5 demonstrates her skills as a poet, for she sang a victory song after Sisera's defeat. In it, she extolled Yael as a heroine for killing Sisera.

187. Gideon defeated the Midianites.

Gideon was another judge. He succeeded in uniting the tribes against the Midianites. God, desirous of convincing the people of his divine protection, insisted that Gideon limit his troops to only 300 men. Despite their small number they then routed the Midianites.

Samson

188. Samson's strength came from his hair.

Samson was the least likely of all judges. According to the TaNaCH, his parents were commanded by an angel that he was never to cut his hair. This prohibition was not unusual in the TaNaCH: the Book of Numbers describes a specific group of people, called Nazirites, who wished to consecrate themselves to the Divine. By taking a Nazirite vow, they were forbidden to cut their hair, consume any grape product, or come in contact with a corpse.

Samson was consecrated by never cutting his hair. Because of this, he had tremendous strength which he used to wipe out as many Philistines as possible.

189. In the TaNaCH, the major enemies of the Hebrews were the Philistines.

The Philistines, united into a five-city oligarchy, were the greatest threat to the Hebrews. They had migrated from Crete at about the same time the Hebrews escaped from Egypt. The Philistines settled along the Coastal Plain (see fact 476) at Ashkelon, Ashdod, Gath, Gaza, and Ekron. They were particularly threatening because they had weapons of iron which cut right through the Hebrews' bronze weapons.

190. Delilah tricked Samson and had his hair cut.

The Philistines finally defeated Samson by hiring Delilah to discover the secret of his strength and neutralize him. After two unsuccessful attempts, Delilah achieved her goal by discovering that Samson's enormous power was connected to his uncut hair. She arranged for the Philistines to shave his head, thus depriving him of his strength. They blinded Samson and made him a slave. As his hair grew back, however, so did his strength. At a celebration to Dagon, the Philistine god, Samson pushed against the supporting pillars of the building and brought the house down, killing himself and the Philistines.

The United Monarchy

191. Hannah was the mother of Samuel.

A woman named Hannah was barren. She went to the yearly meeting of the Hebrews at Shiloh, where she prayed for a son. God heard her prayer and, on Rosh HaShanah (according to the sages), Hannah gave birth to a son, whom she named Samuel. He became the leader of Israel and was called a prophet, a spokesman for the Divine (see fact 207).

192. Saul was the first king of Israel.

The stories about Saul are found in the First book of Samuel, in the Nevi'im division of the TaNaCH. When the people demanded a king, like the Philistines had, Samuel warned them against such a move, seeing their desire for another master as a lack of faith in God. However, they insisted.

God told Samuel to select Saul, a tall Benjaminite, to be king, and Samuel anointed him. King Saul, the first Hebrew king, was able to unite the tribes briefly, and they held off the Philistines, who had used their iron weapons to defeat the Hebrews after the death of Samson (see fact 190).

God ordered Saul to utterly wipe out the Amalekites (see data to fact 158). Following that battle, Saul disobeyed by keeping the best of the Amalekite sheep and oxen and sparing Agag, the Amalekite king. Samuel prophesied that all of Saul's family would be destroyed because of this sin. Samuel then executed Agag.

193. As a prophet, Samuel declared Saul king and, later, anointed David as king to follow Saul.

Following God's command, Samuel went to the family of Jesse of the tribe of Judah. There he selected Jesse's youngest son, David, and secretly anointed him as the next king.

Our rabbis emphasized that David was selected because he was humble and cared for his flocks (see data to fact 583).

194. David killed a Philistine giant named Goliath.

There are two different traditions in the TaNaCH about the death of Goliath, the giant. In the book of 1 Samuel, Saul and his army were challenged by the Philistine champion, who towered over them with his huge iron spear. David, the shepherd lad, volunteered to fight the giant. He took five smooth stones from the nearby brook and slowly approached the roaring giant. Using his sling, he struck Goliath in the forehead, stunning him. He then cut off Goliath's head. This act represented the major victory of Saul's army over the Philistines.

The book of 2 Samuel 21:19 credits someone else with this feat, just mentioning it in passing.

At any rate, it was soon after this victory that David was brought into Saul's court as a singer. Saul suffered from melancholia, and David was able to soothe the sovereign.

195. David and Saul's son Jonathan and were good friends.

While serving King Saul, David became good friends with Saul's son Jonathan. Jonathan saved David from Saul a number of times. Saul feared that David meant to appropriate his kingdom and plotted to kill him. Jonathan warned David of his father's plans, and David fled. Hiding from Saul, he lived as a bandit in the Judean wilderness. Finally, when Saul's search became too threatening, David fled to the Philistines, who gave him a city. David became a mercenary for the Philistines. Our tradition has idealized the relationship between David and Jonathan, using it as a paradigm of selfless friendship.

196. Saul and Jonathan were killed by Philistines on Mount Gilboah.

Saul prepared to do battle against the Philistines. He visited a woman magician at En-dor (a practice forbidden by his own laws). She called up the spirit of Samuel, who informed him that the next day he and his sons would be killed.

Saul and Jonathan died on Mount Gilboah fighting the Philistines, thus ending the line of Saul. According to the text, Saul, fearing that he would be captured, ordered his armor guard to kill him. The guard refused. Saul then took his own sword and killed himself. Our rabbis had a problem with Saul's death. Suicide is forbidden in Judaism because our lives are not considered ours. Life is a gift from the Divine, and no person may take it, not even ourselves. They justified Saul's action by showing that the Philistines would have sinned against the Divine by humiliating the Hebrew king. They declared that, given a choice between death or breaking three commandments, a Jew must choose martyrdom. Those three forbidden acts are murder, forbidden sexual acts, and idolatry (see data to fact 383).

197. David was the second king of Israel.

With Saul's death (and a brief civil war), David became the second king of Israel. In all likelihood, he did so with the blessings of the Philistines, who viewed David as a lackey. He had been working for them from the Philistine city of Ziklag. They probably felt it was politically wise to place a Hebrew on the throne who would keep Israel submissive. It was not an easy succession for him, but David finally defeated the previous backers of Saul.

The stories about David are found in 1 and 2 Samuel, in the Nevi'im division of the TaNaCH. Because they were written by King David's people during his reign, their descriptions of Saul and of David's relationship with him are somewhat suspect. David's anointment by Samuel (see fact 193) obviously justified David's eventual kingship, but we have no way of knowing whether that secret act ever actually took place.

198. David made Jerusalem the capital of Israel.

The twelve tribes had always allied themselves into two separate groups. The North consisted of ten tribes; the South consisted of two tribes, including Judah, the tribe of King David. Even after David had militarily forced his reign upon the north, the followers of Saul, he needed to bring all twelve tribes into a united kingdom. King David brilliantly united the northern and southern tribes by creating a capital, Jerusalem, previously unaffiliated with either group. Jerusalem, located in the middle of the country, had been a city of the Jebusites. Because of its unique physical defenses, it had never been conquered. David took the city by climbing through its exposed water tunnel and taking the residents by surprise.

199. David brought the Ark to Jerusalem.

David succeeded in making his new political capital the religious center of Israel as well. Before his reign, the religious center had been at Shiloh. The Philistines had succeeded in capturing the Ark of the Covenant, but illness broke out in their cities, and they sent the Ark back to the Hebrews. It was stored, unused, at Kiryat Y'arim. David brought the Ark of the Covenant to Jerusalem, making it the religious capital as well as his political capital. He danced before the Ark as it was carried to Jerusalem, thus linking himself as king to the Covenant cult.

Having worked for the Philistines for a period of time, David apparently learned the secrets of iron, and he armed the Hebrews accordingly. When the Philistines discovered David's intentions for Israel's independence, they attacked, but the Hebrews routed them.

David's primary achievement as king was to systematically destroy all of the surrounding enemies of Israel. When he was finished, there were no more Philistines, the Amorites had disappeared, and the Moabites were a cowering vassal state. Thus David brought peace to the area.

He wanted to build a Temple, but Nathan, the prophet, informed him that his hands were too full of blood.

200. The Psalms are 150 poems attributed to King David.

King David is credited by tradition with writing the Psalms, 150 liturgical poems. According to the sages, David's harp was strung with the sinews of the ram sacrificed by Abraham at the time of the Akedah (see fact 130). At midnight the wind would blow across the strings of the harp, awakening David. For the rest of the night he would create special songs to the Divine. The psalms have become essential parts of every Jewish service and are read privately as personal prayers to the Divine.

The twenty-third psalm is the best known. Because it contains the phrase, "Yea, though I walk through the valley of the shadow of death, I shall fear no evil, for Thou art with me," it is read at many funeral services. Many find its opening sentence, "The Lord is my shepherd; I shall not want," a source of comfort in difficult times.

201. Solomon's mother was Batsheva.

David saw a married woman, Batsheva, bathing on the roof of her house. He ordered her to visit him, and she became pregnant. David then arranged for her husband, Uriah the Hittite, to be killed while fighting in battle. Immediately after Uriah's death, David married Batsheva. When confronted by Nathan the prophet with his perfidy, David admitted his guilt and repented.

Although that first child died at birth, Batsheva became pregnant again. Her son was Solomon, who became the third king of Israel.

After wiping out every enemy in sight, David and his reign became associated with peace and prosperity for Israel. Our sages viewed the reign of David as the ideal time. They said that the Messiah would come from the House of David, recreating the Davidic reign of peace and Hebrew power.

202. According to tradition, King David came from the tribe of Judah.

Since David came from the tribe of Judah, the emblem of that tribe, the Lion of Judah, became a symbol of the powerful future kingship of the Messiah.

Moreover, Jerusalem, the City of David, is also known as the City of Peace. David is "officially" buried on Mount Zion in Jerusalem, although historically his grave was probably not there. However, because of the importance of King David, Zion became another name for Jerusalem (see fact 498).

203. Solomon was David's son and the third king of Israel.

With David's death, Solomon became the third king of Israel and killed his brother Adonijah (see data to fact 181). The story of his reign is found in 1 Kings, in the Nevi'im division of the TaNaCH. It describes Solomon as the wisest person on earth, capable of communicating with all living creatures. Despite biblical and rabbinic attempts to portray Solomon as a wise, magnificent ruler, he was a Middle Eastern potentate.

The story of the two women and a baby is a good illustration of this orientation. Two prostitutes gave birth at the same time. One accidentally smothered her child by lying on top of him. Seeing her son dead, she then switched babies with the other woman. They came to Solomon for judgment. He ordered the live baby to be cut in half and given to each mother. Although the story ends with the real mother receiving her baby, thus making Solomon look wise, it is quite possible that Solomon actually intended to have the baby sliced in half.

Solomon lived in a grandiose style with huge numbers of wives and concubines. He had a famous relationship with the Queen of Sheba (see data to fact 468). He conscripted his own people to work at his building projects. His tax levies were overwhelming, and he actually sold some of his towns with their inhabitants to pay for his building projects. In addition, Solomon showed preferential treatment to his tribe (Judah in the south) and overtaxed the northern tribes.

204. Solomon built the Temple in Jerusalem.

Solomon did build a Temple, a beautiful rectangular, cedar structure which housed the Ark. He imported cedar from Lebanon and used foreign workers to create the building. It was divided into three rooms: a narrow entry; a long main room which contained the menorah (see fact 165), the incense altar (see data to fact 165), and the table with the twelve loaves of bread; and an inner square room, the Holy of Holies, which contained the Ark of the Covenant (see fact 165). The sacrifices were performed by the Kohanim outside of the building in the courtyard (see fact 167). The Temple is described in detail in First Kings 6 in the Nevi'im division of the TaNaCH, and it must have been magnificent. However, because of his excesses and insensitivities, Solomon took a powerful kingdom and ruined it.

The Divided Kingdom and Prophets

205. After Solomon, the Jewish kingdom split into two separate nations: Israel in the north and Judah in the south.

When Solomon died, his son Rehoboam became king. Representatives of the northern tribes came to him begging for fair taxes, but Rehoboam responded that he was raising the taxes. Therefore, the northern tribes split from the southern, creating their own kingdom with Jeroboam as their king. They called themselves Israel.

Jeroboam created two new worship sites: one at Bethel (the site of Jacob's ladder dream; see fact 137) and one at Dan. Kingship in the north depended on the backing of the army, and the history of the split kingdom of Israel is filled with revolutions and blood purges.

The two southern tribes formed their own kingdom, called Judah. Judah was a much more stable kingdom because Jerusalem remained the capital, the Temple was the worship site, and the kings came directly from the line of David, thus providing dynastic continuity. The people of Judah also believed that they were the authentic Israel, guaranteed divine protection because of their covenant with God. Neither country, however, was able to maintain the power of the earlier united monarchy.

It was during this period of the Divided Monarchy that the great prophets appeared exhorting the people and the kings to return to their contract with the Divine. Not many people or kings listened.

206. During the period of the divided kingdom, the prophets thundered their demands for social justice.

During the period of the kings, a new institution was introduced to the Hebrews. A group of prophets arose who spoke God's word directly to the people and to the kings. These prophets served as God's spokesmen. Our prophets spoke quite lucidly and directly, albeit in complex, poetic Hebrew. Their prophetic messages remain one of the most important legacies of our tradition because their theme emphasized the Divine's insistence on social justice in our world.

There were non-Jewish prophets as well, but our sages maintained that they were all evil. The most famous was Balaam. Balaam was hired by King Balak to curse the Hebrews. However, instead of cursing them, he blessed them with the words, "How goodly are your tents, O Jacob, your dwellings, O Israel."

207. The prophets spoke the words of God.

There were some generic characteristics common to all the prophets. First, not one of the prophets wanted to be a prophet. Second, every prophet felt the immediacy of the message that he was commanded to convey. Third, every prophet felt deeply the Divine's insistence on ethical behavior. Offering sacrifices wasn't enough. God wanted people involved in social action. Since this emphasis of social justice over ritual was the position of the early Reform Jews, the books of Prophets became an important text source for them (see data to facts 442, 606). Fourth, many of the prophets had an image of what the ideal world should be like, a world where people really cared about and for one another. They described this world as the "End of Days." The prophetic visions of the perfect world became the source of Jewish messianism (see data to fact 326). Finally, each prophet tried to describe the powerful ambivalence of being the Divine's spokesman. They feared it, yet they had to speak out. They couldn't refuse.

208. Elijah defeated the priests of Baal on Mount Carmel.

Elijah lived during the time of the Divided Kingdom (see fact 205), and he served in the north. The king, Ahab, was influenced by his wife Jezebel to hire priests of Baal, a non-Hebrew cultic group.

Elijah thundered against them and challenged them to a ritual duel. Whoever could cause the rains to come to end a serious drought would be the winner.

They met on Mount Carmel, and the priests did their best, but nothing happened. Then Elijah prayed, his offering went up in smoke, and the rains came. The priests of Baal were slaughtered, and, once again, the Divine won the day.

It was Elijah who found the Divine in the "soft voice of silence" rather than in a whirlwind, an earthquake, or fire. We too can search for the divine message in the still, small voice.

The Bible describes Elijah ascending to heaven in a fiery chariot in the midst of a whirlwind. Because it does not mention him dying, our sages assumed that Elijah is still wandering the earth looking for honest people and helping the righteous (see data to fact 579). It is part of our tradition that Elijah will be the vanguard for the Messiah. We therefore welcome Elijah to all events at which the Messiah might appear, specifically at the end of Shabbat and at Passover, the original Redemption. We also welcome Elijah to every Brit Milah, the circumcision ceremony (see fact 270). Three reasons are given: First, our tradition views Elijah as the protector of children. Second, any child could be the Messiah, and Elijah should be there. Finally, according to a midrash (see fact 333), Elijah had to flee for his life because he rebuked the Hebrews for not circumcising their children. We invite Elijah to all circumcisions to assure him that we are maintaining the covenant.

Elijah gave his prophetic ability to his disciple Elisha.

209. Amos said, "Let justice well up as water and righteousness like a mighty stream."

Amos was a prophet from Judah, the south. He came up to Bethel, the shrine in the north, to deliver God's message. In powerful poetry, he warned that the Divine was incensed at the cruel, immoral behavior of the people. As a result, God refused to accept their sacrifices. "Spare me the sound of your hymns, and let me not hear the music of your lutes. But let justice well up like water, righteousness like a mighty stream."

210. Hosea equated idolatry with adultery.

Hosea saw Israel's turning to idolatry as being the same as a wife being unfaithful to her husband. He felt the divine imperative to marry an unfaithful woman to exemplify Israel's sin. He emphasized that the people had sinned through idolatry and dishonesty: "because there is no honesty and no goodness and no obedience to God in the land, false swearing, dishonesty, and murder, and theft and adultery are rife; crime follows upon crime!" In Chapter 14 he quotes God begging his children to return to righteousness. This final chapter is read on Shabbat Shuvah (see fact 23).

211. Isaiah said, "They shall beat their swords into ploughshares and their spears into pruning hooks; nation shall not lift up sword against nation."

Both Isaiah and Micah shared a similar dream of a world at peace. They saw danger in the political alliances Israel was establishing. They saw corruption eating away at their society. Both prophets expressed a desperate need for change, for a return to social justice. Although this famous description of peace is found in both books, it is Isaiah who is credited with this quote where it appears on the wall of the United Nations building in New York City.

212. Jeremiah was thrown into a pit for being a prophet.

It was frequently dangerous to be a prophet. Some of our prophets, in speaking God's word, had to accuse royalty of misconduct. Doing so put their lives in jeopardy. When Jeremiah delivered God's message that Jerusalem was going to be destroyed to punish the people's wickedness, an angry mob threw him into a pit where he almost died. Jeremiah had his own scribe, Baruch, who kept track of all of his messages, including his complaints that he hated being a prophet. Jeremiah was exiled to Egypt when the Babylonians destroyed the Temple. According to tradition, he wrote the Book of Lamentations (see fact 94).

213. Jonah fled, only to be forced to prophesy.

Jonah was commanded to prophesy to the great city of Nineveh. He refused and tried to flee from God on a ship. God created a storm which threatened to destroy the vessel. Jonah, realizing that he was responsible, convinced the crew to throw him overboard. He was swallowed by a large fish and, three days later, was vomited ashore at his destination.

214. Jonah warned the people of Nineveh that they would be destroyed unless they changed their evil ways.

Jonah then fulfilled his assignment of warning Nineveh that they were doomed. The people of Nineveh heeded Jonah's warning and repented. God spared the city. Because of its theme of universal repentance and forgiveness, the book of Jonah is read on Yom Kippur afternoon.

215. Assyria conquered Israel.

In 722 B.C.E (before the Common Era) Assyria invaded and conquered the northern tribes and took their leaders into exile. The ten northern tribes disappeared; they became known as the Ten Lost Tribes of Israel.

The kingdom of Judah was to continue until 586 B.C.E., when Babylonia would conquer the little kingdom, destroy Jerusalem, and take the leadership captive.

There are numerous legends about the Ten Lost Tribes of Israel. One legend is that they exist on an island protected by the roaring Sambatyon River. No one can cross the river except on Shabbat, when the river rests. Since travel on Shabbat is forbidden (see data to fact 97), the Lost Ten Tribes of Israel are stuck. However, when the Messiah comes, they will be released and will rejoin the rest of Israel.

216. King Hezekiah built a water tunnel that saved Jerusalem.

Hezekiah was king of Judah. He (rightly) feared an attack by the powerful Assyrians, who had already destroyed Israel in the north. He therefore ordered a special water tunnel constructed which redirected the water from the Spring of Gihon to inside the city walls. The diggers started to cut through the Jerusalem mountain from each end. To their shock and amazement, they met in the middle. They were so thrilled with their success that they carved a notice on the wall of the tunnel where they met.

When Sennecherib attacked Jerusalem, he couldn't find any water source. Plague broke out in his camp, and he was forced to retreat. Jerusalem was saved thanks to Hezekiah's tunnel. Today Hezekiah's tunnel is one of the favorite Jerusalem tourist sites. Still partially filled with water, it provides a cool touring respite on hot days.

Babylonian Exile and Return

217. Nebuchadnezzar destroyed our Temple and Jerusalem on the Ninth of Av in 586 B.C.E.

In 586 B.C.E. King Nebuchadnezzar of Babylonia (in Mesopotamia by the Persian Gulf) conquered Judah and destroyed the Temple of

Solomon on the 9th of the Hebrew month of Av (see fact 93). He then took the priests, the nobility, and the artisans into exile. He left the farmers, shepherds, and villagers in Judah.

218. The Babylonian Exile followed our expulsion from the Land of Israel, when we were forced to live in Babylonia.

Scholars have speculated a great deal about what happened to us during the Babylonian Exile, which lasted from 586 B.C.E. until 538 B.C.E. (just under 50 years). Market days in Babylonia were on Mondays and Thursdays. Apparently the Hebrews gathered at those times to study about the "good old days" back in Judah. Study became a form of worship and has remained so through the centuries.

Many scholars believe that during these study sessions the Hebrews added some prayers and readings, gradually developing a new form of worship which served as a substitute for the defunct sacrifices.

219. Ezekiel had a vision of a field of dry bones that came to life and symbolized Israel; 2 Isaiah described God working through history.

During the Babylonian Exile the prophet Ezekiel had a vision of a field of dry bones. The bones came to life covered with flesh, a divine sign that Israel would emerge from the exile alive and whole.

At the same time, the prophet in 2 Isaiah, described a revolutionary concept about God: the Divine used other nations to punish or reward Israel. This concept of a God working through history made Jewish theology unique.

Until that time, the Hebrews believed that God's mailing address was Jerusalem. God was in charge of the Land of Israel and nowhere else; thus the Hebrews in Babylonia believed that God was far from them. Isaiah introduced the idea that God transcended space; God was everywhere and controlled all historical events in the world. God was in exile with the Hebrews and, as soon as they truly repented, God would return them to power in Jerusalem.

We don't know historically when the stories, laws, and codes of our people were written in the format we call the Torah. In all likelihood, however, this process also took place during that important Babylonian Exile.

220. Nehemiah became governor of Judea after the exile.

In 538 B.C.E. the Persians conquered the Babylonians, and Cyrus, king of the Persians, permitted the Jews to return to Jerusalem. Very few actually went, however; the vast majority of Jews had settled comfortably in Babylonia and chose to stay there. Those who did return were frustrated by the hard life and the raids by Samaritans and other unfriendly groups. Pushed and prodded by the prophets Zachariah and Haggai, they built a small Temple in Jerusalem on the same spot as the first Temple. The sacrificial cult was revived, but the people remained demoralized, helpless, and miserable.

In the 440s B.C.E. the King of Persia sent Nehemiah to be governor of the weak, miserable region of Judea. Nehemiah's first task was to rebuild Jerusalem to defend itself against the Samaritans (see data to fact 482). He then reorganized the tax districts of the region and established a strong central authority free from corruption. At the same time, he established the authority of his returning group of Jews over the rest of the society. Noting that many of the aristocracy had intermarried, Nehemiah ordered all Jews to divorce their foreign spouses.

The Book of Nehemiah is found in Ketuvim, the Writings section of the TaNaCH.

221. Ezra the scribe brought the Torah back from Babylonia.

While Nehemiah was busy reestablishing a strong Jerusalem, Ezra the scribe returned from Babylonia. The title *scribe* apparently meant someone who was an authority on the Law.

Ezra challenged the authority of both the priesthood and the aristocracy in Jerusalem by ordering them to leave their foreign spouses. He was supported in this effort by Nehemiah.

Most important, Ezra read a scroll called the Torah to the people. The people accepted this set of laws as binding upon them. We don't know a great deal about its development, but it was clearly a new phenomenon brought back from Babylonia by Ezra. The Torah became the constitution of the new province of Judea.

Although Ezra read the Torah text in Hebrew, he instituted the important tradition of having the words translated into Aramaic, the language of the people. Aramaic has many similarities to Hebrew, but the two languages are different enough to require translation. By making the text available to all people, Ezra further undermined the authority of the priesthood. Instead of being the sole caretakers of the Law, the priests were now viewed as a group answerable to the Law, which everyone could study and know.

Politically, however, with sacrifices being offered at the new Temple (see data to fact 220), the priests still held the power. The High Priest ran the country as a theocracy. By the time Alexander the Great came into the region in 332 B.C.E. (see data to fact 38), the High Priest's political power was the same as a king's.

The Book of Ezra is found in Ketuvim, the Writings section of the TaNaCH.

The Writings

222. The Book of Proverbs praises the woman of valor.

The Book of Proverbs is found in the Ketuvim, the Writings section of the TaNaCH. Through poetry, brief admonishments, and proverbs, it strives to teach the reader wisdom. "Reverence of God is the beginning of knowledge; fools despise wisdom and discipline" is the book's theme.

Some scholars believe that the book was used as a text for teaching children the discipline of wisdom. It tried to provide them with insights concerning the right way to behave and respond to their world. Others view it as a form of sound ethical teachings for adults, a series of aphorisms to apply to daily circumstances.

Proverbs 31:10 begins a Hebrew acrostic praising the woman of valor, the capable wife. It beautifully describes the woman's ability to administer and maintain a busy household. Traditional Jewish husbands recite it to their wives at the Shabbat evening meal. Many modern Reform Jews have chosen other selections to read which are less household-oriented in their descriptions of an integrated, sharing partner.

223. Job suffered greatly for no apparent reason.

The Book of Job, found in Ketuvim, the Writings section of the TaNaCH, is an attempt to grapple with the question, "Why do good people suffer?" According to the Torah, the reward for doing the mitzvot is health, prosperity, and long life.

In the Book of Job, the Satan, serving as God's prosecuting attorney, and God make a bet that the righteous man Job can be made so miserable that he will curse God.

Job loses his wife, children, wealth, and health. His "friends" accuse him of being a wicked person because such calamities happen only to wicked people. Job maintains his innocence and repeatedly asks God why such pain is happening to him.

In Chapter 38, God responds out of a storm: the Divine is divine; humans are human and should not have the audacity to challenge the Divine Will. Job is left alone and emotionally crushed on a dungheap.

Scholars believe that the original story ended with Job remaining desolate. However, the sages didn't like that ending and added a chapter that shows Job restored to health and wealth, with a new family, living happily ever after.

The question of why good people suffer continues to be one of the major problems we explore. The rabbinic solution was the concept of the Olam HaBa, the world to come after this earthly life, where the righteous are properly rewarded and the wicked are properly punished (see facts 320, 607).

Some modern writers, such as Rabbi Harold Kushner, author of *When Bad Things Happen to Good People*, offer different solutions to this dilemma. Rabbi Kushner suggests that God is not all-powerful and cannot control the evil things that happen to people. Rather than being responsible for misfortune, God weeps with the sufferers.

224. Daniel was thrown into a den of lions and survived.

The book of Daniel found in the Ketuvim, the Writings section of the TaNaCH, tells how Daniel became an important advisor to the King of Babylonia. For breaking the King's command, Daniel was thrown into a den of hungry lions, but they didn't harm him, proof that the faithful Jew receives Divine Providence.

Many scholars believe that the book of Daniel was written during the period of King Antiochus (see fact 38). It is the only book of the TaNaCH that even hints at Techiyat hamaytim, resurrection of the dead (see fact 607). It also describes Daniel praying three times a day (see fact 295).

225. The Book of Esther tells the story of Purim.

The Book of Esther, found in the Ketuvim, Writings section of the TaNaCH, tells how we were saved from a major disaster. Haman, a descendent of Amalek, wanted to wipe out the Jews because of a personal affront by a Jew, Mordechai. Unbeknownst to Haman, Mordechai's cousin, Esther, was married to Persian King Ahasuerus. Esther's Hebrew name was Hadassah, but not even the king knew that she was Jewish.

When Esther learned that Haman planned to annihilate the Jews, she begged for protection from her husband King Ahasuerus. Haman was hanged, and the Jews were victorious in a mighty battle. The holiday Purim commemorates our being saved from Haman.

There is no historical evidence that the Purim story ever took place. However, we have been saved from annihilation so many times that we celebrate Purim with great energy and joy; it represents every time a tyrant has tried to wipe us out and failed (see facts 51–63).

226. Ruth was the great-grandmother of King David.

The megillah of Ruth, one of the five scrolls (see fact 87) is found in Ketuvim, the Writings section of the TaNaCH. It tells the following story: A Jewish woman, Naomi, had two sons. Because of famine, the entire family went to Moab, where Naomi's sons married Moabite women. Both sons died, and Naomi returned to Judah, ordering her Moabite daughters-in-law to leave her and return to their families. One of her daughters-in-law, Ruth, refused and insisted on taking care of Naomi.

Back in Bethlehem, Ruth went out to gather grain from the corners of the fields of wealthy farmers (see data to fact 579). She caught the attention of Boaz, a relative of Naomi. Boaz married Ruth, and their great-grandchild was David, King of Israel.

Most scholars believe that the Book of Ruth was written as a protest against Ezra's law forcing Jews to divorce their non-Jewish spouses after the Babylonian Exile (see data to fact 220). Its message showed that a non-Jew could actually be part of the Davidic line! Our rabbis resolved this apparent conflict by explaining that Ruth underwent conversion (see facts 586, 587).

The megillah of Ruth is read on Shavuot (see fact 87).

The Apocrypha

227. The Apocrypha are books that weren't accepted as part of the TaNaCH.

Although we don't know a great deal about how the TaNaCH was canonized, most scholars agree that TaNaCH became sacred scripture sometime between 70 c.e. and 135 c.e. The Sanhedrin (see facts 327, 328) apparently had the responsibility of determining which books were accepted into the canon. Other Jewish texts that weren't accepted into the TaNaCH were called *the secular scrolls*. In Greek, they were called the Apocrypha (the outside books).

Although rejected as part of the TaNaCH by the rabbis, the Apocrypha were accepted as part of the Christian canonized books, and they can be found in the Christian editions of the Bible. Only one of the books, *The Wisdom of Ben Sira*, is mentioned in the Talmud (see fact 363).

The Apocrypha includes Tobit, the story of a righteous Jew who is helped by the angel Raphael and a fish; 1 and 2 Maccabees, the sources for most of our information about the Hasmonean Revolt (see facts 38–43); Judith, the story of a Jewish widow who cuts off the head of the enemy general Holofernes, saving her people; Susannah, the story of a righteous woman framed by two lusting elders, whose testimony is shown by Daniel to be corrupt; and Bel and the Dragon, two stories showing Daniel's cleverness in uncovering the deceit of idolatry.

Religious Objects, Dress, and Prayer

Introduction to Customs

228. Beautiful ritual objects fulfill a mitzvah.

Ritual objects play an important role in Jewish life. They are used for daily observance, prayer, and holiday celebration. Our sages have always encouraged use of the most beautiful ritual objects possible to fulfill a mitzvah. Over the centuries, Jewish artisans have produced magnificent candlesticks for Shabbat and the festivals, beautiful challah and matzah covers, illuminated Haggadot, Omer scrolls (for counting the days between Passover and Shavuot), chanukkiyot; Seder plates, etrog containers, and a myriad of other objects used to enhance Jewish ritual.

The ritual objects used in daily Jewish life and those used in the synagogue provide added richness to our tradition. For many of the objects, specific regulations have been created determining how they are to be made.

These rules differed from community to community, since we were never monolithic in our customs, and we have always been influenced by our surrounding cultures. By the eleventh century, customs between two particular groups, Sephardic and Ashkenazic, had changed markedly (see fact 229).

229. Sephardic customs come from Spain and the Middle East, and Ashkenazic customs come from Northern Europe.

Jews under Muslim rule had developed customs and regulations in consonance with their surrounding world. Originating in Babylonia, this culture eventually developed its center in Spain (*Sepharad* in Hebrew). The Jewish culture developed in the Muslim world is therefore called Sephardic.

Jews under Christian rule developed different customs and regulations. Their original center was in Germany (*Ashkenaz*). Therefore, even when the center for this culture spread to Eastern Europe, it was called Ashkenazic.

The vast majority of Jewish laws are the same for these two groups. However, some customs differ (see data to facts 47, 66, 232, 234, 237, 241, 272). Today most of us living in the United States trace our roots to Ashkenazic Eastern Europe. It is important to remember that Sephardic Jewry has an equally rich tradition.

Torah as Ritual Object

230. The Aron HaKodesh is the ark where we keep the Torah.

The Torah scroll is the most central ritual object of our tradition. It is housed at the front of the sanctuary in the synagogue, in a special container called the Aron HaKodesh, the Holy Ark. This obviously symbolizes the Ark which was placed inside the Mishkan in the desert and inside the Temple in Jerusalem (see facts 164 and 204). Traditionally, the ark is beautifully decorated and has a parochet, a decorated curtain, in front. By emphasizing the ark, a symbol of the Temple and the sacrifices, as the central feature of the synagogue, the rabbis successfully transferred the sense of holiness associated with the Temple to the synagogue (see fact 346).

As a sign of respect for our contract with the Divine, we stand whenever the Torah is removed from the Aron HaKodesh. In some communities, it is the custom to remain standing as long as the ark is open. The halachah (see fact 342) is that we remain standing as long as the Torah is being held vertically. Once the Torah has been placed on the reading lectern, even if the ark is open, we may sit. In many communities, men and women kiss the Torah as it is carried past them as a sign of love for our sacred text.

231. A sofer writes Torah scrolls on parchment with a quill pen.

The Torah scroll itself is parchment made from any kosher animal (see fact 590). It is written with a quill pen by a sofer, a scribe. It takes about a year to write a scroll. The text has its own decorative Hebrew script, and the regulations concerning its writing are very detailed. Similar rules apply to the writing of a get (see fact 268) and the parchments found in mezuzot (see facts 247, 248) and tefillin (see fact 249). Although there are rules concerning the writing of the megillot (see facts 34, 52, 78, 87, 94), unlike the other parchment documents, the megillah may be decorated with pictures as well.

232. A Sephardic Torah has the same text as an Ashkenazic Torah, but it is kept in a vertical wooden case.

All Jews use the same Torah text. However, Sephardic and Ashkenazic Jews differ in the way they cover and ornament the scroll (see also fact 233).

Sephardic Jews encase the scroll in a vertical box which opens to reveal the text. The Torah is thus read while it is standing vertically. Congregants behind the baal koray, the reader (see fact 309), can see the parchment from which he is reading.

233. The Torah is dressed to look like the High Priest.

Ashkenazic Jews dress the Torah like the High Priest (see fact 171). The Torah is covered with a mantle, a breastplate, and either finials (called rimonim) or a crown (called a keter). Since the High Priest wore bells at the bottom of his mantle, the keter and finials both have bells. The tradition of dressing the Torah in this manner is fairly recent and wasn't mentioned before the fifteenth century.

234. Atzei Chayim are the wooden poles that hold the Torah scroll.

Both the Ashkenazic and Sephardic Torah scrolls are attached to wooden poles, called Atzei Chayim, the trees of life.

Torah itself is called the Tree of Life. The kabbalists (see facts 355, 417) referred to God as the Tree of Life. Thus, the wooden poles that hold the scroll are physical reminders of the cosmological importance of the Torah. Life, provided through Torah, is our most precious gift from the Divine. A traditional Jewish toast is "L'chayim!" "To Life!"

The Ashkenazic Atzei Chayim unwind the scroll, allowing it to be read on a flat surface (traditionally covered with a cloth). The Sephardic Atzei Chayim poke through the top of the decorated wooden container and are turned to wind the scroll vertically.

235. A yad is a Torah pointer.

It is forbidden to touch the lettered surface of the Torah parchment, so a wooden or metal pointer was created for this purpose. The tip of the pointer is in the shape of a hand with the index finger pointing to the letters. It is called a *yad*, a hand. For anthropological purposes, it is interesting to note that the hand shaped on the yad is traditionally the right hand.

Synagogue Objects and Furnishings

236. Many synagogues contain a seven-branched menorah.

Most synagogue ritual objects serve as reminders of the Temple furnishings and the sacrificial cult. Thus, it has become a tradition to have a seven-branched candelabrum in the sanctuary as a reminder of the seven-branched menorah in the Temple (see fact 165). Because the rabbis forbade making an exact duplication of the Temple menorah, many synagogues created six- or eight-branched menorot (plural of menorah) for their sanctuaries. Don't confuse the Temple or synagogue menorah with the chanukkiya, the nine-branched candelabrum used on Chanukkah (see fact 45).

237. The ner tamid is the eternal light.

It became a tradition to have a ner tamid, an eternal light, burning at the front of the synagogue. Although some sources cite the ner tamid as a reminder of the menorah in the Temple, it is more frequently associated with the Temple's continuously burning incense altar in front of the ark (see data to fact 165). Our sages also associated the ner tamid with the symbolic idea of God's ongoing Presence.

Some Sephardic synagogues have two nerot tamid (plural of ner tamid). One symbolizes the incense altar, and one symbolizes the pillar of fire which guided the Hebrews through the wilderness. According to Exodus 40:34–38, a pillar of cloud led the people by day and a pillar of fire led them at night. The Sephardic second ner tamid reminds us of that special guidance.

238. A mechitzah is a wall that separates men and women in an Orthodox synagogue.

Our tradition maintains that since talmudic times (see facts 360–367), the synagogue has been partitioned, with a men's section (usually in the front) and a women's section (usually above in a gallery or behind the men's section). The latticed wall which divided the two sections was called a mechitzah, a partition.

Rabbis cited the Temple in Jerusalem as the origin of this custom. There, even in the court set aside for all ritually impure people, the women were separated from the men. Our sages stated that at Mount Sinai the women kept apart from the men.

The Reform Movement was vehemently opposed to the mechitzah because one of the fundamental principles of modern liberal Judaism is egalitarianism. Therefore, men and women sit together in Reform synagogues and in most Conservative congregations.

Some recent research into early synagogues indicates that men and women might not have been separated in the earliest synagogues.

239. A mizrach is a wall hanging in a synagogue or home denoting the eastern wall.

With few exceptions, it became the custom for the congregation to face toward Jerusalem during the prayer service. Synagogues were therefore built so the wall on which the ark was placed was in the direction of Jerusalem.

Since the vast majority of our communities were west of the Land of Israel, the natural focus of our prayers was to the east. The Hebrew word for east is "mizrach."

The eastern wall of the synagogue was special because it was closest to the ark and closest to Jerusalem. It became the custom in Eastern Europe for the community's dignitaries to have their seats by the eastern wall. This wall was frequently decorated with a beautiful panel or parchment to show its importance. The panel was called a mizrach.

It became a custom also to have a mizrach on the eastern wall in the home because it indicated which wall faced Jerusalem when an individual or a minyan (see fact 289) prayed at home. Frequently the mizrach served as a charm against the Evil Eye and illness.

240. The sheliach tzibbur is the leader of the service.

It has always been a great honor to be the sheliach tzibbur, the representative of the community, who leads the prayer service. According to tradition, any educated male Jew over the age of 13 and of good character can be the sheliach tzibbur. Rabbis, who were primarily teachers and judges (see data to facts 426, 466), rarely served as the sheliach tzibbur. It was a function for laypeople.

Maintaining the value of egalitarianism, liberal Jews encourage women to lead services, and a woman can be a sheliach tzibbur in most Reform synagogues. The Conservative Movement is still in conflict over this issue, and each congregation establishes its own rules for the participation of women (see data to fact 466).

Part of the celebration of becoming a Bar/Bat Mitzvah is having the Bar/Bat Mitzvah lead the service as sheliach tzibbur (see fact 277).

241. The bimah is the raised area where the sheliach tzibbur leads the service.

The bimah is a raised platform in the synagogue from which the baal koray reads the Torah (see fact 309). There were no regulations about the architectural style of the bimah, so synagogue artists were very creative in making these platforms.

In Sephardic synagogues, the bimah stands facing the ark in the center of the sanctuary with no seats in front of it. The sheliach tzibbur, the leader of the service (see fact 240) leads the service from the bimah.

In many Ashkenazic congregations, only Torah is read from the bimah; the sheliach tzibbur leads the service from a little stand called an amud next to the ark.

Many bimot (plural of bimah) were magnificently decorated. Some were enclosed by a metal railing and stood in the middle of the sanctuary.

In the eighteenth century some synagogues moved the bimah to the front to allow more seating for the congregation. Although this innovation led to some arguments, no bitterness arose over it until the rise of the Reform Movement (see fact 442). When the founders of the Reform Movement followed the architectural pattern of the Protestant churches and moved the bimah to the front of the congregation, placing the ark on the bimah, the Orthodox community was outraged.

Today the placement of the bimah is as varied as artistic styles of congregations. Although the sheliach tzibbur in some traditional synagogues still faces Jerusalem, it has become the custom in many Orthodox and non-Orthodox synagogues for the prayer leaders to face the congregation.

242. A chazzan is a cantor.

Originally, the sheliach tzibbur was a man of status in the community, holding an official position called "chazzan." The chazzan was the synagogue administrator, similar to synagogue president or executive director today. Over the years, the rules for the prayer services increased (see data to facts 292–294). People expressed a desire to hear fine voices leading the prayers. New liturgical music developed which gained popularity but required a knowledgeable prayer leader. This led to a new professional: the chazzan, the cantor.

TaNaCH Translations and Objects

243. The Septuagint is the Greek translation of the TaNaCH.

One of the consequences of Alexander the Great's conquest of the Middle East was that the upper classes began speaking Greek (see data to fact 38). They didn't know Hebrew, and they viewed Aramaic as the language of common people.

The language of commerce, philosophy, and art was Greek. This was especially true for the Jewish community in Hellenized Alexandria. At their urging, a Greek translation of the Torah was written at the beginning of the third century B.C.E. By the year 100 B.C.E., all of the Prophets and much of the Writings were also translated from Hebrew into Greek. It was the first official translation of the TaNaCH, a revolutionary event. Part of the essence of the Torah, one of the aspects that made it sacred, was the fact that it was written in Hebrew. By creating a translation, the Jews of Alexandria were saying that it was more important to understand the words than to ritually read the text. They recognized the dilemma caused by a translation, and they attempted to justify their actions.

According to tradition, King Ptolemy II invited seventy-two scholars to Alexandria to write a Greek translation of the TaNaCH. Each was put in a separate room and, behold, all seventy-two Greek translations were exactly the same. Moreover, because the translators were helped by revelation, their text was superior to the original. Because of the legend concerning the seventy-two scholars, the Greek translation of the TaNaCH is called the Septuagint, the Seventy.

The Septuagint became the Bible text for the early Christians and, as a result, lost favor with the Jewish community. In the second century C.E., therefore, a new Greek translation was written for the Jewish community.

The Septuagint remains the official Bible for the Greek Orthodox Church. Jerome used this text when he wrote the Latin translation of the Bible, the Vulgate. The Catholic Church still prefers the Septuagint over the Hebrew text.

244. The Targum is the Aramaic translation of the TaNaCH.

Before the Babylonian Exile (see fact 218), the Hebrews spoke Hebrew. When they were forced to move to Babylonia, they discovered that the official language of trade and commerce was Aramaic. Aramaic was a Semitic language related to Hebrew, but it was different enough to cause linguistic difficulties for the Hebrews. The exiled Hebrews quickly learned Aramaic. By the time they returned to Judea (see fact 220), the vast majority of them could not understand Hebrew.

When Ezra read the Torah text to the people, he had it orally translated into Aramaic at the same time (see fact 221). This became the accepted way to read Torah. The reader would read the Hebrew, and an official translator gave the Aramaic translation for the people. Gradually, these oral translations got written down.

In the second century C.E., a convert named Onkelos wrote an Aramaic translation of the Torah. It was called *Targum Onkelos*, the Translation of Onkelos, and it became the official rabbinic Aramaic version of the Torah. At about the same time, an official Aramaic translation of the Prophets the *Targum Yonatan*, the Translation of Jonathan was written. Together, they are called simply the Targum, and they can be found in *Mikraot Gedolot* (see data to fact 245).

Although Aramaic ceased to be the Jews' spoken language, some Jews still read the weekly Torah portion in both Hebrew and Aramaic.

245. A Chumash is a printed book that contains the Torah.

In 1517 a Christian named Daniel Bomberg printed the first Hebrew Bible with commentaries. He included the *Targum* (see fact 244) plus explanations by Rashi (see fact 386), Ibn Ezra (see fact 387), and RaMBaN (see fact 403). It was called *Mikraot Gedolot*. To differentiate between the text and the commentaries, Bomberg created a second Hebrew typeface, which became known as Rashi script. (It could have just as easily been called Ibn Ezra script, but it wasn't.)

Bomberg also printed the Torah portion of the TaNaCH (see facts 104, 105) separately with the Targum and Rashi's commentary. This book was called the *Chumash*, from the Hebrew root for *five* because the Torah is the first five books of the TaNaCH (see fact 105).

Today a *Chumash* is any printed text of the Torah. It usually contains a translation into the vernacular plus traditional and/or modern commentaries.

246. A Haftarah is a set portion from the Prophets read after the Torah portion on Shabbat and festivals.

The word Haftarah means additional. Despite its mispronunciation by people, the word is not related to the word *Torah* at all. It is not a Half-Torah.

The sages assigned a specific reading from the Prophets to correspond to each Torah portion. When possible, they selected prophetic portions that contained the same word or theme as the Torah portion.

On numerous occasions, however, they chose the Haftarah portion to correspond to a significant seasonal event. There are special Haftarot (plural of Haftarah) for the Shabbat before Rosh Chodesh (see fact 1); for the festivals (see fact 27); for the weeks before Purim (see fact 59), Tisha B'Av (see fact 93), and the Yamim Nora'im (see fact 9); and for Shabbat Shuvah (see fact 23) and Shabbat HaGadol (see fact 67). Sometimes the Sephardic Haftarah selection is different from the Ashkenazic selection.

No one knows when the tradition of reading set portions from the Prophets after the Torah reading began. The most popular assumption is that it came about when Antiochus had made the study of Torah illegal (see fact 38).

The reader of the Haftarah is called the maftir. Traditionally, the maftir is given the final few verses of the Torah portion to repeat before beginning the Haftarah. These repeated sentences are also called the maftir. It became a minhag (custom) for the Bar (or Bat) Mitzvah to read the maftir as part of the Bar (or Bat) Mitzvah celebration (see fact 277).

Personal Ritual Objects Mentioned in Torah

247. Mezuzah means doorpost.

The Torah mentions only three ritual objects for private use: mezuzah, tefillin (see fact 249), and tzitzit (see fact 250).

Mezuzah means *doorpost*. We are commanded in Deuteronomy 6:9 to "write them (the commandments) on the mezuzot of your house and on your gates." Our sages understood this to be a commandment to place the Shema (see fact 300) and its subsequent paragraph and Deuteronomy 11:13–21 on the doorpost of our dwellings.

248. The mezuzah contains the Shema and V'ahavta written by a sofer on parchment.

The Shema, the V'ahavta, and Deuteronomy 11:13–21 (see data to fact 300) were traditionally written on parchment. Rolled into a container and placed on the right side of the doorway, they became known as a mezuzah. It is written by a sofer, a scribe, with a quill pen.

There was a disagreement over whether the mezuzah should be placed vertically or horizontally. As a result, tradition declared that it should be angled with the bottom facing out.

On the outside of the parchment, the word *Shaddai* is written. It is the Hebrew word for one of the biblical names of God. In addition, SH, D, Y stand for the initial letters of the Hebrew words, "Protector of the Doors of Israel."

From the time of the Talmud, the belief developed that the

mezuzah, besides fulfilling a positive mitzvah, served as a talisman guarding the Jewish home. Strict regulations were developed to ensure that the mezuzah was ritually acceptable; otherwise, it would lose its protective power.

On the back of some mezuzot, the Hebrew letters כוזו במוסין כוזו are written. They are a cryptogram. By substituting the previous letter in the alphabet for each of them, they create the words יהוה אלהינו יהוה, Adonai, our God, Adonai.

249. Tefillin are leather boxes containing Torah passages written on parchment by a sofer, commanding us to bind the mitzvot on our hand and have them between our eyes.

In four places the Torah commands us to put the commandments on our hand and have them as symbols (totafot) between our eyes (Exodus 13:9; 13:16; Deuteronomy 6:8; 11:18). The two paragraphs in Deuteronomy specifically state to bind them as a sign on our hand and between our eyes.

According to our sages, the ritual objects needed to fulfill this mitzvah are the tefillin. Tefillin are two cubical leather boxes which contain the four Torah passages commanding the wearing of tefillin. The paragraphs are written on parchment by a sofer, a scribe, with a quill pen.

The parchment for the hand tefillin is made of one long strip containing the four paragraphs. The head tefillin has four separate compartments, each containing a separate parchment of one of the paragraphs. Sages disagreed over the order of these four parchments.

The hand tefillin, which is actually placed on the bicep, is attached by a long leather strap, which is wrapped around the arm seven times and then wrapped around the hand to form the letters SH, D, Y, one of the names of God.

The head tefillin is attached at the forehead by a leather band which encircles the head.

Traditionally, tefillin are donned every day except Shabbat, festivals, and fast days. Some scholars believe that our sages encouraged wearing the tefillin all day. Ironically, during the Talmudic period there were many Jews who did not put on tefillin. During the twelfth and thirteenth centuries in France and Spain, Jews were very lax about wearing tefillin.

The tefillin are viewed as a physical affirmation to do the mitzvot (the hand tefillin), to think about the mitzvot (the head tefillin), and to do both with a loving heart (the proximity of the hand tefillin to the heart).

Tefillin have mystical implications for Kabbalists. They envision God putting on tefillin just as Jews do. When a Jew dons tefillin, he brings added holiness into the world. For this reason, the tradition developed that if every Jew in the world put on tefillin on the same day, the Messiah would have to come.

Because women are traditionally exempt from positive mitzvot that have a time limit connected to them, women did not traditionally put on tefillin. (We are told that Rashi's daughters did, but they were an exception.)

As part of the Reform Movement's ongoing dedication to the principle of egalitarianism, some Reform congregations encourage women to learn how to put on tefillin. Women in the Conservative Movement, notably rabbinical and cantorial students at the Jewish Theological Seminary (see data to fact 449), are also wearing them.

250. Tzitzit are the fringes on the corners of a tallit.

Numbers 15:38 commands: "Make . . . fringes on the corners of (your) garments throughout the ages; let them attach a cord of techelet, royal blue, to the fringe at each corner. . . ." The Hebrew word for fringe is *tzitzit*. The regulations for making the tzitzit are quite specific. Each tzitzit consists of one long and three short white threads which are passed through holes at the corner of the tallit (see fact 251) and folded, thus making eight threads. They are tied with a double knot. The long thread is wound around the others seven, eight, eleven, and thirteen times and the four sets of braiding are each separated by a double knot. The resultant eight threads left hanging are the tzitzit.

Techelet, the royal blue, was derived from the chilazon, a snail found near Tyre. The Phoenicians were experts at extracting dye from it, and it was famous throughout the Middle East.

251. A tallit is a shawl with tzitzit on the four corners.

Originally, our major piece of clothing was a cloak, a large square of cloth, called a tallit. It had four corners, and it was easy to attach the tzitzit to the four corners, thus fulfilling this mitzvah (see fact 250).

As clothing styles changed, it became difficult to find clothes with four corners. We therefore created a small tallit with a hole in the middle for the head. Traditionally worn all the time like an undershirt, this square of cloth has tzitzit on the corners.

In addition, at all morning services and on the eve of Yom Kippur we wear a large shawl with tzitzit attached to the corners. We call this shawl a tallit. Traditionally, the sheliach tzibbur, the leader of the service, wears a tallit at evening services as well (see fact 240).

In the second century our sages waived the requirement of the techelet, the royal blue/purple thread in tzitzit (see fact 250), because the dye was too expensive and they feared counterfeit dyes would be used. In fact, the dyed tzitzit found in the Bar Kochba caves (see data to fact 352) proved to be made with indigo, a counterfeit dye. As a reminder of the techelet, however, we traditionally include either blue or black stripes in the tallit itself. These tallit stripes of techelet became part of the emblem of the Israeli flag.

It became a tradition to bury a Jew with his tallit, but with one of the tzitzit cut off, thus making it *pasul*, unfit.

Traditionally, any positive mitzvah (commandment) that has a time limit for its performance is reserved for men. Therefore, women were traditionally exempt from wearing tzitzit. Because egalitarianism is such an important principle within the Reform Movement, many congregations encourage women to wear tallitot (plural of tallit). Some women in Conservative and Reconstructionist congregations also wear tallitot.

Jewish Clothing and Hair Customs

252. Two words for a skullcap are kippah (Hebrew) and yarmulke (Yiddish).

Originally Jews did not cover their heads. The early Egyptian and Mesopotamian pictures of Hebrews showed them long-haired and bareheaded. Even pictures from the Greek and Roman periods show Jews to be bareheaded.

There were, of course, some special people who viewed covering the head as a way to show respect for God. The Hebrew term for this respect is *yirat shamayim*, fear of heaven. One rabbi stated that he never went more than four feet without having his head covered.

We don't know the origin of the word yarmulke. Some believe that it is related to the Latin word for skullcap, "armucella." Others theorize that its origin is Slavic, noting that the Hungarian word for a skullcap is yarmulka.

In the Middle Ages it became the custom of the Catholic high clergy to wear a skullcap. The sages saw this as a sign of authority, and they began wearing skullcaps also. When the Christians saw the rabbis wearing skullcaps, they forbade the Jews from wearing them and ordered them to wear silly-looking hats called the "Jews' hats." Jews naturally began wearing the yarmulke secretly under these hats.

Today wearing a yarmulke remains a controversy between different groups of Jews. Traditional Jews see the yarmulke (or kippah in Hebrew) as one of their self-identifying symbols. They insist that it is now a mitzvah (commandment) to wear a kippah. They derive this idea from the traditional rule that we are not to observe the same customs as the non-Jews. Since non-Jews pray with their heads bare, traditional Jews maintain that it is a mitzvah to pray with our heads covered.

Many Reform Jews identify themselves as such by not wearing a kippah. There was a time when Reform congregations refused to allow anyone to wear a yarmulke, viewing it as an outmoded primitive custom which separated the Jew from the cultured, modern society. Today most Reform synagogues provide a yarmulke for whoever wishes to wear it.

In contrast to Jewish men, married Jewish women have always had their heads covered. A woman's uncovered head was a sign of humiliation and punishment. Some of our sages declared a woman's hair to be her most private and sexiest parts. In some communities a bride cuts off her hair before the wedding ceremony. In talmudic times, if a woman walked bareheaded in public, her husband could divorce her without having to pay her ketubah (marriage contract) price (see fact 263).

Although modestly dressed during the week, for the past two thousand years Jewish women have covered their heads in the most stylish decorative finery possible on Shabbat and festivals. The styles of these head coverings were based on the contemporary styles of the surrounding cultures.

In the late eighteenth century, women began covering their heads with a wig (a sheitel). Ironically, many rabbis opposed this innovation because they saw it as being indecent. Today the sheitel is worn only by traditional Jewish women. They wear it as a sign of modesty, keeping their real hair covered. Many Jewish women keep their hair covered by a scarf called a tichel.

In addition, because most Christian women wore hats when they attended church, it became the custom in many liberal Jewish congregations for women to cover their heads when they came to synagogue.

253. A shtreimel is a round fur hat worn by Chasidic Jews.

In addition to the kippah (see fact 252), chasidic Jews (see facts 427–430) follow the custom of wearing special clothes on Shabbat and festivals. The clothing was in the style of the Polish nobility in the sixteenth century. These include a round fur hat called a shtreimel, usually made of mink, and a black, glossy silk or satin robe called a kapoteh (or kaftan). In addition, they wear a special belt called a gartel, which symbolically separates their minds and hearts from their baser needs. For the same reason, many Chasidic men will not wear a tie or scarf while praying because it symbolically separates their minds from their hearts.

254. A kittel is a white robe worn on the Yamim Nora'im, on Pesach, and at a wedding.

It became a custom during the time of the Temple for Jews to wear white on Shabbat and the festivals. The appropriate garment was a white robe called a kittel. As a reminder of that special white robe worn during Second Temple times, the leader of the seder at Pesach traditionally wears a kittel.

By the 1200s it was understood that evil spirits hated the color white, possibly because of its association with purity. For that reason, Jews got married in their kittels and also were buried in their kittels. Since the Days of Awe were judgment days, it became a custom for the community to wear kittels on that day as well.

255. Sha'atnez is the mixture of wool and linen.

Although the sacral garments to be worn by the High Priest (see fact 171) were constructed by weaving linen and wool together, both Leviticus 19:19 and Deuteronomy 22:11 prohibit the wearing of linen and wool in the same garment. Such a garment is called Sha'atnez. No one knows what the word actually means.

As with many commandments, no reason is given for this prohibition. One theory is that other peoples used Sha'atnez in their clothes and this was a way to avoid assimilation. This theory doesn't explain why the priestly garments were then permitted to be made of Sha'atnez.

Another theory suggests that Sha'atnez is forbidden because it is an attempt to improve upon God's creation. For that reason, hybridization is also forbidden by the Torah.

At any rate, traditional Jews today continue to have their new clothes checked by special chemists to make sure that there is no mixture

of wool and linen in them. This seems to be one of the traditional
customs that the liberal Jewish community has not found meaningful.

256. Payot are side curls worn by traditional Jewish men.

Leviticus 19:27 commands, "You shall not round the corners
(payot) of your heads, nor mar the corners of your beard." Traditionally,
"the corners of the head" meant the hair directly above the ears, and this
was not cut. As a result, Jews grew side curls, payot (*payes* in Yiddish).

There are many customs connected with hair. The Nazirite was
forbidden to cut it; Samson got his strength from his hair (see fact 188).
It is clear from Egyptian pictures of Hebrews that we let our hair grow
long. Long hair even resulted in the death of Absalom, King David's
son. Absalom plotted a revolt against his father but was defeated. As he
was fleeing, his hair became caught in a tree. David's general Joab found
him and put him to death (2 Samuel 18).

Traditionally, a boy's hair was not cut until he was 3 years old. That
first haircut took place on Lag BaOmer, and the hair was tossed onto
bonfires on Mount Meiron (see fact 82).

Ironically, it would appear that the prohibition found in Leviticus
was directed against wearing the beard style of the Assyrians and
Babylonians, who carefully trimmed the bottoms of their beards into a
neat square. The rabbis understood the payot to be at the top of the
beard, by the ears, an entirely different location.

The Importance of the Divine Name

257. A Magen David is a Jewish star.

The six-pointed star, now called a Magen David, "shield of David,"
was not originally a Jewish or Hebrew symbol. Many civilizations used
the two equilateral triangles as a mystical sign. Examples have been
found in India dating back to the Bronze Age, about 3500 B.C.E.

The Talmud speaks of the star as "seal of Solomon" and mentions that Solomon had it on his signet ring as a sign of his control over the demons. However, as late as the fourteenth century the six-pointed star was interchangeable in our tradition with the five-pointed star, and both were used as symbols in the Church as well.

The concept of David having a special shield appears in the tenth century, but even by the twelfth century the shield was not yet connected with the six-pointed star. The term *Magen David* did not yet refer to a star. The shield was said to have the divine name of 72 letters engraved on it along with the letters M, CH, B, Y, (the letters of Maccabee; see fact 41). It served as a powerful amulet against demons.

By the fourteenth century, the six-pointed star was included as central to the Magen David, shield of David, and it was viewed as powerful protection. However, as late as the sixteenth century some rabbis still believed that David's shield contained the menorah, not a six-pointed star. Gradually, the six-pointed star became known as Magen David, and it appeared on many amulets.

The Magen David didn't really become a common Jewish symbol until the late eighteenth and early nineteenth centuries. At that time, trying to find a striking Jewish symbol to counteract the Christian cross, many synagogues began using the six-pointed star as ornamentation. It became ubiquitous on ritual objects and was recognized by the Christian world as a Jewish symbol.

An early Zionist organization, Hibbat Zion, used the Magen David on its emblem, and the settlers of Rishon L'Tziyon displayed it on their flag in 1885 (see data to facts 502, 503). Today, of course, the blue Magen David is found on the flag of Israel.

258. A chamsa is a charm shaped like a hand.

Although many rabbis were vehemently opposed to the practice, one of the most common Jewish folk customs was the use of amulets to ward off illness, demons, and the Evil Eye. The Evil Eye was supposedly vulnerable to the colors blue and red.

The chamsa, a metal amulet shaped like an open palm, was one of the most popular protections against the Evil Eye.

In the Middle Ages, amulets containing Psalm 16:8 were used. These were either made from metal or written out on parchment. Since verse 8 of Psalm 16 begins "Shiviti," "I have set (Adonai always before me)," these amulets were called "shiviti."

Frequently the menorah was used as a protection against the Evil Eye, as were magical triangles, squares, and hexagrams.

259. The name of God is so precious that once it has been written, we don't ever want to erase or destroy it.

According to our tradition, the Divine Name has power. The Ineffable Name was mentioned only once a year, on Yom Kippur, when the High Priest would go into the Holy of Holies, and proclaim that Name (see data to fact 24).

According to legend, it was through use of the Divine Name that Rabbi Yehudah Loew of Prague created the golem (see fact 418).

In order to avoid misusing the Divine Name, it became a tradition to use the name Adonai whenever the name of God appeared. Many traditional Jews are uncomfortable using even that word when not praying, and resort to calling God *HaShem*, which means *The Name*. They also never write the complete word *God*, rendering it as *G-d*.

Jewish tradition forbids the destruction of the Divine Name in any form, including its initials. If there is a fire on Shabbat, we are commanded to save all books and scrolls that contain the name of God, even if that means performing one of the forbidden activities (see fact 97). The only other time we are permitted to work on Shabbat is to save a human life (see fact 585).

260. A genizah is a room where damaged scrolls and books containing the name of God are stored.

When books and scrolls containing the Divine Name become unusable, rather than throwing them out, we either bury them or place them into a special room found in many synagogues and cemeteries. This room, called a genizah (*hidden place*), serves as a storage place for all writings containing the name of God. The documents, called *shemot* (names), remain in the genizah until they can be properly buried.

Genizot dating from the Middle Ages have become magnificent resources for scholars trying to understand the traditions and texts of that period (see data to fact 449).

Ritual Purity

261. A mikvah is a ritual bath.

Jewish tradition has always been tremendously concerned with ritual purity. When the Temple existed, the laws were intricate and voluminous because anyone approaching the Temple Mount had to be ritually pure. One Jewish sect in particular, the Essenes, was extraordinarily concerned about maintaining ritual purity (see fact 321).

The primary means of becoming ritually pure was to be immersed in running water. Springs and rivers were used for this purpose, but our sages instituted a means for immersion for those not near a spring or river; they created the mikvah.

The mikvah is a permanent pool or bath of clear spring or rain water. Since the water was not permitted to be placed in a container to be transported, cistern and pipe systems were used to catch rain water where it could flow into pools. The minimum size of a mikvah was 40 seahs, about 73 gallons.

After the destruction of the Temple, our sages ordained that the only aspect of ritual purity to be maintained via the mikvah concerned the niddah, the menstruant woman and the woman who recently gave birth. According to our tradition, a woman was ritually impure during her menses and for seven days after. At that point, in order to become ritually pure, she had to immerse herself in a mikvah. Since it was forbidden for her to have sexual relations until after her immersion, building a mikvah became one of the first responsibilities of a Jewish community.

Many traditional Jews today immerse themselves in a mikvah before Shabbat, the festivals, or marriage as a means of achieving a level of spiritual purification. The mikvah was used as a ritual declaration of a change in personal status, from ritually impure to pure, from secular to sacred. It must be emphasized that the mikvah and immersion in it have nothing to do with physical cleanliness. Anyone using the mikvah must bathe prior to entering it. The concern was and is for ritual purity.

Liberal Jews have philosophically opposed the belief that menstruation causes ritual impurity and have not made going to a mikvah an ongoing part of their lives.

Marriage, Divorce, and Associated Laws

262. Kiddushin is the marriage ceremony.

Originally the marriage ceremony was in two parts: kiddushin (betrothal) and nissu'in (marriage). In the talmudic period these two ceremonies were a year apart. By the Middle Ages, however, the two rites had been combined into one, with rare exceptions.

Kiddushin comes from the Hebrew root for holiness, or separateness, and marriage is the legal procedure for a man to make a woman apart, sacred to him.

We know nothing about the marriage ceremony in biblical times. The verb used in the Torah is to "take" a woman. The Mishnah noted that a man acquires a woman in one of three ways: (1) money, (2) contract, and (3) sexual intercourse (see also fact 263).

Money was defined as anything of known value. If a man handed such an object to a woman in front of two witnesses, and she accepted it, they were married. Originally this buying process involved a coin. Early on, this coin was hollowed out to make a ring. In order for the ring to be of known value, it had to be of solid metal and could contain no jewels.

263. A ketubah is a marriage contract.

One of the three ways a marriage took place in Jewish tradition was through money (see fact 262). A second means was by contract. The marriage contract was called the ketubah, the written document, and its form was defined quite stringently by the sages. It included the complete names of the participants, defined the marital status and price of the bride, stated the terms of the dowry, and included the price of a divorce. Its primary purpose was to note how much the husband must give his wife should he ever divorce her. In case of his death, that amount became her inheritance. This divorce amount was based on the status of the bride. A virgin bride received twice as much divorce settlement as a nonvirgin bride. Upon the signing of the ketubah by the groom and the father of the bride, it became a binding contract. The document itself was usually beautifully illuminated or decorated.

In some communities a betrothal contract was made by the parents when their children were born; in order to be binding, it had to be accepted by the couple when they reached the age of maturity (13 and one day for the boy, 12 and one day for the girl).

American Reform laity had problems with the sections dealing with the sexual status of the bride (virgin/nonvirgin), the terms of the dowry, the divorce price, and the very idea of a man acquiring a woman. They therefore created their own, nontraditional wedding document. Over the past thirty years many new texts of ketubot (plural of ketubah) have been written by liberal Jews. A couple planning on getting married has a wide choice. The most important element of the ketubah is that it is a contract between two Jews binding their lives together.

The third means of acquiring a wife was by sexual intercourse. Our sages opposed this method as immoral and demeaning, but they recognized sexual intercourse as legally binding a couple in marriage.

Our tradition included all three of these methods within the marriage ceremony. Before the wedding, the ketubah is signed and read as part of the ceremony. The groom gives the bride a ring and says, "With this ring, you are consecrated to me as my wife according to the law of Moses and Israel." In most modern, liberal ceremonies, the bride and groom exchange rings.

Two wedding customs developed as a result of biblical stories about our ancestors. The Book of Genesis notes that when Rebecca first saw Jacob (see fact 133), she took a veil and covered herself. It therefore became traditional for the bride to put on a veil prior to the marriage ceremony. This ritual is called badeken, the covering.

The Torah also describes, however, how Jacob was fooled into marrying Leah instead of Rachel (see data to fact 138). In order to ensure that bride switching didn't take place, it became a minhag (custom) for the groom to confirm that the woman being veiled was, in fact, his wife. Therefore, traditionally the groom places the veil on his bride.

264. A chuppah is a wedding canopy.

In talmudic times the wedding ceremony would end with the bride being escorted into the wedding chamber to fulfill the third means of acquiring a wife. This chamber was called the chuppah. In Palestine it was made from the branches of a cypress tree planted by the girl's parents at the time of her birth and a cedar tree planted by the boy's parents at the time of his birth.

The guests then partied while waiting for proof of the bride's status. Contractual money, after all, was at stake. Thus began the tradition of having a wedding feast.

Gradually, the chuppah changed from a bridal chamber to a canopy held over the bride and groom as a symbol of the marriage chamber. Some communities had the groom hold his tallit over the head of his bride as a sign of his role as protector. Today we rarely relate the chuppah to the bridal chamber. We focus more on it being a symbol of "the home the couple is going to create."

265. Sheva Brachot, seven blessings, are recited to celebrate a wedding.

The actual ceremony as described in facts 262–264 would take less than one minute. That's just not enough ritualizing time. Our sages added seven blessings called the Sheva Brachot (Seven Blessings). Legally, they are not necessary for the marriage to be binding, but they include the Divine more directly in the proceedings by praising God for creating man and woman.

Many customs developed around the wedding ceremony. Rav Ashi once attended a wedding feast where there was too much levity. He took an expensive glass and smashed it. In reply to the shocked silence, he said, "Into every joyous occasion, there should be some sorrow," and left. This is one explanation regarding the origin of breaking a glass at a wedding.

New meanings were added to it, of course. Primary was the interpretation that the glass was a symbol of the destroyed Temple. In the 1200s many believed that the glass breaking was an excellent way to get rid of evil spirits, who hated loud noises. It was at that time that the tradition also developed of yelling, "Mazel tov!" which means literally, "Good planet!" (see fact 601). The guests were hoping for a good astrological sign for the bride and groom.

Another anti-evil spirit custom was to have both bride and groom wear white, a color the demons despised (see data to fact 254). In addition, the bride would circle the chuppah seven times, and the guests would carry lit candles, all believed to be very effective at keeping away evil spirits.

The carrying of two candles was also explained as a way to guarantee fertility. In gematriya (see fact 604) the numerical value of the word *candle* is 250. By carrying two candles, the accompanying celebrants thus get the number 500, which is equal to the Hebrew words " פרו ורבו ," "be fruitful and multiply," the first commandment in the Torah.

In Sephardic Jewish communities, on the night before the wedding women would participate in a special rite (the chinnah) to keep away the Evil Eye. It included painting the bride's hands red with henna to protect her against the Evil Eye.

There are numerous marriage customs associated with wishing the couple fertility. The most common is throwing rice, wheat, nuts, or candies at the groom, especially after he is called to the Torah (see fact 308) on the Shabbat before the wedding (called the aufrauf, the calling). Others include serving fish at the wedding meal; having the bride jump over a brass bowl filled with live fish as people call, "May you be as fertile as the fish"; and having the bride hold a baby boy at the wedding feast.

In ancient times the wedding took place outdoors at night, to serve as a reminder that God had promised Abraham that his descendants would be as numerous as the stars (Genesis 15:5).

One of the strangest customs, apparently common in both Ashkenazic and Sephardic communities, was that at the end of the wedding ceremony the bride and groom would try to step on each other's foot. The one who succeeded was assured dominance in their life together.

266. A mamzer is the offspring of a forbidden sexual union.

Our tradition forbids two kinds of sexual unions: adultery and incest. Adultery is sexual intercourse between a man and a married woman (not his wife). According to halachah (see fact 342), if the woman is not married, it is not adultery! Leviticus 18 defines the forbidden sexual relationships that constitute incest.

A mamzer is the offspring from either an adulterous or an incestuous relationship. In order for a person to be legally declared a mamzer, there had to be two witnesses to the illicit sexual act. According to Jewish tradition, a Jew may not marry a mamzer or a mamzer's offspring for ten generations.

In biblical times, if a man suspected his wife of committing adultery but he lacked one witness, the woman was called a sotah, a suspected adulteress. She was brought before the priest, who performed the only trial by ordeal described in our tradition. The priest wrote a curse on a piece of parchment, indicating that if she was guilty, her belly would distend and she would get sick. The priest dissolved the ink in an earthen bowl with some dust from the Mishkan and some "bitter water." The woman then drank the potion. If she was innocent, then nothing would happen, and her name was cleared. Numbers 5:28 mentions that, as a reward for going through the ordeal, she would be able to become pregnant. If she was guilty, however, she became sick, and everyone would know that she had committed adultery. Her husband could divorce her without paying her ketubah price (see fact 263).

We don't know if the "bitter water" itself caused illness or whether the subconscious guilt of the woman affected her in the ritual. The author suspects the latter, since the ritual of the sotah ended when the rabbis feared people no longer felt guilty enough to make the ritual efficient.

267. Chalitzah is the ceremony that annuls a man's responsibility to marry his childless brother's widow.

One of the great losses in Judaism is the ending of a family line. Deuteronomy 25:5 therefore commands that if a man dies childless, the brother of the man must marry his widow. She is called a yevamah. The first child of their union receives the name of the dead man, thus continuing his family line. This is called Levirite marriage (from the Latin word *levir*, brother).

In Genesis 38 the story is told about Judah's sons Er and Onan. Er married a woman named Tamar. He died, so it became Onan's responsibility to marry Tamar. Onan, knowing that the child would legally be considered his brother's, spilled his seed on the ground and was immediately struck dead. This is a Torah example of a Levirite marriage that didn't work. The Catholic Church noted Onan's spilling his seed on the ground as clear proof that masturbation is forbidden and even called the act "onanism." In truth, it is clear from the story that Onan was punished because he refused his responsibility to maintain his brother's line.

Deuteronomy 25:7–10 also provides a ceremony for a brother to avoid the responsibility of marrying his brother's widow. It consists of the brother and the widow appearing before the "elders of the city." He states his refusal to marry his brother's widow. She then loosens his shoe, spits in front of him, and says, "Thus is done to a man that doesn't build his brother's house." She is then permitted to marry anyone she chooses. Because the word for loosen (his shoe) is ch-l-tz, the ceremony is called chalitzah, the loosening.

Although Torah clearly considered it shameful to refuse Levirite marriage, Jewish law (see fact 342) now requires traditional Jews to perform chalitzah rather than actually perform a Levirite marriage. A special chalitzah shoe, a form of sandal, is ceremoniously tied and then formally untied. The ceremony is performed in front of a court of five rabbis rather than three (see fact 425).

Since the widow may not remarry unless the ritual of chalitzah is performed, Jewish courts were permitted to force her brother-in-law to undergo the ceremony.

Few, if any liberal Jews perform chalitzah, much to the distress of the Orthodox community. Reform Jews tend to view the ritual as degrading and unnecessary, since Levirite marriages no longer take place.

268. A get is a divorce document written by a sofer.

It is ironic that the only marriage document mentioned in the Torah is the writ of divorce. It is mentioned as an aside in a specific law dealing with a twice-divorced woman (Deuteronomy 24:1–4). It is clear that Hebrew society knew the details of a divorce document and didn't need them spelled out in the Torah.

Our sages, however, supplied us with those necessary details. The divorce document, called simply *get*, the Hebrew word for document, is twelve lines long. It is written on parchment by a sofer (a scribe) with a quill pen. It must specify both the man and woman involved and note the geographic location in terms of the nearest body of water. It emphasizes that the woman is free to go with any other man. When the man gives the get to the woman, she is divorced, and he must pay her the divorce price mentioned in her ketubah (see fact 263).

Only a man may divorce a woman in Jewish law. There were circumstances under which the court could force the man to give his wife a get, but the action remained his.

Until the tenth century a man did not even need his wife's agreement. In fact, a case is mentioned in the Talmud of a wife running away to avoid receiving the get. One rabbi suggests that if the husband throws the get and it lands within 24 inches of her, she is divorced.

Rabbenu Gershom, a great rabbi in Germany (see fact 384), ordained that the woman had to accept the get in order for the divorce to be valid, and that has been the law since the end of the tenth century.

269. A woman whose husband has left her without giving her a get is called an agunah.

Should a man disappear without giving his wife a get, she is stuck. She may not remarry until she receives a get or a witness appears to testify that her husband is dead. She is called an agunah, an anchored one. The problem of the agunah was especially serious in war time. Our rabbis solved the problem during World War II by encouraging soldiers to write a conditional get. This document authorized a beit din (see fact 425) to issue the wife a divorce should the husband not return within a designated period of time. If he was missing in action, the court could issue his wife a get, enabling her to continue with her life.

In Jewish law, if a couple gets a civil divorce but the man doesn't give the woman a get, they are still married. Should she marry someone else, according to Jewish law, she has committed adultery, and subsequent children are mamzerim (bastards) (see fact 266).

The Orthodox rabbinate does not recognize any get written by a liberal rabbi. As with any issue, there are a number of Reform Jewish positions. There are rabbis who, for the sake of *klal Yisrael* (the unity of the Jewish people) (see fact 611), send divorcing couples to an Orthodox beit din, a court of three rabbis, to receive a formal get. There are rabbis who, offended by the sexist implications of a man divorcing a woman, refuse to give a get. There are rabbis who have written documents for the divorcing couple to share jointly. There are rabbis who write their own traditional gittin (plural of get), acknowledging its nonacceptance by the Orthodox community. There are rabbis who have written a document for a woman to sign, contrary to tradition, divorcing her absent husband.

The Central Conference of American Rabbis (see data to fact 448) has created a new ceremony called Seder HaPreidah, the Order of Release, which enables a divorcing couple to ritualize their separation in a nonsexist, nondemeaning ceremony.

The underlying value of all these options is that marriage is a sacred contract, entered into with Jewish ritual and serious commitment. Its dissolution deserves similar sacred ritual.

Birth and Entering the Covenant

270. The ceremony of circumcision is called brit milah.

Circumcision, the removal of the foreskin of the penis, has for the past 3,000 years been the sign of a Jewish boy's contract with God (see fact 126). For that reason, the ceremony is called brit milah, the covenant of circumcision.

Circumcision has played an important identifying role in our history. The Bible refers contemptuously to the Philistines as the *uncircumcised* (see fact 189).

During the pre-Hasmonean period, Jews tried to be accepted into the Greek world. One way was to participate at the gymnasium. There, both work-outs and games were done naked. Since the Greeks viewed circumcision as a barbarous mutilation, many of these Jewish men underwent the terribly painful operation of removing the sign of circumcision.

When Antiochus made circumcision illegal (see data to fact 38), many Jewish mothers had their male children secretly circumcised, and it became a rallying point for the Hasmoneans. Since that time, the brit milah has been a joyous celebration.

271. A mohel performs the circumcision.

The responsibility for the mitzvah of circumcision is the father's, but since talmudic times, communities have generally relied on an expert in circumcision called a mohel.

Following the Torah command to Abraham, the brit milah takes place on the eighth day after the birth of a boy, unless there are health problems. The mitzvah of circumcision transcends even Yom Kippur. If that is when the brit milah should take place, the child is circumcised on Yom Kippur.

Despite a period in the nineteenth century when a group of Reform Jews opposed circumcision, the rite of brit milah is among the most widely practiced in Jewish tradition. Some liberal Jews do not use a mohel, but rather employ a surgeon to perform the circumcision, with a rabbi present to perform the religious ritual; but the act itself is almost universally performed by Jews.

The Reform Movement recently established a series of classes for Jewish doctors to become mohalim/mohalot (masculine and feminine plural of mohel). There are now more than seventy Reform mohalim/mohalot in the United States. The Conservative Movement also trains Jewish doctors to be mohalim.

Traditionally, the brit milah takes place as early in the day as possible. At the beginning of the ceremony, the baby is placed in a specially designated chair called "Elijah's chair." Some synagogues have elaborately carved and embroidered chairs for this purpose. According to our sages, one of Elijah's complaints against the Hebrews in Israel was that they had ceased circumcising their children. The Book of Malachi calls Elijah, "the Angel of the Covenant," so our sages saw his attendance at every brit milah as being appropriate. Folklore also viewed Elijah as the protector of children against evil spirits. Moreover, Elijah is responsible for announcing the Messiah and, since every child is potentially the Messiah, we invite Elijah to join us.

272. The sandak is the person who holds the baby during the circumcision.

During the actual circumcision, the baby is held by a person called the sandak, "the holder." This honor traditionally went to a grandfather. Under Christian influence, this person took on the role of the child's godfather, called *kvatter*. The woman who handed the baby to the sandak was called the *sandakit*, now understood as godmother, or *kvatterin*. Today it is possible for the kvatter to be a separate person from the sandak. This provides a potential honor to all grandparents or especially close friends.

Following the circumcision, it became the custom to name the child. Ashkenazic Jews traditionally did not name a child after a living relative for fear of tempting the Evil Eye. Sephardic Jews do name their children after living relatives.

273. According to the rabbis, a Jew is someone whose mother is Jewish.

Circumcision does not change the status of a child. According to traditional Judaism, a child is Jewish if his/her mother is Jewish. This status is unchangeable. A Jewish child who is uncircumcised remains a Jewish child.

274. Since 1983 the Reform Movement has declared that a Jew is someone whose mother or father is Jewish, and who lives and acts like a Jew.

In 1983 the Central Conference of American Rabbis (see data to fact 448) declared that a child is presumed to be Jewish if his or her mother *or* father is Jewish. This presumption of Jewishness then had to be established through the performance of mitzvot and a Jewish lifestyle.

The encouraged lifestyle included Jewish study, family participation in celebrating the Shabbat and the festivals, celebrating life cycle moments as a Jew, and being recognized by the Jewish community as a Jew.

275. In the Torah, a Hebrew was someone whose father was a Hebrew.

The Reform Movement's position on patrilineality relates directly to the Torah's position. In the Torah, a Hebrew was someone whose father was a Hebrew. Despite rabbinic revisionist attempts (see data to facts 140, 146), it is clear from the Torah text that Hebrew lineage was patrilineal, not matrilineal.

We still find a vestige of this system in traditional Judaism. The lineal designation of Kohayn, Levi, or Israel depends on the father, not the mother (see data to fact 169).

276. A brit banot is one of the names of a covenant ceremony for a girl.

Traditionally, the only rite connected with the birth of a daughter is a naming. This is done by the father in the synagogue after he is called up to the Torah (see fact 308).

In an effort to emphasize equality between the sexes, Reform Jews have tried to create a ceremony of equal significance for girls. Usually called brit banot, "covenant for daughters," this ritual is still in the developmental stages. Many creative rituals have been attempted, but there is not yet a universally accepted ceremony. It is difficult to create a tradition; certainly, doing so takes time.

Bar/Bat Mitzvah

277. A Bar/Bat Mitzvah is responsible for his or her actions.

Our sages declared that a father was responsible for the actions of his son until the boy reached the age of 13 and one day. At that point, a Jew became a full member of the community. He was counted as part of a minyan (see fact 289), he was obligated to put on tefillin (see fact 240). A full member of the community, responsible for his actions, was called a Bar Mitzvah, Son of the Commandment.

Every Jew becomes a Bar Mitzvah automatically. It is a change of legal status; it has nothing to do with how much an individual knows or has learned.

Our sages selected the age of 13 as the time of attaining legal maturity because of the physical changes involved with puberty. Legal responsibility was thus linked to physical maturation. Girls were considered mature at 12 years and a day.

Until the fourteenth century, we have no records of this change in legal status being ritually celebrated. Then in the 1300s, Eastern European Jewry initiated the custom of calling the new Bar Mitzvah to recite the blessings before and after the Torah reading (see fact 308), recognizing his legal right to do so. This event usually took place on the nearest Monday or Thursday after the boy's thirteenth birthday. When the Bar Mitzvah finished the blessings, his father recited a brief blessing, thanking the Divine for removing the responsibility of his son's sins from him.

In Western Europe the ceremony became more involved. The celebration usually took place on Shabbat rather than on Monday or Thursday. The new Bar Mitzvah was called up to read part of the Torah (see facts 306–309), chant the Haftarah (see fact 246), and, during the meal afterwards, deliver a lecture on some aspect of Talmud (see fact 363). The father recited the blessing thanking the Divine for freeing him from the responsibility for his son's sins.

Originally, the Reform Movement was opposed to the Bar Mitzvah ceremony, because the Reform leaders felt that age 13 was too young for a boy to understand the significance of becoming an adult Jew. They therefore instituted Confirmation as a substitute (see fact 89). Gradually, during the second half of the twentieth century, many Reform congregations reinstituted the Bar Mitzvah ceremony and kept the confirmation ceremony for a later date.

Today the customs celebrating a Jew's becoming a Bar Mitzvah continue to be fluid. Each congregation determines what the Bar Mitzvah is expected to do. In many congregations, rather than reciting the traditional blessing, the parents now recite the Shehecheyanu (see data to fact 287). Some communities have created the tradition of elaborate parties following the ceremony. The important issue, however, remains that the Bar Mitzvah is now responsible for his actions.

In modern times, a ceremony celebrating a girl's change in legal status was instituted, recognizing her becoming a Bat Mitzvah. It too varied from community to community. Traditionally, this ceremony took place when the girl reached 12 years and one day. Many Reform congregations, following the value of egalitarianism, celebrate a girl's becoming a Bat Mitzvah at 13 rather than 12. In addition, they insist that the ritual be the same as the ritual celebrating a boy's becoming a Bar Mitzvah.

Some modern Orthodox congregations are also beginning to encourage the Bat Mitzvah to participate more fully in the service. Traditionally, women are not counted as part of a minyan (see fact 289), nor are they permitted to function as a sheliach tzibbur (see facts 240, 466). However, in some Orthodox communities women have established their own prayer groups, and they pray together. They also study from the Torah but do not recite the blessings before or after their Torah reading. In some of these congregations, a Bat Mitzvah is encouraged to lead the women's prayer group and lead the Torah study, thus showing her new Jewish maturity.

Death and Mourning

278. K'riyah is the ritual tearing of one's clothes as a sign of mourning.

All traditions relating to death were established to achieve two purposes: (1) to encourage the mourner to reaffirm that there is order in his or her world, and (2) to comfort the mourners.

K'riyah, the tearing of one's clothes, is a natural response to a death in the family. Jacob tore his clothes when he believed Joseph was dead. Torah forbids the Canaanite custom of actually gashing ourselves to express our anguish at a loss, but the prophet Jeremiah mentions it as a natural rite.

Today k'riyah has become a symbolic act. Although some Orthodox Jews still actually rip their clothing, most mourners attach a black ribbon to their garment. Prior to the funeral, we affirm God as a righteous judge (Dayan HaEmet) and tear the ribbon. This ribbon is transferable to any garments we wear during the mourning period, and traditionally it is worn throughout the period of Sh'loshim, the first 30 days after burial (see fact 282). Although any mourner may perform k'riyah, the ritual is traditionally limited to the spouse, parents, siblings, and children of the deceased.

279. The Kaddish is a statement that God is all-powerful.

The Kaddish is the God-praising formula par excellence. It ascribes praise to God using a long series of adjectives. It was written in the language of the people, Aramaic, and not in the prayer language, Hebrew.

We don't really know the origin of the Kaddish. According to the Talmud, a group of sages were discussing what words of praise God appreciated most, and one of them quoted a line from the Kaddish. He clearly was using an already-known formula as an example of special God-praising. Traditionally, the Kaddish separates each service into distinct parts and is therefore recited a number of times.

By the eighth century c.e. the Kaddish was already associated with mourners. We have stories from the middle of the eleventh century c.e. indicating that children helped their dead parents through the judgment stage of death by saying the Kaddish (see data to fact 607).

According to an aggadah (see fact 334) written long after his death, Rabbi Akiva (see fact 347) talked to the spirit of a dead Levite whose son had not said Kaddish for him. The spirit was wandering around lost and punished. Akiva got the son to say Kaddish, and the spirit lived happily ever after.

There is nothing about death in the Kaddish; just the opposite: the Kaddish is an unequivocal affirmation of God and God's world. The sages wanted a mourner to recite it twice a day because it helped him reaffirm order and meaning in his life even during the time of mourning.

At the cemetery, the mourners recite the Kaddish as a statement of faith. Originally the period for the bereaved to recite the Mourner's Kaddish was a year. However, that implied that the dead person had been wicked, needing a year's worth of Kaddish. Therefore our sages instituted the tradition of reciting Kaddish for only eleven months.

Traditionally, the Kaddish is recited only by males. However, following the principle of equality, most Reform and Conservative congregations encourage women mourners to recite the Kaddish as well.

Traditionally, only the mourners rise in the synagogue to recite the Kaddish. However, there were communities where everyone would stand to express support and comfort for the mourners and lessen their feeling of self-consciousness. Today many Reform congregations have everyone rise to recite the Kaddish. The reason given is that being a congregation of all Israel, one family, we are all mourners as we remember the Holocaust and our lost families. Therefore, as a reminder of the 6 million lives lost during the Holocaust (see facts 458–463), we rise as a congregation and reaffirm our faith in the Divine when it is time to recite the Kaddish.

280. Shivah is a seven-day period of deep mourning.

Following the funeral, the family begins the deepest period of mourning, called Shivah. Shivah means seven, and this period traditionally lasts for the first seven days of mourning. There is a Torah precedent for this intense seven-day mourning period. We are told that Joseph mourned for his father Jacob for seven days.

281. It is a mitzvah to bring food and comfort to a house of mourning so that the family doesn't have to do any work.

The primary obligation of the mourner during Shivah is to do nothing for him or herself. The entire purpose of Shivah is to free the bereaved to think only about the loss that has been suffered and to grieve. Therefore, it is a mitzvah, a commandment, for people to provide the family with food. The first meal after the funeral is called Seudat Havra'ah, the Meal of Healing. Traditionally, it included eggs or lentils, round foods which symbolized the cycle of life, death, and life: eternity.

Since the bereaved are not supposed to do anything, people enter the house of mourning without knocking or ringing a bell. The bereaved should not feel like hosts. Traditionally, the bereaved sit on the floor, a sign of mourning. For Americans, that is extreme, so they sit on wooden stools or cardboard boxes created especially for that purpose.

Other traditional signs of mourning include not bathing, not wearing leather (always considered a luxury), not shaving, not studying Torah, abstaining from sexual relations, and not leaving the house except to attend Shabbat services. Traditionally, when the family returns home from the cemetery, a candle is lit which burns for seven days.

The tradition developed of covering all mirrors in a house of mourning. Many reasons for this are offered. First, it was believed that the soul of the deceased would try to return home during Shivah. Jews believed that the soul could be seen reflected in mirrors. To avoid that trauma, we cover them. We are not supposed to groom ourselves during the mourning period. Mirrors are covered to keep us from unthinkingly fixing ourselves up or to spare us the pain of seeing how ghastly we look in our unkempt state.

A custom arose that should a person leave his home, he put sand in his shoes so the discomfort would keep him aware of his mourning status. The entire purpose of Shivah and its customs is to force the bereaved to face the wrenching loss in their lives, to mourn freely without worrying about the day-to-day concerns which normally occupy their lives, and to accept the comfort and caring of friends, who help to console them. Some modern, liberal Jewish families do not find the traditional restrictions helpful; instead of aiding them in their mourning, these restrictions inhibit the process, and they therefore don't follow them.

282. Sh'loshim is the first thirty days of mourning.

After the sharp initial grief of Shivah, our sages instituted a second, transitional level of mourning called *Sh'loshim* (Thirty). This second period, less intense than Shivah, lasts three weeks and two days after Shivah. During that time, the mourner returns to work but is discouraged from participating in any entertaining activities. Our sages tried to help the bereaved focus on the loss and continue the therapeutic task of mourning.

The final period of mourning continues for eleven months. During that time, the bereaved traditionally recite the Mourner's Kaddish at both morning and evening services.

According to halachah (see fact 342), the family may put up a tombstone to mark the grave any time after the first 30 days of mourning. Our rabbis recommended, however, that the family wait at least until the end of the eleven months of mourning. For almost three thousand years there was no ritual associated with setting up the tombstone, but in Western Europe and the United States it became a minhag (custom) to "consecrate" the stone with a brief service. This ritual is called an unveiling.

A number of customs developed concerning the stone itself. The letters פ״נ are usually carved into the top of the stone. They stand for the Hebrew words meaning "here lies." At the bottom of the stone many communities include the letters תנצב״ה. These are the first letters for the phrase, "May his soul be bound up in the bond of life."

A Levite's stone (see fact 168) would sometimes have a pitcher carved on it, a reminder that the Levites were the traditional water carriers for the Temple cult. A Kohayn (see fact 169) would sometimes have two hands carved on his stone, symbolizing the Priestly Blessing (see fact 304).

283. A Yahrzeit candle is lit in memory on the anniversary of the death of a close relative.

Jewish tradition added another ritual to help resolve the loss of a close family member. On the yearly anniversary of the death, the family commemorates its loss by lighting a candle at home which burns for 24 hours. The family then recites the Kaddish at services. The anniversary of the death is called Yahrzeit.

284. Yizkor is a memorial service.

There is a tradition of having a memorial service on the last day of Pesach and Sukkot, on Shavuot, and, in the Sephardic tradition, on the afternoon of Yom Kippur as well. Today most Ashkenazic communities also have a memorial service on Yom Kippur afternoon. The major prayer of this service begins with the word *Yizkor*, "May (God) remember," so the service is called informally Yizkor.

Yizkor gained prominence during the Crusader period, when thousands of Jews were slaughtered (see fact 382). The communities remembered them and honored them at the Yizkor services. The Ashkenazic custom is to have people whose parents are living leave the synagogue so they don't participate in the Yizkor service. This was based on the belief that they might bring the Evil Eye down on their living parents by thus "tempting fate." It is the custom in Sephardic communities for everyone to remain during Yizkor.

In addition to Yizkor, the other major prayer recited during the Yizkor service is the El Malay Rachamim, which asks God to guard the souls of the dead under the "wings of the Shechinah," the Divine Presence. The El Malay Rachamim is also said at funerals and can be recited when one is visiting gravesites.

Blessings

285. A traditional Jew says 100 blessings a day.

Although the only formalized worship in the Bible was the sacrificial cult, there are many examples of individuals praying to God.

These private petitions and praises emphasized a basic premise of our tradition: everything belongs to God. "The earth is Adonai's and all of its fullness," declares Psalm 24. Awareness of this fact, dependence upon it, gratefulness for it became part of Jewish ritual. All moments in our lives, even the bitter or painful ones, are blessings when viewed in the perspective of the Divine's miracles. Therefore we are commanded to say a blessing even when a close relative dies (see data to fact 278).

Our sages instituted the custom of reciting a blessing, a statement of praise to the Divine, when we experience something new or special in God's world. Since we view every action and experience as being new and miraculous, Rabbi Meir recommended a minimum of 100 blessings every day. The beginning formula of these "blessings concerning enjoyment" includes blessing God's name and recognizing the Divine as sole sovereign of the universe. Thus all blessings of enjoyment begin, "Blessed are You, Adonai, Ruler of the universe. . . ."

Some examples of moments deserving blessing include waking up and still being alive, discovering that all parts of the body still function in the morning, hearing thunder and seeing lightning, getting dressed, smelling a sweet odor, and seeing a rainbow. Originally these blessings were said by individuals at the proper moments, but gradually many of them were included in public worship as well.

Two controversial traditional morning blessings included thanking God for not being a non-Jew, and thanking God for your not being a woman. The Reform and Conservative prayerbooks put the first of these into a more positive form ("who made me an Israelite"). The Reform prayerbook removed the second entirely. The Conservative prayerbook changed the wording to "who made me in Thine image."

In addition, our sages created separate blessings of praise for different categories of foods. These blessings are recited before eating any specific food. Bread was viewed by the sages as being food par excellence. At a meal where bread is served, the blessing "who brings bread out from the earth," includes all other foods. No other blessings over specific foods are needed after the blessing over bread has been said.

As part of their celebrations, some Sephardic Jews try to say as many blessings over food as possible. They therefore serve numerous appetizers, each requiring its own blessing, before they serve bread.

286. Birkat HaMazon is the blessing said after eating.

Any meal calling for the blessing over bread traditionally ends with a series of four blessings praising and thanking God. This collection of prayers is called Birkat HaMazon, the Blessing of Sustenance. It fulfills the Torah commandment found in Deuteronomy 8:10, "When you have eaten your fill, give thanks to Adonai your God. . . ." It's easy to be aware of the miracle of food when we are hungry. To praise the Divine when we are already sated takes effort and makes those blessings special. When three or more people have eaten together, the Birkat HaMazon includes an introduction which is recited responsively.

Our sages viewed this ongoing awareness of the miracles surrounding us as payment for the privilege of life and enjoyment. Anyone who takes anything for granted in our world is viewed as a thief who steals from God. The Yiddish for reciting Birkat HaMazon is to *bench*, (bless), thus making Birkat HaMazon the blessing par excellence.

287. We say a blessing before we do a mitzvah.

Another form of personal blessing recognizes that we are about to do a mitzvah, a commandment. These blessings begin with the same formula as blessings of enjoyment but include the words, "Who has made us holy with His commandments and commanded us to. . . ."

Not all mitzvot have designated blessings, but many do. Examples of daily mitzvah blessings include studying Torah, washing our hands ritually before eating, putting on tefillin, and putting on a tallit.

Whenever a mitzvah is performed for the first time in a year, a special blessing is added, the Shehecheyanu. It praises God for giving us life and giving us the opportunity to perform the mitzvah.

Prayer and Prayerbooks

288. Kavannah is focusing on our prayers and their meaning.

Tradition has always recognized the importance of kavannah, of intent and focus. For the past two thousand years sages have emphasized that kavannah is necessary for true prayer. Gradually, however, the text of the traditional words themselves developed a sanctity of its own. Our sages were very concerned that we not take God's name in vain. Therefore they discouraged "wasted prayers." For example, a blessing said over the wrong food was viewed as taking God's name in vain. A blessing said incorrectly was viewed as being worse than saying no blessing at all.

It became a mitzvah (commandment) not simply to recognize the miracles in our world, but to use the "correct" words as well.

Many modern liberal Jews do not accept the premise that only specific words are acceptable as prayers. We feel that the kavannah, the intent of the individual, is much more important than the words themselves; there is room for new, creative words to express our feelings and our responses. Thus the Reform Movement has always encouraged the use of creative prayer formulas, a practice discouraged by traditional Jews.

289. A minyan is a quorum of ten Jews, traditionally needed to recite specific communal prayers.

There are two kinds of Jewish prayer: private and public. In order to recite some prayers connected with public worship, our tradition requires a minyan, a Jewish quorum. Ten Jewish men make a traditional minyan.

Our sages understood that ten Jews were needed to create a community from the infamous moment in the desert when the ten scouts convinced the Hebrews that it was impossible to conquer the Land of Israel (see fact 177). God responded angrily, "How much longer will that wicked community mutter against Me?" Since the Divine referred to a group of ten as a "community," that became the official number for a minyan.

A tradition maintains that if there are nine Jews and a child under the age of 13, the Torah can be held by that child and thus create a minyan.

One of the modern controversies between liberal and traditional Jews focuses on who may be counted in a minyan. Traditionally, only Jewish men (over the age of 13) counted. In maintaining the value of equality between men and women, liberal Jews insist that women (over the age of 13) be counted as part of a minyan as well. Some liberal congregations are not concerned at all with the number of worshippers and are comfortable conducting services with fewer than ten adult Jews.

The Conservative Movement continues to struggle with the question of whether women should be counted in a minyan. Each congregation establishes its own rules (see data to fact 466).

290. A Siddur is a daily and/or Shabbat prayerbook.

Our prayer services developed over a long period of time. Although our tradition attributes the actual words of our prayers to early sages, it appears that our prayers were quite individualistic even at public worship.

Originally, the public prayer service was led by the sheliach tzibbur, the representative of the community (see fact 240). Parts of the service were done as responsive chanting, and these, obviously, were known by the community. For most of the service, however, the sheliach tzibbur would take fixed themes and, from these, create the prayers for that day. The language of prayer was Hebrew. There were a few additions which were said in Aramaic, but Hebrew became associated with holiness and the Divine because the Torah was written in Hebrew.

Gradually the prayers themselves became fixed. It is believed by most scholars that, by the time the Temple was destroyed, the general order of the prayers was set; their final sentences were established and, for some prayers, the actual text was set. There are enough variant prayer texts dating to the eleventh century, however, to support the thesis that many prayers texts were not actually fixed until much later.

In the ninth century, Rav Amram in Babylonia wrote a collection of the prayers, including all the laws concerning them (see fact 375). This was called Seder Rav Amram, the Order of Rav Amram, and it was the first known fixed order of prayers.

291. Piyyutim are liturgical poems that have become part of our prayer service.

The Jewish prayer service did not remain static. Through the centuries, Jews continued to add poems and liturgy to the service. These probably never served as substitutes for the set prayers but rather became additions. Their beauty and religious allusions made them very popular, and gradually they were incorporated into the tefillah, the prayer service. These poems were called piyyutim, and they came in many styles and forms.

Although the original piyyutim were written in the East, by the tenth and eleventh centuries there were numerous ones being written in

Europe as well. Piyyutim were written in Hebrew because they were intended for liturgical purposes.

During this entire development, there was not yet a printing press, so all siddurim (prayerbooks) were written by hand. They continued to contain not only the prayers and piyyutim, but the laws concerning them as well.

292. A Machzor is a festival prayerbook.

Gradually, a distinction was made between prayerbooks that contained daily and Shabbat prayers, the Siddurim (plural of Siddur), and prayerbooks that concentrated on piyyutim used primarily at special occasions and the festivals. The festival book became known as a Machzor, a cycle, reminding us of the cyclical nature of the festivals.

This distinction between the Siddur, the ordered daily and Shabbat prayerbook, and the Machzor, the ordered festival book which contained the piyyutim, is apparently very recent and developed in the Ashkenazic community.

Communities continue to create prayerbooks which meet their needs and make a statement about their beliefs and attitudes. The physical format, language, inclusions, and deletions of these prayerbooks all serve to send a message to the praying group about themselves and their identity as a community.

With printed Siddurim, the text of the prayers became regulated and fixed for each community using that prayerbook. This led to the traditional belief that in order to fulfill the mitzvah of praying, the specific words found in the Siddur had to be said.

293. Davvening is traditional praying.

Although kavannah (intent and focus on the meaning of the words) was extremely important (see fact 288), the rabbis decreed that the mitzvah of prayer was fulfilled merely by saying the specific words. Many Jews didn't understand Hebrew and the recitation became the entire process. Familiarity with the prayers sometimes led to very fast, rhythmical chanting of the service. This process of speedily chanting the prayers is called davvening, the Yiddish word for praying. We don't know its etymology.

294. Shuckling is swaying rhythmically while praying.

To apply greater intensity to the process of davvening, many traditional Jews sway in rhythm to the chanting. This movement is called shuckling.

We are told that when Rabbi Akiva prayed in private, his intensity was so great that he started in one corner of the room and ended up in another corner (see fact 347).

The Reform Movement began with a different principle concerning prayer. The early Reformers felt that the purpose of prayer was to elevate the person praying, spiritually and emotionally. To accomplish this, the person had to understand what the prayers meant. This concept led to prayers read in the vernacular. Prayers that were deemed to be no longer meaningful or that contained beliefs no longer acceptable were deleted. In order to provide a service with more decorum, the Reformers changed the davvening pattern to prayer readings. They introduced the practice of both congregational readings and leader readings, following the pattern of the Protestant churches (see data to fact 442).

The tension between fixed prayers and personalized prayers continues. Siddurim continue to be written that express the assumptions of the group; many provide room within the service for private meditation and prayer.

Prayer Services and Their Rubrics

295. Traditionally, there are three daily prayer services.

No one knows when our tradition began creating fixed, communal, prayer services at stated times. The most popular theory is that when it became physically impossible for everyone from a district to take sacrifices to the Temple, designated groups, called ma'amadot, went. Everyone else assembled in their villages during the times of the sacrifices and recited prayers and praise, thus identifying with the Temple worship even though physically absent. Prayer and Torah study became two added forms of worship.

Torah reading apparently took place three times a week: on Mondays, Thursdays, and Shabbat. Mondays and Thursdays were market days in Babylonia, and it was a convenient time for Jews to gather. It was expected that Jews would gather on Saturdays, Shabbat, as well (see data to fact 218). Because few people understood Hebrew, these readings were accompanied by translations in Aramaic and Greek (see facts 243, 244).

When the Temple was destroyed, the sacrificial cult disappeared, and these communal prayer meetings became the primary form of worship. Our sages emphasized that as long as there was no Temple, prayer and study were the media for Jewish worship (see fact 346).

There is no question that our tradition associated the prayer services with the Temple cult. The times for the two original daily prayer services, Shacharit and Minchah, corresponded to the times of the two daily sacrifices.

In addition, our sages retrojected the prayer services back to the Patriarchs. They believed that Abraham created the morning service, because Genesis 22:3 says, "Abraham got up early in the morning" (obviously to pray); that Isaac created the afternoon service, because Genesis 24:63 says, "Isaac went out meditating in the field toward evening"; and that Jacob created the evening service, because Genesis 28:11 says, "He came to that place and stopped there for the night."

296. Shacharit is the morning service.

Shacharit became a reminder of the tamid, the morning offering. It is the longest service. It begins with the morning blessings (see data to fact 285) and traditionally includes passages about the sacrificial cult. There was an assumption that studying about the sacrifices was the next best thing to doing them (see fact 346).

The leaders of the Reform Movement systematically removed any mention of the sacrifices from their services. They viewed them as primitive, antiquated reminders of a worship form no longer appropriate for a modern religion.

It is for this same reason that Reform Jews called their synagogues temples. It was understood that the new, modern Judaism required sacrifices of the heart, not animals. Therefore the Reform Movement offered the new, modern sacrifice in their buildings and removed any indications that they hoped to return to the more primitive offerings.

297. Minchah is the afternoon service.

Minchah became a reminder of the second tamid, the afternoon offering. It is the shortest of the three daily prayer services, consisting of

Psalm 145 (surrounded by single verses of three other psalms), the Amidah (see fact 302), and the Alaynu (see fact 305). According to tradition, it must be said before sunset.

298. Maariv is the evening service.

Maariv, also called Arvit, was not associated with any sacrifice. It originated to fulfill the mitzvah of saying the Shema in the evening (see fact 300). According to our rabbis, the commandment to "speak of 'them' [the mitzvot]. . . . at your lying down and your rising up" meant that the Jew was commanded to say the Shema twice a day: in the morning and the evening. It became customary to include a full service after the evening Shema, because Daniel, according to the TaNaCH, prayed three times a day (see data to fact 224).

For a period of time the Maariv service was optional. Our sages noted only the Shacharit and the Minchah services as being mandatory. Today it has become attached to the Minchah service.

299. Musaf is an additional service on Shabbat and festivals.

An additional sacrifice was offered in the Temple on Shabbat and the festivals. It was called the Musaf, the Additional. As a reminder of that additional offering, our Rabbis instituted a brief, additional service on Shabbat and the festivals called the Musaf, which includes prayers explicitly asking for the restoration of the Temple and the sacrificial cult. Because the founders of the Reform Movement were opposed to reminders of the sacrificial cult, they deleted the Musaf service in its entirety.

300. The Shema and its blessings are recited twice a day.

The Shema and the V'ahavta, Deuteronomy 6:4–9, are recited as part of the Shacharit and Maariv services. They are not prayers, but a Torah passage containing six mitzvot: to love Adonai, our God; to speak of the mitzvot at all times; to teach them systematically to our children;

to recite them in the morning and evening; to put on tefillin; and to write them on the doorposts (mezuzot) of our houses.

The Shema became the most important theological statement in Jewish tradition. It affirms the unity of God, and for traditional Jews also emphasizes God's rule over us. For that reason, it became a tradition to recite the Shema sitting down with a hand covering the eyes. However, it is equally acceptable to recite the Shema standing up, and this issue became a source of conflict in different Jewish communities.

Traditionally, two more paragraphs of Torah are added to the Shema and the V'ahavta during Shacharit and Maariv: Deuteronomy 11:13–21; and Numbers 15:37–41.

The founders of the Reform Movement didn't agree with the theology of the first of these two paragraphs, which emphasized that there is materialistic reward for doing the mitzvot and natural punishment for breaking the mitzvot. They therefore deleted that paragraph from the Siddur.

The third paragraph of the Shema contains the mitzvah to wear fringes on the corners of our garments. The early Reformers were opposed to particularist dress which separated them from the cultured secular world. They therefore deleted that portion as well.

Eventually they attached the last sentence of the third paragraph to the end of the first paragraph. Thus the Shema found in the Reform Siddur consists of the first paragraph of the traditional Siddur plus the last sentence of the third paragraph of the traditional Siddur.

Our sages connected the Shema to Jacob and his sons. According to a midrash (see fact 333), just before Jacob died, he was worried that his children in Egypt would forsake their heritage. They responded, "Listen, Israel, Adonai is our God, Adonai alone" (Shema, Yisrael. . . .).

Our tradition maintains that the priests, as part of the sacrificial cult, recited the Ten Commandments and the Shema.

Traditionally the Shema is surrounded in the Shacharit service by three blessings, two before and one after. These blessings focus on (1) God's creation of light and darkness, order in the universe (see fact 111), (2) God's love of Israel, demonstrated by giving us Torah, and (3) God's redemptive power, symbolized by His saving us at the Sea of Reeds.

In the Maariv service (see fact 298), a second blessing is included after the Shema, asking for divine protection when we lie down.

Besides the two fixed times for reciting the Shema, it became a tradition to recite the Shema and its blessings immediately before going to sleep. In Yiddish this act was called Kriyas Shema (reciting the Shema), frequently mispronounced "Krishma."

301. The Mi Chamocha reminds us of having been saved at the Sea of Reeds.

When the Hebrews were saved at the Sea of Reeds, they sang a song of thanksgiving (see fact 157). Since we responded at that moment of redemption by singing God's praises with the words, "Who is like you, Adonai, among the gods," this poem, the Mi Chamocha, is included in the morning and evening service as one of the fixed prayers connected to the Shema. It has become a symbol of our hope for divine protection and redemption. Just as God saved us then, may he save us now.

302. The Amidah is the Standing Prayer consisting of nineteen prayers on weekdays.

The Amidah is the central prayer of every Jewish service. Though called the *Shmoneh Esrei* (the Eighteen), it actually has nineteen blessings, probably because one blessing was split into two in the third century. Our tradition incorrectly credits Rabban Gamliel with adding a nineteenth benediction at the end of the second century c.e.

The Amidah is traditionally recited standing up. At the Shacharit and Minchah Services, the Amidah is repeated out loud by the sheliach tzibbur (see fact 240). It is not repeated at the Maariv Service.

The first three blessings and the last three blessings are recited at every Jewish service. The thirteen middle benedictions of the Amidah are petitions for a variety of needs and aspirations: knowledge, repentance, forgiveness, redemption, healing, abundance, liberation, justice, defeat of the slanderers, support for the righteous, rebuilding of Jerusalem, the coming of the Messiah, and hearing our prayers.

Our sages determined that since Shabbat and the festivals were days symbolizing perfection and completion, it would not be appropriate to include petitions on those days. They therefore included in the Shabbat and festival Amidah a short middle blessing that emphasizes the holiness of the day, and deleted the thirteen middle blessings.

After the middle petitions, the Amidah concludes with three final benedictions:

1. A petition that the Divine will accept our worship (the Avodah).
2. A prayer of thanksgiving noting our dependency upon the Divine every moment (Birkat Hodaot).
3. A prayer for peace (Birkat Shalom).

The first two prayers of the Amidah contain themes and theology that the Reform Movement has, on principle, rejected. The first benediction, the Avot, reminds the Divine of the special relationship between the Patriarchs and God. Relying on their merit, we ask for a similar special relationship (see fact 599).

Traditionally the Avot includes the phrase "umayvee Goel," "and brings a Redeemer." The phrase obviously refers to the Messiah. Since the Reform Movement was opposed to the belief in a personal Messiah, the editors of the Reform prayerbook changed the phrase to "umayvee G'ulah, and brings redemption." The state of redemption is one of the powerful goals of our tradition, but we recognize it as being our personal responsibility to achieve it. We have always striven to create a world of social justice and equality. Such a world would be a world redeemed, and we use the Avot as a reminder of that imperative.

Many Reform congregations object to the prayer's focus on solely the Patriarchs. They have therefore included in the Avot references to Sarah, Rebecca, Rachel, and Leah, the wives of Abraham, Isaac, and Jacob (see facts 122–142).

The second prayer of the Amidah, the G'vurot, notes God's power and greatness. Traditionally the prayer focuses on the Divine's ability to resurrect the dead (see fact 607). The oft-repeated phrase is "m'chayei maytim," "gives life to the dead." The editors of the Reform prayerbook were philosophically opposed to this concept. The vast majority of Reform Jews do not believe in physical resurrection in the End of Days. They therefore changed the Hebrew to "m'chayei ha-kol," "gives life to all."

These changes are more than cosmetic. They emphasize the value of using words in prayer that represent the actual beliefs and feelings of the congregation. In Reform Judaism, personal belief becomes an important criterion for determining the text of the prayers, not tradition.

303. The Kedushah quotes Isaiah quoting the angels: "Holy, holy, holy is Adonai."

The third prayer of the Amidah (see fact 302) is called the Kedushah. Its Hebrew root, Holiness, is the same as that of the Kaddish (see fact 279), the Kiddush (see fact 6), and Kiddushin (see fact 262). It emphasizes the holiness of God by referring to the famous theophany of Isaiah 6:2–3: "Fiery angels stood above him, each with six wings; with two each covered its face, with two each covered its feet, and with two each fluttered about; And each called to the other and said, 'Holy, Holy, Holy is Adonai Tzvaot (sometimes translated the Lord of Hosts); The whole earth is full of His glory."

The Kedushah quotes Isaiah's fiery angels: "Holy, Holy, Holy is Adonai Tzvaot; The whole earth is full of His glory." It is this quote which provides it with its name Kedushah. In addition, our sages included two more quotes. The first, from Ezekiel's vision (3:12), quotes the heavenly hosts: "Blessed is the glory of Adonai from its place." The final verse of the Kedushah is taken from Psalm 146 and declares, "Adonai will live forever, your God, Zion, from generation to generation; Halleluyah."

These three quotes make up the core of the Kedushah. Around it our sages added introductory sentences and statements, based on different services for different occasions. Traditionally the Kedushah is one of the prayers that can be said only in the presence of a minyan (see fact 289).

A form of the full Kedushah appears in every Shacharit and Minchah service. A shortened one-line statement of God's holiness comprises the Maariv Kedushah.

304. Duchenen is giving the Priestly Blessing.

The Priestly Blessing is found in Numbers 6:23–27. It consists of fifteen Hebrew words. Traditionally, the priests blessed the people every morning after the sacrifice. Because the priests delivered this blessing from a platform called the duchan, the custom of reciting the Priestly Blessing today is called *duchenen*. In traditional synagogues it is one of the rituals that is done only by Kohanim, descendants of the priestly line (see fact 169). In Ashkenazic communities it became the custom for the Kohanim to recite the Priestly Blessing only on the Yamim Nora'im and the festivals at the Musaf Amidah.

In Israel the Priestly Blessing is done every day as part of the morning Amidah. All Kohanim, shoeless, ascend the bimah. After a blessing recognizing that they are about to perform a mitzvah, they turn toward the congregation with their tallitot (see fact 251) over their faces. They raise their arms and repeat the ancient formula: "May Adonai bless you and keep you; May Adonai let His face shine upon you and be gracious to you; May Adonai bestow His favor upon you and grant you peace."

In some congregations it became the custom for the Levites present to wash the hands of the Kohanim prior to the Priestly Blessing, a reminder of the sacrificial rituals when this was one of the levitical functions.

The hands of the Kohanim are held in a special way during the Priestly Blessing: The hands are raised, palms out. The thumbs of the two hands are outspread but touching. The other four fingers on each hand are held split into two sets of two fingers each. This became the emblem of the Kohanim (and was used by "Star Trek" as Mr. Spock's greeting).

Since the name of God is used in the Priestly Blessing, from ancient times tradition forbade looking at the Kohanim as they blessed the congregation. Tradition went so far as to warn that anyone who looked at the Kohanim would go blind.

The founders of Reform Judaism were opposed to any distinctions between Kohanim, Levites, and Israelites and so removed all rituals that reminded them of the sacrificial cult. They therefore removed the ritual of duchenen from the service.

305. The Alaynu is a statement of God's majesty.

The Alaynu, the Adoration, was originally recited only as part of the shofar service on Rosh HaShanah (see fact 20). By the fourteenth century it was being recited at the conclusion of every service. According to tradition, it was written by Rav in the third century (see fact 360). Some sages maintained that the prayer was created by Joshua (see fact 183).

Its inclusion in the daily service may have developed from the Alaynu's association with Jewish martyrdom. We are told that in 1171 the Jews of Blois, France, trapped in their synagogue, were put to death by a mob which set fire to the building. As the flames rose, the crowd outside heard an eerie sound. The congregation dying within sang the Alaynu, and its music impressed the murderers.

The Alaynu began with a paragraph praising God's rule and emphasizing the special relationship Israel has with the Divine "Who did not make our portion like theirs nor our fate like that of all their multitude for they prostrate themselves before vanity and emptiness and pray to a God that doesn't save."

The second paragraph expressed the fervent hope for the speedy arrival of God's Messianic era which would bring a united humanity.

Needless to say, once the Jews began using prayerbooks with fixed prayers, the first paragraph of the Alaynu got them into trouble. The Christian authorities had censors who could read the prayerbooks, and the offending passage, "for they prostrate themselves before vanity and emptiness and pray for a God that doesn't save," was cut. The original paragraphs remained in the Sephardic Siddurim.

The Alaynu mentions *prostration* as the form of physical worship, a mode used in the Temple. Traditionally, on Rosh HaShanah when the Alaynu is recited, the community does fall prostrate to the floor. On all other days a simple bending of the knees suffices.

Torah Reading as a Ritual

306. The Torah is traditionally read on Shabbat, festivals, Mondays, and Thursdays.

The reading of Torah is a central part of our ritual, and traditionally there has to be a minyan to read it as part of the service. Torah is read on Shabbat, festivals, and Monday and Thursday mornings. Monday and Thursday were Babylonian market days, so people could gather to study our contract with the Divine (see data to fact 218). Our rabbis added a midrash to this pragmatic reason. We are told in Exodus 15:22 that the Hebrews were demoralized because "they traveled three days in the wilderness and found no water." Torah, said our rabbis, is life-giving like water. Therefore, going with Torah for three days demoralizes Jews. By reading Torah on Shabbat, Mondays, and Thursdays, Jews never have to suffer Torah deprivation.

307. Trop are the cantillation notes for chanting Torah and Haftarah.

Both the Torah and Haftarah are traditionally chanted. The proper melody for each word is designated by cantillation signs called trop. Originally the reader had a helper who provided hand signals called ta'amim, telling him how to sing the words. Gradually these ta'amim became standardized and were written down. Scholars dedicated their lives to studying every aspect of the TaNaCH: the number of letters, the number of times each letter was used, the number of times each word was used, grammatical constructions, different spellings of words, and so on. All of this knowledge was transmitted from one generation to the next and was called the Masorah, the Transmitted Text. By the Middle Ages, the rules for writing and chanting the TaNaCH were set. The resulting TaNaCH was called the Masoretic Text.

Since the Torah scroll itself does not contain the trop, the ability to chant the Torah was and is an impressive skill.

308. The honor of being called to recite the blessings before and after the Torah reading is called an aliyah.

Originally, as part of the service, people were called up by their Hebrew names to the bimah to chant the text. This honor was called an aliyah, a going up. People were honored as a recognition of piety or generosity to the congregation; to celebrate getting married (see data to fact 265); to celebrate becoming a Bar Mitzvah (see fact 277); to celebrate the birth of a child; to commemorate a Yahrzeit (see fact 283); to celebrate recovery from an illness; to offer a prayer for a relative who was sick; to note the end of a Shivah period (see fact 280).

Our rabbis determined the number of people who could be honored with an aliyah at various services: on Mondays, Thursdays, and Shabbat afternoon, three people were permitted to read Torah; on Rosh Chodesh and the intermediate days of the festivals, four people were called up; on the festivals, five people were permitted to read Torah; on Yom Kippur, six people were called up; on Shabbat morning, seven people were called to read Torah. On Shabbat every Torah portion was divided into seven separate readings, each containing a minimum of three verses.

Traditionally, the first person called to read Torah was a Kohayn, the second person called was a Levite, and the third person was an Israelite. To avoid the Evil Eye, a father and son or two brothers were not called to read consecutively. Most Reform congregations do not take these customs into account when they call people to the Torah.

Today, an aliyah usually consists of reciting a blessing before and after the Torah reading, rather than actually reading from the Torah (see data to fact 309).

309. The baal koray chants the Torah.

As Torah knowledge deteriorated among lay people, it became difficult to find appropriate honorees who could chant the Torah text correctly. Therefore a synagogue official was given the responsibility of chanting. He was called the baal koray, the master of reading. People honored by being called to the Torah chanted a blessing before and after the reading and left the Torah chanting to the skilled baal koray. Today an *aliyah* consists of reciting blessings before and after the Torah reading.

Traditionally, when a person has had an aliyah, he or she is greeted by well-wishers with the words, "Yasher Kochacha," "May your strength go straight." It is a form of congratulations reserved for someone who has done something special.

310. Hagbahah is the honor of lifting the Torah, and Gelilah is the honor of rolling the Torah.

In Ashkenazic services, after the Torah reading is completed, someone lifts the Torah vertically and turns to face in each direction, revealing at least three columns of the text to the congregation. This honor is called hagbahah, lifting. The person holding the Torah sits, and someone else rolls the scroll back together and ties a sash around the two atzei chayim (see fact 234). This honor is called gelilah (the rolling).

History, Jewish Texts, and Tradition

Roman Period and Herod

311. Josephus was a Jewish historian who wrote about the Jews for the Romans during the Greek and Roman periods.

The period that involved the most changes in our religion, the Greco-Roman period, is also the period most obscure to historians. We don't know a great deal about Jewish history from the time of Alexander the Great until the Bar Kochba Revolt (see facts 39–42, 349–351). Our sources are few, and the ones we have tend not to be historically reliable. They include:

1. Brief incidents in the New Testament.
2. Brief references by the sages in rabbinic literature.
3. Obscure texts found at Qumran (see fact 322).
4. Some brief mentions by Greek and Roman writers.
5. The writings of Josephus Flavius.

Josephus was a Jew who lived during the time of the Great Revolt against Rome (see data to fact 336). He was well educated, knowing both Jewish texts and the Greek language. During the Great Revolt, Josephus served as general of the Galilee. When the Roman army overcame his forces, Josephus and 40 compatriots fled to a cave. They agreed to commit suicide. Josephus fixed the lots so that his name would come out last. After the others killed themselves, Josephus convinced the remaining fighter to surrender with him.

As a prisoner of the Romans, Josephus volunteered to write the history of the Great Revolt. General (later Emperor) Vespasian agreed. Josephus thus provided the Romans (and now us) with a first-hand account of the fall of Jerusalem (see fact 336). It must be emphasized that Josephus was writing for Vespasian, so his work is definitively biased.

Following the end of the war, Josephus was taken to Rome, where he wrote *The Jewish War*. His second major work, *Jewish Antiquities*, described the entire history of the Jews. It included a great deal of material from the time of Alexander the Great to the destruction of the Second Temple. However, because of Josephus's proclivity to depend on hearsay and legend, scholars are never sure what to accept as fact.

Be that as may be, Josephus's works are the most thorough histories of the period that we have, and they serve as the basis for most theories about the Jews in the Greco-Roman world.

312. After the Hasmoneans, Rome conquered Judea.

Corruption within the Hasmonean family speeded the fall of the Hasmonean Empire (see facts 38–43). By 67 B.C.E. there was civil war in Judea, and the land was ripe for conquest. Rome took advantage of the situation and, in 63 B.C.E. Pompey conquered Judea.

Confusion ensued. Rome was in a state of flux, with power struggles between Pompey and Julius Caesar; and after Caesar's death, Cassius, Mark Antony, and Octavian all struggled for control of the Roman Empire.

The Hasmonean family wasn't willing to give up and, with the support of the Parthians (a nation in Asia Minor), there was a mini-revolt which was brutally suppressed.

313. Rome made Herod king of Judea.

After brutally suppressing a Judean revolt against their rule, Rome appointed Herod king of Judea. Herod had complete authority, and he used it ruthlessly. He established an enormous secret police force, brutally killed anyone suspected of plotting against him, and created Roman peace by slaughtering all dissidents.

Herod controlled the sacrificial cult by placing a lackey in the position of High Priest. If any of his appointees was foolish enough to displease him, Herod killed him and replaced him with another lackey.

314. King Herod was responsible for an enormous number of building projects in the Land of Israel.

The vast majority of popular tourist sites in present-day Israel were originally built by Herod. Herod was security conscious. He built fortresses throughout the land just in case he should ever need sanctuary. These included Sabaste in the Hills of Ephraim, the central region of Israel; Herodium, just east of Bethlehem; and Jericho. Each of these fortresses was architecturally unique.

Sabaste was originally called Samaria. It had been the capital of Israel during the Divided Kingdom (see fact 205), and Samaria became the name for the entire northern region. Herod built over the ruins of Samaria, which had been built atop a mountain. He ordered the construction of an enormous colonnade of imported marble starting from the base of the mountain and rising to the summit.

The mountain Herod had chosen for the fortress Herodium was too low. Herod had his architects raise the summit and build his palace inside this man-made cone. It is generally believed that Herod was buried in Herodium, but no grave was ever found. Equally puzzling is the fact that archaeologists have been unable to discover a water source there.

To supply water for the Jericho fortress, Herod had an enormous aqueduct built which carried water from Ein Kelt.

Herod continued to build. In honor of Octavian (Augustus Caesar), Herod took the ancient port city of Straton's Tower just south of

Haifa and renamed it Caesarea. There he created a deep sea port, surrounded the city with a wall, and constructed an amphitheater. To supply the port with ample water, Herod built another enormous aqueduct.

Although Herod was a terrible tyrant, his buildings and fortresses remain awesome architectural achievements even today.

315. Herod enlarged the Temple Mount to make the Second Temple larger.

One of Herod's greatest building projects was in Jerusalem. He wanted to enlarge and embellish the Temple, but the mountain on which Solomon had built the First Temple and on which Zachariah and Haggai had built the Second was just too small for his plans. That didn't stop Herod. He dramatically increased the size of the Temple Mount by constructing huge encasement walls and filling them with pure dirt, creating a large trapezoid. He was then able to proceed with his architectural plans to enlarge the Temple and its courtyards.

Herod protected the Temple Mount with a large military fortress called the Antonia, honoring Mark Antony. He protected the western entrance of Jerusalem (and, incidentally, his villa situated nearby) with a huge tri-towered fortress called the Citadel.

316. Herod used hundreds of thousands of Jews as slaves to build the structures and cities he wanted.

Herod's projects were built through the use of thousands of Jews as forced laborers moving enormous blocks of limestone. Many of these blocks weighed more than ten tons. Because of his despotic actions, the Jews despised and feared Herod. Even projects that he commissioned to endear him to the people failed to change their hatred for him.

317. Herod built Masada overlooking the Dead Sea.

Herod's most famous fortress was Masada. Located on the shores of the Dead Sea, Masada was built on a high plateau. Access was only along a steep, sharply winding path called the Snake Path. At the top, Herod had two palaces: a magnificent three-tiered northern palace complete with columns and frescoes offered a spectacular view of the Dead Sea. A larger mosaic-decorated western palace was probably planned as an administrative headquarters.

Herod's architects created water channels and cisterns to provide drinking water during the long, dry summers. Huge storehouses guaranteed food in case of siege. A strong casemate wall enclosed the entire summit of the plateau. It was an awesome fortress and appeared to be invulnerable.

Roman Period and Jewish Political Groups

318. The Sadducees were the political party of the priests during Roman rule.

As early as 151 B.C.E. there were clearly different political groups of Jews in Judea. Under the rule of the Hasmoneans (see data to fact 42), these groups vied for power. Most of the documentary materials describing these different political forces were written by the winning political group, the Pharisees, so their descriptions of their political adversaries are suspect.

The first of these groups was the Sadducees. They came primarily from large land-owning aristocratic families and priestly families. Many were involved in the sacrificial cult of the Second Temple. For most of the Hasmonean period, and probably until the year 70 C.E., they were politically powerful. However, they did not write anything for posterity, so we know about them only from their opponents, the Pharisees.

The Sadducees recognized the authority of the written Torah and viewed the sacrificial cult as the primary form of worship. They viewed the priests as the only authoritative representatives of Jewish law.

319. The Pharisees were the political party of the sages during Roman rule.

The Pharisees represented a new stream of Jewish thought. They maintained that, in addition to the written Torah, God had handed down an Oral Tradition at Mount Sinai. The Pharisees claimed divine authority for this Oral Tradition. They challenged the priests and maintained that the priests didn't know the correct laws because they didn't study the Oral Tradition. This tension between Pharisees and Sadducees may have started as early as the time of Ezra (see fact 221).

It was the Pharisees who were involved with the people in the synagogues, teaching and encouraging study and prayer as Jewish forms of worship. So long as the Temple stood, the Pharisees never denied the importance of the sacrificial cult, but they accused the priests of performing the sacrifices incorrectly because the priests ignored the Oral Torah.

Although apparently supported by most Jews, the Pharisees did not enjoy real political power during the Hasmonean period. However, their representatives did eventually write down a great deal of material that provides us with our historical understanding of that period and forms the core of rabbinic Judaism.

320. Olam HaBa is the Hebrew term for life after earthly life.

One of the most important beliefs of the Pharisees (denied by the Sadducees) was reward and punishment in the World-to-Come, the Olam HaBa. The Pharisees developed the concept that the reward for doing mitzvot in this world would take place in the Olam HaBa. They described a Divine Court where the Divine judged the soul of each person based on his or her actions. This emphasis on mitzvot leading to the Olam HaBa became a primary belief within Jewish thought. It met a deeply felt need. Most Jews during the Roman period suffered physical hardships. Reward in the Olam HaBa explained apparent injustices in this world. The righteous, despite their immediate suffering, were guaranteed eternal bliss because they followed the mitzvot.

Many modern liberal Jews have difficulties with this belief. We like to emphasize that Judaism focuses on our immediate lives. Our sages have always maintained that doing mitzvot is the most important part of being Jewish. However, it is necessary to note their emphasis on receiving a reward in the Olam HaBa as well. This belief has given Jews strength and courage for two thousand years.

321. The Essenes were a group who dropped out of Jewish society.

In addition to the Sadducees (see fact 318) and Pharisees (see fact 319), a third political group, the Essenes, emerged during the Hasmonean period. The Essenes viewed both the Sadducees and the Pharisees as corruptors of Jewish law.

Many Essenes were celibate and viewed the world as a conflict between the spiritual (good) and the physical (bad). They were tremendously concerned with ritual purity. The group that lived in Jerusalem kept itself separate from other Jews, fearing ritual contamination. Some scholars believe that Essenes lived in small communities separated from the rest of the Jewish world. There, they wore carefully washed white garments and frequently immersed themselves.

322. The Dead Sea Scrolls were found in caves at Qumran.

About 2,200 years ago, there was a group of Jews who created a community at Qumran, located on the shore of the Dead Sea. Some scholars identify them with the Essenes (see fact 321). Whoever they were, they kept themselves ritually pure (see data to fact 261), studied texts, wrote texts, and prepared for the Final Spiritual Battle between the Sons of Light (themselves) and the Sons of Darkness (everyone else). Hundreds of parchments have been found at Qumran. Because of the location of the caves in which they were found, these parchments are called the Dead Sea Scrolls.

Although they were discovered as early as 1947, research on the Dead Sea Scrolls is still in its beginning stages. Because of political conflict among the scholars involved, it will take many decades before we fully understand their significance. Some parchments and scrolls found at Qumran are now housed in the Shrine of the Book in Jerusalem.

Jesus and Christianity

323. When Herod died, some Jews wanted to rid Judea of the Romans.

Herod left Judea in ruins. People were starving, angry, and frustrated. Rome tried to administer the province through a series of procurators, but these men tended to be mediocre.

There was unrest between the Sadducees and the Pharisees; groups like the community at Qumran were predicting the Final Battle any day. Followers of self-proclaimed prophets and saviors roamed the Galilee (see fact 477) and the Jordan River valley (see data to fact 485) announcing the imminent end of time. One of these, John the Baptist, associated the End of Days with ritual purity. He advocated ritual immersion as a form of spiritual cleansing, in a doctrine similar to the one described in the Dead Sea Scrolls at Qumran.

Another group fomented unrest in Judea and encouraged violence to expel Rome from their land. They viewed all Jews who cooperated with the authorities as traitors. This group punished those "traitors" by approaching them in crowded areas and stabbing them to death with sharp knives called sicarii. These "dagger men" also were called Sicarii.

Scholars believed until recently that the Sicarii were the same group as the Zealots and the "brigands" mentioned in Josephus's *The Jewish War* (see data to fact 311). It is now believed that they were different groups. That probably didn't matter very much to the Roman authorities, who viewed all the groups as threats to their control. Into this milieu came Jesus.

324. Jesus lived during the Roman period.

The only information we have about Jesus comes from the Christian texts themselves. Hundreds of books have been written about the "historical Jesus," all based on the same data.

It is important to note that descriptions of Jesus' life, teachings, and beliefs certainly fit into the bubbling cauldron of unrest which was Judea at the beginning of the Common Era.

Jesus was a Jew apparently influenced by John the Baptist, although there is no indication that either Jesus or John ever spent any time at Qumran. He emphasized that the Messiah would come any day. He preached a Judaism that valued personal charity and love, but he still believed that the Law was the cornerstone of Judaism. He was obviously charismatic, and most people who heard him believed that the End of Days was near.

When Jesus came to Jerusalem, he entered a city where the Sadducees and Pharisees wielded political clout. He preached against the way the Temple was being operated and threatened the priestly class. Jesus was arrested and taken to the High Priest and the Temple Committee on Dangerous Jews. For many historic reasons, this ad hoc court could not have been the Sanhedrin, the Jewish Supreme Court (see facts 327, 328). Jesus was handed over to Roman authority Pontius

Pilate, who ordered him crucified. Crucifixion was common all over the Roman Empire.

In every spot in Israel where Christian tradition maintains Jesus did something or said something, a church or monastery has been built as a commemoration (see data to fact 370).

325. The Holy Sepulchre in Jerusalem is the spot where many Christians believe Jesus was killed, buried, and rose on the third day.

The most important Christian site in Israel is in Jerusalem, where Jesus was crucified, anointed, buried, and, according to Christian tradition, came back to life on the third day. Since Jesus' death and resurrection are primary Christian doctrines, these sites hold special holiness for Christians and have resulted in two thousand years of pilgrimages to Jerusalem.

The sites of these events are housed in one enormous Church, the Church of the Holy Sepulchre. The specific spots, originally pointed out by Helena, the mother of Emperor Constantine (see data to fact 370), have become holy shrines for Christians.

Protestants have designated a separate site, the Garden of Kings, as the burial spot of Jesus.

326. Christians believe that Jesus was the Messiah; Jews believe that Jesus was neither the Messiah nor divine.

Although Judaism and Christianity have evolved into very different religions over the past two thousand years, there are really only two major theological differences in the religions.

Christianity begins with the belief that humans are separated from God because of Adam's sin of eating the forbidden fruit. This separation is called Original Sin. With the sacrifice of Jesus on the cross, God provided humans with the means to rejoin God and be saved from Original Sin. The method for this salvation is faith in Jesus as the Savior and undergoing baptism, ritual purification with water. This belief is called the Doctrine of Salvation.

Jews, on the other hand, believe that humans don't need Jesus as an intermediary. We don't believe in the existence of Original Sin, and therefore we believe that humans don't need "saving." We often focus on God's willingness to forgive us because we miss the mark so frequently in our contract with the Divine (see facts 11, 12, 26), but that is very different from the belief in Divine Grace and Salvation.

The second major difference between Judaism and Christianity has to do with the Messiah. While both traditional Judaism and Christianity have specific beliefs about the Messiah, they are very different. The word *Messiah* comes from the Hebrew *Mashiach* (Anointed). Originally the term referred to either a king or a priest, both of whom were anointed. Gradually the term came to mean a king from the Davidic line who would restore Israel to its previous national greatness. The original Jewish understanding of Messiah was this-world and politically oriented.

During the Second Temple period many Jews believed that the Messiah would free them from Rome. Although some Jewish splinter groups (such as the Essenes) believed that the Messiah would be superhuman and transcend the physical into an apocalyptic struggle, most of our sages recommended that we not worry about the Messiah and instead concentrate on doing mitzvot.

An essential belief of Christianity is that Jesus was the Messiah, the anointed. Belief in this doctrine is the defining element for being a Christian. We believe that Jesus was not the Messiah, however. Traditional Jews are still waiting for the Messiah to come. There have been numerous cases of false Messiahs over the past two thousand years, and Jews have suffered after each disappointment (see fact 423).

Reform Jews tend not to believe in a personal Messiah. We speak about the Messianic Age, a time when there will be universal peace, cooperation, and sharing.

Anyone who believes that Jesus was the Messiah automatically puts him-or herself into the faith system of Christianity and removes him or herself from Judaism. It is not possible to believe in Jesus as the Messiah and retain Jewish identity. The two are in direct opposition to one another (see data to fact 542).

The Mishnaic Period

327. During the Roman period, the Jewish Supreme Court was called the Sanhedrin.

We don't know much about the history of the Sanhedrin. It is probable that during the Hasmonean period the Sanhedrin was a national court headed by the High Priest.

The term is used loosely before the year 70 c.e. to refer either to an ad hoc court convened for capital crime cases or to a national court called to make major political decisions. It met in the courtyard of the Temple.

According to our sages, the Sanhedrin had always been a legislative body headed by two sages. This idea appears to be a retrojection back in time from the post-100 c.e. reality.

328. The Sanhedrin consisted of 71 rabbis.

After the destruction of the Temple (see fact 336), the Sanhedrin actually became a legislative Supreme Court of 71 rabbis, guaranteeing that most of the Sanhedrin members were Pharisees. The Sanhedrin decided both specific legal questions and general problems, and their decisions became the foundation of precedent law within Jewish society. Thus, after 70 c.e. the Sanhedrin became the major law-creating body for the Jews. It was also responsible for   the New Moon (see fact 1).

329. We call our sages who lived during the Roman period Tanna'im.

During the Greek period and much of the Roman period the Jewish community relied on the interpretations of the sages to determine what God's commandments really were. These sages were called Tanna'im. Many of them served on the Sanhedrin, the Jewish Supreme Court consisting of 71 rabbis.

330. For 200 years the Tanna'im made laws that were not officially written down.

The decisions of the Tanna'im were transmitted orally. This oral transmission allowed for fluidity in the legal interpretations and also guaranteed that no group of Tanna'im got too politically powerful: Oral traditions were easily changed. Moreover, frequently one group of Tanna'im disagreed with other groups. With the decisions kept oral, they were more easily reconsidered by the next generation of Tanna'im.

Special memorizers, human tape recorders, called tanna'im (yes, it's the same word), memorized the dicta and rulings of the various rabbis. Frequently they relied on mnemonic devices to help them recall all the legal statements.

Although our tradition maintains that Tanna'im transmitted Oral Law for 500 years, most modern scholars believe that they did so for only 200 years.

331. Hillel said, "What is hateful to you, don't do to anyone else."

Hillel was a sage of the first century B.C.E. who served as a leader of the Sanhedrin. He was famous for many legal decisions. His most famous decision was called the prozbul. According to the Torah, at the end of seven years during the Sabbatical Year (see fact 174), all debts were automatically cancelled. As a result, people were unwilling to lend money in the fifth and sixth years of the seven-year cycle, causing serious problems for the poor. Hillel declared that while all debts were cancelled between individuals, the court could take over the responsibility of the debt, thus guaranteeing that the debt would eventually be repaid even after the seventh year. This was a revolutionary change from Torah law and had a huge effect on the authority and legitimacy of the Oral Law.

According to tradition, Hillel was once accosted by a scoffer who challenged him to teach him all of Torah while standing on one foot. Hillel replied, "What is hateful to you, don't do to anyone else. That's the whole Torah. The rest is commentary; go and learn it." Note that Hillel's statement has two parts. In the first sentence, he identified the essence of our tradition. However, in the second sentence Hillel emphasized the imperative to know all of Torah: "Go and learn it." People frequently quote the first statement but conveniently leave off the second part.

Hillel was also the creator of the sandwich, insisting that on Passover Jews had to eat the lamb, bitter herbs, and matzah together. This innovation became part of the seder (see fact 73).

332. The two most famous law schools of the Pharisees were the School of Shammai and the School of Hillel.

Shammai was a brilliant scholar who lived at the same time as Hillel. He was also a leader of the Sanhedrin. The Talmud frequently compares the two men: Shammai was viewed as being quick to anger while Hillel was credited with being very patient. According to tradition, these two sages disagreed on only three legal matters during their lifetimes.

Their students, called the School of Hillel and the School of Shammai, had more than 350 legal controversies, however. These two groups of Pharisees contested law between them until the end of the second century C.E. According to tradition, the School of Hillel tended to give the lenient legal decisions, whereas the School of Shammai tended to be stricter. Many scholars have tried to explain the differences between the two schools. One theory was that the School of Hillel represented poorer Jews and therefore was more lenient. Another theory suggests that the schools represented their founders: Hillel was kinder and gentler than Shammai.

In fact, we have no way of knowing why the two schools disagreed the way they did. We don't know the names of the individual sages involved in the disputes. They are identified simply as School of Hillel and School of Shammai. Tradition does insist that, with very few exceptions, halachah, Jewish law, goes according to the School of Hillel, rather than the School of Shammai. These two groups of Pharisees were the most influential in determining halachah through almost the entire period of the Tanna'im.

333. Midrashim are TaNaCH-based stories written by the sages.

At the same time that the sages were creating the Oral Law from the Torah, they were using Torah as the source material for their sermons to the people. The characters in the Bible served them as role models in stories as they taught the common people the important values and beliefs inherent in Judaism. Because they believed that the Torah was written by God, they believed that it contained all truth. It was their responsibility to squeeze from the text the hidden truths. They therefore tried to interpret, explain, and fill in the gaps left in the text.

For example, we first meet Avram when he is 75 years old. The sages created an entire childhood for Abraham in which his adventures served as sermons and lessons for the common people. The people loved these stories and understood their significance as paralleling their own struggles to survive in the Greco-Roman world. These stories told by the sages and based on the Torah are called 'midrashim' (plural of midrash). They have become overlays in the way our tradition views the Torah text. The Torah characters were no longer limited by their simple portrayal in the Torah text; they became the personalities portrayed by the rabbis with all of their philosophical understandings and insights.

It is from the midrash that we get the story of Avram (see fact 122) breaking his father's idols and blaming the large idol for the destruction. When his father challenges his story because "idols can't move or do anything," Avram then asks his father why anyone would worship anything so useless.

It is from the rabbis that we get the tradition that Esau is all-evil and Jacob is all-good (see facts 134–136). The Midrash dramatically influenced the way Jews viewed their world, and it helped create the values that we have always treasured. The first step in studying Torah Jewishly is to understand what the rabbis said the Torah said. That's Midrash.

There are two kinds of midrashim. The majority of midrashim consist of stories and sermons that answer philosophical or value questions of the people. There was also midrash that resulted in a legal decision. We call the story Midrash "aggadic midrash," and we call the legal midrash "halachic midrash."

334. Aggadah included rabbinic stories not based on the Ta-NaCH.

Our sages, in addition to telling stories based on the TaNaCH (see fact 333), told stories about one another to illustrate ethical points. These stories not based on the TaNaCH are called aggadah, tellings. They provide us with wonderful insights into the lives, personalities, and feelings of our sages. The Talmud is rich in aggadah, stories about the rabbis.

335. Philo was a Jewish philosopher during the Roman period.

During the Roman period one of the greatest threats to Jewish leadership was the popularity of Greek culture among young, wealthy Jews. The Jewish community of Alexandria was apparently one of the most assimilated of the time. Most of the well-to-do families didn't know Hebrew and relied on the Septuagint (see fact 243). More disturbing was their interest in Greek philosophy.

Greek philosophy was grounded in the assumption that humans could understand the truths of the universe through reason. These truths included the exploration of creation and God. Judaism was grounded in the assumption that truth was available in written form: the Torah. However, Torah did not appear to be compatible with the principles and assumptions of Greek philosophy, and many young Alexandrian Jews toyed with the idea of rejecting Torah.

In the first century a wealthy Alexandrian Jew, Philo, began writing a series of philosophical treatises on Torah. His purpose was to show that Torah was compatible with basic Platonic thought. He did so by emphasizing that Torah was not to be read literally: it consisted of allegories. All anthropomorphisms about the Divine were not to be taken literally. Moreover, the stories themselves were not literal. In the story of the Garden of Eden, for example, the snake is really lust; Adam is reason; Eve represents the physical senses. Lust appeals to the senses and eventually conquers reason.

This style of creating allegorical meanings within meanings was very popular among the early Church Fathers, and they made great use of Philo's work. Philo also provided modern scholars with insight into the beliefs and lifestyles of the Alexandrian Jews in the first century.

Although Philo's writings may have convinced some Alexandrian Jews to remain within the community, they were neither accepted nor cited by traditional Jewish sources. Most rabbis did not read Greek. Moreover, Philo's lack of Hebrew knowledge, his insistence on Torah as allegory even when it came to law, and his Platonic world view all combined to make his works foreign to the rabbis.

336. The Roman general Titus destroyed the Second Temple in 70 c.e.

The Jews initiated the Great Revolt against Rome in 66 c.e. and it began successfully. The Sicarii took Masada (see data to facts 317, 323) and other Roman strongholds. The Roman garrisons at Caesarea (see data to fact 314) and Jerusalem were slaughtered. The Jews defeated a small army sent down from Syria at Bet Horon, just as the Maccabees had done a century earlier.

Emperor Nero could not let a revolt pass unnoticed. He sent his general Vespasian with four legions, about 60,000 troops. The Jewish aristocracy joined in the revolt and sent generals to prepare Jewish defenses. One of those generals was Josephus (see fact 311).

The Jews had hoped for support from Diaspora Jews in Egypt, Persia, and Rome. It never happened. Judean Jews were isolated in their revolt.

Worse, none of the separate Jewish fighting groups liked one another. Rather than uniting their forces, Jews attacked Jews. During the war against Rome, the Jews continued a civil war inside Jerusalem.

There was no way for Jewish armies to attack the enormous Roman forces. At best the Jewish generals tried defending strongholds. The Great Revolt became a series of Roman sieges and slaughters.

With Nero's death in 68 c.e., Vespasian's campaign paused outside Jerusalem. A popular general, Vespasian had a chance to become emperor. When word came that he had been selected, Vespasian returned to Rome, leaving his siege forces in the hands of his son, Titus.

In 70 c.e. (according to tradition, on the 9th of Av; see fact 93) Titus's forces finally smashed through the final defenses of Jerusalem. They destroyed the entire city, including the Temple. They razed the Antonia fortress (see data to fact 315). However, they couldn't tear down Herod's retaining wall around the Temple Mount (see fact 337); the dirt would have crushed their own workers. Nor did they tear down the Citadel (see data to fact 315); Titus used it as a legion barracks.

Victorious, Titus returned to Rome with prisoners and some furnishings from the Temple, including, apparently, the Temple menorah. The Arch of Titus in Rome shows carvings of that scene.

337. The kotel is the Western Wall of the Temple Mount.

Although Titus destroyed Jerusalem and the Temple in 70 c.e., the retaining wall around the Temple Mount (see fact 315) has remained to this day. It is called the Western Wall, or just the kotel (the wall). The kotel, symbol of the destroyed Temple, has been the holiest spot for Jews for the past two thousand years. Jews flocked to the kotel to mourn the destruction of the Temple. For that reason, the kotel was known as the Wailing Wall.

Until June 1967 (see fact 553) the only visible part of the wall was 91 feet long. Since that time, much of the area has been excavated to reveal fascinating ruins from the Roman period and the continuation of Herod's wall. The encasement wall, not surprisingly, encircles the entire Temple Mount, but only the section on the western side which had been visible for the past two thousand years retains special emotional importance for Jews. After the Six Day War it became customary to refer to the kotel as the Western Wall, not the Wailing Wall.

338. The Romans built a huge ramp up the side of Masada to conquer the Jewish rebels.

Despite the fall of Jerusalem in 70 C.E., Rome was forced to retain a large force in Judea. Zealots, rebels, and Essenes continued the struggle against Rome. Few in number, they could only harass the Romans through small raids, but it was bad for the Roman image to be unable to stop the outbreaks completely.

The Romans couldn't totally crush the rebels, because the rebels' camp was on top of Masada, and after each raid the rebels fled back to that awesome fortress. They made one of the buildings into a synagogue; they built mikvaot (see fact 261). The summit of Masada became a Jewish community, a base for Sicarii to continue the fight against Rome.

Titus ordered Flavius Silva to destroy the rebels at all costs. It became a huge undertaking.

The only path up the mountain was so narrow and twisting that it was called the Snake Path, and it was impossible for the Romans to use it to attack the Zealots successfully. Therefore Silva's first action was to lay siege to the mountain. The Romans built a wall around the entire base of the plateau and set up their camps around that perimeter.

It quickly became clear, however, that the defenders were more comfortable than the soldiers. All Roman water had to be imported from Ein Gedi; the Jews had huge cisterns filled with water. The Masada storehouses also were full, and there was no threat of hunger on top of the mountain. Silva had to do something else and quickly for the emperor was impatient.

Silva had his architects plan a ramp up the western slope of the mountain. This ramp, built by Jewish slaves, enabled Silva to send up a mobile battering ram and ended Jewish resistance at Masada (see data to fact 339).

339. At Masada, more than 900 Jews chose to die rather than be made prisoners of the Romans.

When it became clear that the Romans were going to succeed in breaching the Jews' defenses (see fact 338), the Jewish leader Eleazar ben Yair called the 960 Jews together and proposed, just as Josephus had in the Galilee (see data to fact 311), that everyone commit suicide rather than be captured by the Romans, and they did so. Breaking through the fortifications the next morning, the soldiers found all the inhabitants dead.

The capture of Masada in 73 or 74 c.e. marked the end of the Great Revolt. Masada has become a symbol of Jewish heroism and determination to live free and proud.

When archaeologists excavated Masada from 1963 to 1965, they found the bodies of some of the defenders and their families, as well as coins, weapons, food, clothing, and some potsherds which might have been used as lots.

340. Rabbi Yochanan ben Zakkai established a law school at Yavneh.

With the destruction of the Temple, the focus of worship switched from sacrifices (now impossible) to prayer and study. These functions took place in synagogues and in scholars' academies (*yeshivot*). The most important academy was established by Rabbi Yochanan ben Zakkai at Yavneh.

341. General (later Emperor) Vespasian gave Yochanan ben Zakkai permission to establish his law school at Yavneh.

According to Jewish lore, while Jerusalem was still under siege, Yochanan ben Zakkai slipped out of the city (tradition says he was carried out, wrapped in a shroud) and gained an audience with the general. Their meeting resulted in Vespasian's giving Yochanan ben Zakkai permission to establish his legal academy at Yavneh. Ben Zakkai's school became the site of the Sanhedrin, and he was named head of that august body of seventy-one Tanna'im. The title for head of the Sanhedrin was nasi, prince or president.

The great sages continued to teach their disciples in their separate academies and, for an unknown length of time, retained their independent authority over their students. The authority of the Sanhedrin was not established overnight.

342. Halachah is the Hebrew word for Jewish law.

At the same time that the sages were teaching, they were also becoming the legislators of Jewish law, halachah. After 70 c.e. the official title in Judea for a legislative sage was rabbi. The rabbis' decisions eventually became binding upon the Jewish world.

Halachah actually means *way*. It encompasses the entire process of determining the limits and requirements set upon a Jew, and it includes all legal decisions spanning the past two thousand years. Halachah defines every aspect of a traditional Jew's life.

In addition to halachah, individual communities of Jews developed local customs. A local Jewish custom is called a minhag. According to tradition, a minhag is binding upon anyone visiting that community even though it is recognized that the custom isn't halachah for the entire Jewish world. Thus, for example, Sephardic and Ashkenazic (see fact 229) minhagim (plural of minhag) differ. When one is in a Sephardic community, it is proper to follow Sephardic customs; when visiting an Ashkenazic community, we follow Ashkenazic minhagim.

343. When the Temple was destroyed in 70 C.E., there was a power shift in Judaism from the priests to the rabbis.

The destruction of the Temple marked the end of priestly rule and power within Judaism and the rise of rabbinic authority. According to post 70 C.E. Judaism, the decisions of the rabbis were as authoritative as the commandments found in the Torah. The Sanhedrin even had the authority to supersede Torah law in certain cases.

Since there were no more sacrifices, the priests served no political function. The rabbis did include prayers for the restoration of the Temple (see data to facts 295, 299), but until that time came, actual political power in the Jewish world was placed in the hands of the rabbis.

344. S'michah is the ceremony of ordaining a rabbi.

According to tradition, a Jewish legal scholar became a rabbi through a special ceremony called s'michah. This ordination ritual included the rabbi's teacher placing his hands on the student's head, thus making him a rabbi. Some modern scholars doubt whether this ritual actually took place during the Roman period. They suggest that it probably developed at a later time when the authority of the rabbis was more firmly established. At any rate, our tradition definitely retrojects s'michah to the Roman period, whether it happened then or not.

345. The first assumption of rabbinic Judaism is that all halachah was given at Mount Sinai and the rabbis have the authority to explain it.

To understand how Judaism developed, it is essential to remember that the rabbis did not see themselves as creators of Jewish law. For them, the Oral Law and the Written Law (Torah) were both given to the Jewish people by God at Mount Sinai. Moses received the Torah, the Written Law, and used the Torah as his notes for delivering all of the Oral Law as well to the entire Jewish people. The rabbis saw themselves as explainers of Divine Law already given at Mount Sinai.

346. The second assumption of rabbinic Judaism is that studying Torah and halachah serves as a substitute for the sacrificial offerings until another Temple is built.

People don't change their fundamental religious beliefs. Since the only form of worship practiced in Judaism was the sacrificial cult, people panicked when the Temple was destroyed. One of the revolutionary accomplishments of the rabbis was their emphasis that, with the destruction of the Temple, God accepted temporary substitutes for the sacrifices: study and prayer. According to the Tanna'im, study and prayer were the acceptable Jewish routes to achieve holiness in our contract with the Divine until the Temple was rebuilt and we returned to sacrifices. This concept was extremely important. In most ancient religions, when the site of worship was destroyed, the religion disappeared from the face of the earth. By substituting study and prayer for physical sacrifices, the rabbis kept Judaism alive.

347. According to tradition, Rabbi Akiva didn't begin studying until he was 40 years old.

One of the most famous of the Tanna'im was Rabbi Akiva. According to Jewish tradition, he grew up an ignorant shepherd. The Talmud states that he was jealous of scholars and would throw stones at them. Then he met a woman named Rachel and fell in love. She indicated that she had no intention of getting involved with an illiterate shepherd, so after they married, Akiva began studying. Tradition says he was 40 at the time.

His first step was to learn to read. Akiva learned by asking his son to teach him what he learned in school. Quickly he learned from older and older children until he knew enough to present himself to a sage as a student. His first teacher was Rabbi Eliezer ben Hyrcanus, a great scholar. After thirteen years of solid studying, Akiva became a teacher himself. Tradition claims that he had 12,000 students. When he returned home after his twelve-year absence, he heard his wife say that if his being away meant that he would be a greater scholar, she was willing to wait another twelve years. Without greeting her, he turned around and went back to his studies for another twelve years.

Akiva was the first important systematizer of Oral Law. He began with the principle that nothing in the Torah could be redundant since it was written by God. Therefore every change in grammar, spelling, even the lettering, had legal implications and significance for him. He was one of the first to note specifically the rules for interpreting the Torah. He influenced the legal decisions of the Sanhedrin, he was tremendously important in the creation of Midrash, and he was instrumental in guiding the path of halachah, Jewish law. He believed deeply that the most important commandment for a Jew was to study, "because study leads to practice." Akiva was responsible for the retention of the Song of Songs in the TaNaCH, maintaining that it was an allegory of God's love for Israel, not a sensuous love poem (see fact 78).

348. Rabbi Akiva supported the Bar Kochba Revolt.

As one of the leaders of the Sanhedrin, Akiva became actively involved in diplomacy with the Romans. As the political situation deteriorated, he even took a ship to Rome to try to convince the authorities to change their rigid policies concerning Judea. When his entreaties failed, Akiva encouraged the Bar Kochba Revolt (see fact 349) and was martyred when he refused to stop teaching Judaism.

349. The Bar Kochba Revolt, an attempt to rebel against Rome, began successfully.

The Bar Kochba Revolt against Roman rule broke out in 132 c.e. There had been years of discontent prior to actual war. Back in 115–117 c.e. Jews had started uprisings against Rome's authority in Alexandria and other major cities, and they had been brutally suppressed. Jews were still resentful of Roman rule, and the governor of Judea was ruthless, creating greater tension.

Despite what some history books maintain, war would probably have broken out even without provocation from Emperor Hadrian. However, in 132 c.e. Hadrian declared Jerusalem to be a Roman city. To emphasize this point, he ordered the building of a temple to Jupiter on the Temple Mount. Rumors spread that Hadrian also intended to save Jewish babies from mutilation by forbidding circumcision.

Hadrian regularly vacationed in Judea. When he left in 132 c.e., war broke out. The Jews were led by a single man, Shimeon Bar Kosiva. Several leading rabbis including Rabbi Akiva believed he was the Messiah; they gave him the Messianic name Bar Kochba, son of a star. Thus his war was called the Bar Kochba Revolt.

It was different in many ways from the Great Revolt of 66 c.e. (see data to fact 336). First, all Jews were united under one leader, Bar Kochba; there was no civil war. Second, Bar Kochba was apparently a ruthless general. Stories describe his method of selecting troops: they had to cut off one of their fingers to prove their dedication. Even if just a legend, it certainly describes a dedicated fighting force. Finally, the revolt had the support of Rabbi Akiva and other Jewish authorities, which lent Messianic authority to the war.

The Jews were successful for several years, took Jerusalem, and proclaimed a free Judea. Hadrian was forced to call in his greatest general, Severus, who had been busy subduing the Britons. Rather than engaging the Jewish armies directly, Severus surrounded the Jewish strongholds and systematically starved out the Jews. In 135 c.e. the final Jewish stronghold, Beitar, fell. Bar Kochba and all his fighters were slaughtered. More than 580,000 Jews were killed in the revolt, which marked the end of Jewish hopes for an independent state for almost two thousand years. We didn't have our own country again until May 14, 1948 (see fact 537).

350. The Roman emperor Hadrian made Judaism illegal.

Following the defeat of Bar Kochba (see fact 350), Hadrian issued many cruel edicts against the Jews. Circumcision was banned. Jews were forbidden to enter Jerusalem, and the entire southern part of Judea was abandoned. By forbidding Jewish ritual practices and study, Hadrian hoped to wipe out Judaism, thus ending a tradition that he had viewed as tremendously troublesome. He didn't succeed, but his edicts caused tremendous suffering for the Jews living in Judea.

351. Following the Bar Kochba Revolt, the Romans executed ten rabbis including Rabbi Akiva.

Hadrian made the teaching of Judaism a capital offense and, according to tradition, ten of the leading sages, including Rabbi Akiva, were put to death. Their martyrdom for Kiddush HaShem, the Sanctification of the Divine Name (see fact 383) is recalled every Yom Kippur.

After the revolt, although many Jews remained in Judea, poor and oppressed, huge numbers of Jews fled the country. In addition, the split between the Jews and the Christians, who had not participated in the war, became permanent.

352. Shimon bar Yochai said, "Kill the best of the non-Jews."

During the Bar Kochba Revolt one of Rabbi Akiva's greatest students, Shimon bar Yochai, was forced to flee from the Romans. According to tradition, he escaped by hiding in a cave (some say buried up to his neck in dirt) for twelve years. He naturally viewed everything Roman as an abomination, and he was quoted as saying, "Kill the best of the non-Jews." This rather extreme position is important simply as a balance against all of our tradition's wonderful expressions of ecumenism and acceptance of the non-Jew. We had angry leaders. We were not always understanding and gentle.

353. Tradition says that Shimon bar Yochai wrote the *Zohar*.

Ironically, tradition credits Shimon bar Yochai with the writing of the *Zohar*, the central book of kabbalah, Jewish mysticism. However, the *Zohar* was probably written in Spain in the late thirteenth century, more than a thousand years after the time of Shimon bar Yochai. Because of his credited authorship, Shimon bar Yochai is venerated by all Jews interested in Kabbalah, Jewish mysticism, and the belief in hidden secrets in the Torah. He was buried on Mount Meiron near Tzfat. Tradition says that he died on Lag BaOmer (see fact 82). As part of their Lag BaOmer celebration, thousands of Jews make a pilgrimage each year to his burial site and celebrate Lag BaOmer there.

354. The *Zohar* is the central book of Kabbalah.

The *Zohar*, written in the late thirteenth century, had a tremendous influence on the Kabbalah, Jewish mysticism. It is an Aramaic commentary on a variety of verses from the Torah and includes long narratives, legends, and conversations of Shimon bar Yochai. The sections follow the weekly Torah portions from Genesis through most of Numbers, and it also contains four commentary portions for the book of Deuteronomy. Followers of Kabbalah believe that there are hidden messages written within the text. It is not possible to just read the *Zohar*; it must be studied with a teacher who knows the meaning of the text.

355. Kabbalah is Jewish mysticism.

Early Kabbalah, Jewish mysticism, was apparently greatly influenced by the Persian apocalyptic religions. Groups such as the Essenes (see fact 321) describe what would happen in the final battle of good versus evil.

Influenced by the Greeks, early kabbalists (Jewish mystics) also speculated about creation and the "End of Days." Like all mystical traditions, Kabbalah was stringently limited to an elitist group of scholars capable of understanding its mysteries. The Mishnah (see fact 357) states, "Whoever thinks about four things, it would have been better if he had never been created: what is above, what is below, what was before time, and what will be hereafter." However, this rule did not apply to the Tanna'im themselves.

Gradually the focus of Kabbalah switched to envisioning the divine realm itself. Our sages viewed the Divine as being both close and yet impossibly remote. It was impossible ever to actually understand the Divine, but it was possible to catch glimpses of the spiritual world which held the Divine throne. This concentration led to angelology.

The Book of Ezekiel (see fact 219) begins with the prophet's vision of the divine chariot, the Merkavah. The Merkavah became the symbol of early Kabbalah's search for the heavenly realm, and there are numerous descriptions of the Divine Throne and the angels' activities. This kabbalistic study is called Merkavah mysticism.

Early Kabbalah also concentrated on ways to ascend to the heavenly world (a process ironically called "descending to the Merkavah, the

Chariot,") while still alive. This process always involved asceticism and meditation.

It is important to note that Kabbalah was not a fad for kooks, as was once believed. We are told of four Tanna'im, involved in the Sanhedrin, who explored the transcendent realm, called "pardes" (paradise; see data to fact 105). One died; one looked and became mentally ill; one looked and became a heretic. Only Rabbi Akiva "ascended in peace and descended in peace." The fact that Rabbi Akiva and other sages were involved in this spiritual exploration emphasizes how "mainstream" Kabbalah was for the great scholars of that time. It continued to play a significant role in Jewish tradition, reaching its zenith in the 16th century (see fact 417).

356. Judah HaNasi edited the Mishnah.

At the end of the second century the Nasi of the Sanhedrin, Judah, had so much political influence with both the Roman authorities and the other rabbis that he succeeded in accomplishing a revolutionary legal step. He systematically wrote down the 500 years' worth of Oral Laws created by the rabbis, the Tanna'im. This huge task resulted in a six-volume set of laws called Mishnah.

357. The Mishnah is the written Oral Law.

The Mishnah, written in Hebrew, immediately became a Jewish best seller. Judah HaNasi (the Prince) edited all of the Oral Law material and presented it in the Mishnah, organized into topics. Groups of topics (called a tractate) were then placed into larger categories of related topics, called orders. Judah HaNasi (the Prince) included in his Mishnah both the majority viewpoints and the minority views. His writing style was terse and assumed legal knowledge on the part of the reader.

The six volumes of the Mishnah dealt with six major orders of Jewish law: agriculture, festivals, women's issues, civil/criminal law, sacrifices, and ritual purity. Within each order were the tractates (topics) further divided into chapters, and then into paragraphs. A paragraph was also called a mishnah.

358. Laws of the Tanna'im that didn't get into the Mishnah are called B'raitot.

Not every statement by the Tanna'im was included in the Mishnah. The rabbinic laws that didn't make it into the Mishnah were called B'raitot (the singular is Braitah). While originally preserved by the students of the Tanna'im, these legal statements were eventually redacted into a text of their own, the Tosefta. So long as they didn't contradict a law in the Mishnah, the B'raitot were considered to be legally authoritative.

359. *Pirkei Avot* (the Ethics of the Fathers), contain rabbinic wisdom about how to live.

Within the Mishnah there is one tractate that contains pithy sayings of the sages. Called *Pirkei Avot* (the Chapters of the Fathers), this tractate contains no halachic material. It serves as a moral blueprint for how a Jew should view the world, similar to the wise aphorisms in the Book of Proverbs. Because of its ethical focus, its common sense, and its simplicity, *Pirkei Avot* became very popular within Jewish tradition. Some scholars believe that it originally had five chapters and that a sixth was added to enable Jews to read a chapter each Shabbat during the weeks between Pesach and Shavuot (see data to fact 81). The tractate now consists of six chapters, and it is a custom to read a chapter a week between Passover and Shavuot.

In some cases, these simply stated, deeply thoughtful sayings provide our only insights into the personalities and thoughts of our sages. Even when we have aggadic material about some sages (see fact 334), no text makes our rabbis' ideas as clear as this tractate. The sayings in *Pirkei Avot* make our early leaders real for us when we read their aphorisms. The tractate is found at the end of the volume dealing with Civil/Criminal law.

The Talmudic Period

360. Rav took the Mishnah to Babylonia, where he established a Jewish law school.

As a written text of Oral Law, the Mishnah (see fact 357) became authoritative for all Jews. One of Judah HaNasi's students, Rav, took a copy of the Mishnah and headed for Babylonia, where a large community of Jews had been living since the exile (see facts 218, 220). This community, while relying on Palestine's rabbis for certain decisions, had established its own Jewish hierarchy. Rav united with Samuel, the leading Jewish authority in Babylonia, and set up a legal academy. His primary topic was, of course, the Mishnah. The system for learning Mishnah included asking questions and talking with the text. Statements of previous sages were quoted and discussed. Arguments over the Torah origin for each Tanna'itic statement raged. The law students in the academies created conversations with the now-dead Tanna'im and continued the debates over generations.

361. Amora'im were Jewish law students who discussed and argued about the laws in the Mishnah.

The law students who discussed and fleshed out the Mishnah were called Amora'im. One of the significant assumptions of the Amora'im was that generations closer to the revelation at Mount Sinai understood Torah better than later generations. It therefore became a rule that Amora'im were not permitted to contradict the Tanna'im concerning a specific law. This principle of later generations not superseding earlier halachah (see fact 342) has continued to this day in the traditional Jewish community. It is because of the assumption that the farther we are from Sinai, the less we know, that modern Orthodox rabbis are either unwilling or tremendously cautious about initiating changes within the tradition.

362. The discussions about the Mishnah by the Amora'im are called the Gemara.

According to tradition, the ongoing discussion and exploration of the Mishnah by the Amora'im continued in oral form for three hundred years, with each generation of scholars continuing the discussion from previous generations. These discussions included personal stories about the Amora'im, their beliefs, their lives, and their relationships. These discussions, stories, comments, and arguments of the Amora'im are called the Gemara.

363. Mishnah + Gemara = the Talmud.

The Mishnah plus the discussions, arguments, comments, and stories of the Amora'im are what we call the Talmud. Frequently we will emphasize the discussions and arguments by referring to the Talmud as the Gemara. It is also called the "Shas," an acronym for *Shishah S'darim* (*The Six Orders*).

The ongoing explorations of the Mishnah by the Amora'im took place in both Babylonia and Israel. The result was two separate works: the Babylonian Talmud (see fact 364) and the Palestinian Talmud (see fact 365).

364. According to tradition, Rav Ashi in Babylonia wrote down the Gemara and the Mishnah in 500 C.E.

According to tradition, Rav Ashi edited and wrote down the Gemara as it related to each mishnah (paragraph) of the Mishnah. His editing was finally finished (according to tradition) by a scholar named Ravina.

Most modern scholars believed the process continued long after Rav Ashi. As a matter of fact, in all likelihood the contents of the Babylonian Talmud (the Mishnah and the discussions of the Babylonian academies) remained fluid until the time of Yehuddai the Gaon in the 760s C.E. if not later.

The only written copies of the Talmud were on parchments, and most communities had only small portions of the enormous work. Because of his good relations with the Muslim authorities, Yehuddai was able to make the Talmud authoritative for the Jewish community by firmly establishing many of the laws dealt with in the Talmud.

365. The Jewish law school in Tiberias also created a Talmud.

While Rav and Samuel were creating their Babylonian academy, the Palestinian Amora'im were involved in their own exploration and discussion of the Mishnah and the statements of the Tanna'im. The Amora'im in Palestine succeeded in only partially editing and redacting their discussions of the Mishnah. The resultant document of Mishnah plus Gemara (discussions) from Palestine is called the Palestinian Talmud (or the Yerushalmi, the Jerusalem Talmud, although it was not created there). Scholars do not agree about the reasons for the partial editing of the Palestinian Talmud (see fact 370).

Thus there are two Talmuds: a Babylonian Talmud, much larger and more fully edited with more discussions and materials included, and a Palestinian Talmud. When we refer to The Talmud, we usually mean the Babylonian Talmud.

366. Most of the Gemara is written in Aramaic.

The Talmud was written in the language of the people, Aramaic. However, the legal arguments are in "legalese," understandable to the "professionals," the rabbis. Just as we would have difficulty picking up and understanding a case book of law, it is hard to understand the Talmud without studying it with a knowledgeable teacher.

Moreover, in its arguments the Talmud rarely provides a conclusive answer. It contains the questions, challenges, and discussions of the Amora'im but frequently leaves the discussion without a stated solution. It is not possible to read Talmud: one must study it.

367. The Talmud is the beginning resource book for all Jewish law.

With a huge ocean of rabbinic ideas recorded on parchment, the Talmud became the resource book for learning Jewish law. All points of halachah, Jewish law, were first referred back to the Talmud, the combination of Mishnah and Gemara. Because the Babylonian Talmud is more complete and better edited than the Jerusalem Talmud (see fact 365), it became the authoritative resource for the Jewish people. It helped that Babylonia had become the recognized center of Jewish thought.

368. The exilarch represented the Babylonian Jews to the non-Jewish authorities.

We don't know the political structure of the Jews in Babylonia before 226 c.e. In all likelihood there was a political liaison between them and the Parthians, the rulers of the country. In 226 c.e. the Sassanids conquered the country. It was at that time that Samuel (see data to fact 360) succeeded in becoming the political head of the Jewish community, answerable to the Sassanid leader. His position received an official title: Exilarch. The exilarch became a dynastic position because, according to tradition, Samuel's family could trace its roots back to King David, thus placing him and his family in line for eventual Jewish kingship (which never happened, of course). At the same time, Rav (see fact 360) became the head of the legal academy. His title was Rosh Yeshivah.

369. From 200 to 1000 C.E. the greatest Jewish cultural centers were in Babylonia.

Because of the secure relationship between the Sassanid leaders and the exilarch (see fact 368), the Babylonian Jewish community thrived. When the Muslims took over (see fact 371), they retained the same political organization. The exilarch was the liaison between the Jews and the caliphate. The Rosh Yeshivah (see fact 368) was the authority on Jewish law and its interpretation in the academies. From the academies in Babylonia came legal decisions that affected world Jewry. Influenced by the rich Muslim culture, Babylonian Jews became involved in medicine, astronomy, mathematics, and poetry.

370. The Jews suffered under Byzantine rule.

In 325 C.E. after the Council of Nicea, Emperor Constantine declared Christianity to be the official religion of the Roman Empire. Five years later he moved the capital of his kingdom to Constantinople, thus creating what we call the Byzantine Empire. From 330 until 1453, when the Ottoman Turks conquered Constantinople (see fact 499), Jews lived within the Byzantine Empire. For the vast majority of that time, they suffered. Because of Christian doctrine, the Jews were viewed as a base, vile group, and they were brutally discriminated against. The Byzantine emperors regularly established new laws to restrict and punish the Jewish community. These restrictions set the precedent for later brutality against the Jews in Western Europe. It was a capital crime for a Jew to convert a Christian (see data to fact 586), and it was a capital crime for a Jew to marry a Christian.

Constantine's mother, Helena, became a devout Christian and traveled to the Holy Land. There, she pointed out the exact spots where

Jesus performed many of his miracles, and she found the cross on which he was crucified. Helena's visit resulted in the creation of numerous churches and monasteries, which became holy sites for Christian pilgrims who now flocked to the Holy Land (see data to facts 324, 325).

Soon thereafter, the Amora'im in Tiberias wrote down their discussions, thereby creating the Jerusalem Talmud. Some scholars believe they did so because their community was threatened. Other scholars do not accept this theory. At any rate, the Tiberias Jewish academy continued to function, writing piyyutim (see fact 291), midrash, and some responsa (see fact 376). Gradually, however, the Babylonian Jewish leaders gained political power throughout the Jewish world (see facts 371–374). Communities turned to the legal academies in Babylonia for authoritative Jewish decisions.

In the sixth century in Palestine, Jews were officially forbidden to build new synagogues. Ironically, it was during this period that the beautiful synagogues with mosaic floors were created (see fact 481), proving that the Byzantine laws weren't necessarily enforced.

In the seventh century, Jews living in the Land of Israel united with the Parthians in a revolt against the Byzantine Empire. The Byzantine emperor, Heraclius, defeated the Parthians and began a systematic slaughter of the Jews. The Jews were spared only because a new power, Islam arose in the Middle East (see fact 371).

The Geonic Period

371. In the seventh century, Muslims from Africa conquered the Middle East, North Africa, and Spain.

While Heraclius was punishing the Jews in Jerusalem, the Middle East was overwhelmed by a new religion, Islam. Coming from Arabia, the followers of Mohammed, Islam's founder, conquered Spain, North Africa, Egypt, Syria, Israel, Babylonia, India, and parts of Afghanistan. They gave their victims a choice: convert or die. The two exceptions were Jews and Christians, who were permitted to keep both their religion and their heads.

From 661 to 750 the Ummayad dynasty ruled the Muslim world. They kept administrative powers in their own hands and kept foreigners out of government. The Ummayad government center was in Damascus, but Jerusalem was always considered a holy city because it was from there that Mohammed leaped into heaven (see data to fact 495). In order to attract pilgrims on their way to Mecca, the Damascus caliph ordered a large shrine to be built on the Temple Mount on the spot from whence he leaped. He also built a magnificent mosque to dwarf the Christian's Holy Sepulchre. Through these projects, the caliph succeeded in making Jerusalem the third holiest site for the Muslims (see facts 494–496).

In 750 c.e. the Abbasid dynasty took over. They relied on local leaders to administer their own groups and established their headquarters in Baghdad, Babylonia. They were willing to allow Jewish leaders to run their own community, thus providing the exilarch in Babylonia with tremendous authority over the Jewish world.

372. The gaon was the head of the Babylonian law schools.

The Rosh Yeshivah (see data to fact 368) received a new title: the head of the Babylonian academies was called Gaon. He was generally recognized as the greatest scholar of his generation, and his decisions were viewed as authoritative. With the editing and codification of the Talmud, the authority of the gaon increased.

Even after the Babylonian academes lost their authority (see data to fact 384), the title Gaon was used to designate an outstanding scholar and legalist.

373. The gaon was responsible for making the Talmud available to world Jewry.

The gaon's first responsibility was to disseminate the newest Jewish best seller, the Babylonian Talmud, to Jews around the world. Since all texts were still handwritten, this alone was a huge task. Equally important, these texts had to be amplified and explained by the gaon. By concentrating on the decisions found in the Babylonian Talmud, each gaon succeeded in diminishing the authority of the Jerusalem Talmud.

374. Answers to questions about halachah are called responsa.

The Talmud rarely gives a definitive legal decision. Doing that became the authoritative responsibility of the gaon. Moreover, many of the Talmudic discussions led to further questions which needed legal decisions. As new situations arose, rabbis from North Africa, Rome, Egypt, and even Palestine would send their questions to the gaon. His answers were recognized as being authoritative halachah. These questions from rabbis to the gaon and his subsequent answers were called responsa, teshuvot. From the seventh through the eleventh century more than 100,000 responsa were written, creating an ocean of legal decisions that formed the practices we are familiar with today. Unfortunately, the vast majority of these responsa were lost, since the geonim (plural of gaon) rarely kept copies of their answers.

375. The Gaon Amram wrote the first Siddur.

The first Siddur was originally part of a responsum (see fact 374) by Amram the Gaon. He was asked by a Spanish rabbi to list the necessary prayers in order, and he did so, thus creating the first official prayerbook (see fact 290).

376. The responsa helped unify world Jewry for a while.

Because of the responsa process (see fact 374), the authority of the gaon became paramount and, more important, world Jewry was united under a single legal authority. This unity had tremendously beneficial consequences for the Jewish community. They could serve as merchants between warring nations and be guaranteed credit from their Jewish brethren. They didn't have to carry cash, which could be stolen by pirates and robbers. Universal Jewish law, halachah, guaranteed Jewish merchants fair trade practices among their foreign brethren, and this protection provided them with tremendous advantages over the disorganized non-Jewish merchants.

377. Saadia Gaon wrote the first medieval book of Jewish philosophy.

Probably the greatest gaon was Saadia (882–942 c.e.). Living during the Muslim period, when the Jewish intelligentsia spoke Arabic and were fairly easily accepted into the Arab culture, he had the job of keeping Jews Jewish. This was not an easy task. Think about America today. We dress, speak, and think American Western culture. We know some Jewish tradition, but not much. Our primary concentration is on American matters. Wealthy Jews in Babylonia, North Africa, and Spain in the tenth century had a comparable situation. Like the Jews of Alexandria, they were attracted to the rediscovered Greek philosophers and many were considering rejecting their Jewish practices.

Saadia met this cultural crisis head-on and won. The high points of Muslim culture were its beautiful use of Arabic and its fondness for the Greek philosophers. Saadia wrote a philosophic work, *The Book of Beliefs and Opinions*, in magnificent, flowing Arabic. In it, he defended the rational underpinnings of Judaism and showed logically that every rational Jew could believe in the Torah as well as Aristotle and Plato. By applying both the accepted philosophical methodology and the language revered by the Muslim culture, Saadia succeeded in refocusing many semi-assimilated Jews back on Torah and halachah.

In addition, Saadia wrote the first Hebrew grammar book which explained how the holy language worked. He provided a Hebrew dictionary plus a compendium of rhyming words for Hebrew poets.

Saadia Gaon was the first to write an Arabic translation of the Bible. He included commentaries, explanations, and grammatical notes as well. His translation continues to be the authoritative Bible for Jews in Arab lands.

Saadia thus brought a new, rich understanding of Jewish tradition to the Babylonian academies and the Jews living in the Muslim world. His philosophical work paved the way for future Jewish thinkers, and his approach to Torah influenced a century of Jews.

378. The Karaites were Jews who believed that the TaNaCH was divine but who didn't accept the authority of the rabbis.

Beginning in the eighth century, the rabbis encountered a major challenge. A group of Jews led by Anan ben David declared that they didn't accept the authority of the rabbis to interpret Torah. This group, originally called the Ananites, developed their own understanding of Jewish law based only on the Written Torah.

The Ananites were stricter and more rigid than the rabbis in their understanding of Torah law. Most Ananites believed it was prohibited to have any fire on Shabbat, even Shabbat candles. Many emphasized that Shabbat and holidays should be solemn, joyless times because of the destruction of the Temple. They were not really reformers of Judaism;

they simply didn't accept the rabbis as legitimate authorities of Jewish law. They denied the authority of the Mishnah and the Talmud.

It is difficult to determine the authoritative Ananite doctrines because the Ananites relied on their personal ability to interpret the Torah text. Anan's famous adage was, "Search thoroughly the Torah and don't rely on my opinions."

In the ninth century the major group of Ananites combined with other anti-rabbinic groups and became known as the Karaites, the followers of mikra, the Torah text.

379. Saadia Gaon opposed the Karaites.

The major rabbinic opponent of the Karaites was Saadia Gaon. He issued articles, letters, and responsa attacking the doctrine of the Karaites and even declaring that they were not Jews. The fury of his attack must have shocked the Karaites. They responded with their own letters and attacks, but their Arabic wasn't as good as Saadia's, and their defenses were less convincing. Saadia successfully defended rabbinic authority against the Karaite philosophical invasion.

The conflict between the Karaites and the Rabbanites (supporters of rabbis as authorities of Jewish law) continued in the Muslim-held lands into the eleventh century. The conflict then shifted to Europe. Karaites and Rabbanites didn't achieve some level of rapprochement until the sixteenth century. According to rabbinic law, Karaites are considered heretical Jews; they were treated as Jews in every country they lived in until the eighteenth century, when Russia annexed Poland (see fact 437). Catherine the Great then declared that Karaites were exempt from the double tax for Jews. From that time to the present, European countries, including Nazi Germany, distinguished the Karaites as being non-Jews. During the Holocaust, the Karaites were not slaughtered.

Karaites continue to view themselves as the true Jews.

The Crusader Period

380. The Golden Age of Spain lasted from 900 to 1300 c.e.

Despite high taxes under the Ummayads and the Abbasids, Jews prospered in Spain after the Arabs took over in 711 c.e. Jewish culture thrived next to Muslim culture, and the wealthier Jews assimilated many of the studies of their rulers. Thus in the tenth century, Jews in Spain, equally fluent in Hebrew and Arabic, studied medicine, poetry, the Koran, Jewish law, mathematics, astronomy, and philosophy.

Under tolerant Muslim rulers, Jews of Spain attained high political and social positions.

381. The Muslims who slaughtered Jews in Spain in the 1100s were the Almohads.

The Golden Age of Spain (see fact 380) had its brass side as well. The average Jew was still considered a second-class citizen. There were laws discriminating against him, and there were political tensions. In the twelfth century a group of zealous Muslims streamed through Spain giving Jews the choice of converting or dying. Many of our most famous Jewish scholars of that period fled before the Almohads.

382. Thousands of Jews were slaughtered in Europe during the First Crusade.

In 1095 Pope Urban II declared a holy war, a Crusade, against the Muslims to make the Holy Land Christian again.

Meanwhile, the feudal system in Europe was beginning to break up. The common folk were starving and undirected. There were serious droughts and a famine in 1095.

With Urban's call and the Church's support, thousands of towns-people found a direction for their frustration and hate. With rabble-rousers leading them on, mobs formed intending to march to the Holy Land and kill the enemies of Christ.

According to many of the rabble-rousers, however, there was a traditional enemy of Christ much closer than the Holy Land: the Jews in the Rhineland. Before the knights of Europe had even started to get organized, a "Crusade" of Christian mobs was declared. From these ranks were heard the words of a respected knight, Godfrey of Bouillon, stating that he wouldn't leave his country for the Holy Land until he had avenged the crucifixion by spilling a Jew's blood with his own hands.

The mobs attacked the wealthy Jewish communities in the Rhine-land. More than 1,000 Jews were slaughtered at Worms. In Mainz, more than 1,300 Jews lost their lives. Before the Crusaders ever left Europe, more than 10,000 Jews lay murdered.

383. Kiddush HaShem was Jewish martyrdom.

Kiddush HaShem means literally, the Sanctification of the Name (of God). In the Talmud it was understood as the willingness to die as a Jewish martyr. Kiddush HaShem was declared obligatory for only three commandments. A person had to suffer death rather than (1) commit idolatry, (2) commit a forbidden sexual offense, (3) commit murder. Given the choice between committing one of those three acts or dying, our sages declared a person must choose, as Kiddush HaShem, the Sanctification of God, to die. For all other forced transgressions, our sages emphasized, a person should commit the transgression and live.

Although it was historically connected to the Hasmonean Revolt (see facts 39–41) and to the persecutions of Rome, Kiddush HaShem became commonplace during the Crusades. The Crusades created the first experience of large numbers of Jews dying for Kiddush HaShem. Jewish women fearing rape and violation chose to die for Kiddush HaShem.

The Crusaders, in their zealous efforts to rid their countries of infidels, frequently tried forcing Jews to convert. Although some acquiesced, most Jews viewing conversion as idolatry, chose to die instead, thus making Kiddush HaShem a historical reality.

384. Rabbenu Gershom limited all Ashkenazic Jewish men to one wife at a time.

By the middle of the tenth century the authority that Babylonia held over the other Jewish communities had begun to diminish. Rabbis had established their own legal schools in Spain, North Africa, and Germany. For a while, these new Jewish centers relied on the responsa from the geonim (plural of gaon; see facts 372–374) of Babylonia. Gradually, however, the differences in lifestyle and the distance from Babylonia to Spain and Germany encouraged the heads of the German and Spanish legal academies to issue their own authoritative decisions. These became binding on their communities and marked the beginning of the end of the period of the Babylonian Geonate. Babylonia's academies lost their authority over the rest of the Jewish world.

The most obvious split between the Babylonian academies and the German academy in Mainz took place at the beginning of the eleventh century. The leading German rabbi was Gershom, known by German Jewry as Rabbenu Gershom (our Rabbi, Gershom). According to tradition, Rabbenu Gershom wrote four special ordinances which differed with Babylonian halachah (and Spanish halachah, for that matter). First, Rabbenu Gershom declared that a man could have only one wife at a time. This ruling was revolutionary. According to the Mishnah and the Talmud, a man could have four wives at the same time (provided he could keep them fed, clothed, and sexually satisfied). This law continued in both Babylonia and Spain, where Muslim law permitted more than one wife. In Germany, however, where Christian law definitively forbade bigamy, Rabbenu Gershom decreed that only one wife was permitted. This law became binding for all Ashkenazic Jews and established a major cultural split between Sephardic and Ashkenazic Jewry.

In addition, Rabbenu Gershom decreed that a woman had to agree to a divorce before a man could give her a get (see fact 268). He also made it a major sin to open and read someone else's mail, thus ensuring the privacy and safety of mercantile transactions between Jewish communities (see data to fact 376). Finally, Rabbenu Gershom forbade Jews to remind a Jew forced to convert to Christianity of his previous shame (see data to fact 383).

Modern scholars challenge whether all these ordinances were actually decreed by Rabbenu Gershom. However, they so clearly marked a change in German Jewry's reliance on Babylonia that they remain significant.

385. Samuel HaNagid was a Jewish general for the Muslims in Spain.

The most successful of the Jews living in Spain in the eleventh century was Samuel HaNagid. Born in Cordoba, Samuel received traditional Jewish training. In addition, like many upper-class Spanish Jews, Samuel also learned Arabic, the Koran, and philosophy.

The vizier of Granada was so impressed with Samuel's Arabic, that he advised King Chabbus to hire him. From tax collector to scribe, to assistant to the vizier, Samuel rose through the political ranks.

In 1027 the Jews of Granada recognized Samuel as the head of the Jewish community, the Nagid. By 1038 Samuel HaNagid was both vizier of Granada and commander of the Muslim army. For the rest of his life Samuel HaNagid led the army in a series of successful wars. He wrote poetry and was the top advisor to the king. He was an authority on Jewish law in Spain and maintained good relations with the Jewish authorities in Babylonia.

According to some scholars, Samuel HaNagid became the patron of a young, brilliant poet and philosopher, Solomon Ibn Gabirol. However, after subsidizing this brash young poet, Samuel dropped his patronage because Ibn Gabirol criticized his poetry. It has been suggested that tension increased between the two because Ibn Gabirol's works were viewed more favorably than Samuel HaNagid's. This is all conjecture.

Warrior, poet, Jewish authority, patron of the arts, and vizier, Samuel HaNagid epitomized the ideals of the wealthy Spanish Jews in the tenth and eleventh centuries.

386. Rashi wrote the most important commentary to almost every verse in the TaNaCH.

Rashi was the outstanding biblical commentator of the Middle Ages. He was born in Troyes, France, and lived from 1040 to 1105, surviving the massacres of the First Crusade through Europe.

He was a fantastic scholar and studied with the greatest student of Rabbenu Gershom in Mainz. At 25 he founded his own academy in France. Rashi's commentary on the Bible was unique. His concern was for every word in the text which needed elaboration or explanation. Moreover, he used the fewest words possible in his commentaries. Most of his explanations were not written by him. Apparently, students would ask him questions about the text, or he would rhetorically ask questions about specific words, and a student would write his short, lucid answers in the margin of the parchment text. These answers comprised Rashi's commentary. We now have the answers, but the trick to studying Rashi is to figure out what the problem was with the text or the grammar of a given word. Besides explaining individual words, Rashi also made use of the great oceans of midrash. However, instead of just quoting the early rabbis, Rashi applied the stories specifically to the Bible text, often abridging them. He assumed that his students knew the midrash; he just emphasized its immediate relevance to the TaNaCH.

Rashi is also important for students of French. Many words in the Bible were unknown to Rashi's students, and obviously they would ask what a particular word meant and Rashi would give the answer in Old French using Hebrew transliteration. These transliterations provide important insights into the development of French and its pronunciation.

The original printed Bible text by Bomberg (see data to fact 245) included Rashi's commentary. That commentary became so popular that there are now more than 200 commentaries on his commentary. It is assumed in traditional circles that when you read the TaNaCH, you also read Rashi.

387. Ibn Ezra was a great TaNaCH commentator.

The Golden Age of Spain produced some magnificent Jewish scholars. One of these was Abraham Ibn Ezra. Born in 1089, Ibn Ezra was a friend of Judah HaLevi (see facts 392, 393). Tradition maintains that Ibn Ezra married Judah HaLevi's daughter. After three of his children died and one son converted to Islam, Ibn Ezra became a wanderer. It was during his self-chosen exile that he wrote his brilliant works.

Ibn Ezra was a poet, astrologist, scientist, and Hebrew grammarian. All the Hebrew grammar books to that time had been written in Arabic. When he discovered that the Jews of Italy didn't understand Hebrew grammar, he wrote an excellent Hebrew grammar book which became a best seller.

In his travels, he met Rabbenu Tam in France (see data to fact 390), and they apparently discussed halachah and Torah.

Ibn Ezra's most famous work was his commentary on the Bible. Unlike Rashi, Ibn Ezra didn't want to use midrash in his explanations. He concentrated on the grammar and the literal meaning of the text. His most controversial beliefs were all couched in very careful language; scholars suspect that Ibn Ezra did not believe that the Torah was written by Moses on Mount Sinai. He found seams and grammatical problems which indicated that the Torah was written over a period of time. He didn't dare proclaim this opinion openly; it would have meant his death. However, there are hints of his suspicions within his commentary.

388. On every page of a traditional TaNaCH, the commentaries of Rashi and Ibn Ezra surround the text.

Ibn Ezra's biblical commentary was considered so important that when Bomberg printed Rashi's commentary on the inside margin of each TaNaCH page, he printed Ibn Ezra's commentary on the outside margin of the page (see data to fact 245).

389. Rashi wrote the most widely read commentary to the Talmud.

Rashi's commentary on the Talmud was even more important than his TaNaCH commentary. The Talmud was written in legalese: terse, unexplained language with no punctuation. Rashi provided a simple explanation of all Gemara discussions. He explained all of the terse phrases; he explained the principles and concepts assumed by the Amora'im. His simple, brief explanations for practically every phrase of the Gemara made the Talmud understandable to the nonscholar. It became an instant best seller and, to this day, it is unthinkable to study Talmud without studying Rashi's commentary at the same time.

390. Surrounding the text on every page of the Talmud is Rashi's commentary on the inside and the Tosafot on the outside.

Rashi's explanations and commentaries on the Talmud were so important that for almost a hundred years after his death, Talmud students in France and Germany concentrated their brilliant minds on discussing and elaborating on Rashi's commentary. Just as the monks were concentrating on deep philosophical discussions of Christian theology, France's Jewish scholars were focusing on the Talmud and its text. Their complicated (and sometimes convoluted) commentaries were called Tosafot (Additions). The scholars who created these additions were called the Tosafists (Those Who Added).

The most famous of these Tosafists was Rashi's grandson, Rabbenu Tam, who frequently disagreed with his grandfather. Today on every page of Talmud you can find Rashi's commentary surrounding the text on the inside of the page, and the Tosafot surrounding the text on the outside of the page.

391. Meir of Rothenberg was one of the great Tosafists.

Meir ben Baruch (1215–1293) was considered the greatest Jewish scholar and judge in Germany during the thirteenth century. By the time he was 34, despite the fact that he held no official title, Jewish communities were already turning to him for authoritative judgments.

Almost a thousand of his responsa are extant, and they had a tremendous impact on Ashkenazic customs and law. Moreover, his students became recognized authorities on halachah, and they frequently cited his legal positions, customs, and habits.

In 1286 Rudolph I of Hapsburg became emperor of Germany. He insisted on taxing the Jews as slaves of the treasury. Rabbi Meir, outraged, led a mass exodus of Jews from Germany. He was betrayed, and Rudolph I imprisoned him, insisting that the Jews of Germany recognize his right to tax them as slaves of the treasury before he released their beloved rabbi. The Jews offered Rudolph 23,000 pounds of silver as a ransom but not as a tax. Rudolph refused, and Rabbi Meir remained in prison until his death.

Rabbi Meir's commentaries (see fact 390) to the Talmud covered eighteen tractates, an impressive amount of legal material.

Spanish Jewry

392. Judah HaLevi wrote poems about Zion.

One of the greatest poet/doctors produced during the Golden Age of Spain was Judah HaLevi (1075–1141). He made his living as physician to the Spanish king and his nobles, specializing in diseases of the rich and powerful. In his spare time he wrote more than 800 poems in as many styles as were known in Arabic-loving Spain. He wrote more than 350 piyyutim (see fact 291) and many poems mourning the fact that he and other Jews were not in their Holy Land. Judah HaLevi's religious attachment to the Land of Israel influenced Jews for almost a thousand years. His eloquent longing for a return to Zion resonated in the hearts of all Jews who saw themselves living in exile.

393. Judah HaLevi wrote *The Kuzari*.

Judah HaLevi elaborated his position on Israel in his brilliant philosophical book, *The Kuzari*. Basing his plot on the true story of a tribe, the Chazars, who converted to Judaism, he described how the king of Chazar decided to choose a religion.

The king invited a Muslim, a Christian, and a Jewish philosopher to his court to describe their religions. Obviously, the Jewish philosopher was the most convincing, and the book ends with the king of Chazar becoming a Jew. Judah HaLevi describes, through the book's Jewish philosopher, the unique traits of the Land of Israel: just as some land is more fertile than other land, the Land of Israel is the only place in the world where prophecy can occur. Just as some languages are more capable of expressing poetic feelings and emotions, only the holy tongue, Hebrew, was capable of receiving divine prophecy. In addition, according to Judah HaLevi, just as some beings are more naturally adept at physical prowess or intellectual pursuits, only the Jew has the elevated soul to allow him to achieve a special covenant with God. Thus the most special relationship a human could have with the Divine would be attained by a Jew in the Land of Israel speaking the holy tongue. *The Kuzari*, while using traditional Platonic logic to show the natural distinctions between land, language, and living beings, thus became a powerfully particularistic treatise affirming the special nature of the Jew. It is not a book we quote during National Brotherhood Week.

394. Benjamin MiTudelo traveled around the world describing different Jewish communities.

We don't know why Benjamin MiTudelo journeyed around the Jewish world in the 1100s. Since he left at the time of the Almohads (see fact 381), he might have been fleeing their persecution. Yet he traveled leisurely for more than five years (some scholars believe fourteen years). There is some speculation that he was a gem dealer. We know nothing else about him except that he wrote a detailed, fairly impersonal description of everything he saw and heard. His book became invaluable to scholars interested in the lifestyles of communities in the twelfth century. Benjamin traveled around the entire north coast of the Mediterranean (the south coast would have put him into Almohad country), stopping in major communities in France, Italy, Greece, Turkey, and the Land of Israel. Like other Jewish travelers, Benjamin associated all Roman and Greek ruins with moments in Jewish history. He was especially interested in the economic conditions and professions of the different communities, and his book has detailed descriptions of daily Jewish life in those communities. He was interested in the Jewish political hierarchy and in Jewish scholars.

From Israel, Benjamin headed north around the Fertile Crescent to Baghdad, where he spent a great deal of time, awed by the size and wealth of the community. He included in his book stories he heard about China, India, and Ceylon (much of it fantasy). His description of

Egypt (on his way home) was excellent. We know nothing about Benjamin once he returned to Tudelo and stopped writing. His book, however, is one of the most important twelfth-century documents for scholars.

395. Maimonides was the greatest medieval Jewish philosopher.

Maimonides (Moses ben Maimon) lived from 1135 to 1204. He was a brilliant doctor and Jewish legalist and the greatest Jewish scholar and philosopher of the Middle Ages. He had a more powerful impact on Jewish tradition than any other man. Maimonides was the quintessential rationalist, and he used his sharp, logical mind to systematize different aspects of Jewish life. He broke down complicated matters into simple lists, a brilliant pedagogic device. He was born in Spain (so he is a member of the Golden Age of Spain group), but when he was 13 his family fled the Almohads and settled in Fostat, near Cairo, where he quickly gained prominence.

396. Maimonides is called RaMBaM in Hebrew.

By taking the first letters of his name (Rabbi Moses Ben Maimon) and inserting vowels, tradition gave him the acronymic name RaMBaM. Most of the Jewish scholars during the Middle Ages received acronymic names.

397. RaMBaM wrote thirteen statements of Jewish faith.

One of RaMBaM's first major works was a commentary to the Mishnah (see fact 357). As befitted a scholarly Jew living in the Muslim world, he wrote it in Arabic. As an introduction to one tractate, RaMBaM wrote thirteen statements of Jewish faith. Our rabbis had always shied away from creedal statements, since our tradition emphasized Jews doing mitzvot. The Shema was understood as a bottom-line statement of faith, and it remained a mitzvah to say it, but it wasn't a controversial theological position (Adonai is our God, Adonai is one; see fact 300). With pressure from the Karaites and Muslim sects, RaMBaM felt that it was necessary to delineate philosophically the fundamental

Jewish beliefs. After much controversy, they became accepted by the traditional Jewish community, and they are sung today at services in the Yigdal hymn. They are as follows:

1. There exists a perfect God who created everything.
2. God is one.
3. God cannot be viewed in bodily terms.
4. God is eternal.
5. Jews pray directly to God with no intermediaries.
6. The prophets are true.
7. Moses was the greatest prophet.
8. The entire Torah was given to Moses.
9. The Torah is eternal and unchanging.
10. God knows what we do.
11. God rewards and punishes according to our actions.
12. The Messiah will come.
13. There will be a resurrection of the dead.

These thirteen statements of faith enabled Jews to determine who was a true believer and who a heretic. Obviously, they cause difficulty for some modern Jews. Many of us feel uncomfortable talking about God, and these articles of faith feel rigid. However, if we can view them as an attempt to fit Jewish belief into a logical set of measurable statements rather than as requirements for being part of the religion, they become less imposing. There is no imperative to accept the beliefs of a brilliant man in the twelfth century as binding upon us. It is important, however, to understand how Jews have viewed their faith over at least the past 850 years.

398. RaMBaM wrote the *Mishneh Torah*.

RaMBaM was a workaholic. He served full time as a famous physician for the vizier of the Caliph. He wrote influential letters to various Jewish communities which affected Jewish law. He wrote, in beautiful Arabic, the *Sefer HaMitzvot*, which listed the 613 command-ments found in Torah. In 1180 he completed his first enormous work, the *Mishneh Torah* (see fact 399), the Repetition of the Torah (or, more probably, the Second Torah). RaMBaM was not a particularly modest man. He intended that his *Mishneh Torah* would become the final word on all major halachic questions, and he wanted it to be as authoritative as the first Torah. He was concerned that all of the Talmudic arguments and subsequent responsa were overwhelming scholars and students, and he wanted them concentrating on more important issues such as Jewish philosophy and truth.

399. The *Mishneh Torah* is a fourteen-volume law code.

RaMBaM, (see facts 396–398) took all of the Talmudic arguments, all of the responsa, and all of the customs that had developed over the years in the Sephardic world, and he codified them *by topic* in fourteen volumes, the *Mishneh Torah*. He wrote in beautiful, simple Hebrew, thus making the halachah (see fact 342) available to anyone who wanted to read it. He left out all proof texts, and all rabbinic discussions. He thus created the first code of Jewish law. It was revolutionary, it was brilliant, and it infuriated the rabbinic world. How dare RaMBaM assume what the law was without citing Talmudic arguments! With the *Mishneh Torah*, normal Jews could understand halachah without the help of rabbis. It was outrageous! Despite the tremendous controversy created by the *Mishneh Torah*, it became the cited source for most subsequent Jewish legal works. All later codes of law referred back to the *Mishneh Torah*.

In Hebrew numerology, the number 14 is written Y D. Therefore, the *Mishneh Torah* is also called the Yad.

400. RaMBaM described eight rungs of tzedakah (giving to the needy).

RaMBaM included sections on medicine, metaphysics, astronomy, and science in his *Mishneh Torah* (see fact 399). He included a long section on the Messiah, with arguments proving that Christians and Muslims were mistaken in their beliefs. He also included a section about tzedakah, the mitzvah of giving to the poor. (see fact 579). Tzedakah means righteousness. In Jewish law it was understood that Jews were required to help the poor, not only because they felt sorry for the needy, but because it was their religious obligation to give. RaMBaM in the *Mishneh Torah* noted eight levels of giving, each more virtuous than the previous. These are giving:

1. reluctantly
2. less than one should, but cheerfully

3. enough, but only after being asked directly
4. before being asked
5. in a way so the giver doesn't know who receives the tzedakah
6. in a way so the receiver doesn't know who gave the tzedakah
7. in a way that neither knows who the other was
8. in the form of providing work or money so the receiver will not need tzedakah again.

401. RaMBaM wrote *The Guide of the Perplexed.*

Having set the rabbinic world into an uproar with his *Mishneh Torah* (see fact 399), RaMBaM proceeded to write what he considered his most important book. It took him ten years, but in 1190 he finished *Guide of the Perplexed*. Written in beautiful Arabic, the *Guide* was a brilliant book of Jewish philosophy. It was not intended for the masses. In RaMBaM's view, philosophy was reserved only for the intellectual elite, who would not be misled by it. The book was not meant simply to be read; it was RaMBaM's insights into the world and its truth written in a convoluted form utilizing brilliant contradictions.

In his introduction, RaMBaM explained how he hid truths among necessary falsehoods. Maimonides intended his book to be understood only by philosophers who understood his method. As a result, Jews have been arguing for 850 years over what RaMBaM really meant. He was an Aristotelian, and his brilliant mind systematically presented Judaism as a religion of reason. His philosophical proofs for the existence of God influenced Thomas Aquinas. His systematic description of the prophets fit into the Platonic framework of the philosopher-king. In short, his *Guide of the Perplexed* synthesized Jewish and Greek thought and made them mutually compatible.

His opponents suspected him of heresy (it is possible or even probable that RaMBaM did not believe in creation from nothing and certainly didn't believe in Divine Providence, a gap that contradicted his own Thirteen Statements of Faith (see fact 397), but the *Guide* was written so skillfully and subtly that it was impossible to create a concrete case against RaMBaM.

In many Jewish communities, however, his book was banned; in Montpellier, France, it was burned. To everyone's horror, RaMBaM's grave in Tiberias was desecrated.

Some communities tried to protect their impressionable youth from RaMBaM's *Guide*. It was ruled that only someone over 25 years of age was permitted to read it because younger minds might misunderstand its meaning and become corrupted. The *Guide* was definitely the most influential Jewish book of the Middle Ages.

402. Nachmanides is called RaMBaN in Hebrew.

One of the last great Spanish-Jewish scholars was Moses Ben Nachman, Nachmanides (1194–1270). He was known in Jewish tradition by the acronym RaMBaN (Rabbi Moses Ben Nachman). RaMBaN lived in Christian Spain and was greatly influenced by the French Jewish academies, especially the Tosafists (see data to fact 390). Living in Gerona, he was recognized as a brilliant scholar, and even the Christian king of Spain accepted his advice on some Jewish matters. He was a prolific writer of legal decisions and Talmudic discussions, and more than fifty of his treatises are extant.

In 1263 RaMBaN was involved in a disputation in Barcelona. An apostate, Christiani, had been failing at convincing Jews to convert to Christianity. He succeeded in getting the king to order a debate between him and RaMBaN to prove that Jewish texts actually recognized that Christianity was the superior religion. RaMBaN agreed on condition that he would have complete immunity for what he said. The king agreed. RaMBaN won the debate, which infuriated the Christian leaders. They charged RaMBaN with denigrating Christianity (which he had). RaMBaN appealed to the king, who protected him and recommended that RaMBaN leave Spain for a while. RaMBaN wisely fled.

403. RaMBaN was a great TaNaCH commentator who established a synagogue in Jerusalem.

RaMBaN, after fleeing Spain (see fact 402), eventually landed in the Land of Israel in 1267 and traveled to Jerusalem. There he found the Jewish community reduced to two animal-skin dyers. He immediately set about to establish a synagogue and yeshivah there. According to tradition, his fame was so great that hundreds of scholars flocked to Jerusalem to study with him.

RaMBaN continued to write on many Jewish topics, including mysticism. His most important work was finished when he was already settled in Israel, an old man. It was an enormous commentary on the Torah. RaMBaN included theology, his personal insights into the nature of humans, and his own ideas about the reasons for specific mitzvot. He systematically offered rational explanations for each commandment.

Like the commentaries of Rashi and Ibn Ezra, RaMBaN's commentary is found on each page of *Mikraot Gedolot* (see fact 245). Unlike their commentaries, however, RaMBaN's commentary is long. He sermonized, exhorted, and enriched his community with his Torah explanations.

Medieval Europe

404. Blood Accusations falsely accused Jews of killing non-Jewish children for Jewish ritual.

For more than two thousand years Jews have been accused of diabolically killing non-Jews for ritual purposes. One of the first Blood Accusations was made to Antiochus ɪv (the Greek king in the Chanukkah story; see fact 38). Antiochus was said to have found a non-Jew who claimed that Jews kidnapped him and held him for a year, fattening him up to be sacrificed.

In Europe the first Blood Accusation was in England in 1144. Jews were accused of kidnapping a child (William) and torturing him exactly as they had Jesus. This accusation led to riots and massacres of Jews. Until the 1600s, the primary Blood Accusation was that Jews needed Christian blood to reenact the crucifixion of Jesus. For this reason, the vast majority of Blood Accusations took place around Easter time. It was also believed that Jews used Christian blood to cure the bad effects of circumcision and prevent Jewish men from menstruating. Although Pope Innocent ɪv wrote a strong letter denying all of the above beliefs, the rumors and subsequent slaughters continued.

In the seventeenth century the Blood Accusations added another motif: Jews needed Christian blood for making their matzah. This became the classic Blood Libel accusation. The rational proofs by gentile leaders and Jews alike that Jews were forbidden to ingest any kind of blood had no effect on the mobs or the continuation of these accusations. Even Pope Clement xɪv was ignored by Christians about this matter. Czarist Russia used the Blood Accusations frequently to keep anti-Semitism high among the peasants.

405. England was the first country to expel all Jews.

Jews didn't settle in England in any significant numbers until 1066, when they followed Norman the Conqueror over from France. They served primarily as money lenders and bankers. Although a royal charter guaranteed them safety and special privileges in the early 1100s, the Jews in England faced tremendous anti-Semitism. The masses and the barons viewed them as part of the royal oppression. The kings viewed them as sources of revenue. After numerous Blood Accusations and riots, Edward ɪ found the Jews so poor that they no longer served any practical purpose. He therefore issued an edict in 1290 that all Jews were to be expelled from England by All Saints' Day. England became the first nation to expel all its Jews. It would not be the last.

406. Jews were forced to wear a "badge of shame" in all Christian countries.

Pope Innocent ɪɪɪ called the Fourth Lateran Council in 1215 in order to get support for a Crusade. At that time, the Council ordered all Christian communities to force all Jews to wear distinguishing markings on their clothes so Christians would not mistake them for fellow Christians. Many communities complied with this order, and for half a millennium Jews wore special badges on their chests. In England this badge was in the shape of two tablets. In some communities it was a yellow badge with a red bull's-eye. In Italy Jews were forced to wear a coarse red cape. French Jews wore a red and white circle on their chests. The most common badge was a circle of yellow cloth, at least a handsbreadth in diameter, which was called the "badge of shame." Although the law went unenforced during the modern years of enlightenment, Hitler reinstituted the order, forcing all Jews to wear a yellow Magen David on their clothes with the word "Jew" written on it. For that reason, many Jews remain sensitive about a yellow Magen David as decoration.

407. Christians burned huge carts filled with handwritten Jewish texts and scrolls, especially the Talmud.

One of the goals of Christian Europe's leaders was to convert the Jews to Christianity. So long as the recognized authoritative religious text was the Bible, they felt that they had a chance to convince Jews that according to their own religion, Jesus was the Messiah. In 1236 an apostate, Nicholas Donin, notified Pope Gregory ɪx that the Jews viewed the Talmud as being authoritative. He also claimed that the Talmud contained blasphemies against Jesus and Mary and attacks against the Church. Pope Gregory ix ordered an investigation of these charges. In France the Christian authorities confiscated all Jewish books in 1240. After a series of rigged disputations over the content of the Talmud and basic Jewish beliefs, the Talmud was condemned in 1242. Twenty-four wagon loads of handwritten texts were burned in Paris. Similar, although smaller, conflagrations took place throughout Europe.

In 1553 the pope declared the Talmud to be a blasphemous book, and a huge pyre of newly printed texts were burned. Over a thousand complete copies of the Talmud were destroyed.

408. Jews were accused of causing the Black Plague.

In 1348 the Black Death hit Europe. It was so devastating that between one-quarter and one-half of the entire population of Europe was wiped out. People naturally panicked. Huge numbers of Christians accused the Jews of causing the plague by poisoning the wells. They tortured Jews until they "confessed," and then they slaughtered or expelled the Jewish communities.

In many towns the Jews were slaughtered before the Black Death ever arrived. Pope Clement vi wrote an official letter decrying this madness. He pointed out that the Jews suffered from the Black Death as much as the Christians did and that the plague was punishment from God against the Christians for their sins. Many nobles and leaders tried vainly to protect "their" Jews, but they failed. Frenzied mobs slaughtered thousands of Jews and tortured thousands of others. Most serious, when the plague was over and Jews returned to their towns, the Christian population continued to view them as dangerous, despicable creatures, a view that was maintained through the centuries.

409. Jews were expelled from France.

The Jews were originally welcomed by the rulers of France. Charlemagne was favorably disposed toward the Jewish community because they brought special mercantile opportunities to his kingdom (see data to fact 376). Until the First Crusade, Jews enjoyed financial success in the various French provinces, but beginning in 1096 that situation began to change.

Despite the continued intellectual richness of Rashi and the Tosafists (see fact 390), the political situation for Jews worsened in France. The twelfth century saw numerous riots, persecutions, and heavy fines levied against the Jewish communities. Philip Augustus was especially harsh, imprisoning all wealthy Jews until they paid an enormous ransom and then expelling them from his kingdom.

The thirteenth century saw Blood Accusations, murders, expulsions from towns and small provinces, and Talmud burnings. During the fourteenth century various kings of the different French provinces blatantly squeezed as much money as they could out of the Jewish community. In 1394, when it became clear that the Jewish population was impoverished and no longer of any financial use to the crown, Charles vi forbade Jews to remain in the kingdom of France. There resulted a mass departure of Jews. Gradually the other French provinces either expelled Jews or made their lives so miserable that they voluntarily left. By 1501 there were practically no Jews within the present borders of France.

Christian Spain

410. Spanish Christians called Jews who had been forced to convert to Christianity "Marranos" (pigs).

In 1391 Christian mobs rioted through the Christian-held parts of Spain. Urged on by pious priests, they gave the Jews of Spain a choice: immediate baptism or death. Thousands of Jews chose death; thousands were fortunate enough to escape the mobs; the rest accepted baptism and officially became Conversos, New Christians.

There were tax and professional advantages to being a Christian in Spain, and many of these New Christians did very well economically. Although some of them did accept Christian doctrine, the vast majority of these forced Conversos maintained their Jewish identity in secret. There was much bitterness between Old Christians and New Christians. The Old Christians called the Conversos "Marranos," or pigs.

The Church was upset about the large number of baptized Christians who were suspected of practicing Jewish rites. That was a capital crime in the Church, and it didn't matter that the baptisms had frequently been forced. The Church tried putting pressure on the Spanish kings to get tough on Conversos and Jews. The kings compromised and added restrictions on Jews, leaving the Conversos alone. In 1415 the Talmud was banned; Jews were forbidden to leave the country, wear fancy clothes, trim their beards, or socialize with non-Jews. Another 35,000 Jews converted to Christianity.

In 1479 the two kingdoms of Aragon and Castille were united when Ferdinand and Isabella married. To maintain Christian support, they turned to the problem of the Conversos. In 1481 they invited the Inquisition (see fact 411) to investigate the Conversos.

411. The Inquisition was an investigative court set up by the Catholic Church to try heretical Christians.

The Inquisition was the investigative branch of the Church, an ongoing institution originally founded by Pope Gregory IX in the thirteenth century. Its job was to investigate cases of Christian heresy. Invited to Spain by Ferdinand and Isabella (see fact 410), the Inquisition began its procedures in southern Spain. A list was compiled of all Christians suspected of performing Jewish rites. These suspects were then either tortured into confession and condemned, or officially reconciled to the Church.

The sentenced Conversos were marched into the main square, where their crimes were cataloged. They were then burned at the stake. This burning was called *auto da fé*, act of faith. In Church doctrine, through death, the souls of the condemned were saved.

412. Torquemada, head of the Inquisition in Spain, caused the death of more than 13,000 people

In 1483 the Grand Inquisitor was Torquemada, the personal confessor to Ferdinand and Isabella. Under his direction, from 1483 to 1495 more than 13,000 Conversos (see fact 410) were put to death. Everyone knew that this number represented only a small group of the Christians actually practicing Jewish rites.

The Inquisition was frustrated in its attempts to purge the Church of this contamination, because of the ongoing ties between the Conversos and Jews. It was clear that the Jews were having a bad influence on Conversos and were a corruption of pure Christian Spain.

413. In 1492 Spain expelled all Jews from the country.

In 1492 Ferdinand and Isabella succeeded in conquering Granada, the final Muslim stronghold in Spain. All of Spain was now Christian.

From this new base of power, they decreed that all Jews were to be expelled from Spain by July 30, 1492. Anyone who wished to convert was welcome to stay in Spain. Conversos were forbidden to leave the country.

We don't know how many Jews were expelled from Spain. Estimates range from 100,000 to 250,000. According to tradition, the last Jews left Spain on August 2, corresponding to the Ninth of Av (see fact 93). In their desperate need to escape, thousands of Jews were cheated and slaughtered by ship captains and crews. Jews went to North Africa, Italy, Greece, and Turkey. Many found refuge in Holland. Scholars have been fascinated by the coincidence of three ships sailing under Christopher Columbus on August 2, 1492. Arguments continue over how many Conversos and Jews were involved in Columbus's voyage.

The expulsion from Spain marked the official end of an incredibly rich Jewish culture. The surviving Jews carried this culture to every haven and community they found. The Edict of Expulsion of the Jews from Spain was not rescinded until December 1968.

The vast majority of Spanish Jewry fled to Portugal. Some scholars believe that at least 150,000 Jews paid a special head tax to John II, the Portuguese king, to permit them temporary residence. In 1496 a new Portuguese king, Emanuel I, contracted to marry Spain's Princess Isabella, Ferdinand and Isabella's daughter. One of Ferdinand's conditions for his marriage was that Emanuel rid Portugal of all Jews. Emanuel reluctantly agreed and ordered all Jews to leave by November 1497. However, as Jews began to flee, Emanuel realized the financial losses he would incur with their departure. He devised another scheme: He ordered all Jews to be baptized as Christians. Nevertheless, the new Conversos continued to flee the country, so Emanuel issued an edict forbidding their departure. He then proposed that the Inquisition be brought into Portugal. It wasn't until 1531 that Pope Clement VII finally authorized an Inquisition in Portugal. Thousands suffered from the Portuguese tribunals. Conversos desperately tried to leave the peninsula, and the trickle continued through the sixteenth, seventeenth, and eighteenth centuries. Their primary haven became Amsterdam (see data to fact 433). The Portuguese Inquisition officially ended in March 1821. It was a horrendous time for Jews.

Ladino and Yiddish

414. Ladino, a combination of Spanish and Hebrew, was the language of Sephardic Jews.

The Jews expelled from Spain (see fact 413) had their own language, Ladino. Ladino began as a natural dialect of Castilian Spanish which included some Hebrew words. Sephardic Jews who found refuge in countries where Spanish was still spoken maintained Ladino as an almost-pure Spanish. The farther away from Spain they went, the more the Sephardic Jews changed the vocabulary, pronunciation, and morphology of Ladino. As a result, the Ladino dialects of Turkey and Italy are markedly different from the Ladino of Holland. Sephardic Jews incorporated a large number of Turkish, Arabic, Greek, and French words into Ladino. They also added some Hebrew. Ladino remains the language of many Sephardic Jews today. Until the twentieth century, Ladino was written with Hebrew characters rather than the Latin alphabet.

415. Yiddish is German mixed with Hebrew and Slavic words.

From the tenth to the end of the eighteenth century, Yiddish was the language of Jews from Holland all the way to the Ukraine. It was a primary unifying element for Ashkenazic Jews. Being able to communicate with fellow Jews across Europe provided us with a sense of community even though accents, words, and customs were different from region to region.

Yiddish was Middle German mixed with biblical Hebrew words. As Jews moved to the Slavic countries, and specifically to Poland, the Yiddish language incorporated more Slavic words and grammatical forms. Each regional dialect influenced the Yiddish of that particular area. Both Hebrew and regional words were merged into Yiddish, and Yiddish grammatical forms were used.

Like Ladino, Yiddish was written with Hebrew characters. Early Yiddish (900–1300) concentrated on translations and commentaries of the Bible. In the fourteenth century, biblical tales, midrashim, and homilies were written in rhyme. This form reached its zenith in the late sixteenth century with the famous book *Tzena Urena*, which became a very popular book for women.

Although Yiddish was threatened with extinction after the Holocaust (see facts 458–463), it has been making a remarkable comeback, especially at colleges and universities. In 1980 Aaron Lansky, a Jewish graduate student, founded the National Yiddish Book Center, whose purpose was to collect and save unwanted and discarded Yiddish books. By 1990 he and his co-workers had collected almost a million Yiddish books which would have been otherwise lost or destroyed. All duplicates were donated to major libraries.

With the advent of glasnost, Aaron Lansky began his plan to ship

9,000 Yiddish books to the Soviet Union to provide Soviet Jews with once-forbidden books (see data to fact 573). Such efforts guarantee the survival of Yiddish as a living language.

Europe in the Sixteenth and Seventeenth Centuries

416. The first ghetto was in Venice.

Ever since Jews began living outside the Land of Israel, they preferred to live in their own areas of cities and towns. In the Middle Ages they frequently received charters from the rulers of an area to establish their own quarter where they lived under Jewish law. These quarters were usually surrounded by a wall with a gate and tended to be in the poorer sections of the town or city. During the centuries when Jews relied on royal protection from the anti-Semitic lower classes, the wall and gate served to keep people out more than they kept the Jews in.

In 1516 Venice decreed that Jews had to live within the Jewish quarter. Because it was next to a foundry, or *ghetto* in Italian, the Jewish quarter in Venice was called a ghetto. It soon became law throughout Europe that Jews must live within the Jewish quarter of towns and cities. All these Jewish quarters were called ghettos.

417. Lurianic Kabbalah flourished in Tzfat in the 1500s.

Kabbalah, Jewish mysticism, reached its zenith in Tzfat under the charismatic leadership of Isaac Ben Solomon Luria, known as the Ari (1534–1572). Esoteric explorations into the hidden secrets of Torah had been going on among Jewish scholars for over a thousand years (see fact 355).

There are two separate foci of Kabbalah. One form is primarily theoretical: it attempts to understand the hidden secrets of the Divine and understand the Jew's role in the eternal universe. The other form is practical: it attempts to harness the power of the Divine and use it to change the world. Practical Kabbalah involves amulets against illness and evil spirits and even enables the advanced practitioner to bring clay to life (see fact 418). A student of Kabbalah who can commune with the souls of departed righteous Jews is functioning at a theoretical level, while a student of Kabbalah who heals a terminally ill person by using the divine name, is functioning at a practical level.

Through discussions with his disciples, the Ari provided a philosophical system to the discipline of Kabbalah which has influenced Kabbalah even to this day. He did practically no writing himself; his system and his teachings were written down by his primary disciple, Chaim Vital, after the Ari's death.

It is impossible to describe Lurianic Kabbalah, but, with the understanding that all descriptions are already false because words oversimplify, this is an attempt.

Prior to the appearance of the Ari, one of the primary cosmological realities of Kabbalah was that there are ten separate levels (called sefirot) of creation. The lowest and least spiritual level is, of course, our world, the physical. The Divine transcends all of these levels, but the Divine's emanations are the creative force for each of these levels.

The Ari began by noting the interrelationships of these different sefirot. Rather than being independent, they are interconnected and subgrouped, corresponding to five aspects of the Divine.

Luria concentrated on the process of creation. Originally, the Divine created with too much of the Divine's emanation. It was more than any creation could bear (even spiritual sefirot), and that original creation exploded, producing shards which poison all subsequent creations. Those shards are the source of evil in our world. In order for any creation to take place successfully, the Divine had to contract the creative emanations through the filtering sefirot. The sefirot thus acted like a set of screens, limiting the amount of divine emanation that could penetrate. This process of contracting the Divine emanation is *tzimtzum*.

Every Jew is directly linked to the Divine by soul emanations through both the sefirot and the physical world (a much lower level, of course). Through prayer, focus (kavannah; see fact 288), and mitzvot, it is possible for a Jew to be aware of the higher sefirot and, through them, to commune with past souls. The soul is a spark of the divine emanation within us. It is possible, through study, knowledge, and concentration, to send that spark back up through the sefirot while the Jew is still alive. The Ari laid great store in the hidden numerical meanings of Hebrew words to aid in this sefirot exploration.

Most important, the Ari taught that a Jew's actions affect the amount of divine emanation present within the world. Through mitzvot, a Jew can bring more holiness (more divine emanation essence) into the world. Through this process, a Jew can repair the world from the original damage produced by those exploding spiritual shards, that is, evil. This process of being able to repair the world is called tikkun olam (see fact 606). By bringing enough divine emanation into the world (via mitzvot) Jews could cause the Messiah to come.

Luria, with his charismatic personality, brought into his Kabbalah system the assumption that tikkun olam and the arrival of the Messiah were just around the corner. His ideas, disseminated by Chaim Vital, ignited the esoteric Jewish world and indirectly led to the powerful response Jews had to Shabbetai Tzvi (see fact 423).

418. Yehudah Loew of Prague was said to have built a golem.

Yehudah Loew of Prague was one of the outstanding Jewish minds of the sixteenth century. He wrote numerous books on Jewish law, philosophy, and morality.

Ironically, he is credited with the creation of a golem, an activity he would probably have opposed. A golem is a human figure created from clay and brought to life by use of the Ineffable Name of God. Since the letters of that name were considered to be the original source of life, it is thought possible for one knowledgeable in the secrets of the Divine Power to use them to create life (see data to fact 417).

Discussions of golems go back to the Talmud. Rava is said to have created such a man. In the sixteenth century numerous golems were said to have been created, but in each case their power increased and threatened human life, so they were destroyed by their makers.

Yehudah Loew of Prague was said to have created a golem to protect the Jewish community from Blood Accusations (see fact 404). It was close to Easter, and a Jew-hating priest was trying to incite the Christians against the Jews. The golem protected the community from harm during the Easter season. However, the creature threatened innocent lives, so Yehudah Loew removed the Divine Name, thus rendering the golem lifeless.

Today someone who is large but intellectually slow is sometimes called a golem.

419. Joseph Caro wrote the *Shulchan Aruch*.

Born in Spain in 1488, Joseph Caro moved to Turkey with his family. He became a brilliant Jewish scholar, and in 1522 he began writing his major work, the *Beit Yosef*, which took twenty years to complete. The *Beit Yosef*, written as a voluminous commentary to an earlier Jewish code, the *Tur*, was Joseph Caro's attempt to codify all of Jewish law. It was a huge undertaking because Caro tried to show the origins of all halachic decisions in his code before arriving at each decisive ruling. He applied Talmud, the huge ocean of responsa, Maimonides' *Mishneh Torah*, and the post-*Tur* legal decisions. He showed familiarity with all of the great legalists and included varying community customs.

Caro then wrote a short digest of all of the laws he had dealt with so extensively in the *Beit Yosef*. Aimed as a simple guide for young students, this digest listed in concise Hebrew what a Jew was supposed to do in each circumstance of life. Caro called it the *Shulchan Aruch, The Prepared Table*, because it made halachah available to even the simplest Jew. He assumed that the scholarly reader who wanted the legal background discussions would refer to the *Beit Yosef*.

420. The *Shulchan Aruch* is a code of Jewish law.

The *Shulchan Aruch, The Prepared Table*, became tremendously influential in the Jewish world because it was the first code actually to be printed. In the mid-1500s many more printed copies were available to the Jewish populace than were other, handwritten codes. As a result, the *Shulchan Aruch* quickly became popular and was hailed as a magnificent code.

However, because of Joseph Caro's Sephardic background, the *Shulchan Aruch*, did not include Ashkenazic and Polish customs. Therefore, although the text was available to them, Ashkenazic Jews were unwilling to accept the code as authoritative.

421. Moses Isserles wrote the *Mappah*, Ashkenazic additions to the *Shulchan Aruch*.

Moses Isserles, a great Polish rabbi, added a commentary of Ashkenazic customs to the *Shulchan Aruch* (see fact 420). First published in 1569, Isserles' *Mappah* (*Tablecloth*) was responsible for the *Shulchan Aruch's* being accepted as a major legal work.

It took several more commentaries and editions before the *Shulchan Aruch* became the code of Jewish law. However, traditional Jews today view Joseph Caro's *Shulchan Aruch* along with Isserles' *Mappah* as the accepted authoritative starting points for Jewish law. The process of expounding and amplifying halachah through modern responsa and papers continues to this day (see fact 426).

422. Chmielnitzky led Cossacks in riots against the Jews.

The 1600s were a horrific time for Jews in Central and Eastern Europe. The first group to suffer were those Jews who had remained in Germany. They were slaughtered and persecuted by both sides during the Thirty Years' War, from 1618 to 1648. Although this series of wars was primarily a conflict between Protestants and Catholics, the battles took place in villages where Jews and estate stewards lived, and they were indiscriminately attacked and massacred. The German Jewish community was bankrupted.

In Poland the Jews had served the landowners primarily as tax collectors, so the peasants developed the view that the Jews were the source of their poverty and misery. There was great animosity between the Polish serfs, the Cossacks, and the Jews, but the landowners protected their Jews.

In 1648, the year the Thirty Years' War ended, the Ukrainian peasants were organized by Bogdan Chmielnitzky to avenge the high taxes and poverty. Chmielnitzky hoped to establish an independent Poland with the Cossacks in charge. United with the Tatars and too powerful for the wealthy landowners to stop, Chmielnitzky and the Cossacks took revenge upon the Jewish communities of Poland. In two years, Chmielnitzky and the Cossacks savagely attacked and butchered more than 100,000 Jews. Thousands of others fled, creating serious refugee problems in Europe. It was another terrible blow for the Jews.

423. Shabbetai Tzvi was the false Messiah in the 1600s.

Shabbetai Tzvi was born in Smyrna, Turkey. The Jews there knew that he was an emotionally sick person; they tolerated his manic depressions and his fits of exhilaration combined with strange actions. As he grew older, however, some of his actions became too bizarre for them, and they banished him. Shabbetai Tzvi traveled to Palestine, where he met a charismatic self-proclaimed prophet named Nathan of Gaza.

Nathan declared that Shabbetai Tzvi was the Messiah and would throw off the yoke of the Sultan. Shabbetai Tzvi believed him. In 1665, pronouncing the Ineffable Name of God, Shabbetai Tzvi declared himself to be the Messiah. Hundreds of thousands of Jews believed him. Nathan of Gaza served as his press agent and sent reports of wonders and miracles to the entire Jewish world.

Word spread that the Messiah had arrived in the Land of Israel and was on his way to Constantinople to overwhelm the Sultan. In every community the "believers" threatened and cowed the nonbelievers. Major rabbis, wealthy community leaders, and mobs of people all declared Shabbetai Tzvi to be the Messiah. Mass hysteria ensued.

Jews from the Netherlands, Germany, Poland, and Italy sold their homes and began the long journey to Constantinople to join the Messiah. By 1666, hundreds of thousands of Jews were caught up in the madness.

The Sultan finally decided to put an end to this excitement. Shabbetai Tzvi, who had been under house arrest since 1665 as a precaution, was given an ultimatum: convert to Islam or die. Shabbetai Tzvi began studying the Koran. The Jewish world reeled. For the vast majority of his followers, it was inconceivable that the Messiah would be a Muslim. For the most fervent believers, however, this was simply another Messianic sign, and many converted to Islam.

Many reasons are given for his huge impact, and the incredible number of people who believed and followed Shabbetai Tzvi. First, the century had been filled with horrors, and devastated Jews were looking for solace from any quarter (see data to fact 422). The promise of the Messiah was a comfort they couldn't resist.

Second, the teachings of Lurianic Kabbalah, Jewish mysticism, which had developed in Tzfat in the 1500s, emphasized the imminent arrival of the Messiah. Those who studied Kabbalah were emotionally ready for the final redemption (see fact 417).

Third, when Shabbetai Tzvi wasn't depressed, he was apparently a remarkable personality, overwhelming all who met him with charm and emotive power.

Finally, the fact that the rumors began in the Holy Land, spreading from there to Europe, offered plausibility to the stories. Mass excitement convinced the skeptics, and much of Jewry joined in the feverish movement.

By 1667 the madness was over for most Jews. Hundreds of thousands were homeless, impoverished, and lost. The Thirty Years' War and Chmielnitzky devastated us physically; Shabbetai Tzvi, the false Messiah, wiped us out spiritually.

424. Pilpul was a skill to resolve all apparent contradictions in the Talmud.

Pilpul, which means "pepper" in Hebrew, was an accepted talmudic study technique even during the time of the Amora'im (see fact 361). Those engaged in pilpul are intensely aware of every nuance of talmudic language in order to make clever, insightful distinctions in the legal arguments presented.

In the fifteenth and sixteenth centuries pilpul became an art form for talmudic scholars. It was their way of showing their legal brilliance. The Tosafists had been involved in similar examinations of the Talmud (see fact 390). In the late seventeenth century, pilpul became the fad in Polish yeshivot. Students strove to show their knowledge and cleverness even at the cost of changing the intention of the Talmud and the meaning of its text. Students began with the assumption that, like the Torah, every word in the Talmud held its own significance. There could be no redundancy and certainly no contradictions in the text. They therefore used tremendously convoluted (albeit creative and sometimes brilliant) logical arguments to resolve all apparent contradictions and repetitions.

Historians have viewed this leap into pilpul in two different ways. One group (the modernist rationalists) saw pilpul as a symptom of the decline of fluid Judaism after the horrors of the 1600s. They saw the Rabbinic leadership abandoning the day-to-day needs of the common people and escaping into theoretical Talmud. This abandonment led to the rigidification of Jewish tradition and the subsequent need for Enlightenment.

Another group (modern traditionalists) saw pilpul as a symptom of the richness of Jewish life despite abject poverty and misery. Talmud became a Tree of Life to all students who grasped it, bringing comfort and support to our people. The traditionalists noted that legal decisions continued to be handed down, the community leaders continued to care about and for the people, but the level of physical poverty was just too great for most common people and so they turned toward practical kabbalah for succor.

Both viewpoints are probably true. Many great students fled into the Talmud as a refuge from the horrors of daily life, yet the rabbis still tried desperately to help their downtrodden people. At the same time, because of the aftereffects of Shabbetai Tzvi (see fact 423), they tried to limit the influence of charismatic leaders, especially those who were preaching Messianism or practical Kabbalah (see data to fact 417).

425. A beit din is a court of three rabbis.

One of the primary jobs of rabbis in Eastern Europe was to serve as judges and arbiters for the Jewish community. The most common court consisted of three rabbis and was called a beit din. Besides these ongoing courts, special arbitration courts of three rabbis were also established. Each litigant chose one rabbi, and the two rabbis then chose a third. Large cities could have many such courts, each one autonomous.

Smaller towns would depend on a single rabbi to make day-to-day legal decisions. If a serious case occurred, the rabbi would refer to a larger court. In many large Jewish communities, rabbis served quite specific functions. There would be a rabbi responsible for divorce decisions, one who supervised the butchers, one who served as overseer for tzedakah institutions, and so on.

From the mid-1500s to 1765 all of these courts were under the official authority of the Council of the Four Lands. This council served as the buffer between the Jewish community and the ruling governments of Poland, Lithuania, Estonia, and Galicia. It was responsible for providing the tax money. It also handled all serious cases within the Jewish community, and it ruled with an iron hand. The council controlled the punishment of cherem (excommunication), whereby a Jew was cut off totally from the Jewish community. The result was usually starvation, since the Christian community had neither the institutions nor the desire to help ostracized Jews.

The Council of the Four Lands also included rabbis who provided legal decisions which controlled the economic and social activities of the Jewish community. The council provided dowries for poor brides, sponsored yeshivot (plural of yeshivah), tried to help Jewish institutions, protected the jobs of Jews in communities by banning competitors from entering the towns, and jealously guarded its own political power.

426. A posek is recognized as a Jewish legal authority.

Each generation had its great rabbinical minds which were recognized by the community. These brilliant legalists had the authority (bestowed upon them by the community) to make new precedent law to meet new circumstances. Thus the responsa system continued even after publication of the *Shulchan Aruch*. This process of recognizing the great legal authorities of a given generation continues in the Orthodox community to this day. A rabbi with the authority to decide new cases is called a posek.

Chasidic Judaism

427. The Baal Shem Tov founded the Chasidic movement.

Despite all good attempts by the Council of the Four Lands to help communities and institutions, the plight of most Jews in Eastern Europe through the 1700s was almost unbearable. People had nothing. Many families couldn't afford to feed their children, so they sent the oldest boys to yeshivot (plural of yeshivah; see data to fact 340), where they had to fend for themselves. The yeshivot helped the boys establish meal days with families in the community. Each boy would try to get as many such meal days as he could; they were his only source of food. Families with eligible daughters would try to provide a meal day for the best students in the hope that one of the boys would eventually marry into the family, thereby bringing them honor. Talmud knowledge was to them the highest value and the most praiseworthy attribute in the divine order of the universe.

The vast majority of people were illiterate and ignorant and felt hopeless. Many people turned to "practical Kabbalah," magic, and superstition to provide some order in their lives. Miracle workers moved from community to community healing and providing amulets against the Evil Eye. They were called upon to exorcise dybbuks, wicked transmigrating souls which had entered emotionally disturbed people. These practical kabbalists, frowned upon by the rabbis, were called Baalei Shem, Masters of the Name. They used the power from the Divine Name of God to influence the world, producing magic.

Into this situation came Israel ben Eliezer from Moldavia. It is impossible to separate fact from fiction about him personally. However, he definitely had a gentle, special persona which attracted and impressed people. Although he didn't write anything himself, his followers did, and ideas credited to him changed Judaism drastically. His followers called themselves Chasidim, pious ones. Their movement was called Chasidut, the Chasidic movement.

428. Chasidic Jews believe that they can best connect with the Divine through joy.

Using the vocabulary of practical Kabbalah (see data to fact 417), Israel ben Eliezer emphasized that every Jew can get in touch with the Divine through kavannah (see fact 288), focus, and joy. By viewing the world with wonder, by offering one's soul to God, an ignorant Jew could get closer to the Divine than could a coldly logical talmudic scholar. This was a revolutionary idea, and it appealed to the common people for obvious reasons. The people credited Israel ben Eliezer with miraculous capacities. He was called a Baal Shem, a Master of the Name. However, because of his gentle soul and his effect on people, he was called the Baal Shem Tov, the Good Master of the Name (frequently mistranslated the "Master of the Good Name"). Taking the first letters of Baal Shem Tov (B, SH, T), they called him by the acronym BeSHT.

429. Chasidic Jews believe their leader, a Rebbe, has a special relationship with God.

Chasidic Jews believed that their leader was a tzaddik, a wholly righteous man. Originally, Jews followed the BeSHT (see data to fact 428) because of his special personality. They also followed his disciples because of their personalities. This element of personality cult was integrated into the Chasidic Movement.

One of the beliefs associated with Kabbalah is that the soul of each Jew consists of a spark of the divine emanation (see fact 417). In most of us, our physical needs, lusts, passions, and the like prevent us from being wholly in touch with the Divine. It is possible through kavannah (see fact 288), knowledge, and study to elevate our awareness so that we can feel our linkage with the Divine, but we can only be partially successful in this endeavor.

According to the Talmud, in every generation there are thirty-six wholly righteous Jews, tzaddikim (plural of tzaddik). The followers of the BeSHT understood a tzaddik to be someone who is not afflicted with the normal, human shell around his soul. These thirty-six tzaddikim (called lamed-vavniks) are capable of complete unity with the Divine while still alive. They possess insight into the Divine order of the universe unknown to the rest of us. Chasidic Jews believe that each of their leaders is one of those thirty-six wholly righteous men.

The leader of a Chasidic sect is called the Rebbe. The Rebbe's leadership transcends knowledge. It transcends the ability to be a posek. It is based on divine genetics, and Chasidic Jews believe that the trait of being a tzaddik is handed down from parent to son, thus creating dynasties of Rebbes.

430. Mitnagdim were Jews opposed to the Chasidic movement.

It should come as no surprise that the rabbis who were part of the institutions of Poland and Lithuania were horrified by the rise of the Chasidic Movement. Not only was this excitement among the common people personality-oriented (a frightening reminder of Shabbetai Tzvi and its aftermath); but its emphasis was on not needing to know Talmud or rely on the rabbis for getting close to the Divine. This idea threatened their authority because the Rebbes whom their followers considered to be tzaddikim were, for the most part, not great scholars. The rabbinic leaders feared violations of Jewish law through ignorance. They vigorously opposed the practices of the Chasidic Jews and were therefore called mitnagdim, the opposers.

Elijah ben Solomon Zalman, recognized as the most brilliant Talmudic scholar and legalist of the late eighteenth century, led the opposition against the Chasidic Jews. He taught in Vilna, Lithuania, the heartland of talmudic brilliance, and was therefore called the Vilna Gaon. In 1772 he recommended that all Chasidic Jews be placed in cherem (excommunication). He ordered that the books credited to the BeSHT be burned (see data to fact 428). The conflict between the Chasidim and the mitnagdim continued until a greater threat to both of them appeared, the rise of the Haskalah, Enlightenment (see fact 436).

First Jews in North America

431. The first Jews in North America sailed from South America to New Amsterdam in 1654.

Portugal claimed Brazil in 1500. By 1502 there were a number of New Christians (see fact 410) creating sugar plantations in Brazil. Some of them practiced Judaism in secret because Portugal was a Catholic country, capable of calling the Inquisition into Brazil.

In 1630 the Dutch conquered the northeastern part of Brazil. Since the Dutch were lenient toward Jews, the Dutch settlements became havens for New Christians, who professed Judaism.

That decade was wonderful for Jews and New Christians in Brazil. They built a synagogue and prospered economically. The New Christians were involved primarily in the sugar industry. The Jews thrived as slave traders. By 1642 there were more than 1200 Jews living in Brazil.

In 1645 the Portuguese struck back. In a nine-year war, they drove the Dutch from Brazil. All Jews were expelled from Brazil in 1654; the New Christians were sent to Lisbon, where they were tried and put to death.

Many of the remaining 600 Jews returned to Holland. Some settled in the Indies. Twenty-three Jews, however, continued north, and in September 1654 they arrived in New Amsterdam. Ironically, a month earlier a Jew, Simon Barsimon, had arrived there from Holland.

The twenty-three Jews decided to settle in New Amsterdam. The governor, Peter Stuyvesant, was violently opposed to having Jews corrupting his town. He asked for permission to expel them, but the Dutch West India Company, pressured by influential Jews in Holland, refused. Stuyvesant then tried to add a tax on the Jews because he wouldn't allow them to stand guard duty. The Jews petitioned and received the right to stand guard duty and to engage in wholesale and retail trade.

In 1664 the British took New Amsterdam and renamed it New York. The Jews were accorded even more civil rights. By 1706 they had organized their own Jewish community, Shearith Israel.

432. The first Jews in North America were Sephardic Jews.

The first Sephardic Jews settled in six communities: Newport, Rhode Island; New York; Philadelphia; Charleston, South Carolina; Savannah, Georgia; and Richmond, Virginia. Some also headed north into Canada. Although they were not permitted to hold public office, they did establish synagogues and welfare institutions.

In 1700 the Jews were permitted to practice crafts and trade, and many became shopkeepers and merchants. There were also Jewish silversmiths, candle makers, bakers, and the like. A few families became wealthy by selling supplies to the British and by becoming merchant shippers. In Canada the Jews were mostly fur traders; some of the southern Jews were planters.

There were few instances of anti-Semitism in North America. Jews and Christians frequently worked in the same businesses, partly because the number of Jews in colonial America was minuscule. By 1700 there were at most 300 Jews in the country.

In the eighteenth century, German Jews began arriving, and by 1720 the majority of Jews were German, not Sephardic. However, the newcomers did not establish their own institutions but rather joined the Sephardic synagogues. Jews tended to be Whigs and supported the Revolution, hoping for full civic equality. Many Jews fought in the Revolutionary War. One of the most famous was Haym Salomon, who had arrived from Poland in 1775 and became an ardent patriot. He spied for the colonies while pretending to help the British. When discovered, he fled to Philadelphia. His loans to the army helped finance the battle against Cornwallis, which ended the war. Salomon invested much of his fortune in Continental bonds and, sadly, died penniless.

Spinoza

433. Spinoza was excommunicated because of his beliefs.

Spanish and Portuguese Conversos (see facts 410, 413, 432) found physical but not religious haven in the Netherlands. Although anti-Jewish sentiment was high, the authorities in Amsterdam and the other large cities tended not to investigate the backgrounds of people who wanted to settle in the Netherlands. Jews were forbidden religious freedom, and the Marranos kept their religious practices secret. Other Spanish and Portuguese Jews heard about their settlement, and by the late sixteenth century, Amsterdam became the site of a large secret Jewish community. Both the Marranos and Portuguese Jews kept their religion secret until the beginning of the seventeenth century. Then, after much controversy, Amsterdam decided to permit Jews to have a synagogue, a printing press, and a school. However, they were not given citizenship and could not work in the guilds. Still, Jews viewed Amsterdam as a miraculous haven compared with other countries in the 1600s, and they thrived as a highly intellectual, Jewish cultural center. Their Torah school was considered one of the best in Europe, and their synagogue became one of the finest Sephardic structures.

A group of Jewish scholars within this thriving Amsterdam community began discussing unorthodox philosophical ideas. One of the most outspoken of these Jewish free thinkers was Baruch Spinoza. Born in Amsterdam in 1632, he began to attract the attention of both the Jewish and non-Jewish authorities in 1656 by maintaining that Moses did not write the Torah, that natural law transcended Torah law, and that the soul was not immortal. The Jewish leaders were frightened that such positions would offend the Church and bring the Dutch authorities down on the Jewish community. They excommunicated Spinoza, severing all ties with him.

Spinoza changed his name to Benedict and proceeded to write his philosophical works. His *Tractatus Theologico-Politicus* challenged all basic tenents of traditional Judaism. Using rational arguments, Spinoza maintained that Moses did not write the Torah and that it developed over centuries. Therefore, the Bible text and its moral content had to be studied, analyzed, and critiqued like any other book. Biblical stories were not to be believed as literal; they were merely intended to teach abstract concepts through concrete examples. Because nature is governed by eternal acts of the all-encompassing God, miracles were impossible. Spinoza maintained that traditional rituals were superfluous and meaningless for the rational modern man.

Spinoza's *Ethics* attempted to present his rational philosophy. Spinoza was a pantheist. He considered everything in the world to be an aspect of God: God is the only possible substance in the world. God works through the laws of nature, and everything is ordered accordingly. There is no purpose to the world except to be logically ordered as an aspect of God. The human quest consists in trying to understand the logical system of the world.

Spinoza was so radical for his century that everyone attacked his philosophy. However, he began to have influence on philosophers in the eighteenth and nineteenth centuries. He was a tremendously courageous man, insisting on the truth of his positions even as his entire community fearfully rejected him.

The Rothschilds

434. The richest Jewish bankers in Europe were the Rothschilds.

Because of their tremendous wealth and their great philanthropic generosity, the Rothschild family became one of the most famous Jewish names in Europe. Their family history is a rags to riches success legend.

The founder of the dynasty, Amschel Mayer Rothschild, was born in Germany in 1743. He grew up in ghetto poverty, a small antiques merchant who collected old coins. Through manipulation, luck, and some good politics, he succeeded in becoming a provider of old coins to

Landgrave William ix of Hesse-Kassel. He made some money, but, more important, he made some important financial connections.

Amschel Mayer had five sons, and each founded a banking branch in a major European country. They were able to succeed by establishing among themselves excellent communications, something that other financial institutions didn't have at that time.

The most important of the sons was Nathan Mayer, who settled in London, where he was entrusted with large amounts of William ix's money. Through brilliant speculation and insider trading, Nathan amassed a fortune. He arranged a series of flag signals across the English Channel from France. By receiving information faster than others, he was able to make several financial killings which began the Rothschild fortune.

Amschel Mayer's son James set up a branch in Paris. This enabled Nathan in London to provide needed funds to the Duke of Wellington even when other banks were blocked and guaranteed the Rothschilds' political success in England. Karl Mayer founded the Naples branch in Italy, and Salomon Mayer ran the Vienna branch.

Amschel Mayer was in the Frankfort branch. An Orthodox Jew, he supported the followers of Rabbi Samson Raphael Hirsch (see fact 443).

The first two generations of Rothschilds were involved in huge financial activities that included transmitting the French war indemnity to the allies after the Congress of Vienna, financing Austria's first railroad, financing the Crimean War, and purchasing the Turkish viceroy's Suez Canal shares for Britain.

The philanthropic generosity of the Rothschilds was legendary. Edmund de Rothschild, one of the sons of James (the French branch), became the primary supporter of Jews trying to establish farming settlements in the Land of Israel (see fact 503). The Rothschilds were famous for using their financial and political clout to better the conditions of Jews throughout Europe. They were, and are, a remarkable Jewish family.

Enlightenment and Haskalah

435. Moses Mendelssohn introduced European culture into the ghetto.

The eighteenth century in Christian Western Europe was the Age of Reason. The philosophers believed that reason led to complete truth.

Men were writing about the basic equality of all men. They believed in the essential natural goodness of humans, the only animals capable of reason and logic.

Ironically, one of the philosophical outcomes of these beliefs was a strong attempt both to isolate the Jews and to influence them to convert. Since Christianity was seen as the religion of reason, Jews were logically seen as the followers of a religion of nonreason. Therefore there was increased pressure for Jews to assimilate into the Western Christian culture and, if they didn't choose to, to protect "reasonable people" from them. The Jews, meanwhile, remained in their ghettos.

A Jewish champion emerged from Dessau. Born in 1729, Moses Mendelssohn was a brilliant scholar. After receiving a traditional Jewish education, Mendelssohn went to Berlin, where he studied secular subjects while earning a living as a merchant. Despite a severe curvature of the spine, Mendelssohn was charismatic, vibrant, and a great philosopher.

At first he was a secular philosopher, applying his brilliance to the philosophy of the Enlightenment. Many of his ideas paved the way for Kant's *Critique of Pure Reason*, and his great mind was recognized by the leading thinkers in Europe. In 1771, however, after being attacked in print because he was a Jew who refused to convert, Mendelssohn turned his prodigious talents to fight for the civil rights of Jews. Through clear, rational arguments, he succeeded in convincing a number of communities not to expel their Jews.

At the same time, Mendelssohn tried liberalizing the Jewish community. He strongly believed that the Jews should not have their own rabbinic courts but should be answerable to the secular authorities. He emphasized that Judaism should be free from rabbinic punishment, including excommunication because that limited human freedom. Obviously, these ideas were opposed by rabbinic authorities.

Mendelssohn went further. He decided to lead the Jews out of their limited intellectual existence by introducing them to the world of Western thought and ideas. He wrote articles in pure Hebrew in a magazine called *HaM'assef*, the Gatherer, which translated many of the articles and writings of German culture. He also translated the Torah into German using Hebrew letters, and he wrote a beautiful Hebrew commentary which accompanied his text.

Although Mendelssohn was opposed by the rabbinic authorities of his time, his works enabled a generation of young Jews to become familiar with the philosophy of the Age of Reason and to learn German, the language of Western culture. Thus he single-handedly broke down the intellectual ghetto walls before the physical boundaries had been removed.

Mendelssohn emphasized that the ideas of Enlightenment did not mean that a Jew had to convert. He himself remained a strict Orthodox Jew in his private life. His motto was, "Fully German on the street, fully Jewish at home."

Because of Moses Mendelssohn, when the French Revolution was finally successful and Jews were given full civil rights, there was a population of young Jews intellectually prepared to join Western European society.

436. The Haskalah was the Enlightenment movement for Jews.

As early as the 1740s, there were young Jews who wanted to participate in both the world of Western culture and the Jewish world. They were part of the Age of Reason, the world of Enlightenment, and they felt that it was their duty to bring this general culture to the ignorant, particularistic Jewish world. They zealously set out to educate the Jewish masses in Western culture, and they called their movement the Haskalah, the Enlightenment. They were very successful in Germany and France. Jews spoke German and French, the wealthy were accepted into German society, and they became knowledgeable in Western art, music, and literature.

In the late 1700s they focused on enlightening the masses of Eastern Europe. There was a certain messianic fervor in their attempt to introduce Western culture and customs to their fellow Jews: they believed that anti-Semitism existed because Jews looked different and talked and acted differently from the non-Jewish community. To extirpate anti-Semitism forever, they claimed, Jews had to fit into Western culture.

The first German Enlighteners who tried to bring Haskalah to Russia did so in the same way Mendelssohn had done. They printed articles in German about Western culture; they talked with shtetl Jews in German (see fact 438); they dressed as Germans dressed, and they offered elementary school education that included courses in secular subjects such as math and science. This early movement failed. The majority of Jews saw no advantage in trying to enter Russian culture, which was itself painfully backward. The first Haskalah did have one important effect: it united the mitnagdim (see fact 430) and the Chasidim (see facts 428, 429) against the common foe. Both groups saw the Haskalah as a threat to Judaism and joined forces against it.

The second Haskalah attempt changed its focus. It offered courses in Hebrew and Russian as well as courses in agriculture and secular subjects relevant to the young Russian Jews. Against a great deal of opposition, the Haskalah movement began to gain backing among young Russian Jews. Abraham Mapu wrote the first Hebrew novel, *Love of Zion*, and it became very popular, refocusing Russian Jews on the Land of Israel and glorifying the agricultural life.

Philosophical treatises were written in Yiddish to attract larger audiences. The leaders of the Haskalah even got the Russian government's support in establishing secular schools for Jewish children. They exalted in this success until they realized that the goal of the Russian government was to get their children to convert.

The Haskalah, with its emphasis on Western culture, Hebrew, love of Israel, and pragmatic secular studies, laid the groundwork for the eventual Zionist movement, which resulted in the return to Zion and the rebuilding of the Land of Israel (see fact 502).

The Shtetl

437. The Pale of Settlement was the area of Russia where Jews were forced to live.

Russia expelled all Jews at the end of the fifteenth century. In 1772, when Russia annexed a large part of Poland, Catherine the Great continued the Russian policy of keeping the country free of Jews and ordered the expulsion of all Jews from the newly annexed territories. However, when new partitioning occurred in 1793 and 1795, the huge number of Jews in those regions forced her to change her policy. Catherine the Great decreed that Jews could remain within the newly partitioned territories, but they could not move into other areas of Russia.

The area where Jews were permitted to live was called the Pale of Settlement. It ran along the western border of Russia from the Baltic Sea to the Black Sea.

In the nineteenth century when serfs and peasants were permitted to move more freely throughout Russia, Jews were still forbidden to leave the Pale of Settlement.

438. A shtetl was a little village where Jews lived.

In the Pale (see fact 437) Jews were primarily merchants and innkeepers. They also supervised the huge land holdings of the aristocracy just as they had in Poland. The vast majority of Jews lived in small villages and towns called shtetlach. They had developed this living arrangement in Poland prior to the annexations. Small-village living enabled Jews to care for one another and to socialize in both the synagogue and the market. Moreover, Jews were legally answerable to the Jewish courts under rabbinic authority.

Shtetl life, as depicted in *Fiddler on the Roof*, was hard. Poverty was pervasive. In 1804, Jews were prohibited from being innkeepers. Stripped of their livelihood, they resorted to being middlemen between the big cities and the villages. Most Jews were illiterate, ignorant of Jewish texts. However, because of the close-knit community which lived according to Jewish law, even the poorest Jews knew the lifestyle requirements for being a Jew.

Each shtetl had a similar cast of characters. There was always a rabbi. His primary job was to make legal decisions between Jewish litigants. Frequently, there would be political fights between the local rabbi and the rabbi in the next shtetl, often about problems concerning the shochet (the ritual slaughterer), and arguments over whether meat was kosher, that is, permitted to be eaten (see facts 589-597).

The rabbi was helped by a shammash, a sexton. The shammash was the rabbi's secretary, messenger, bailiff, and notary. He served as gravedigger and all-around handyman. He was also responsible for making sure that Jews arose to go to the synagogue; he did so by knocking on their shutters each morning with a mallet.

Most communities had a shadchan, a marriage broker. Originally, this profession was highly esteemed. However, as less reputable people tried their hand at making matches, the now-stereotyped exaggerating, manipulative shadchan became a shtetl reality.

In the shtetl Jews cared for Jews. A stranger was always guaranteed a meal at Shabbat. Orphans were cared for. Poor brides were provided with a dowry. These tzedakah institutions were overseen by a gabbai, the tzedakah collector and shtetl warden (see facts 579-582). In the 1880s, Jews created and maintained vocational and agricultural schools for fellow Jews. This Society for Manual Work, called ORT, Organization for Rehabilitation and Training, became an international organization dedicated to helping Jews learn manual skills.

Shtetl life meant living in a goldfish bowl; everyone knew about everyone. Life in Russia was painfully hard, but the shtetl environment enabled Jews to survive.

439. Sholom Aleichem wrote funny and sad Yiddish stories about the shtetl.

Life in the shtetl was best portrayed by a group of Haskalah writers (see fact 436). Writing in Yiddish, they were able, through humor, poignancy, and sensitivity, to portray the Jewish world of the shtetl and the conflicts and tensions which every Jew faced. The greatest of these writers were Mendele Mocher Seforim, Sholom Aleichem and I. L. Peretz. They enriched the lives of their Yiddish readers, who were able to forget their personal troubles by reading about the pitfalls and adventures of other unfortunates in shtetl life.

Sholom Aleichem's famous stories about Tevye the milkman and his daughters were the source material for the musical *Fiddler on the Roof*.

440. Chappers were Jews who stole children to meet the Russian army quota.

One of the goals of Czar Nicholas I (1825-1855) was to convert all Russian Jews or kill them. He created a simple method: every Jew from age 12 to 25 had to serve in the Russian army for 25 years. Once under the army's authority, these Jewish children were brutally forced to renounce their religion or die. Every Jewish community was given a quota for army recruits, approximately thirty conscripts per thousand males. The community leaders tried filling these high numbers with the children of the poorest Jews, frequently kidnapping children as young as 8 and then swearing that they were 12. The community officers assigned to this horrendous job were called chappers (kidnappers). Between 30,000 and 40,000 Jewish children were thus brutally torn from our religion before the law was abolished in 1856. We don't know how many died or how many succumbed to conversion but it was a terrible time in our history.

The barracks where the children were kept were called cantonments, so the brutalized children were called Cantonists.

Western Europe in the Nineteenth Century

441. Napoleon gave Jews full civil rights.

In 1791, in the spirit of *liberté, égalité, fraternité*, all Jews were given civic rights in France. However, their religious authorities were given no official status. Beginning in 1793, attempts were made to deny civil rights to Jews in France and, in fact, to expel all Jews from the country because they practiced usury.

In 1806 Napoleon convened an Assembly of Jewish Notables, who were asked twelve questions concentrating on the relationship between Jewish authorities and the national state. The Assembly's response indicated that Jewish law was in no way contrary to French law. Then in 1807 Napoleon convened a French Sanhedrin consisting of forty-five rabbis and twenty-six laymen. They codified the twelve answers given by the Assembly of Notables.

With those satisfactory answers, Napoleon then established a national Jewish administration answerable to the state in all religious matters. It consisted of a consistory, or religious council, in each department of France. The national consistory, which was in Paris, consisted of three rabbis and two laymen. All consistories were answerable to the Paris office, and the Paris consistory was answerable to the state.

As flawed and discriminatory as the system remained, it was the first time that European Jews had true civil rights. These rights spread as Napoleon's influence spread. By the 1840s, Jews were viewed as citizens in most Western European countries.

442. The Reform Movement began as an attempt to keep Jews in the modern world from converting to Christianity.

Although Jews were given political rights, socially they were still held in contempt by cultured Europeans. Tremendous pressure was placed on them to give up their strange particularistic ways and leap into the richness of science, music, art, and literature. Many acquiesced, believing that the new nationalism would provide them with full identity. The old ways of superstitious religious rules and regulations were past. The new age of science and reason, of unlimited truth had arrived.

Some educated Jews were horrified by this mass exodus from Judaism. The cream of European Jewry was embracing secular nationalism, and they were determined to stop the flood. They took European anti-Semitism at its word: people hated Jews because Jews acted strangely, differently. This group of educated, modern Jews decided to make Judaism acceptable to intellectual Europeans. They set about to reform Judaism.

They began in the early nineteenth century with four esthetic innovations which they justified within the existing framework of halachah:

1. Some of the prayers were said in the vernacular. The vast majority of the prayers were still in Hebrew.
2. The prayers were either recited or sung; the sing-song davvening system was abolished because it threatened modern decorum.
3. The use of the organ was introduced to make the singing more decorous.
4. The sermon became the most important part of the service, and it was delivered in German.

These changes reformed the Jewish prayer experience into an imitation of the nineteenth-century Lutheran service.

By the 1840s the early Reformers had established some theologies to match their reforming efforts. Led by great minds like Abraham Geiger and Samuel Holdheim, they emphasized that the most important God-given commandments were the ethical imperatives. These were eternal and true. The goal of Judaism was to live a lifestyle that brought holiness into the modern world, a world of science and truth. All outmoded rabbinic legislation had to pass the test of reason, morality, and modernity to be acceptable. If a practice separated the Jew from the modern, secular world, then it was a Jew's religious obligation to renounce it.

Abraham Geiger believed that all of Jewish tradition was an evolutionary process. He saw every generation of Jews creating practices that expressed the eternal ethical laws inherent in Judaism. Samuel Holdheim believed that practically all of the ceremonial regulations established in traditional Judaism had to be abolished in order for pure ethical monotheism to become the center of Reform Judaism. He espoused a revolutionary rather than evolutionary view of tradition.

The founders of Reform Judaism burned with a messianic passion.

They believed that what they were doing would save Judaism from the old-fashioned legislative stagnation of the rabbis and, at the same time, rid Europe of anti-Semitism by offering a Judaism that the secular world could honor and accept.

443. Rabbi Samson Raphael Hirsch showed Jews how they could be both Orthodox and modern.

The debate over reforming Judaism involved only those Jews who were already to some extent involved in the world of Western culture. The unenlightened mitnagdim (see fact 430) and Chassidim (see facts 428, 429) were unaware of the experiments in reforming Judaism except through wildly exaggerated hearsay. However, there were rabbis who had studied Western culture and were alarmed at the excesses proposed by the Reformers. Since the expounders of reform were coming from traditional congregations, all of these Western-cultured rabbis met at a series of conferences in 1844, 1845, and 1846. Their goal was to keep Judaism a unified religion.

One of the major proponents of retaining halachic practices within modern Judaism was Rabbi Samson Raphael Hirsch. Knowledgeable in the Talmud and texts, Rabbi Hirsch also studied at the University of Bonn. He was a good friend of Abraham Geiger, although they remained philosophically opposed. Hirsch believed in the divinity of Torah and the Talmud. He provided rational explanations for each of the mitzvot (see fact 162), showing that they fit into a modern, cultured, Jewish life. Although he was by no means the first to propose the theory, it was Hirsch's argument that the dietary laws (see facts 589-597) were for health reasons that became the accepted argument for their continuation among many German Jews.

Rabbi Hirsch agreed that there had to be reform within Judaism. He was all in favor of delivering sermons in German. He even encouraged students to study TaNaCH (see fact 104) and not simply concentrate on Talmud (see fact 363). He found value in Western cultural studies. However, the proposals among the more radical Reformers to abolish the dietary laws and change the rituals in the service were unacceptable to him.

Sadly, in 1876 he noted that there was a split within modern Judaism. The Reformers went their way, and Rabbi Samson Raphael Hirsch became the proponent of a new modern Jewish stream of Orthodoxy. His movement was funded by the Rothschilds (see data to fact 434). Orthodoxy as a philosophical movement was thus born as a reaction against the first of the modern Jewish movements, Reform.

America in the Nineteenth Century

444. In the 1840s large numbers of Jews from Germany fled to America.

The 1800s were a time of political turmoil in Europe. The educated, cultured classes were demanding more civil rights, and there were revolutions in 1818, 1828, and 1838. After each revolution was defeated, the liberal leaders, many of them Jews, fled to America.

A revolution in 1848 was successful in Austria, and Prince Metternich, the reactionary Austrian chancellor, had to flee. In Germany, however, the revolution was defeated as the earlier uprisings had been, and the liberal leaders of the revolt were hunted down. As in the previous revolts, many of the participants in this failed revolution were Jews, and they fled the country. Their destination was the Land of Promise, the United States. From 1840 to 1880 the Jewish population in the United States rose from 14,000 to 200,000, most of them from German-speaking countries.

These new Jewish immigrants spread across the United States, beginning as itinerant peddlers and eventually becoming merchants. Large Jewish centers were established in New York City, Cleveland, St. Louis, San Francisco, New Orleans, Cincinnati, Albany, and Buffalo. The German Jews brought with them the liberal values and reforms they had espoused in Germany, and many quickly assimilated into American culture. With the freedom available in the United States, they created the open, Jewish society we are familiar with today. They were so successful in their efforts that in 1882, of the 200 known synagogues in the United States, 188 identified themselves as Reform!

445. B'nai B'rith was the first and largest Jewish service organization.

In 1843 there were about 15,000 Jews in the United States. Twelve of them got together to found a Jewish fraternal organization aimed at helping Jews. B'nai B'rith (Sons of the Covenant) was the first Jewish service organization, and it remains the largest, with branches in forty-five countries.

Through the nineteenth century, B'nai B'rith concentrated on philanthropic activities such as building orphanages, old-age homes, trade schools, and hospitals, and funding a variety of Americanization and relief programs for the mass immigration which had begun in 1881 (see fact 452). At the same time, Jewish women began organizing local groups to help meet the needs of their communities. Called Jewish Ladies' Aid Societies, Hebrew Women's Benevolent Associations, or just Community Sisterhoods, these groups provided local Jewish social identity and, on occasion, even became the active founders of small community congregations.

In 1901 Baron de Hirsch, a wealthy philanthropist, encouraged Jews to leave the squalor and congestion of the Lower East Side and spread out across America, especially to the south and west. B'nai B'rith became active in that program and, by 1916, had succeeded in resettling more than 100,000 Jews across the United States. These new settlements of Jews attracted still more Jews, thus spreading the Jewish community across America.

In the twentieth century, while maintaining all of the earlier programs, B'nai B'rith expanded to meet a new American problem: anti-Semitism.

From the Colonial period to the 1860s there was very little organized anti-Semitism in America. The final vestige of civil discrimination ended in 1877 when New Hampshire permitted non-Protestants to become members of its legislature. Jews were assimilated into American culture and, for the most part, were accepted. America in those years concentrated on anti-Catholicism against the Irish immigrants entering the country.

During the Civil War the 150,000 resident Jews tended to side with their respective regions. About 7,000 fought for the Union, about 3,000 for the Confederacy. Before the South's defeat, there were some unpleasant incidents of anti-Semitism, including General Grant's order expelling all Jews from areas under his military control. This order, called General Order Number 11, was promptly revoked by President Lincoln.

Until the beginning of the twentieth century, anti-Semitism in the United States was limited to extreme racist groups like the Ku Klux Klan. However, with the enormous increase of Jewish immigrants and the political pressures leading to World War I, anti-Semitism became a mainstream phenomenon. To counteract it, B'nai B'rith founded its Anti-Defamation League (the ADL) in 1913. The ADL continues to work for improved relations between groups and to fight discrimination wherever it appears.

In 1923 at the University of Illinois, Rabbi Ben Frankel created a new institution which he called Hillel. Aimed at serving the needs of Jewish college students, Rabbi Frankel's Hillel provided social and academic activities on campus. Two years later, at Rabbi Frankel's request, B'nai B'rith voted to sponsor the Hillel Foundation, and today there are more than 300 university campuses with Hillel offices.

In 1924 B'nai B'rith founded its B'nai B'rith Youth Organization, the BBYO, aimed at offering social and athletic programs for Jewish children.

446. The Jewish Chautauqua Society was founded to create better understanding between Christians and Jews on college campuses.

Another attempt to combat anti-Semitism was the founding of the Jewish Chautauqua Society. Rabbi Henry Berkowitz, one of the first rabbis ordained at Hebrew Union College (see fact 448), was concerned by Jews' lack of Jewish knowledge. He was impressed with the Methodist study groups called the Chautauqua Circles, named after the study group founded in Chautauqua, New York. Rabbi Berkowitz began establishing reading groups for Jews. He also created a curriculum for Jewish religious-school teachers.

In 1909 Rabbi Berkowitz was encouraged to make his Chautauqua Circles available to the non-Jewish population as well. Later, with the help of Dr. Julian Morgenstern, the president of Hebrew Union College, Rabbi Berkowitz redirected the focus of the Jewish Chautauqua Society toward college campuses, where lectures were given on the rich contributions Judaism has made to Western civilization. The Jewish Chautauqua Society's purpose thus focused on providing books, lecturers, and courses on college campuses to teach non-Jews about Judaism.

The program was tremendously successful. In 1949 the National Federation of Temple Brotherhoods, affiliated with the Reform Movement, took over the administration of the Jewish Chautauqua Society. As of 1989 the Society has donated more than 100,000 books to college libraries. More than 150 college courses are offered for credit each year, and guest lecturers and rabbis provide information to parochial schools and colleges.

Rise of Jewish Institutions

447. Rabbi Isaac Mayer Wise was one of the great pioneers of Reform Judaism in the United States.

The impetus for reform in America came primarily from laypeople influenced by America's cultural insistence upon radical freedom. The rights of the individual were paramount in nineteenth-century America, and change was encouraged as healthy and natural. Throughout his adult life, Rabbi Isaac Mayer Wise tried to systematize that change and create a single unified American Jewish community. Beginning in 1848 he tried to create a union of all congregations. It failed. In 1855 he called for a rabbinical synod which would become the Jewish authority for all Jews in America. The modern Orthodox (see data to fact 443), represented by Isaac Leeser, were suspicious, and the radical reformers led by Rabbi David Einhorn viewed Wise's compromises with tradition as treachery. Rabbi Wise's hopes for a synod died stillborn. But he didn't give up. In 1856 he published his prayerbook, *Minhag America* (the Custom of America), which he hoped would become the unifying prayerbook for all American Jews. It didn't.

Wise never succeeded in uniting the radical reformers with the more traditional of the Reform Jews. In 1873 the lay leaders of Cincinnati (where Wise served as a rabbi) joined with Wise to organize a union of congregations in the South and West. They called themselves the Union of American Hebrew Congregations. Eventually, this group became the umbrella organization for all Reform congregations in the United States and Canada.

448. Hebrew Union College was the first rabbinical seminary in the United States.

Rabbi Isaac Mayer Wise's (see fact 447) major success occurred in 1875, when he founded a rabbinical school for American rabbis. Called the Hebrew Union College, this seminary provided Reform congregations with rabbis trained in the United States under the influence of their college president, Rabbi Wise. It was the first rabbinical seminary in the country.

Wise's final attempt to unite all of America's Jews was the establishment of the Central Conference of American Rabbis in 1889. Wise hoped that this union of rabbis would serve as an authoritative body for all American congregations. It didn't. Every congregation jealously guarded its own autonomy, and Wise's dream of a single unified American Jewry died. However, his influence as a major pioneer of Reform Judaism in America was tremendous. The institutions he established remain the primary organizations of Reform Jewry. The Central Conference of American Rabbis, while not serving as a synod, has provided ritual and ethical guidelines for Reform Jewry and has created materials which have had a great impact on the Reform Movement.

In 1922 Rabbi Stephen S. Wise (not related to Isaac Mayer) founded a seminary in New York, which he called the Jewish Institute of Religion. In the mid-twentieth century the Hebrew Union College and the Jewish Institute of Religion merged, forming a single Reform seminary in America, the HUC-JIR. Today, HUC-JIR has campuses in Cincinnati, New York, Los Angeles, and Jerusalem (see fact 566).

449. Rabbi Solomon Schechter was one of the founders of the Conservative Movement.

The Conservative Movement, known in Europe as the Historical Movement, was a reaction to what its founders viewed as the overzealous reforms of the Reform Movement. Many modern Jews felt that there should be innovations in Judaism, but they wanted to retain more traditional practices than the reformers were willing to accept. Unlike Holdheim and Einhorn, they didn't view traditional practices as impeding the modern contract with the Divine (see data to facts 442, 447).

They tried to establish a seminary and a movement, but they got very little support. The Reformers weren't interested, and the Russian immigrants arriving after 1882 weren't interested (see fact 452). In 1902 they invited Rabbi Solomon Schechter to become president of a newly revamped school, the Jewish Theological Seminary.

Solomon Schechter was born in Rumania and had a traditional upbringing. Nevertheless, he studied at Berlin University, and he was eventually invited to be a tutor of rabbinics in London, and became a lecturer at Cambridge University. He gained international fame as a scholar when he discovered the Cairo Genizah (see fact 260). The Genizah contained more than 200,000 pages of rare manuscripts, some dating back almost 1,500 years. Schechter brought more than 100,000 documents back to England. These Cairo Genizah pages have provided tremendous scholarly insight into the history of the Jewish world under Muslim rule.

Schechter accepted an invitation to come to America. He succeeded in attracting an outstanding group of scholars to teach, and the Jewish Theological Seminary became a recognized center of Jewish learning.

In 1913 Solomon Schechter was instrumental in founding the United Synagogue of America, the umbrella organization of all Conservative congregations.

450. Rabbi Mordechai Kaplan founded the Reconstructionist Movement.

Mordechai Kaplan's early Jewish education was Orthodox. He was ordained at the Jewish Theological Seminary (the Rabbinical school for the Conservative Movement), where in 1909 he became a professor. He continued teaching there until 1963. Kaplan never saw himself as founding a new movement in Judaism. His followers, however, eventually viewed themselves as a new stream and created their own rabbinical school, a union of synagogues, and havurot (see fact 465).

Mordechai Kaplan's own concept of Judaism fit within the existing synagogue structures. He viewed Judaism as a civilization. Jewish practices became Jewish because Jews did them. Societal concerns became Jewish when Jews worried about them. The mitzvot, traditionally understood as commandments, were for Kaplan, folkways which united Jews into a community. According to Kaplan, God neither commanded nor chose the Jewish people. All Jewish traditions were created and maintained by Jews in their personal and communal attempts to achieve salvation in this life. All social and religious functions of the Jewish people, therefore, should be under the auspices of the synagogue, which should be a Jewish center for the entire community.

In following this theology, Mordechai Kaplan encouraged the creation of a new prayerbook which removed all references to the chosen people, God as a personal deity, revelation at Mount Sinai, and a personal Messiah.

While supporting a Jewish state, Mordechai Kaplan denied any difference in the quality of life between a Jew living in Israel and one living outside the Land. Since Judaism is a civilization, the quality of every Jewish community is as special as its members, and no specific area makes such a community more special.

There are disagreements about when Reconstructionism became a separate Jewish movement. Many believe that it started when Kaplan founded the Society for the Advancement of Judaism in 1922. As a synagogue and a Jewish center, that society encouraged the views now identified with Reconstructionism. Some prefer a later date: The Reconstructionists actually became identified as a new movement of Jews when they established their own rabbinical school in 1967 and began ordaining rabbis.

Mass Jewish Migration to the United States

451. Pogroms were government-organized riots against the Jews in Russia.

Through the nineteenth century, Russia remained a rigid, reactionary nation which encouraged anti-Semitism. The pogroms began in 1881 after Czar Alexander II was killed. Jews were blamed, and riots broke out all over Russia. One of the worst was in Kiev. It lasted for three days while the police simply watched. The first pogroms concentrated on destroying property; there were few deaths.

In May 1882 Czar Alexander III added to the misery by establishing a set of laws which limited where Jews could live and what professions they could hold. The result of these May Laws was further rioting.

From 1903 to 1905 a number of vicious pogroms took place. Encouraged by the government, which blamed the Jews for all revolutionary movements against the Czar, mobs slaughtered Jews in Kishinev, Zhitomir, and hundreds of small towns. The worst pogrom of this period was in Odessa, where thousands of Jews were wounded and more than 300 were killed.

These pogroms, organized, encouraged, and supported by the government, were fiercely condemned by the American Jewish Committee, founded in 1906 (see data to fact 454).

From 1917 to 1921 another series of more than 3,000 pogroms took place in towns, villages, and cities under the auspices of the varying Russian governments, resulting in the deaths of at least 6,000 Jews. These were by far the worst.

There were three major Jewish responses to the new pogroms: (1) Jews began to create defense groups to fight back, (2) Jews became deeply involved in the nationalist movement of returning to the Land of Israel, and (3) Jews fled from Russia.

452. More than 2 million Jews came to the United States between 1880 and 1920.

The vast majority of Jews who fled from Eastern Europe between 1882 and 1920 (see fact 451) came to the United States via Ellis Island. Thousands also joined communities in Canada, Baltimore, and Philadelphia. More than 1,300,000 chose to settle in New York.

Most came without possessions and without vocational training. Most had been untouched by the Haskalah (see fact 436), and the culture shock after leaving their shtetlach was enormous.

453. Emma Lazarus wrote the poem inscribed on the Statue of Liberty.

Emma Lazarus, the daughter of German Jews, began writing poetry as a teenager, and her poems attracted the attention of Ralph Waldo Emerson. She also translated into English the poetry of Judah HaLevi and Ibn Gabirol (see data to facts 385, 392, 393).

She volunteered as an immigrant relief worker in New York and staunchly defended the Russian Jewish immigrants in articles in which she praised them as pioneers of progress.

In 1883 she wrote her famous sonnet, "The New Colossus," expressing her belief that the United States was the haven for Europe's "huddled masses yearning to breathe free." The sonnet was engraved on a plaque and placed on the pedestal of the Statue of Liberty in 1903.

454. When Jews came to America, many settled on the Lower East Side of New York.

Many of the new Russian Jewish immigrants (see fact 452), after being processed on Ellis Island, went to the Lower East Side of Manhattan. There they found tenement lodgings and struggled to survive. Called "greenhorn" by some, they adapted more or less to the new freedoms available to them. Many assimilated quickly into the American culture.

The already-settled middle-class German Jews responded to these new Jewish immigrants in one of two ways: Many were ashamed of being associated with these new, dirty, clearly non-American Jews and tried to limit their immigration; others recognized their responsibility for their fellow Jews and established assimilation programs, soup kitchens, and philanthropic centers for the new immigrants. Old-age homes, orphanages, vocational training schools, and free clinics sprouted on the Lower East Side.

In 1906 a small group of prominent German Jews established the American Jewish Committee, whose purpose was to influence the American government to protest the pogroms taking place in Russia (see fact 451) and to open America's doors to Russian Jewish immigrants. During the 1920s and 1930s the American Jewish Committee fought against anti-Semitism in the United States and tried to pressure the Roosevelt administration to help German Jewry.

In Boston in 1895 the Jewish charities began to set up a federation which unified fund raising and allocation. It was so successful that soon all major cities set up similar programs. In 1917 New York established the Federation for the Support of Jewish Philanthropic Societies.

The new immigrants found some support systems already in place. The Lower East Side was the needle-trade center of New York. By 1909 more than 83 percent of all garment industries were run by Jews using Jewish labor. Owners, bosses, and workers helped new immigrants find jobs.

The hours were long (usually a minimum of 70 hours a week), the physical conditions oppressive. Much of the work was done in private rooms on a contract basis. Warehouses without enough ventilation, light or heat, housed hundreds of sewing machines with workers doing twelve-hour shifts. These factories were called sweatshops.

Sometimes their plight came to public consciousness. In 1911 a fire broke out at the Triangle Shirtwaist Company and 146 young women died in the blaze, a tragedy that shocked New York.

The new Jewish immigrants found work in sweatshops, at peddling, and, like other desperate immigrants, in illegal activities. Prostitution, illegal liquor distribution, and illegal gambling in New York were run by Jewish mobsters for many years.

455. Jews were actively involved in creating the labor unions.

Because of their persecution and poverty, Eastern European Jews became actively involved in the early labor unions in Russia. Revolutionary socialists dedicated to creating an equal, just world, these young Jews organized strike funds and welfare funds. In 1897 they called their independent revolutionary circles the Bund.

Many of the 2 million Jewish immigrants (see fact 452) brought this same socialist spirit with them to America. Although there were already labor unions for skilled workers in place when they came, the Bundists organized separate labor union circles at their jobs, fighting for a reduction in hours, a minimum wage, and safer working conditions. One of the largest of these was the International Ladies' Garment Workers Union, founded in 1900. In 1910 it took part in a strike which lasted two months and involved 60,000 workers.

In 1914, workers in men's clothing formed the Amalgamated Clothing Workers of America. These unions eventually succeeded in reducing the work week to 40 hours, raising wages, and improving working conditions.

Another large union was the Workman's Circle, which also actively supported Yiddish culture.

456. The National Federation of Temple Sisterhoods supports the Reform Jewish Movement, and the Women's League for Conservative Judaism supports the Conservative Movement.

Local Jewish women's groups had been playing a major role in American communities since the 1850s (see data to fact 445). With the encouragement of Rabbi George Zepin, delegates from 52 of these local Reform organizations met in Cincinnati (at the Biennial Convention of the Union of American Hebrew Congregations; see data to fact 447) and established the National Federation of Temple Sisterhoods. It was the first auxiliary organization of the Union of American Hebrew Congregations.

Under the leadership of Mrs. Abram Simon, the women dedicated themselves to provide support to the national Reform Jewish Movement, in addition to continuing their help in their local congregations and communities. They began by creating scholarships for rabbinical students attending Hebrew Union College. They printed a yearly Jewish calendar which reflected the Reform celebration of the holidays (see data to facts 1, 35, 65). During World War I they collected more than $300,000 to build a dormitory for the rabbinical students at Hebrew Union College. During World War II they provided 50 percent of the funds to help build the House of Living Judaism, the headquarters of the Union of American Hebrew Congregations in New York.

Among its many building projects, the National Federation of Temple Sisterhoods also provided a library for the Leo Baeck High School in Haifa (see data to fact 566), a synagogue/library center at the Ben Shemen Children and Youth village, a study center at kibbutz Yahel in Israel, and a reading room at the New York campus of Hebrew Union College-Jewish Institute of Religion. In the mid-1930s, with the encouragement of Jane Evans, they founded the Jewish Braille Institute of America.

One of the National Federation of Temple Sisterhoods' greatest accomplishments was the establishment of the National Federation of Temple Youth. Early on, local Sisterhoods recognized the need to create social groups for the teenagers in their congregations. At their urging, independent Young Folks' Temple Leagues were founded. It was natural that these separate groups get together for dances and other social activities, and informal regional events took place. In 1927 Jean Wise May, daughter of Isaac Mayer Wise (see fact 447), proposed that a national federation of these youth leagues be created to hold debates, forums, and social activities under the auspices of the Union of American Hebrew Congregations. It took another twelve years to make this proposal a reality, but during that time the National Federation of Temple Sisterhoods succeeded in founding more than 350 Temple Youth groups, loosely organized into regional federations.

In 1939 the National Federation of Temple Youth (NFTY) was created. Following World War II, NFTY's programs rapidly expanded. Under the creative direction of Rabbi Samuel Cook, National Camp Leadership Institutes were initiated, regional summer camp sessions were begun, and international exchange programs were instituted. The exciting spirit created among Reform Jewish teenagers by these programs made NFTY and its camps one of the most significant sources for Reform Jewish leadership in the country. In 1965 NFTY established a national camp which provided summer-long dynamic, imaginative programming for its high school campers.

Thanks to the original support of the National Federation of Temple Sisterhoods, NFTY now has eight regional camps, the national camp, an extensive series of programs in Israel for American teenagers, and 21 regions.

Shortly after the founding of the National Federation of Temple Sisterhoods, Mathilde Schechter, wife of Rabbi Solomon Schechter (see fact 449), called on women from Conservative congregations to create a national Women's League. At its first convention in 1918, women from twenty-six congregations gathered and dedicated themselves to the enrichment of Jewish learning and practice.

Today, the Women's League for Conservative Judaism has delegates from more than 700 synagogues and is divided into twenty-eight branches. It supports Conservative congregations in Israel, the Jewish Theological Seminary (see data to fact 449), U.S.Y. (United Synagogue

Youth, the youth program for the Conservative Movement), and has a rich social-action agenda.

The Women's League remains an active force in the Jewish Braille Institute of America as well.

European Anti-Semitism and the Holocaust

457. Mendel Beilis was a Russian Jew victimized in 1911 by a Blood Accusation.

In 1911, to the horror of the rest of the world, Czarist Russia instigated a Blood Accusation. Mendel Beilis, a Jewish brick kiln superintendent was accused and tried for killing a Russian child for ritual purposes. Universal liberal outrage eventually resulted in his release after two years.

The Nazis systematically used the Blood Accusation theme to stir up hate against the Jews. It became a predominant motif of anti-Jewish feeling and continues to this day.

458. The Holocaust lasted from 1933 to 1945.

The Holocaust, called in Hebrew *HaShoah*, was the Nazi systematic slaughter of all Jews. It began officially in 1933, when Hitler and the Nazis came to political power in Germany, and it lasted until 1945, when Germany accepted military defeat at the hands of the Allies. During that time, the Nazis committed atrocities unique in the history of the world.

The policy of brutalizing and tormenting Jews because they were considered a subhuman race went back to the 1920s as a major part of the Nazi platform. In 1925 Hitler wrote *Mein Kampf*, which emphasized the need to punish all Jews for their perfidy. However, until the Nazi policy became the law of Germany, the anti-Semitic actions of the 1920s were viewed as mere thuggery.

The Holocaust is historically divided into three periods. From 1933 to 1939 the goal of Nazi Germany was to make the state free of Jews by making it financially, emotionally, and physically impossible for the

Jewish population to survive there. From 1939 to 1941, Germany engaged in the mass slaughter of Jews (see data to fact 461). From 1942 to 1945, the Nazis perfected their program of genocide (see data to fact 461). Beginning in 1933, Jews were deprived of their citizenship and forbidden to hold public office or have professional jobs. Jewish children could no longer attend public school. It became illegal for non-Jews and Jews to socialize. Jewish businesses were boycotted. Jewish books were burned. There were beatings, tortures, and humiliations. The official policy, however, was to force Jews to flee Germany, not kill them en masse.

American Jewry responded to these oppressive measures with outrage. In the 1930s the American Jewish Congress tried to arouse American public opinion against the Nazis. As part of its anti-Nazi program, it helped establish the Joint Boycott Council against German products. The American Jewish Committee (see data to fact 454) worked desperately to convince the Vatican, American statesmen, and even German officials to help Jews get out of Germany.

459. Kristallnacht was an enormous Nazi pogrom against the Jews.

On the night of November 9, 1938, the Nazis systematically unleashed a nationwide pogrom of unmitigated violence against the Jews. So many Jewish stores and synagogues were destroyed that the riots were called the Night of Broken Glass, Kristallnacht. To add insult to injury, the Nazis then forced the Jewish community to pay for the damages. More than 15,000 Jews were rounded up and sent to German work concentration camps. The intensity of the destruction was so great that many Jews were finally convinced that there was no longer any hope for them in Germany.

Unfortunately, there was no place to run. Countries, including the United States and the British in Palestine, locked their doors against Jewish immigration. During the Holocaust years neither Pope Pius xi nor Pope Pius xii condemned the Nazi atrocities, even when the Jews of Rome were rounded up and sent to the death camps (see fact number 461). Not wanting to alienate German Catholics, the Catholic Church carefully remained neutral throughout the Nazi atrocities.

Aliya Bet, the Jewish movement to transport Jews to Palestine past the British, desperately tried to help Jews escape from the horror of Germany, but only a trickle succeeded (see fact 528).

460. The Nazis planned to exterminate all Jews.

With the conquest of Poland in 1939, Germany's policy towards the Jews changed, and the second of three periods of the Holocaust began (see facts 458, 461). The Nazi High Command secretly decided on "The Final Solution," the total annihilation of world Jewry.

The first step was to isolate all Jews from the rest of society. Hundreds of thousands of Jews were crowded into tiny areas of large Polish cities, thus creating disease-ridden ghettos. At the same time, the German army gathered large groups of Jews from the conquered areas, and began systematically to shoot and dump them into large mass graves. The extermination of the Jews had begun. From 1939 to 1941, especially in Russia, there were mass slaughters of Jews. While these slaughters were enormous in scope, the Nazis began to realize that these mass murders were being accomplished with only limited efficiency. The army complained about the cost of bullets needed for the killing. Moreover, officers noted that some soldiers became demoralized at shooting naked men, women, and children day and night.

Some concentration camps were set up to work the Jews to death. As an experiment, Jews were killed with carbon monoxide from the trucks transporting them, but this method proved too slow and too costly.

All of this was accomplished in official secrecy. The world didn't know of the plan; Jews in the ghettos didn't know of the plan. It was too inhuman to be believable.

461. More than 6 million Jews were slaughtered during the Holocaust.

In 1942 at the Wannsee Conference, the Nazis smoothed out the logistics needed to slaughter all Jews, thus beginning the third period of the Holocaust (see facts 458, 460). Extermination camps using poison gas and crematoria were created under the direction of Heinrich Himmler. Adolf Eichmann took responsibility for the transportation, administrative coordination, extermination, and burning of all Polish and other foreign Jews, about 7 million people. This meant moving them from the ghettos where they had been placed and transporting them to the death camps. It entailed organizing train schedules to move Jews efficiently from France, Greece, Italy, Rumania, and Hungary to the death camps and timing their schedules so as not to create wasteful, long lines of unloaded train cars.

The Nazis wasted nothing. Clothing, hair, jewelry, gold- and silver-teeth of the dead and near-dead were all collected and used for the military effort. Things had to run efficiently and smoothly. Eichmann was good at his work. By 1943 at just one extermination camp, Auschwitz (the largest), 10,000 Jews a day were killed every day, 365 days a year. Eichmann succeeded in increasing the rate to 12,000 Jews a day. Other death camps, never to be forgotten, included Majdanek, Treblinka, Bergen-Belsen, Buchenwald, Belzec, Sobibor, and Riga.

In addition, Jews were worked to death in camps. These labor camps were excuses for more torture and starvation. They also provided cheap labor for Germany's industries, including I.G. Farben and Krupp. For that reason, many Jews still refuse to buy German products produced by those firms. The death rate in the labor camps was about 80 percent.

By the end of the Holocaust, more than 6 million Jews had been slaughtered. The attempt by some moderns to "prove" that the Holocaust was a Jewish hoax is one of the great obscenities of our generation. The Nazis, always clerically efficient, kept voluminous notes on all of their actions. The piles of eye-glasses, hair, shoes, and clothing carefully stored by the Nazis were silent proof of their atrocities.

462. The Jews in the Warsaw Ghetto fought back with tremendous bravery.

Although conditions were practically unbearable in the Polish ghettos where Jews had been forced to move, the majority of Jews didn't believe that the Nazis intended to slaughter them all. They had heard rumors about death camps, but the concept simply wasn't believable to normal people. There were numerous small attempts to organize defense groups against the Nazis, but these were rarely successful at uniting the Jewish populace, which had always believed in law and order. Moreover, Jews desiring to resist were hindered by the lack of weapons and support by the non-Jewish anti-Nazi groups, who were also virulently anti-Semitic. Frequently, if the partisans in Poland, Russia, Yugoslavia, and Hungary (anti-Nazi groups) found a Jew hiding in the woods, they would kill him.

The best-known act of Jewish resistance took place in the Warsaw Ghetto. The Germans had been transporting Jews from the ghetto for "resettlement," a Nazi euphemism for the gas chambers. By 1943 the Jewish population in Warsaw had fallen from 500,000 to 40,000. Finally, the younger people in the ghetto convinced the population that the

Germans weren't sending them to work camps; they were slaughtering them.

On April 14, 1943, the first night of Passover, the Jews opened fire on German troops as they entered the ghetto. They beat back a tank force. Led by Mordechai Anilevitz, the Jews hid in underground bunkers and cellars and emerged to fight the Nazis with small arms and gasoline bombs. The Germans bombed the ghetto, leveling every building in the area, but the Jews continued to resist underground. The Nazis systematically searched out each bunker, filling it with poison gas. In June 1943, three months after resistance began, the Nazis announced that the last of the fighters were killed. They didn't know that several hundred fighters had made it out of the ghetto through the sewers.

The kibbutz Yad Mordechai (the Hand of Mordechai; see data to facts 476, 539) was founded in 1943 in memory of Mordechai Anilevitz. When some of the survivors of the uprising made it to Palestine, they joined that kibbutz and in 1949 created a second kibbutz, Lochamei HaGhettaot (the Fighters of the Ghettos). Both have museums showing the horrors of the Holocaust and the bravery of the Jewish fighters in Europe.

463. Until the Holocaust, the greatest yeshivot and Jewish cultural centers were in Poland.

In 1939 more than 3 million Jews lived in Poland, where there were wonderful yeshivot, Jewish theaters, and synagogues. Hitler ordered that the finest examples of Jewish art from Poland, Czechoslovakia, Hungary, and Rumania be saved for a museum of the destroyed subhuman race. Thus, hundreds of thousands of ritual art pieces from Eastern Europe survived the Holocaust. The people weren't so fortunate. In 1946, fewer than 105,000 Polish Jews remained. Even smaller percentages of Jews survived in Czechoslovakia and Hungary. Hitler's plan effectively destroyed Eastern Europe's Jewry, and they have remained small in number and socially impoverished into the 1990s.

1945–1991

464. Jews have been prominent in the civil rights movement in the United States.

In mid-twentieth century, American Jews were actively involved in the struggle to protect the civil liberties of all American citizens. True, they saw this activism as being a way to guard their own rights, but their commitment to equal rights for blacks went far beyond their own self-interest.

Joel Spingarn was one of the founders of the NAACP and its chairman from 1913 to 1919. His brother, Arthur Spingarn, continued as honorary president through 1966.

After 1954, with the new thrust toward economic and political equality for blacks, many Jewish college students became active in the civil rights movement. They headed south to challenge segregation at its roots. As part of the New Left, they also worked in northern urban centers to achieve economic equality for blacks.

In 1964 James Chaney, Michael Schwerner, and Andrew Goodman, three student civil rights workers, were murdered in Philadelphia, Mississippi. Two of them were Jews.

Rabbis were prominent in the civil rights movement in the South. Abraham Joshua Heschel (see fact 578) marched at Selma, Alabama. Joachim Prinz used his political influence to push for civil rights legislation.

Positive Jewish involvement changed in the late 1960s as blacks became both more militant and more particularist. Many blacks identified with the Arab cause against Israel, creating a rift between black and Jewish leaders. The blacks complained that the Jewish leaders were patronizing them.

In addition, the civil rights movement shifted its focus from political enfranchisement to economic and social equality in the North. This refocus put blacks in direct conflict with Jews in their neighborhoods, deepening the rift. Many Jews opposed legislation that gave special privileges to minority groups, because they saw this as threatening their children's chances of getting into Ivy League colleges. They had personally suffered from quota systems in the 1920s and 1930s and thus had a long-standing hatred for them. Their opposition focused on the Bakke case.

Allan Bakke, a white engineer, claimed that the University of California Medical School had denied *his* equal rights because of their special admission program for minorities. In 1978 the U.S. Supreme Court ruled that "discrimination in reverse" was illegal. Most Jews favored the ruling, while blacks were vehemently against it. This led to ill-feeling between the two groups.

Although some black leaders continued to use anti-Semitic statements as a means to gain support among militant black followers, there were active attempts made in the early 1990s to heal the rifts in black-Jewish relations. It was difficult; both sides remained wary and suspicious.

465. Havurot are small groups of Jews who study and celebrate Judaism together.

In the 1960s some young left-of-center American Jews complained about the "sterility" of the large suburban synagogues with their impersonal professional staffs. They wanted to be liberal Jews and, at the same time, experience the emotions generated by traditional Judaism. Inspired by some theoretical ideas about creating small, informal communities of sharing egalitarian Jews, they formed their own havurah, a friendship study/davvening/celebrating group. The first havurah began in Cambridge, Massachusetts, and was called Havurah Shalom.

The havurah functioned without rabbi or cantor; the members took responsibility for deciding how they would pray, what they would say, and what they would study. Members led study sessions, and all members were encouraged to take on leadership roles.

The idea of warm, supportive, emotionally uplifting Jewish experiences gained popularity, and a number of congregations formed such groups within the synagogue structure, thus making havurot (plural of havurah) mainstream institutions. There are now a variety of havurot; some members take responsibility for teaching their children; some provide a wide assortment of different study/experiential programs. Some concentrate on helping the elderly and visiting the ill. Most havurot emphasize the special benefits of being part of a warm, caring community of Jews eager to experience Judaism together. The unique element of the havurah is the merging of traditional experiences in a small group of liberal, egalitarian, self-leading Jews.

466. Sally Priesand, the first woman rabbi, was ordained in 1972.

The role of rabbi in our tradition included serving as a judge, a legislator, a teacher, and a community authority. Until 1972, only men were rabbis.

Traditionally, women were exempt from any positive commandment that is time-bound. Our sages believed that child care and home care transcended those time-oriented commandments and that obligating women to perform them would be overwhelming. For that reason, women were exempt from participating in daily services, wearing a tallit, waving the lulav, dwelling in the sukkah, listening to the shofar, and putting on tefillin.

Traditionally, a woman was forbidden to serve as a sheliach tzibbur (see facts 240, 277) because she was exempt from the mitzvah of participating in the service. Our sages maintained that only those obligated to perform a mitzvah may represent others in that mitzvah.

Moreover the Talmud maintains that men should not listen to a woman's voice because it distracts them from prayer. Our sages declared that women could not serve as court witnesses; many sages recommended that women not be taught too much Torah. Since they couldn't be witnesses, women couldn't be judges.

According to one argument in the Talmud, women are theoretically permitted both to be called up to the Torah and to read the Torah publicly. However, later talmudic sages forbade this practice because it jeopardized "kvod hatzibbur," the dignity of the public.

Given these legal considerations and the second-class position of women in the non-Jewish society, it was unthinkable that a woman could be a rabbi.

In 1846 at the Breslau Conference, the leaders of the German Reform Movement declared that there should be total religious equality for women. The movement then began implementing this philosophical position.

The Reform Movement didn't function within a vacuum. Although many Reform Jews were eager and willing to give women full religious equality and recognition, most were not prepared to have their religious leader be a woman. This feeling took more than a century to overcome. In a number of instances, a woman had studied to become a rabbi but the leadership of Hebrew Union College had chosen not to ordain her.

In 1972 Rabbi Sally Priesand was ordained by the Hebrew Union College-Jewish Institute of Religion. By 1990 more than 150 women had been ordained as rabbis in the Reform movement.

The Conservative Movement continues to struggle with the issue of religious egalitarianism. In 1973 the Rabbinical Assembly Committee on Law and Standards established the minority position that permitted each congregation and rabbi to decide whether women could be (1) counted in a minyan, (2) called to the Torah, and (3) serve as a sheliach tzibbur.

In 1984 the faculty of the Jewish Theological Seminary voted to ordain women rabbis. Many Conservative rabbis strongly objected to this position for the traditional reasons mentioned above. They felt that the Conservative leadership institutions were no longer legitimately applying halachah (see fact 342) to their decisions. Therefore a group of Conservative rabbis, while maintaining membership in the Rabbinical Assembly, set up an advocacy institution called the Union for Traditional Conservative Judaism. The Union for Traditional Conservative

Judaism saw itself maintaining the traditional (and therefore "norma-tive") principles of Conservative Judaism.

In 1987 the Jewish Theological Seminary invested the first women as Conservative cantors. This too led to strong feelings and controversy because the primary function of a cantor is to be the sheliach tzibbur (see data to fact 242), a role traditionally forbidden to women.

In 1990 the Union for Traditional Conservative Judaism established its own rabbinical school and changed its name to the Union for Traditional Judaism. For all intents and purposes, it thus became a new stream of Judaism, separating itself from the Conservative Movement.

467. WUPJ is the World Union for Progressive Judaism.

Although the Reform Movement in the United States is the largest numerically and most influential financially, there are Reform Jewish communities in more than thirty countries all over the world. Most call themselves Progressive, not Reform, and many are more traditional in their ritual practice than are American Reform congregations.

In 1926 the World Union for Progressive Judaism was founded as the umbrella organization for all Reform congregations around the world. Besides HUC-JIR (see facts 448, 566), there are seminaries in London and Paris which train Reform rabbis. WUPJ's headquarters are located in Jerusalem and New York City.

468. The Falashas are black Jews from Ethiopia.

The word *Falasha* means "the Exiled," and it is viewed by the Jews of Ethiopia as a pejorative term. They refer to themselves as Beta Esrael (House of Israel). According to their tradition, they are descended from King Solomon and the Queen of Sheba. They have been frequently linked to the tribe of Dan, one of the Ten Lost Tribes (see data to fact 215). Most historians believe that they originated from the Agau tribe, already in Ethiopia. They came in contact with Jews 1,500 to 2,300 years ago, and the Jews assimilated into their family, thus creating Ethiopian or black Jews.

Although the Beta Esrael don't know Hebrew, they do have as their sacred book the TaNaCH written in a special Ethiopian dialect, Ge'ez. The book is handwritten on parchment, but it is not a scroll. According to their tradition, they had a Hebrew Torah scroll until the 1600s, when it was destroyed during a persecution.

The Beta Esrael follow many customs found in the Torah but do not know any of the laws developed by the Tanna'im or Amora'im (see facts 329, 361). They still offer the Passover sacrifice (see fact 71) and have their own priesthood. They strictly follow the laws of ritual purity (see fact 261). They celebrate Sanbat (Shabbat) by praying in their synagogues the entire day, coming out only to participate in a communal meal. They follow the basic laws of kashrut (see facts 589–597) and, unlike most Ethiopians, they do not eat raw meat.

In 1975 Israel's Chief Rabbinate (see fact 565) declared that the Beta Esrael were Jewish and welcomed them to Israel under the Law of Return (see fact 542).

The Beta Esrael had been persecuted for the past 1,500 years. Like most Ethiopians, they were bitterly poor and suffered starvation. Christians and Muslims have frequently tried to wipe them out. During the reign of Emperor Haile Selassie, there were laws requiring the Beta Esrael to listen to Christians trying to convert them. With the overthrow of Haile Selassie in 1974, a communist government took over. There were constant skirmishes between government and anti-government forces, and the Beta Esrael were caught in the middle. The government refused to allow Ethiopians, including the Beta Esrael, to emigrate. Desperate, many undertook the terrible trek to escape to the Sudan. In 1984, about 12,000 Beta Esrael were being held in refugee camps in the Sudan, leaving about 26,000 Jews in Ethiopia, most of them elderly or sick. That year Israel succeeded in airlifting large numbers of Beta Esrael from the Sudan (see fact 568).

In May 1991 the Communist government of Mengistu fell. Miraculously, even as he fled the country, arrangements were made to allow the remaining Ethiopian Jews to fly to Israel in a huge airlift called Operation Solomon. Israel processed and transported almost 14,500 Ethiopian Jews in thirty-two hours. One plane carried more than 1,000 people in a single flight.

There are now more than 36,000 Ethiopian Jews in Israel, and the problem of absorbing them has become an exciting challenge for the 1990s.

469. The Conference of Presidents of Major American Jewish Organizations is the umbrella organization for forty-six Jewish institutions.

After World War I the number of Jewish organizations skyrocketed. As more institutions became involved in Jewish concerns and began getting in one another's way, there was a need to establish some form of unified Jewish representation. In 1955 a group of representatives of Jewish organizations got together to found an umbrella organization which could speak for all of them. By 1970 the Conference of Presidents of Major American Jewish Organizations included twenty-four Jewish groups whose members represented the majority of the Jewish community in the United States.

In 1990 the Conference represented forty-six national Jewish organizations, including Hadassah (see fact 526); the American Jewish Congress, which in the 1930s focused public awareness on Nazi atrocities in Germany (see data to fact 458), actively fought against anti-Semitism, and later became a defender of civil liberties in the United States; the Zionist Organization of America; B'nai B'rith (see fact 445); and the rabbinic and lay organizations for the different Jewish movements. The American Israel Public Affairs Committee, an organization that educates American politicians and lobbies Capitol Hill for Israeli causes, is also a member of the Conference.

Israel:
The Geography and History
of the Modern State

Importance in the Ancient Middle East

470. Israel connects Africa and Asia Minor.

The Land of Israel (Eretz Yisrael) connects Asia and Africa. It is part of the famous Fertile Crescent, that banana-shaped piece of fertile land that runs from the Persian Gulf to Egypt and is surrounded on both sides by enormous deserts. In ancient times Eretz Yisrael was called Canaan. People have been moving around the Fertile Crescent for the past 100,000 years.

When Sumer and Akkad became great powers in Mesopotamia 5,000 years ago, they established trade routes to the other great civilization of that time, Egypt. Merchants traveling from Mesopotamia to Egypt had to go through the Land of Israel, the only safe land route, making it significant to every nation in the region.

471. Ancient merchants had to go through the Yizrael Valley to get from Mesopotamia to Egypt.

In ancient times there were two routes through the Land of Israel. The main route was called the Way of the Sea. It used the natural passes through Israel's mountain ranges. The Way of the Sea used the mountain pass north of Lake Kinneret, and crossed the flat Yizrael Valley (perfect for caravans), went through a second mountain pass to the Mediterranean coast, and then followed the coast all the way to Egypt.

The second route, called the Way of the King, cut through the first mountain pass near Lake Kinneret (see fact 479), then headed south through the Jordan Valley, following the Great Rift (see facts 485–487, 491) until it turned west to join the Way of the Sea along the northern coast of Africa.

472. Three ancient cities guarded the Yizrael Valley: Hatzor, Megiddo, and Beit Shean.

Control of the merchant routes between Mesopotamia and Egypt meant power and money, and, not surprisingly, huge wars have been waged for more than five thousand years over these routes. The easiest way to control both routes through the Land of Israel at once was to plug up the Yizrael Valley at the passes.

The Canaanites built three cities to do this. North of Lake Kinneret stood the city of Hatzor, blocking the northern pass. Just south of Lake Kinneret looking over the Jordan Valley stood Beit Shean. Blocking the pass on the western end of the Yizrael Valley stood Megiddo.

These cities rarely remained stable. Mesopotamia, Egypt, other Canaanite nations, and, when they arrived on the scene, Hebrews, all fought to control them. Megiddo, the "plug" to the coast, controlling the entire Yizrael Valley and its trade, was conquered and rebuilt twenty-six times. Because so many battles have been fought in the Yizrael Valley near Har Megiddo (Mount Megiddo), that city became the symbol for the Final Battle described in Christian theology: Armageddon.

473. A tel is a hill consisting of layers of old cities.

Frequently, when a city fell, it was rebuilt by the conquerors. Because the ancient civilizations didn't have bulldozers, they rarely leveled the conquered cities but rather built directly on top of the old ruins. Gradually this process of building city upon city created large artificial mounds, which are called tels. By digging vertically into a tel, archaeologists are able to learn about the different layers of occupation and the culture of each level. The work is slow and painstaking because the process destroys the evidence of everything above it. To double-check themselves, archaeologists leave vertical walls between their digging squares. These walls showing the various levels that the archaeologists are digging through are called baulks.

Geography of Israel

474. Jaffa has been a port in Israel for more than 4,000 years.

The Land of Israel (Eretz Yisrael) is small, about the size of New Jersey, yet it has a wide variety of extreme geographic regions. In a single day it is possible to drive from a snow-peaked mountain through a fertile valley filled with orange orchards, through a desert, and end up swimming in the Mediterranean Sea.

Israel's western border is the Mediterranean Sea. For more than 4,000 years, until 1936, the main port of Israel was Jaffa. Israel's Jaffa orange was fittingly named after this original port.

The coast provides a number of other ports which the modern state has enlarged for major shipping. In 1936 the British allowed Tel Aviv to become a Jewish port (see data to fact 530). The main British port and base, however, became Haifa (see fact 475).

475. Haifa is the main port in Israel.

In 1934 the British completed Haifa's large harbor and it became an important seaport. Today it is the major shipping port in Israel. Haifa is built on the side of the Carmel mountain range at three levels. It contains Israel's only subway, the Carmelit, which goes through the Carmel mountain.

The Technion, Israel's Institute of Technology, is located at the top of Mt. Carmel. The Leo Baeck School, Israel's only Reform high school, is also in Haifa (see data to fact 566).

In biblical times it was from Mt. Carmel that Elijah challenged the priests of Baal (see fact 208). The Cave of Elijah, where tradition says he hid from Jezebel after killing her priests, is a Jewish shrine in Haifa.

Haifa is considered one of the better integrated cities in Israel, where Arabs and Jews get along pretty well.

476. Israel's coastal plain has been the site of numerous battles.

Along the Mediterranean coast is the fertile coastal plain. It contains the vast majority of Israel's citrus orchards and vineyards. Rishon L'Tzion, the town in which Baron Rothschild founded his wine-making industry (see fact 503), is located here.

Three thousand years ago the Philistine cities were located along this plain; they included Ashdod (now a port city) and Ashkelon (now an absorption town for Ethiopian Jews; see facts 468, 568). The fertile coastal plain was the usual merchant route between Mesopotamia and Egypt, and many wars were fought along this coast.

When Egypt attacked Israel in 1948 (see fact 539), its tank force advanced along the coastal plain. It was slowed down remarkably at kibbutz Yad Mordechai and stopped at kibbutz Negba (see data to fact 539).

From 1948 until 1967 Israel was only 9 miles wide at the narrowest spot along the coastal plain. Therefore it was in constant danger of being cut in half by an attacking Jordanian army. Arab terrorists regularly tried to raid along that narrow strip of land. During the Six Day War Israel took the west bank of the Jordan River, thus gaining a natural border almost 50 miles wide (see fact 551).

477. The north of Israel is called the Galilee.

East of the coastal plain is a hilly region which quickly becomes rocky mountains running north-south through central and northern Israel (all mountain ranges in Israel run north and south). This mountain range has three names, each for a different section. In the north, above the Yizrael Valley (see fact 471), it is called the Galilee. The other two sections are the Hills of Ephraim (see data to fact 482) and the Hills of Judea (see data to fact 483).

The Galilee is remarkably rugged land. Two thousand years ago Jewish farmers barely scratched out a living from its rocky soil. As a result, the Galileans were a very tough group of people. The city of Nazareth, where Jesus probably grew up, is located in the Galilee.

478. Tzfat is the city of Kabbalah, Jewish mysticism.

The major Jewish city in the Galilee is Tzfat. Because Tzfat is situated next to Mount Meiron (see data to facts 82, 353), it became the center of Kabbalah, Jewish mysticism. Isaac Luria lived in Tzfat (see fact 417), as did Joseph Caro (see fact 419). The Shabbat song, "L'cha Dodi," "Come my Beloved," to welcome Shabbat as a bride, was written and first sung in Tzfat (see fact 100).

Because Tzfat is built on the side and crest of a mountain, and the Arabs held the upper ground in 1948, the Jews feared that they would lose the city in the war. However, with the help of a home-made mortar, the Davidka, the Jews took and held Tzfat (see data to fact 537).

Today, along with sixteenth-century synagogues of kabbalist Jews, there is an artists' colony in Tzfat.

479. Lake Kinneret is the only fresh-water lake in Israel.

In the Eastern Galilee lies Lake Kinneret, the only fresh-water lake in Eretz Yisrael. Shaped like a harp, *kinnor* in Hebrew, Lake Kinneret gets its water from the Jordan River, which has its three sources farther north at Banyas, Dan, and Hatzbiya. Lake Kinneret is called the Sea of Galilee in the Christian Bible.

It was there, according to the Christian New Testament, that Jesus gave his first sermon at Kfar Nachum (Capernaum), gave his Sermon on the Mount, multiplied loaves and fishes, walked on its water, and attracted a group of disciples. Helena, Constantine's mother, lent authority to the traditional spots for these miracles, and all are marked today by churches and monasteries (see data to fact 370).

480. Tiberias was the Roman capital in the Galilee.

Tiberias is located on the banks of Lake Kinneret. Originally the Roman capital in the north, Tiberias was the site where the Amora'im wrote the Jerusalem Talmud (see fact 365).

According to tradition, Tiberias is the burial site of both Rabbi Akiva (see fact 347) and RaMBaM (see facts 395–401).

Under the Ottoman Turks in the 1500s, the Jews were permitted to surround the city with a wall. They hoped in this way to create their own independent city. An earthquake destroyed the fortress completely.

In the sixth century a synagogue was built at Tiberias that had a beautiful mosaic floor complete with a full zodiac sign. The zodiac clearly meant a great deal to our people because it appears on a number of synagogue mosaic floors built during the Byzantine period (see fact 481 and data to fact 601).

481. A beautiful mosaic floor was found in the ancient synagogue of Beit Alfa.

The finest example of a mosaic (small stones set into a design) floor in a synagogue was found at Beit Alfa where the Akedah is depicted (see fact 130). It shows the donkey, the two servants, Abraham with his knife, Isaac, the altar, and a hand from the clouds. The words "Don't reach out your hand (against the boy)" are written into the mosaic.

The same floor shows an ark replete with cherubim, birds, a lulav, two menorahs, and fire pans. The center consists of a large zodiac sign, a reminder that astrology was important to Jews during the Byzantine period (see data to fact 601). Similar floors have been found at Tiberias (see fact 480) and at Beit Shean (see fact 472).

482. Nablus is the city of the Samaritans.

The second of the three parts of the mountain range in central Israel (see fact 477) is called the Hills of Ephraim and is bounded on the north by the Yizrael Valley. Because the major ancient city, fortressed by Herod (see data to fact 314) was Samaria, the area is also called Samaria. It includes the major portion of the West Bank (see fact 552).

In the center of Samaria is the city of Nablus (known in Hebrew as Shechem), a major site of Arab unrest and attacks on the West Bank. Nablus is also the city where most of the Samaritans live. The Samaritans consider themselves descendants of the tribes of Ephraim and Menasheh who were never taken into captivity by the Assyrians (see data to fact 215). When the Jews returned from the Babylonian Exile (see data to fact 220), they were attacked by the Samaritans. The rabbis have not considered them Jews for the past 2,000 years.

The Samaritans have their own Torah scroll written in ancient Hebrew and their own priesthood. They celebrate the holidays mentioned in the Torah but have their own post-Torah halachah unrelated to rabbinic laws. Their practices tend to be stricter and more rigid than halachah.

They make pilgrimage to their holy mountain, Mount Gerizim, three times each year on the Shalosh Regalim (see fact 27). On Passover they hold their annual Pesach sacrifice on their holy mountain, slaughtering and consuming their Pesach sheep (see fact 71). There are still more than 500 Samaritans living in Nablus.

483. Bab El Wad is the mountain pass between Tel Aviv and Jerusalem.

Just south of the Hills of Ephraim are the Hills of Judea, the third and southernmost section of the central mountain range (see fact 477). They rise to 3,000 feet above sea level. Jerusalem is located in the center of the Hills of Judea. There is a single pass from the coast through the mountains, in Hebrew called Shaar HaGai and in Arabic called Bab El Wad, both meaning the Gate of the Valley. It was at that pass that the Arabs set up their roadblocks in 1947 and 1948 to strangle Jerusalem (see data to fact 537).

484. The Cave of Machpelah in Hebron is holy to both Muslims and Jews.

The ancient city of Hebron lies in the Hills of Judea south of Jerusalem. Abraham bought a cave there to bury his wife Sarah (see fact 131). The cave was covered with a large crusader building and was holy to both the Muslims and Jews because of their shared ancestor Abraham, who was buried there. According to Jewish tradition, Abraham, Sarah, Isaac, Rebecca, Jacob, Leah, Adam, and Eve were buried in the Cave of Machpelah in Hebron.

From 1948 to 1967 Hebron was part of Jordan, and Jews were forbidden even to set foot in the city. Israel took Hebron in the Six Day War, and now both peoples may visit their holy shrine. Jewish settlers built a new city above Hebron called Kiryat Arba.

Hebron has been one of the sites of tension and conflict between Arabs and Jews on the West Bank (see fact 552).

485. The Jordan River is the largest river in Israel.

East of the central mountain range (consisting of the Galilee, the Hills of Ephraim, and the Hills of Judea), there is a deep valley 112 miles long which runs from Lake Kinneret down to the Gulf of Eilat, at the southern end of Israel. Geologists call it the Great Rift. In the northern part, east of the Galilee and the Hills of Ephraim, it is called the Jordan Valley. The Jordan River, the longest river in Israel, meanders through this valley, making it tremendously fertile. Although the distance from Lake Kinneret to the Dead Sea is only about 60 miles, the Jordan River is more than 100 miles long, twisting back on itself as it goes through the valley.

486. Jericho is the world's oldest city.

Just north of the Dead Sea (see fact 487) lies the city of Jericho. Archaeologists have uncovered 8,000-year-old ruins of a tower dating back to 6800 B.C.E. making Jericho the oldest known city in the world. Jericho exists because of a fresh-water spring making fertile an otherwise desolate area.

Because it is located in the Great Rift, Jericho enjoys a warm climate during the winter. The Muslim caliph Hisham took advantage of this weather and built a magnificent palace at Jericho in the eighth century. Soon after he built it, however, an earthquake destroyed the palace, leaving only the ruined remnants to show the level of his opulence.

The remains of a mosaic floor of a synagogue have been uncovered at Jericho. It shows a menorah and contains the words "Shalom al Yisrael," "Peace to Israel."

487. The Dead Sea is the furthest below-sea-level area on earth.

The Jordan River runs into the Dead Sea, the lowest spot on earth. The Dead Sea, 50 miles long and 11 miles wide, is 1,280 feet below sea level. It receives less than one inch of rain per year. There is a tremendous evaporation rate, resulting in huge accumulations of chemicals in the Dead Sea. As a result, the Dead Sea is ten times saltier than the Atlantic Ocean. Its ratio of chemicals to water is so high that it is impossible to sink in it. It remains as warm as bath water and leaves a coating of chemicals on the skin. Dermatologists have discovered that the chemicals are beneficial for many skin ailments, and numerous resort hotels have been built to accommodate tourists coming for treatments.

Today the Dead Sea is mined for its chemicals and is the site for experiments in solar energy.

In ancient times the area was famous for its salt and bitumin. According to tradition, it used to be fertile and green. After the incident of Sodom and Gemorah (see facts 127, 128), however, it became the desolate wasteland it is today.

Both Masada (see facts 317, 338, 339) and Qumran (see facts 322, 323) are located near the Dead Sea.

The famous oasis of Ein Gedi is located on the western shore of the Dead Sea. David fled there while being pursued by King Saul (see data to fact 197). Today Ein Gedi has a kibbutz as well as a nature preserve famous for its ibex and panthers. The waterfall at Ein Gedi, hidden among the desert mountains, is wonderful.

488. The Negev is a large desert in the south of Israel.

The whole region south of the Hills of Judea and west of the Aravah (see fact 491) is called the Negev, the Dry Area. The Negev is a large desert which receives less than four inches of rain a year. However, as has been proved by the numerous kibbutzim thriving there, the land can be fertile when supplied with enough water. David Ben Gurion's kibbutz, S'dei Boker, is located in the Negev (see data to fact 538).

489. Be'er Sheva, in the middle of the Negev, is a thriving modern city.

The modern city of Be'er Sheva is in the middle of the Negev desert. Originally an oasis with a well, it is now a modern city with a university and more than 100,000 residents.

According to the Torah, Abraham settled in Be'er Sheva for a period of time. Also, Isaac is said to have dug seven wells at Be'er Sheva (Genesis 26). The name means either Seven Wells or the Well of Promise.

490. Bedouin still live in the Negev near Be'er Sheva.

The Bedouin are nomadic Arab tribes. For the past 1,500 years they have followed their traditional routes from the Negev through the Sinai Desert. Each Bedouin tribe has its own resting spots, wells, and oases. The Bedouin never recognized arbitrary international boundaries and, even when Israel and Egypt were at war, traveled as they wished across the borders.

Today many Bedouin live in Israel, forsaking the nomadic life. There are still nomadic tribes, however, who live in the Negev near Be'er Sheva. They continue to ignore international borders and spend part of their time in Jordan. It is possible to visit the Bedouin market on Thursday mornings in Be'er Sheva.

491. Kibbutz Yahel and Kibbutz Lotan are two Reform kibbutzim in the Aravah.

The Great Rift south of the Dead Sea is called the Aravah. It is extremely hot and barren except for occasional oases along the way to the Gulf of Eilat (see fact 492). Bar Kochba and his men hid in caves along the Aravah while fighting the Romans (see fact 349). Many of their artifacts, found in caves, have provided us with insights into their lifestyle and struggle. Those artifacts, like the Dead Sea Scrolls, are now housed in the Shrine of the Book in Jerusalem.

The two Reform kibbutzim Yahel and Lotan are located there. Besides exporting dates, the kibbutzim provide experiential programs for visiting youth groups and offer tours into the desert and Sinai. Through their ongoing struggle to find an acceptable group Jewish lifestyle, the members of Yahel and Lotan are creating a live-in havurah (see fact 465), working together to combine traditional religious experiences with a vibrant, egalitarian Reform Judaism.

492. The southernmost city in Israel is Eilat.

Israel's southern port is Eilat, located on the Gulf of Eilat (called by Arabs the Gulf of Aqaba). In ancient times, Solomon had his port of Etzion Gever there and had fleets sailing the Red Sea to Ethiopia.

From 1948 to 1967 Eilat was a small military outpost guarding the triple border of Egypt, Jordan, and Saudi Arabia. After the Six Day War (see fact 552), Eilat became a starting point for tours into the Sinai Desert.

When Israel returned the Sinai to Egypt (see data to fact 559), Eilat assumed high tourist status and today is a sea resort. Besides scuba diving in tropical reefs, sailing, glass-bottomed boat rides, and snorkling, Eilat offers a unique look at its tropical reefs through an underwater aquarium.

493. The Crusaders built more than 250 forts in the Land of Israel.

In 1096, after the Crusader mobs had slaughtered the Jews in the Rhineland (see fact 382), the knights finally headed for the Holy Land. They arrived in 1098 and moved quickly down the coast. In 1099 the Crusaders attacked Jerusalem. Using siege machines, they broke into the city and committed another blood bath, massacring more than 20,000 men, women, and children. The Jews who survived the first onslaught were herded into synagogues, and the buildings were set on fire, destroying much of the Jewish population.

By 1120 C.E. the Land of Israel was totally in Crusader hands. Most of the Crusaders returned to Europe while others remained and proceeded to build fortresses and manor estates similar to those in Europe, planning to make the land into a feudal state.

The Crusaders left more structures in Palestine than did any other group. Castles and fortresses can be seen all over the country. Huge walled cities were created at Akko, Caesarea (see data to fact 314), and Banyas. Smaller forts were built at Belvoir, Beit Guvrin, Atlit, and Monfort. The Crusaders built more than 250 forts and churches during their stay. They were not properly defended, however, since the average castle held only ten to fifteen knights. When the Moslems counterattacked, the Crusaders lost almost all of their carefully built forts.

Significance for Muslims, Christians, and Jews

494. Jerusalem is holy to Muslims, Christians, and Jews.

Located in the middle of the Judean Hills, Jerusalem would have remained a small out-of-the-way town if it weren't for its religious significance. When King David conquered the city and brought the Ark to Jerusalem, he made it the capital of Israel, the religious beacon for Jews for three thousand years (see fact 199).

Because Jesus spent his last days there and it is the traditional site of his death and resurrection, Jerusalem became a holy site for the Christians (see fact 325).

According to Muslim tradition, Mohammed leaped into heaven from a stone on the Temple Mount, thus making Jerusalem the third holiest site for Muslims (see data to fact 371).

495. The Dome of the Rock stands on the Temple Mount.

When Mohammed began preaching his religion of Islam, he believed that the first group to accept his doctrine would be the Jews in Yathrib. He therefore ordered that all prayers be made facing Jerusalem. When it became clear that the Jewish tribes in Arabia were not accepting him, he changed the worship to be directed toward the Kaaba, a great black stone in Mecca. However, Jerusalem continued to be a holy site for Muslims.

The third holiest spot for Muslims is the large rock on the Temple Mount. According to Jewish tradition, this rock is the center of the world and the site of the Akedah (see fact 130). According to Muslim tradition, the rock was the spot from which Mohammed leaped into heaven after miraculously traveling from Mecca to Jerusalem in a single night.

To commemorate this miracle, the caliph Abd al-Malik built a magnificent structure called the Dome of the Rock. It is sometimes (incorrectly) called the Mosque of Omar; it was not built by Omar, and it is not a mosque. However, its gold dome (now made of a special aluminum) dominated the landscape of the Old City of Jerusalem for the past 1,300 years. It has been suggested that Abd al-Malik's intention in building the Dome of the Rock was to make the Muslim structures more spectacular than the Christian Church of the Holy Sepulchre (see fact 325). He apparently succeeded. The interior, paneled in marble, contains magnificent stained glass windows, decorated ceilings, and, of course, the beautiful dome rising over the rock which stands in the center of the building.

The Dome of the Rock is situated on the spot where, according to one Jewish tradition, the Temple's Holy of Holies once stood (see the data to fact 204). There have been a number of attempts by extremist Jews to get rid of the Dome of the Rock to enable the Temple to be rebuilt. Israel's army has been successful in preventing any damage to the building.

496. The Mosque of al-Aqsa, third holiest spot for Muslims, also stands on the Temple Mount.

In 693 C.E. a mosque on the Temple Mount was completed by Caliph Abd al-Malik. It is called the Al-Aqsa Mosque, the "furthermost mosque," as a reminder that it was the farthest spot that Mohammed reached on his night journey from Mecca to Jerusalem (see fact 495). The mosque of Al-Aqsa can easily hold 3,000 people. It once contained a preacher's magnificent pulpit, but this was damaged in a fire set by a mentally disturbed Australian in 1969 which resulted in a UN Security Council censure of Israel.

King Abdullah, the first king of Jordan, was assassinated by an Arab terrorist in the Al-Aqsa mosque in 1949 because he was willing to sign a treaty with Israel.

497. The Mount of Olives, opposite the Temple Mount, has a huge Jewish cemetery.

Just east of the Old City of Jerusalem is found the Mount of Olives, separated from the Temple Mount by the Kidron Valley. According to the TaNaCH (2 Samuel 15:32), King David worshipped at the top of the Mount of Olives.

In the Torah (Numbers 19), Aaron's son Eleazar is commanded to take a totally red heifer, kill it, and burn it to ashes, which in turn were used to purify both people and objects that had come in contact with a corpse. According to tradition, during the time of the Second Temple, the red heifer was burnt on the Mount of Olives. In Roman times there was a bridge from the mountain to the Temple Mount. From the top of the mountain, fires were lit to notify the community that it was Rosh Chodesh (see fact 1).

Most important, the prophets Zechariah and Ezekiel proclaimed that the glory of God will stand on the Mount of Olives at the End of Days. The Mount of Olives therefore became an important burial site for Jews, an ideal spot to wait for the End of Days and resurrection (see fact 607).

The Mount of Olives was holy for Christians as well. It was from its height that Jesus was said to have risen to heaven. At its base was the garden where Jesus was arrested (Gethsemane).

During the Muslim period the Rosh Yeshivah (see data to fact 368) would sit on the Mount of Olives during the Shalosh Regalim (see fact 27), and there would be ceremonies on the mountain.

When Jordanian soldiers took the Mount of Olives in 1948, they desecrated the Jewish cemetery and used the area as a latrine. They also bulldozed part of the cemetery and used Jewish tombstones to pave the road leading to the Intercontinental Hotel, built atop the Mount of Olives. After Israel took the Mount in the Six Day War, restoration of the graves and headstones to their proper places began.

498. Zion became another name for the whole country of Israel.

For the past 2,000 years, Jews have turned toward the Land of Israel, their land. In prayer and poem, Jews remember the idealized time when King David was ruler and the Hebrews were a great power. They remember the Temple, the site of holiness, and they regularly pray for a return to the Land.

According to tradition, King David was buried on Mount Zion, a hill just west of his city and south of the Temple Mount. Because of the importance of King David, who made Jerusalem the capital of Israel, his burial mountain, Zion, became another name for Jerusalem. Later it became synonymous with the entire Land of Israel.

Judah HaLevi (see fact 392) focused on the special religious nature of Zion. With hindsight, we call him a *religious* Zionist. The history of the modern state of Israel depended on a different insight, however. Modern Israel was founded by Jews who strove to establish a politically recognized homeland for the Jews. We call them *political* Zionists. The history of political Zionism began 500 years ago.

From Ottoman Turks to British Mandate

499. The Ottoman Turks ruled Palestine from 1520 to 1920.

When the Jews were exiled from Spain in 1492 (see fact 413), many of them escaped to Turkey. They brought with them Spanish culture, administrative and trade experience, and technical knowledge which included the use of cannon and gunpowder. The sultan of the Ottoman Turks encouraged their immigration. In 1516 the Turks won a great victory at Aleppo and took over control of the Land of Israel.

The Land of Israel was important to the Turks as a strategic site on the pilgrimage route to Mecca. It was also their link with Egypt. However, the Turks couldn't afford to leave a standing army there to keep the peace. Therefore, from the sixteenth century on, the Ottomans relied on the Bedouin chieftains to keep the peace and collect the taxes. The wealthy landlords living in Constantinople rented the land to poor Arabs, who had to pay back a large portion of their crops. The Bedouin chiefs were not interested in maintaining the land, and they extorted as much money as they could from the poor tenant-farmers and the Jews trying to survive in the country.

Through the seventeenth, eighteenth, and nineteenth centuries, conditions increasingly worsened. In the 19th century, Ottoman Turkey was called "The Sick Man of Europe." The sultan lacked funds, power, and organization. Bribery was such a large part of every administration that it became impossible to get anything done in the government. The local authorities in the Land of Israel were totally independent and took advantage of their capacity to squeeze money out of the poor. Every powerful chieftain in the Land of Israel mercilessly taxed the weak, poor farmers. The landlords in Constantinople didn't care so long as they got their yearly taxes. The land deteriorated horribly; erosion stripped the mountains of soil, and malarial swamps covered large portions of the north.

500. The Old City of Jerusalem is surrounded by a wall.

The first Ottoman sultan, Suleiman the Magnificent, loved Jerusalem. In 1537 he ordered the entire city surrounded by a wall with seven well-defended gates which were locked each night. The city was divided into a Christian quarter, a Jewish quarter, a Muslim quarter, and an Armenian quarter. All Jerusalem residents lived inside the city, where, as the centuries passed, they became more cramped for space. No one thought to move outside the Old City walls because wild beasts, Bedouin, and robbers roamed the Judean Hills at night, attacking anyone foolish enough to be caught outside the locked gates.

501. Sir Moses Montefiore built the first set of houses and a windmill outside the Old City of Jerusalem.

The Jews in the Land of Israel couldn't survive on their own. The taxes were too high; they didn't have the means to become financially independent. Therefore, they relied on the Jews of Europe to send them funds. These funds, used for bribes, soup kitchens, Shabbat food for the poor, and fuel for the winter, were called the chalukah, the distribution. It was an ongoing example of Jews taking care of Jews. It mattered to European Jews that fellow Jews in the Land of Israel survive. Even though many of them were suffering financially, they contributed to the chalukah.

In addition, wealthy European Jews tried to help the Jews of Palestine become financially independent. One of the most famous Jewish philanthropists was Sir Moses Montefiore. During his life he visited the Land of Israel seven times. He tried unsuccessfully to buy some land there in 1838 so Jews could begin farming. He donated money for a textile mill, but it failed.

In 1856 Sir Moses Montefiore succeeded in encouraging a small group of Jews to create their own settlement outside the walls of Jerusalem, despite the physical danger from robbers and wild animals. He built a line of houses and included a windmill to grind flour, hoping to make those few settlers self-sufficient. He then offered money to anyone willing to stay in his new settlement overnight.

Although not a great success this settlement, called Yemin Moshe (the right hand of Moses), introduced to Jerusalem's poor Jewish population the idea that they could safely settle outside the city walls. Yemin Moshe began the new modern city of Jerusalem.

In 1870 one of the Jewish self-help organizations, the Alliance Israelite Universelle, bought some land from the Turkish authorities and founded an agricultural school at Mikveh Israel. In 1878, settlements were started at Petach Tikvah and Rosh Pinna. Because of malaria, both were abandoned as independent farming sites, but the seed of the idea of Jews becoming farmers in the Land of Israel was beginning to take root.

502. The First Aliyah began in 1882, led by the BILU.

Anti-Semitism continued in cultured Western Europe and Eastern Europe through the nineteenth century. Some intellectual Haskalah Jews (see fact 436) tried to solve this dilemma.

In 1860 Moses Hess wrote a book called *Rome and Jerusalem*, in which he noted that the world consisted of two races: Aryans and Semites. The Aryans described the world and tried to make it beautiful. The Semites tried to make the world moral. Since these two groups were really separate, rather than living in conflict within the same borders, the Semites should fulfill their destiny and create their own nation. Although basically ignored at the time of its writing, *Rome and Jerusalem* was the first printed expression of the political need for Jews to have their own country in Palestine.

In 1882 Leon Pinsker, a Russian Haskalah writer, wrote a book called *Auto-Emancipation*, in which he said anti-Semitism existed because Jews were a minority without their own land. So long as they tried living among non-Jews, they would be persecuted. Jews needed to return to the Land of Israel and become independent. Pinsker was a major leader in a group called Lovers of Zion.

At this time, a group of fifteen idealistic Jews sailed for Palestine in 1882 to found their own agricultural settlement. This marked the first Jewish immigration to Palestine for the political purpose of establishing a Jewish homeland. It was called the First Aliyah (Going Up). The group of fifteen called themselves the BILU, an acronym for the Hebrew "House of Jacob, let us go up." They arrived at Mikveh Israel, the agricultural school, where they suffered terrible privations. They built an independent settlement called Rishon L'Tziyon, The First of Zion, but it almost failed because it lacked sufficient fresh water. In desperation, they turned to Baron Edmund de Rothschild for help (see fact 503).

503. The Jews returning to the Land of Israel were helped by Baron Edmund de Rothschild.

One of the principal financial supporters of the BILU was Baron Edmund de Rothschild (see date to fact 434). He provided the BILU with funds, agricultural experts, and French vines to create a wine industry in Palestine. Under his supervision, the settlement of Zichron Yaakov was founded. Rishon L'Tziyon was revitalized when Baron de Rothschild provided money to dig a deep water-well (see data to fact 502). In exchange, the settlers tried to cultivate the Baron's grapes.

Unfortunately, things did not go smoothly. The French vines were not well suited to Palestine's climate or soil. The agricultural experts viewed the BILU as hired laborers and refused to let them participate in planning. At best, the Jews were made to oversee the real workers, Arab laborers who worked for less. The ambitious, idealistic BILU were frustrated. They wanted to branch out on their own, but Baron de Rothschild opposed their doing this as financially unsound. Gradually, more Russian Jews came over under the auspices of Pinsker's Lovers of Zion (see data to fact 502), and by the 1890s they numbered more than a thousand. The settlers succeeded in creating settlements at Gederah

(1884), Mishmar HaYarden (1890), Hadera, and Rechovot (both in 1891).

The BILU didn't succeed in establishing a Jewish political presence but, at great personal sacrifice, the idealistic Jews of the First Aliyah did create the first self-sufficient Jewish agricultural settlements in 2,000 years.

504. Eliezer Ben Yehuda created the modern language of Hebrew.

Eliezer Perelman was a Lithuanian Jew who joined the Haskalah movement (see fact 436). In the 1870s, believing deeply that Jews had to have their own country and their own language, he changed his name to Eliezer Ben Yehuda and began his life-long crusade to encourage Jews to speak Hebrew. This idea was revolutionary. Traditionally, Hebrew was used only for prayer, for it was considered a sacred language. Orthodox Jews were horrified at the thought of secular Jews speaking Hebrew as a national Jewish language.

Eliezer Ben Yehuda persevered. He was enthusiastically supported by the BILU, who adopted Hebrew as their official language. The problem, however, was that Hebrew hadn't been used in conversation for almost 2,000 years. It had no vocabulary to meet the day-to-day needs of the modern world. Moreover, Hebrew literature tended to be flowery and verbose. Eliezer Ben Yehuda focused on writing in a direct, succinct style and proceeded systematically to create the needed modern vocabulary. Through his weekly magazine, his dictionary, and his enthusiasm, Eliezer Ben Yehuda succeeded in making Hebrew a modern spoken language, the national tongue of the Jewish people.

505. Alfred Dreyfus was a French captain framed by the army because he was a Jew.

The most controversial trial at the end of the nineteenth century resulted from the case of Alfred Dreyfus. Dreyfus was a captain on the French general staff, an extraordinarily high position even for an assimilated Jew. In 1894 a document sent by French Major Ferdinand Esterhazy, who was working for the Germans, was intercepted. Because he was a Jew, Dreyfus was accused of the crime. The prosecution went so far as to forge documents to frame him, and in a closed court-martial Dreyfus was found guilty and condemned to life imprisonment on

Devil's Island. In 1895, amidst cries of "Death to the Jews," he was publicly humiliated.

Even when the frame-up was proven, the French army refused to change its verdict. The incident caused an international scandal because France, the European birthplace of liberty, justice, and liberalism, had sunk to such depths of anti-Semitism. On January 13, 1898, Emile Zola wrote an outraged article, "J'accuse!" which accused Dreyfus's opponents of malicious libel. Despite world horror, it wasn't until 1906 that the French Court of Appeal admitted that there had never been a case against Dreyfus, and he was completely exonerated.

506. In response to the Dreyfus trial, Theodor Herzl wrote *The Jewish State.*

One of the people most shaken by the Dreyfus case was Theodor Herzl. Theodor Herzl was born in Budapest and attended the Liberal Temple there. He received a law degree but chose to concentrate on writing. He was 31 years old in 1891 when he moved to Paris as the correspondent for the Vienna *Neue Freie Presse.* Encountering anti-Semitism, he assumed that the solution was for Jews to totally assimilate. He believed that anti-Semitism occurred because Jews looked and acted different.

Herzl was covering the Dreyfus trial as a correspondent when he witnessed the vitriolic anti-Semitism of the French. When he observed the humiliation of Alfred Dreyfus and heard the mobs screaming, "Death to the Jews," he was flabbergasted. Dreyfus was a totally assimilated Jew, high-ranking in the French army, a man of culture and French idealism.

Moreover, the French were the most sophisticated, cultured people in the world. Their anti-Semitic responses couldn't spring from ignorance. (As it happens, Herzl assumed at the time that Dreyfus was guilty; it was the vehemence of the hatred that stunned him.) Herzl concluded that the only solution for anti-Semitism was the exodus of Jews from hostile nations and their resettlement onto their own land. Anti-Semitism would cease, he believed, only when Jews had their own country.

Obviously, this was not an original thought. Both Hess and Pinsker had written about it earlier (see data to fact 502). However, Herzl, a man of incredible energy, proceeded to create the necessary political framework to achieve that goal. He knew that the first step to creating a Jewish homeland had to be an international Jewish institution responsible for funding and organizing the new nation.

Having been turned down by major Jewish philanthropists who viewed him as a zealous madman, Herzl presented his plan to the Jewish people. In 1896 he wrote a pamphlet, "The Jewish State," which described his goal of creating a separate nation for the Jews. Herzl believed that the non-Jewish countries would recognize the benefits of ridding their territories of anti-Semitism and would help him get an internationally recognized charter. It didn't happen.

507. The First World Zionist Congress convened in 1897.

Through his pamphlet, "The Jewish State," (see fact 506), Theodor Herzl was able to excite enough thoughtful European Jews about his plan to convene a World Zionist Congress, to begin establishing a Jewish nation. The First World Zionist Congress met in Basel, Switzerland, in 1897. It was the first time that Jews from different nations had ever met with a political agenda. The official language of the Congress was German.

Although the philosophical differences among the representatives were tremendous, all agreed that the purpose of the World Zionist Congress would be to represent the needs of all Jews in their goal of establishing an independent Jewish nation. It was understood that their major function was to create the political organizations needed to found a new country. They elected Herzl president of the organization and agreed to meet once a year.

Richard Gottheil, who attended the First World Zionist Congress, returned to the United States and, in 1898, helped form the Federation of American Zionists. Other Zionist organizations, including Hadassah (see fact 526), joined this American Zionist umbrella organization, and in 1918 the Federation became the Zionist Organization of America.

508. Theodor Herzl was the father of political Zionism.

Buoyed by the success of the First World Zionist Congress (see fact 507), Theodor Herzl then tried meeting with the Turkish sultan (see fact 499) to convince him to allow Jews to migrate en masse to Palestine. He believed that the movement to create a Jewish homeland could not accomplish its goals through illegal immigration. The Jews had to get a charter from the Turks. Herzl did meet the sultan in 1898 but was disappointed at the lack of enthusiasm he encountered.

Despite a weak heart, Herzl continued to spend the last years of his life struggling to amass the capital needed for establishing a nation and trying to convince the heads of European states to help the Jews.

England refused to give the Jews permission to settle on Cyprus. However, Foreign Minister Lord Chamberlain did offer Herzl the option of settling in Uganda. Herzl brought this proposal back to the World Zionist Congress. While many Jews seriously considered the offer, the representatives of Russian Jewry, dedicated to the dream of a return to Zion, threatened to leave the Congress. The proposal was defeated.

Herzl died in 1904. Because of his single-focused devotion to the need for a Jewish state, he is credited with being the father of political Zionism and is buried on Mount Herzl in Jerusalem.

509. The Jewish National Fund plants trees in Israel.

Although the creation of the Jewish National Fund was originally proposed by Judah Alkalai in 1847, it is credited to Hermann Schapira. It was established at the Fifth Zionist Congress in 1901, when the new Zionist anthem, "HaTikvah," was officially played for the first time.

The purpose of the Jewish National Fund (JNF) was to collect money from every Jew in the world to purchase land in Palestine. Doing this would make the land the property of the entire Jewish people.

By distributing little blue-and-white-metal boxes worldwide to collect coins, the Jewish National Fund provided every Jew with the opportunity to contribute to the Zionist movement. With the monies collected, the Jewish National Fund purchased tracts of land in Palestine from the Turkish landlords in Constantinople.

This created a serious problem. Although the Turkish government was opposed to Jews immigrating to Palestine, the Turkish and Arab landlords were glad to sell their land to the Jews because they considered much of it unusable swamps. They got more money by selling the land than they did from the Arab tenant farmers who toiled in Palestine.

These tenant farmers were placed in an impossible position. For centuries their families had worked the land for the Turkish landowners and paid the landowners yearly rent. Suddenly a group of Jews arrived claiming they owned the land the Arabs had worked for centuries. Instead of hiring the tenant farmers to work the land, the pioneers moved them from it. This situation was the foundation of the Arab cry of Zionists "stealing" their land from them.

The Jewish National Fund, by controlling the funds for the settlements, became the overseer for the New Jewish community in the Land of Israel. In 1920 it also began to collect monies to help reclaim the swamps of Palestine. There quickly followed afforestation efforts. Since 1920, millions of trees have been planted in Israel by the Jewish National Fund. It has become a custom to buy trees to be planted in Israel on Tu BiShvat (see fact 50).

The Jewish National Fund continues to play an active role in creating new agricultural settlements in Israel, including the Reform Jewish kibbutzim of Yahel and Lotan (see fact 491).

510. Young idealists hoping to create a new world in Palestine were involved in the Second Aliyah.

The BILU had succeeded in starting some poor settlements with the help of Baron de Rothschild (see facts 502, 503), but they were nowhere near establishing a community that could seriously be considered a Jewish nation. They desperately needed a large influx of Jews.

Because of the severe pogroms in Russia in 1903 and 1904 (see fact 451), many Jews fled that country. Although the majority headed for the United States, about 40,000 arrived in Palestine between 1904 and 1914. The vast majority of them came illegally, because Turkey had forbidden Jewish immigration. Jews were permitted to stay only three months in the Land of Israel, but bribes kept the Turkish officials in Palestine silent.

Although a number of these new Jewish immigrants were religious and joined the large traditional community in Jerusalem, the vast majority of this second major immigration, called the Second Aliyah, consisted of idealistic young, secular Jews, eager to build a new Jewish homeland. They were influenced by the ideas of Ber Borochov and other Socialist Zionists, who demonstrated that Zionism could be compatible with democratic socialism.

Many of them had read Ahad HaAm, a Zionist writer. In his book *The Wrong Way*, Ahad HaAm criticized the Zionists who had been simply talking about going to Israel. In his opinion, creating a Jewish nation wasn't enough. The Jewish nation had to encompass a whole new value system of equality, egalitarianism, and utopianism. The Jewish state had to be a light to the other nations. To accomplish this new society, Jews had to purify themselves and live the values espoused within Judaism. The new nation couldn't be just a nation for Jews; it had to be a Jewish nation. The young pioneers of the Second Aliyah were determined to create the society envisioned by Ahad HaAm.

Inspired by one of their members, A. D. Gordon (see fact 511), they studied farming and began establishing new settlements. Influenced by Eliezer Ben Yehuda (see fact 504), they adopted Hebrew names and spoke only Hebrew. They were dedicated to equality of the sexes. Some of them overtly renounced marriage and simply lived together. They felt it was their obligation to create a new utopian society, fulfilling their socialist dreams. It was the Second Aliyah group that established many of the political institutions needed by an independent nation. Political committees, organizations, and societies were founded, all under the umbrella of the World Zionist Organization.

511. A. D. Gordon believed that making the Land of Israel green was the highest imperative for a Jew.

One of the members of the Second Aliyah was a middle-aged idealist named A. D. Gordon. Although Gordon had never done manual labor, he insisted on joining the young farmers. He suffered all of the deprivations—malaria, unemployment, physical hardships—yet he insisted on working the land. Inspired by the Russian peasant's traditional love of the land, A. D. Gordon worked out a philosophy which emphasized as the ideal Jewish goal actually working the land to make the Land of Israel green. He inspired a huge number of young Second Aliyah members to work the land themselves. Until then, many settlements had relied on cheap Arab labor. Through his encouragement, the Jews of the Second Aliyah found inspiration in getting their own hands into the soil.

512. HaShomer was the first Jewish defense group in Palestine.

Traditionally, Jewish settlements had relied on Bedouin and Arabs to protect them from raiders. It was really a form of blackmail; the Jewish settlers paid the Arabs not to attack their settlements.

This system was reprehensible to the idealistic Second Aliyah pioneers who had been involved in Jewish defense groups in Russia. In 1907 they formed a small group of ten Jews assigned to protect one settlement. They were successful, and in 1909 they expanded into a larger defense organization called HaShomer (the Guard). Their motto was, "By blood and fire Judah fell, by blood and fire Judah will rise up."

They were a wild bunch, dressed in Arab garb with bandoliers of ammunition slung over their shoulders like Mexican bandits. They were expert horsemen, spoke fluent Arabic, and gained the respect of the Bedouin clans for their ferocity and fairness. The HaShomer inspired the settlements: Jews could successfully defend Jews. Although never large in number (in 1914 it had fifty members), HaShomer was a symbol of the new Jewish society being created in the Land of Israel.

513. Degania, the first kibbutz, was founded by members of the Second Aliyah.

The original settlements of the Second Aliyah relied on funds from the Jewish National Fund. The JNF watched these funds carefully and viewed innovations with distrust. In 1909, with concern, the JNF allowed seven men and women to move from the farming settlement of Kinneret a mile down the road to Degania and create a new format of settlement. Called a kevutzah, it was basically an enlarged family where everyone worked together, made decisions together, and depended upon one another. A second kevutzah was founded at Kinneret in 1911.

The intimacy and intensity of these small socialist communal farming settlements met the needs of the idealistic young pioneers. They shared everything, lived together, and fought together. The Second Aliyah thus created the kibbutz movement.

514. In 1909 Tel Aviv was founded on the sands just north of Jaffa.

The accomplishments of the Second Aliyah didn't remain solely agricultural. All Jews entering Palestine had to come through the port of Jaffa. Many First Aliyah pioneers settled in this Arab port city, causing large rent increases.

When the Second Aliyah pioneers arrived, the Jewish population of Jaffa rose to over 8,000, and housing became extremely difficult to find. In 1906 a group of more than a hundred Jews met to plan a garden suburb north of Jaffa, built on the sandy shore of the Mediterranean. Despite tremendous hostility from the Turks, they succeeded in finding the necessary bribe money, and they purchased land for their project. In 1909 they drew lots and set up sixty tents. These quickly became houses. Despite forced expulsion by the Turks during World War I, by 1925 the Jewish suburb north of Jaffa had become an all-Jewish city of more than 34,000: Tel Aviv.

Today Greater Tel Aviv is the largest city in Israel, with a population of more than 1.5 million. Seeing its skyscrapers and modern hotels and cultural centers, it is hard to believe that it was only a sandy beach less than a hundred years ago.

In 1991 U.N. allied forces attacked Iraq to force her to leave Kuwait. Iraq immediately made Tel Aviv a target for Scud missile attacks. More than $100,000,000 of damage was inflicted on the city.

For more than a month, citizens of Tel Aviv, fearing chemical attacks from Iraq, wore gas masks every day.

515. The modern Jewish community in Palestine was called the Yishuv.

By 1914 the majority of Jews living in the Land of Israel were secular European Jews who had come to create a new Jewish nation. Jerusalem still contained a large number of pious Jews willing to continue the chalukah system of receiving aid from Jews around the world (see data to fact 501), but they were now in the minority. Most Jews were striving to convince Turkey to grant them a charter and permit legal Jewish immigration en masse. This group, organized and politically prepared, was called the New Yishuv, the dwellers (in contrast to the pious Jews, the Old Yishuv). By 1920 the modern settlers, represented by the Jewish Agency and an executive committee, were called simply the Yishuv.

516. Jews joined the British in World War I to fight the Turks.

Many of the New Yishuv felt that the way to convince the Turks to grant them a charter was by participating in their political process. They studied law in Constantinople, paid bribes to officials, and represented the Jews in Turkey's Parliament.

In 1909 a new group of Turks revolted against the sultan. They took over political control in Constantinople and forced the sultan to accept a constitution. The response of the Arab tribes under Turkish rule was to oppose the "Young Turks." The Turks, after all, weren't Arabs.

The Arab tribes, Muslim and Christian, united through the common language of Arabic. A nationalistic Pan-Arabism was created which violently opposed both Turkish rule and Jewish immigration into Palestine. The new Arab nationals viewed the Jews as Europeans who were threatening their creation of an Arab nation.

This situation became more complicated when World War I broke out in 1914. Although most of the fighting was focused in Europe, a large part of the stakes consisted of the Middle East. England, France, and Germany all wanted control over the Suez Canal and its access to the Red Sea. All three wanted to wrest control of the Persian Gulf from Turkey. All three wanted the convenient access to the Red Sea which Palestine offered. This territorial conflict became greatly complicated because England and France were officially allies during the war, and Germany and Turkey were allies.

The Arab nationalists decided that they could achieve their goal of creating a national Arab state by joining the British in their fight against the Turks.

The Jews of Palestine were on the spot. Should they join the Turks, hoping for a charter when the grateful Turks won, or should they join the British and hope that a grateful Great Britain would give them a homeland? The Yishuv split bitterly over this dilemma. Two of the Yishuv's leaders, David Ben Gurion (see fact 538) and Yitzchak Ben Zvi, pushed for creating an alliance with the Turks. Zeev Jabotinsky, writing from Europe (see fact 518), urged joining the British in Egypt. Most of the Yishuv wanted to stay neutral and avoid the wrath of both the Turks and the British.

The problem was taken out of their hands when Turkey condemned all Second Aliyah settlers as foreign invaders and expelled more than 12,000 Jews from the country. Most fled by boat to Egypt, where the British army was garrisoned.

517. Josef Trumpeldor founded the Zion Mule Corps.

The Jews in Egypt tried to convince the British to let them fight. The British were skeptical and suspicious; they didn't believe that Jews could fight. One man, Joseph Trumpeldor, convinced them.

Trumpeldor grew up in Russia and enlisted in the Russian army. Fighting in the Russo-Japanese War (1904–1905), he volunteered for dangerous missions, was badly wounded and lost an arm. Undaunted, he volunteered for more missions and was captured. He survived and immigrated to Palestine. During World War I he was deported to Egypt. There he convinced the British that they should give Jews a chance to serve in the army. Impressed, the British allowed the Jews to establish a 500-man Zion Mule Corps, responsible for bringing supplies to soldiers. After showing outstanding bravery at Gallipoli, Turkey, the Zion Mule Corps convinced the British to consider allowing Jews to carry arms.

518. Zeev Jabotinsky helped found the Jewish Legion, which fought for the British.

The idea for a Jewish fighting force was first proposed to the British by Zeev Jabotinsky. He was a fervent writer with a charismatic personality. Impressed by the courage of the Zion Mule Corps (see fact 517), the British agreed to the creation of an all-Jewish regiment. Jabotinsky actively enlisted volunteers, and in 1917 the Jewish Legion marched under the flag of the Yishuv, the blue Magen David. The Jewish Legion was the first recognized Jewish fighting force in two thousand years.

519. The NILI were Jewish spies working for the British against the Turks in World War I.

The Turks persecuted the 56,000 Jews who remained in Palestine. Many starved. Led by Aaron Aaronson, the Jews created a spy ring to work for the British. They were called the NILI, an acronym for the Hebrew phrase, "the pride of Israel will not be extinguished." Despite their brave efforts, some of them were caught, tortured, and killed. The Turks assumed that all Jews were involved in spying, and further restrictions were placed on the Yishuv (see facts 515, 516). Tel Aviv was forcibly evacuated.

520. The Balfour Declaration promised the Jews a homeland in Palestine.

Britain wanted control of the Middle East. In order to achieve it, the Foreign Ministry made a series of secret treaties with different allies, but they were all contradictory.

In 1915, in the Anglo-Hejaz treaty, Britain promised the Arab nationalists that the Middle East would become an Arab state.

In 1916 the secret Sykes-Picot treaty with France divided the Middle East between England and France. England would protect Egypt and the newly created Saudi Arabian state; France would protect the Syrian-Lebanon state. Palestine would be international.

An Anglo-Jewish chemist, Chaim Weizmann, had contributed greatly to the British war effort by showing how to synthesize acetone, needed to make TNT into a controlled explosive (see data to fact 541). In appreciation, the British listened to his plea for the establishment of a

Jewish state in Palestine after the war. Realistically fearing an alliance between the 56,000 Jews in Palestine and Germany, in 1917 the British agreed to advocate a Jewish homeland in Palestine.

On November 2, 1917, Lord Lionel Rothschild received a letter from Arthur Balfour, who represented the British government. The letter stated that England approved of a Jewish homeland in Palestine, provided the religious and ethnic rights of all sects and groups were upheld. This simple three-paragraph letter was called the Balfour Declaration.

World Jewry believed that Herzl's dream had been fulfilled: the Jews had their internationally recognized charter.

521. Arabs destroyed the settlement of Tel Chai.

In 1917 General Edmund Allenby led a victorious British army (including the Jewish Legion) into Jerusalem. In 1918 he succeeded in pushing the German-Turkish forces out of Palestine. Meanwhile, T. E. Lawrence (Lawrence of Arabia) led his Arab forces into Damascus. It was time to divide the spoils, and Britain's perfidy became clear.

Britain occupied the entire area and, following the plan outlined in the Sykes-Picot Treaty, agreed that France should oversee the newly created Arab states in Syria and Lebanon. Chaim Weizmann met with Emir Faisal, the leader of the Arab nationalists, and they agreed that Jews and Arabs could live peacefully together.

Many Arab nationalists furiously rejected the results of these talks. They had expected to be given the entire Middle East as an Arab state, and they viewed the deals being made between Britain and France as a major double-cross (which it was). They blamed the Yishuv for the political mess.

Both the Yishuv and the Arab nationalists expected to receive Palestine from the British as a national home. France placed pressure on Britain to make Palestine an international territory, and England agreed to remove herself from the Eastern Galilee. In that territory were four Jewish settlements which found themselves in no-man's land, unprotected by either France or England.

In 1919 the Arabs united to try to throw the French out of the Middle East and forcibly take Palestine. They began with the four unprotected settlements, claiming that they contained French soldiers. In 1920 they attacked the settlement of Tel Chai. The Jewish defenders repulsed the charge. The Arabs attacked again and took the settlement, killing eight of the settlers. One of the casualties was Josef Trumpeldor, the founder of the Zion Mule Corps (see fact 517).

522. Trumpeldor's last words were, "No matter; it is good to die for our country."

The surviving defenders of Tel Chai (see fact 522) retreated south to better-protected settlements. Two months later, when the French took over control of the area, the settlers were able to return. They brought with them the blood-stained flag which had hung over Tel Chai. They made a statue of a roaring lion and placed it in the cemetery where the eight casualties were buried. On the lion they engraved the words, "It is good to die for our country." Tel Chai and Trumpeldor became symbols of Jewish courage and determination to create and defend their own homeland. Today Tel Chai is a museum showing the defense of the settlement in 1920. The roaring lion is a field trip site for Israeli children.

In addition, Trumpeldor symbolized the burning desire of Jewish youth in Eastern Europe for a Jewish state. Under the leadership of Jabotinsky (see facts 518, 523), they established a Youth Movement, Betar (Brit Trumpeldor, the covenant of Trumpeldor), which trained Jews in Zionism and self-defense. Many of the futile attempts at resistance during the Holocaust were organized by Betar. In Israel Betar tended to be the preparation organization for Jews wishing to join the Irgun (see fact 531).

523. The Haganah was originally founded by Zeev Jabotinsky.

In April 1920, traditional Arabs made their yearly pilgrimage to Nebi Mussa, the Muslim site of Moses' burial (see data to fact 182). There the Mufti, the Muslim religious leader of Jerusalem, urged them to slaughter the Jews. With cries of "Kill the Jews," Arab mobs went on a rampage through Jerusalem for three days, killing and raping. The British authorities did nothing.

Zeev Jabotinsky organized veterans of the Jewish Legion (see fact 518) and HaShomer (see fact 512) to fight back. The British arrested the Jewish defenders for illegally carrying weapons. Jabotinsky proudly admitted that he was responsible for the defense, calling the group the Haganah (the Defense). He was sentenced to fifteen years' hard labor, but his sentence was commuted. He was expelled from the country and never returned.

The Yishuv, following Jabotinsky's lead, saw the need for an ongoing Jewish defense force even though the British had declared it illegal. Under the auspices of the Histadrut, Israel's labor union, they founded their underground army, the Haganah.

The British Mandate

524. The British were in charge of the Land of Israel from 1920 to 1948.

The League of Nations finally met to decide the fate of Palestine. A group of American Jews established a delegation to represent Jewish interests at Versailles. They called themselves the American Jewish Congress (see data to facts 458, 469).

In 1920 the League of Nations stated that Britain should have mandatory control over Palestine until Arabs and Jews could live peacefully together. Britain got exactly what she wanted: control over the area. The British Mandate lasted from 1920 to 1948, and it marked a time of tremendous friction, tension, and fighting among the English, Arabs, and Jews.

It was in Britain's best interest to keep disorder in the region. She wanted to maintain political control because of her interests in the Near East: access to the Red Sea via the Suez Canal. If there were peaceful relations between Arabs and Jews, there would be no need for British "protection" and Britain would be forced to leave. The Balfour Declaration promised the Jews a homeland as long as all other ethnic and religious groups were agreeable. By encouraging Arab unrest, the British were able to undercut their commitment to allow a Jewish homeland.

The British also recognized that there were many more Arabs than Jews in Palestine. The Arab population was nearly ten times as large as the Yishuv when the Mandate was founded. Britain had to appease the majority, and this influenced her policies.

Moreover, the Arab farmers made good colonial subjects. They didn't have a central authority. The vast majority of the population were poor tenant farmers, so British control was very easy. The Yishuv consisted of strong-willed, hard-headed idealists who wanted to found a modern industrial state in Palestine. They made difficult colonial subjects.

The British therefore found it expedient to support the Arabs, to maintain tension and friction between the two groups, and to under-mine the Yishuv whenever it could. At the same time, the British pretended to be fulfilling her Balfour Declaration commitment.

525. The chalutzim (pioneers) comprised the Third Aliyah.

Despite British interference, Arab riots, and economic crises caused by World War I, the Yishuv grew by leaps and bounds. New kinds of settlers began coming to the area. Calling themselves chalut-zim, pioneers, these settlers came prepared. They were being trained to be farmers in Poland, Russia, and even the United States, and they arrived with agricultural skills. Between 1919 and 1924 more than 50,000 chalutzim arrived in Palestine: the Third Aliyah.

The Jewish National Fund continued to buy large tracts of land, much of it swamps. The Third Aliyah founded new settlements, large kibbutzim, and moshavim (settlements). They drained the swamps and made the once-devastated land green.

In addition, the Yishuv had founded the Histadrut, Israel's labor union, which encouraged the building of roads and large housing projects. Modern electric generators were built, and factories were created. The Yishuv leaped forward to become a modern industrial society.

In 1924 more than 35,000 Jews streamed in from Poland and Germany. Rather than being pioneers, these new immigrants were upper-middle class professionals, doctors and lawyers. They brought capital to build even more new industries in Palestine. Between 1924 and 1928 the Fourth Aliyah, more than 62,000 Jews, entered Palestine. One of the reasons for this large influx of immigrants was the closing of America's doors in 1924 to unlimited immigration.

526. Henrietta Szold founded Hadassah.

Henrietta Szold was born in Baltimore in 1860. She became involved in serving the needs of the immigrants streaming into the United States from Eastern Europe (see fact 452). In 1909 she visited Palestine for health reasons and fell in love with the country. At the same time, she was horrified by the lack of medical facilities for the Second Aliyah settlements. She returned to the United States to orga-nize an International Women's Zionist Organization. She was able to get thirty-eight women involved in 1912, but it wasn't until 1914 that the first convention of Hadassah met. Henrietta Szold was elected president. By 1916 Hadassah had 4,000 members, and Henrietta Szold was given the responsibility of organizing the American Zionist Medical Unit in Palestine.

When Hebrew University was founded in 1925, Henrietta Szold quickly encouraged the medical unit to join forces with the educational unit, thus creating a modern medical institution. In 1936 this unit became Hadassah Hospital, one of the most respected, modern medical centers in the world.

Today Hadassah is the largest Zionist organization in the world and one of the largest women's organizations in the United States. Through dues, contributions, and fund-raising activities, Hadassah continues to support the Hadassah Medical Center as well as providing funds for a myriad of programs, including vocational training schools.

527. The British prevented Jews from freely entering the Land of Israel.

Britain's two greatest blows against the Yishuv were to limit immigration and to limit the Jewish National Fund's ability to purchase land. Following major Arab riots in 1929 in which the Jewish community of Hebron was massacred on a Shabbat, the British issued a White Paper which noted the unrest caused by Jewish immigration and recommended severe restrictions on such immigration. World Jewry was outraged, and the British retracted the White Paper. It was lucky for many Jews that such restrictions were removed. Between 1933 and 1936, more than 164,250 Jews fled Germany and entered Palestine, thus doubling the size of the Yishuv. Called the Fifth Aliyah, these German Jews came with money to build businesses in the cities. By 1936 Tel Aviv had more than 150,000 inhabitants and Haifa had become a major port city with more than 50,000 Jews.

528. Youth Aliyah saved thousands of children from the Nazis.

The Yishuv (see fact 515) recognized the need to help save Jewish children in Europe. In 1933 Henrietta Szold and Hadassah established Youth Aliyah, an institution to bring German Jewish children to Palestine and provide them with homes. Between 1933 and 1942 more than

5,000 children were brought into Palestine and integrated into kibbut-zim. Another 15,000 were sent to Western countries by Hadassah because the British refused to allow them to enter Palestine. Since its founding, Youth Aliyah has provided homes for more than 140,000 Jewish children in Israel.

529. Aliyah Bet smuggled Jews into Palestine.

The Yishuv was outraged by Britain's callous refusal to open the gates of Palestine to Jewish immigrants (see fact 528). With Hitler in power in Europe, thousands of Jews desperately needed refuge imme-diately. Britain adamantly refused to increase its immigration quota for Jews.

The Yishuv and European Jewry organized Aliyah Bet, the insti-tution responsible for smuggling Jews into Palestine against the orders of the British. The British called this illegal immigration; the Jews called it legitimate immigration based on the promise of the Balfour Declara-tion.

Youth movements and Zionist organizations set up transport systems to get Jews to small ports in Southern Europe. From there, a part of the Haganah (see fact 523) called the Mossad L'Aliyah Bet tried to sneak boatloads of Jews into Palestine. By the end of 1939 thousands of Jews had arrived in Palestine illegally.

530. The Jews protected themselves from the Arabs by building tower and stockade settlements.

In 1936, despite all British attempts to placate them, the Arabs of Palestine set up a revolt against both the British and the Yishuv. Mobs attacked and ransacked the Jewish quarter of Jaffa. The Arabs declared a countrywide work strike, and the Yishuv took over all necessary civil occupations. With the permission of the British High Commissioner, the Yishuv established a port in Tel Aviv, thus replacing Jaffa, which was on strike.

The Arabs began a policy of terrorism against the British and the Yishuv. The Haganah announced a policy of restraint: defend but don't attack. The Yishuv developed a new defense measure. They chose sites which the Arabs would have to pass to get to a Jewish town or village. In the middle of the night, groups of young Jews would race to the selected site with prefab walls. Working through the night, they would set up a defense wall (made of the prefab wooden frames filled with gravel) and a watch tower with a searchlight. Protected from immediate Arab attack, they then added houses within the walls and planted fields, creating permanent settlements.

In this way, 52 settlements formed a fence around the older Yishuv neighbors protecting them from Arab attacks. They were called tower and stockade settlements, and they saved many towns from possible massacres.

In addition, a British captain, Charles Orde Wingate, trained Jewish volunteers from the Haganah to counterattack against the Arabs and protect the British oil pipeline. Many of his students, such as Moshe Dayan (see fact 554) and Yigal Allon, eventually became the military leaders of Israel. For his friendship with the Yishuv, Wingate was banished by the British from Palestine and never permitted to return. He was killed in Burma during World War II.

531. Zeev Jabotinsky founded the Irgun.

For one group of angry young Jews, the defense policy of restraint in the face of Arab attacks wasn't acceptable. They wanted to follow the biblical injunction, "An eye for an eye." Led by Jabotinsky, who was still living in exile (see fact 523), this group broke away from the Haganah to create a separate Jewish military force called the Irgun Tz'vaei Leumi, referred to as either the Irgun or Etzel, the acronym of its full title.

The Irgun responded to every terrorist attack with its own terrorist attack. The Yishuv, fearing political reprisals from the British and the loss of world sympathy if Jews were seen as terrorists, opposed the Irgun and their raids.

In 1939, when the Haganah and many in the Yishuv decided to help the British fight the Nazis (see fact 532), the Irgun declared that the British were as much an enemy as Germany or the Arabs, and they began terrorist raids against the British. Again the Yishuv and the Haganah opposed these actions.

The political and military actions of the Irgun so angered some of the leaders of the Yishuv that they never forgave Jabotinsky. He died in New York of a heart attack in 1940 while trying to get funds for the Irgun's efforts. His will requested that he be buried in Eretz Yisrael only at the invitation of a Jewish government. He had faith that there would one day be a Jewish state.

It is a sign of the deep levels of disagreement among the different

Jewish movements that Jabotinsky's final request was not fulfilled for twenty-five years. He was finally buried with his wife on Mount Herzl in 1964.

532. Jews joined the British in World War II to fight the Nazis.

In 1939 when Europe's Jews most desperately needed a haven, Britain issued another White Paper further limiting Jewish immigration to Palestine. Seventy-five thousand Jews would be permitted to enter over a five-year period, and then a fixed ratio of two Arabs per Jew would be maintained. This White Paper shattered the Yishuv's hopes of attaining a Jewish state under the British Mandate. The Irgun increased its attacks against British troops.

With the outbreak of World War II, the Yishuv found itself once again in a conflict. It was clear that the British would always double-cross them, and they were dedicated to saving Europe's Jews, despite the White Paper. However, armed attacks against Britain would subsequently help Germany and the Axis Powers, which was unthinkable. Therefore the Yishuv joined forces with the British. As David Ben Gurion declared, "We shall fight side by side with Britain in our war against Hitler as if there were no White Paper, and we shall fight the White Paper as if there were no war." The majority of the Irgun also agreed to help the British. One group, however, led by Avraham Stern, determined that the British were as dangerous as the Arabs. Called the Stern Gang (or LECHI, an acronym for the fighters for Israel's freedom), this group continued terrorist raids against the British throughout World War II. One of LECHI's officers was Yitzchak Shamir (see fact 571).

The Arabs, meanwhile, wholeheartedly supported Germany. The Mufti of Jerusalem went to Berlin to help the Nazis. Between 1941 and 1945 he broadcast from Berlin in Arabic encouraging the Arabs to expel the British and slaughter the Jews.

533. Top Jewish troops, trained by the British, became the leaders of the Palmach.

Within the first week after the beginning of World War II, more than 130,000 Jews from the Yishuv had volunteered to enter the British army. The British refused to take Jewish volunteers without accepting an equal number of Arab volunteers. The Arab leaders, however, had already pledged their support to Germany. The British therefore reluctantly accepted Jewish recruits, but they balked at permitting the Jews to establish their own recognized brigade.

In 1941 the situation for the British in Palestine was very serious. Their major front was in North Africa, trying to stop Rommel. The Vichy French were in Syria and Lebanon, threatening Palestine's borders. The British turned to the Yishuv for help. Within the Jewish units were special fighting forces called the Palmach, the assault companies, famous for their bravery and their rigorous training. Many of them had trained under Orde Wingate (see data to fact 530). Very macho, their personal hallmarks were thick handlebar mustaches.

The Palmach was assigned to stop the Vichy French from crossing from the north into Palestine. They did so, suffering enormous casualties. Their reputation as courageous fighters was enhanced. Throughout World War II the Palmach trained rigorously and became the broad base of fighting reserves needed to provide the backbone of the Haganah (see fact 523). The Palmach cooperated closely with the British until after the battle of El-Alamein in North Africa. With the German threat diminished, the British tried to disband the Palmach, knowing that the troops would eventually be used against them. The Palmach therefore went underground and continued to train and prepare the Yishuv for the struggle against Britain which they knew was imminent. Many famous Israeli generals received their training and experience in the Palmach.

534. Hannah (Szenes) Senesh wrote, "Blessed is the match."

In 1944 the Yishuv finally convinced the British to let them have their own brigade. In addition to more than 26,000 Jews from Palestine serving in the British army, the Yishuv created the Jewish Brigade, consisting of 5,000 men. The Jews in the Brigade performed double duty in the army. At the same time that they were working for the British, they organized and trained for their eventual opposition to British control of Palestine. While they fought in Italy, they arranged escape routes to get Jews out of Europe after the war. All Jewish Brigade members were in the Haganah.

Jews worked on similar projects in Central Europe while in the British army. An excellent example of this two-way action was a group of paratroopers who volunteered to drop behind Axis lines to work with the nationalist patriots in Czechoslovakia, Hungary, and Yugoslavia. While fighting against the Nazis, they were also finding ways to get Jews out of those countries.

One of these, a young Jewish poet named Hannah Szenes (pronounced Senesh), parachuted into Yugoslavia, where she helped the partisans. She tried sneaking across the border into Hungary, her native land, but was captured, tortured by the Nazis, and put to death.

One of her most famous poems was written while she was in Yugoslavia:

Blessed is the match consumed in kindling flame.
Blessed is the flame that burns in the heart's secret places.
Blessed is the heart with strength to stop its beating for honor's sake.
Blessed is the match consumed in kindling flame.

535. Menachem Begin became the leader of the Irgun.

At the end of World War II the conflict over Palestine rapidly gained momentum. As early as 1942, the Yishuv had turned to the United States for support of a Jewish state in Palestine.

Even after the horror of the Holocaust, Britain refused to change its policy of allowing no further Jewish immigration. Despite the hundreds of thousands of Jews languishing in Allied displaced persons' camps, the British locked the gates to Palestine. British ships stopped Aliyah Bet ships and forced the refugees into camps they had established on Cyprus. Despite expressions of world outrage, the British interned more than 51,500 Jews who were desperately trying to get to Palestine.

Jewish resistance increased dramatically. The Yishuv gathered weapons for the war they knew was coming. Despite British intervention at every turn, the Haganah prepared for military conflict, hiding guns in kibbutzim and training volunteers in orange groves.

Arab terrorism increased. The Irgun and Stern Gangs retaliated. The Irgun turned its forces against the British as well. In 1944 Menachem Begin became the head of the Irgun. Having escaped from the Nazis in Poland, Menachem Begin was subsequently arrested by the Soviets but survived. When he arrived in Palestine, he declared armed warfare against the British. Many in the Yishuv were angry because they feared that Jewish terrorist reprisals would turn world sympathy from their cause. Begin responded that the world didn't really care; the Jews would have to kick the British out themselves.

On June 29, 1946 (now called Black Saturday), the British arrested the leaders of the Jewish Agency, the organization responsible for running the Yishuv (see data to fact 540). This further radicalized the country. On July 26 the Irgun, after first warning the British, blew up their headquarters in Jerusalem located in the King David Hotel. More than 100 British, Arabs, and Jews were killed.

536. On November 29, 1947, the United Nations voted for the establishment of a Jewish state and an Arab state in the Land of Israel.

In order to keep the peace, Britain had more than 100,000 top troops in the country. Their efforts were in vain. Arab snipers were killing people, Jews and British, daily. The Stern Gang was setting bombs regularly. The Irgun was attacking British supply lines, bases, and compounds. On May 5, 1947, a combined Haganah/Irgun raid blew a hole in the British prison at Akko, and 251 prisoners escaped. The British had considered the Akko prison invulnerable, and they were shaken by the audacious, successful attack.

The British lost even more world support when they stopped the *Exodus 1947*, a ship loaded with 5,200 Jewish refugees sailing toward Palestine from Marseilles. Hand-to-hand fighting took place, but the Jews were overcome. The British transported the Jews back to France. At Port-de-Bouc the Jews refused to get off the two British ships and the French refused to force them. The British then sailed the two ships back to Hamburg, Germany, where they forced the Jews back into DP camps. The *Exodus* scandal shook the British government. Although still allied with the Arabs, the British had to admit that things were out of control. There was tremendous pressure from both the British Parliament and the United States to end the mandate.

Finally the British invited the United Nations to make recommendations to solve the Palestine problem. They still hoped that the United Nations would recommend that the British retain control of the area. After many debates and compromises, the United Nations Special Committee on Palestine (UNSCOP) recommended that there be two states in Palestine, an Arab state and a Jewish state. The Jews would get most of the coastal plain, with Jaffa being an Arab "island" (see facts 474, 476). They would also get the Yizrael and Hulah Valleys and much of the Negev (see facts 471, 488, and data to fact 545). The rest of the country would be Arab. Jerusalem would be an international city.

On November 29, 1947, by a 33–13 majority, the United Nations voted that, beginning on May 15, 1948, if the Yishuv agreed, there would be two independent states in Palestine, and the British Mandate would end.

537. On May 14, 1948, the State of Israel was born.

The British and the Arabs wasted no time preparing to make it impossible for the Jews to declare an independent state. From November 30, 1947, to May 14, 1948, the Arabs waged an unofficial war against the Yishuv. Soldiers from Iraq, Syria, Jordan, and Egypt stole into the country to organize Arab attack forces. The Arab Legion, Jordan's army, was under British protection, and it joined attacks prior to British evacuation.

The only fighting forces that the Yishuv had were the Haganah and the two terrorist groups, the Irgun (see fact 531) and the Stern Gang (see data to fact 532). They were all forced to work underground because Britain declared it illegal for Jews to own or carry weapons. There were constant inspections, check points, and patrols all trying to disarm the Jews.

The Yishuv became a military camp. Almost every member of the population was in some way involved in the Haganah and other defense units. The Haganah policy from November through March was: "Defend every outpost, every settlement. Don't give anything up. The fighting stops here." The Palmach (see fact 533) sent units and, on occasion, individual men and women to help protect attacked points.

The first major battle took place at kibbutz Tirat Tzvi, which was attacked by thousands of Syrian and Iraqi irregulars. The kibbutz repulsed the attack. The winding road up to Jerusalem became the site of bloody massacres as food convoys were attacked at Shaar HaGai (see fact 483). To this day, the rusted ruins of the destroyed trucks remind Israelis of the sacrifices made to keep Jerusalem from starving.

The Old City of Jerusalem was cut off from the New City, and the Arabs systematically starved the Jewish inhabitants. The British sat and watched, waiting for the Yishuv to admit defeat.

In March 1948 the Haganah policy changed. Although they had no artillery, the Yishuv had smuggled enough small arms into the country to begin an offensive against the Arabs. Their first goal was to open the road to Jerusalem. In a surprise raid, 1,500 men cleared the hills above the road to Jerusalem. The dominating fort, Kastel, was taken, lost, and retaken. A large convoy rushed supplies to Jerusalem. During that operation, the Irgun attacked an Arab village, Deir Yassin. More than 200 villagers were killed, including women and children.

On April 13 the Arabs slaughtered and mutilated a convoy of 100 doctors and nurses heading for Hadassah Medical Center. The British did nothing. It was a brutal time.

Fighting continued in the north. Haifa and Tiberias fell to the

Yishuv. Using a home-made mortar, the Davidka (named after its inventor, David Leibovitch), the Haganah attacked and took Tzfat (see fact 478). Although inaccurate, the Davidka created a great deal of noise, which frightened the Arab population into fleeing. All of this fighting took place while the British were still officially in charge of the country.

The Yishuv was in trouble politically as well. The U.S. State Department was planning to remove its vote from the UN resolution on Palestine, arguing that the declaration of a Jewish state would result in a massacre of the Jews. Chaim Weizmann hurried to Washington to speak with President Truman about keeping faith with the Yishuv. With the help of Truman's friend Eddie Jacobson, Weizmann succeeded in meeting with the president. Truman promised that the United States would continue to support the UN resolution.

As May 15 approached, the Yishuv had to decide whether they should proclaim an independent Jewish state. One side rightly pointed out that when the Yishuv declared itself a state, five well-equipped, very angry Arab armies would attack with planes, tanks, and artillery. The Jews had no large weapons and no air force. There could be a massacre. As if to emphasize this point, news reached the meetings in May that the Arab Legion had succeeded in destroying Gush Etzion, a group of settlements just south of Jerusalem.

The majority view, however, was to take the opportunity for a state because there might never be another. After a long debate, the committee agreed to name the country Israel. It was agreed that the word "God" would not appear in the Declaration of Independence; the term "Rock of Israel" appeared instead.

One of the few humorous difficulties was an organizational one. The day scheduled for the end of the Mandate turned out to be a Saturday, the Shabbat. A Jewish state couldn't declare itself on Shabbat. On the 5th of Iyyar—May 14, 1948—the British left Palestine, officially ending the Mandate. Just before sundown, David Ben Gurion read the new Declaration of the State of Israel. *Hatikvah* was played. Eleven minutes later President Truman officially recognized the State of Israel and was followed almost immediately by the USSR. For the first time since Bar Kochba (see fact 349), Jews had their own country.

Israel as a State

538. David Ben Gurion became the first prime minister of Israel.

The most influential individual in the creation of the Jewish state was David Ben Gurion. His life embodied the institutions that resulted in the state of Israel. Born in Poland in 1886, David Gruen became an ardent Zionist and came to Palestine as part of the Second Aliyah in 1906 (see fact 510). Inspired by Eliezer Ben Yehuda (see fact 504), he changed his name from Gruen to David Ben Gurion and campaigned for Hebrew to be the language of the Yishuv. He argued for the independence of Jewish workers and became a member of HaShomer (see fact 512).

He strongly believed that the key to gaining a Jewish state was the permission of the ruling government. Therefore he was in favor of supporting Turkey during World War I until he was expelled. After a stay in the United States, Ben Gurion went to Egypt, where he joined the Jewish Legion (see fact 518). He was one of the founders and organizers of the Haganah (see fact 523).

Tremendously charismatic, he helped found Israel's labor union, the Histadrut, and was on the Executive Committee of the Jewish Agency (see data to facts 515, 535 and 540) through years of frustrating negotiations with the British. He vigorously opposed the Irgun because he saw terrorist acts as an obstacle to achieving statehood (see fact 531). It was largely his influence that prevented Jabotinsky from being brought back to Israel for burial on Mount Herzl until 1964 (see data to fact 531).

Ben Gurion was chiefly responsible for gaining U.S. Jewry's support for Israel and collecting the large sums of money needed to buy arms for the Yishuv. In 1946 he took charge of the Yishuv's defenses. On May 14, 1948, he read the Declaration of Independence and became the first prime minister and secretary of defense.

His insistence that there be only one army led to a showdown between him and Menachem Begin. The Irgun had purchased weapons and were transporting them to Israel on a ship, the *Altalena*. When Begin refused to turn the weapons over to the Israeli army, insisting that they were for the Irgun, Ben Gurion ordered the *Altalena* to be blown up, even though Israel desperately needed the arms.

Ben Gurion was dedicated to the realization of Herzl's dream that Israel be the homeland for all Jews. In 1951 he traveled to the United States and launched the first Israel Bond Drive.

In 1953 Ben Gurion resigned from the government and went to work on his desert kibbutz, S'dei Boker. In 1955 he was named defense minister again and in that same year was elected prime minister. He resigned in 1963. In 1965 he split from the Labor Party and formed a new political party, RAFI. In 1970 he retired from the Knesset (see fact 540) and returned to his kibbutz, where he worked until his death on December 1, 1973. Israel's international airport at Lod is now named David Ben Gurion Airport.

539. On May 15, 1948, Israel was attacked by seven Arab armies.

On the day after Israel declared statehood, the armies of Egypt, Syria, Lebanon, Jordan, Iraq, Yemen, and Saudi Arabia attacked the new Jewish state. Military strategists were in agreement: there was no way for Israel to win. The British had succeeded in limiting the number of Israel's weapons. Israel had four anti-tank guns when war broke out. The British had left almost all of the high defense fortresses and police stations in the hands of the Arabs, so they held most of the high ground.

The most serious problem, however, was numbers. There were only 650,000 Jews in Israel. They had already lost more than 900 people in the "pre-war war." They faced a potential force of 30 million Arabs. The Irgun agreed to join the no-longer-underground Haganah, which provided Israel with a fighting army of 51,000 men and women.

Although the War of Independence lasted officially until February of the next year, the war was decided by June 11, 1948. Egypt attacked the Negev with a large tank force and bombed Tel Aviv daily. The scattered settlements between Egypt and Tel Aviv put up desperate resistance. Kibbutz Yad Mordechai held out for six days. Kibbutz Negba was never taken. Egypt's drive was halted 14 miles south of Tel Aviv.

The Syrian army was stopped at kibbutz Degania by settlers who used Molotov cocktails, a flame-thrower, and one anti-tank gun.

The Jordanian army was stopped in its attempt to cut the coastal plain in two. The Lebanese army was pushed back in the western Galilee.

After tremendous fighting, the Arab Legion was pushed back from the New City of Jerusalem. However, the Old City was isolated, and Israel couldn't get supplies or reinforcements through. The Jordanians slowly squeezed the fighters into a tiny clump of houses, systematically destroying every building they took. On May 28, 1,300 civilians and 40 Haganah defenders surrendered, the only major victory that the Arab armies were able to claim. Jerusalem remained divided from May 28, 1948, until June 1967 (see fact 553).

The situation in the New City of Jerusalem was very serious. The Arabs blocked the road from Tel Aviv to Jerusalem by holding the police station at Latrun. After two desperate attacks failed, Israel began considering the horror of losing Jerusalem.

Led by an American colonel, David "Mickey" Marcus, the Israelis found a way to save their spiritual heart. Following a shepherd's path lost for centuries, the Israelis flattened out a road which went around Latrun and enabled them to send food convoys to Jerusalem. The first convoy arrived on June 11, the date of the first truce.

In July the Israeli army went on the offensive. They took the high defense fortresses in the north. They surrounded the Egyptian army and took the Negev. Their only failure followed repeated attempts to take the Old City of Jerusalem. By February 1949, Israel held the entire coastal plain, the Negev, the Galilee, and a significant portion of the Sinai Peninsula. Jordan held the Old City, East Jerusalem, and the West Bank of the Jordan River and incorporated them into Jordan. No Palestinian state came into being. It was a miraculous military victory which stunned world strategists. Israel had survived and became the fifty-ninth member of the United Nations. By the summer of 1949, under the directions of United Nations Acting Mediator Ralph Bunche, Israel signed armistice agreements with her Arab neighbors and returned the Sinai to Egypt. For his efforts in the negotiations, Ralph Bunche received the Nobel Peace Prize in 1950.

540. Israel's parliament is called the Knesset.

From the beginning of the Mandate, the World Zionist Organization administered the programs for world Jewry's settlement and development in Israel. It did so through an executive office in Jerusalem, called the Jewish Agency, which was founded in 1929. With the declaration of the State of Israel, the responsibilities of the Jewish Agency had to be redefined. It was, after all, a nongovernmental, international office, not a legislative organization for Israel. However, the majority of Israel's leaders had served in the Jewish Agency; its president was Chaim Weizmann (see fact 541). In November 1947 the Jewish Agency established a National Council as part of its organization. On May 14, 1948, this council became the independent legislature of Israel. The Jewish Agency continued to be responsible for immigration, land settlement and development, and youth work.

In November 1948, while the war was still going on, Israel took a census and determined that 506,567 Jews and Arabs had the right to vote in Israel's first election. On January 25, elections were held. Almost 87 percent of the population voted.

Rather than voting for individuals, the electorate voted for parties. On the basis of percentage of votes received, the parties then chose their Assembly representatives. To no one's surprise, David Ben Gurion's party, Mapai, received the most votes, providing it with 47 out of 120 seats in Israel's Assembly. Because Mapai did not receive a majority vote, Ben Gurion had to establish a coalition with other parties to create his government. Menachem Begin's party, Herut, refused to consider joining Mapai, so Ben Gurion made alliances with the religious political parties, establishing a precedent which continued into the 1990s. The 120 members met for the first time in February 1949. The Assembly was called the Knesset.

541. Chaim Weizmann became the first president of Israel.

On February 14, 1949, Israel's parliament, the Knesset, met and elected Chaim Weizmann as the first president, an honorary post.

Chaim Weizmann, born in the Pale of Settlement in 1874 (see fact 437), was one of fifteen children. He showed an early aptitude for science and was sent to Germany to study. After studying biochemistry in Berlin, he moved to England in 1904.

He was an ardent Zionist and attended the Second World Zionist Congress as a delegate. While he was tremendously impressed with Herzl (see fact 508), he also agreed with Ahad HaAm that the Jewish homeland needed institutions to make it unique (see data to fact 510). He pushed for the creation of a Hebrew university and urged that Hebrew become the national language, even for science.

In 1906 Weizmann had the opportunity to speak with Arthur Balfour about Zionism, and he apparently impressed Balfour. Through his biochemistry contacts, he also met British statesman Lloyd George and convinced him that the Jews needed a homeland.

Although Weizmann did not hold any executive position in the Zionist movement, in 1917 he suddenly became extremely important. Lord Balfour became Britain's foreign secretary and Lloyd George became prime minister. Influenced by Weizmann, they pushed for a positive British statement about Palestine, and the result was the Balfour Declaration (see fact 520). This brought Chaim Weizmann world recognition as the representative of Zionism, and he was sent to Palestine to negotiate with Emir Faisal, the leader of the Arab nationalists (see data to fact 521).

Weizmann was made president of the World Zionist Organization and tried to make it the authoritative body for all Zionists. He failed. Although recognized as the spokesman for World Zionism, Weizmann had no real influence in Britain and, ironically, lost influence in the World Zionist Congress because he was viewed as an Anglophile. Moreover, because of poor health, his activities had to be limited.

Despite having little real political influence, Weizmann was pivotal in convincing President Truman to recognize the State of Israel (see data to fact 537). He did fulfill one of his dreams when, in 1949, he established the Weizmann Institute of Science in Rehovot. It has become one of the world's great scientific research centers. Weizmann died in 1952 and was buried in Rehovot.

542. The Law of Return states that any Jew who comes to Israel, can become a citizen.

On July 5, 1950, the Knesset (see fact 540) passed the Law of Return, fulfilling Herzl's dream. The Law of Return states that every Jew in the world has the inherent right to settle in Israel as an automatic citizen; it emphasizes the purpose of Israel as a homeland for all Jews.

Since 1950, the Law of Return has been the source of many controversies in Israel because it didn't define the term *Jew*. Orthodox Jewry tried to include in the original law the phrase "Jew according to halachah" (see fact 342), but the secular Jews in the Knesset refused to allow the amendment.

According to halachah, a Jew is anyone born of a Jewish mother (see fact 273) or someone who converted under the auspices of an accepted beit din, Jewish court (see fact 425). Since Jewish identity comes with birth, halachically there is no way to cease being a Jew.

In 1962 Oswald Rufeisen applied for Israeli citizenship as a Jew. He was born in Poland and both his parents were Jewish, but in 1942 he had converted to Catholicism and in 1945 had entered the Carmelite order as Brother Daniel. Knowing that according to halachah he was still a Jew, he applied for Israeli citizenship under the Law of Return.

This issue became a major one in Israel because it challenged the very definition of "Who is a Jew?" Israel's Supreme Court finally decided that even though halachah would declare him to be a Jew, in the eyes of the secular world Brother Daniel was not a Jew. For modern Jews, a Jew was someone associated with the beliefs, rituals, and people of Israel. Someone who had converted to another religion couldn't be considered a Jew.

Since the founding of the State, the major political party has always had to rely on coalitions with other smaller parties to attain a majority. The coalition has always included the National Religious Party. The National Religious Party has been pressuring the larger political parties to change the Law of Return to include the words "according to halachah." This change would mean that any person who converted to Judaism under the auspices of a Reform or Conservative rabbi would be viewed as non-Jewish and would not be allowed to become a citizen under the Law of Return.

Needless to say, every time the attempt has been made to amend the Law of Return, there have been enormous outcries from Diaspora Jewry, protesting the possible change. Yitzchak Peretz, Israel's minister of interior in the late 1980s, consistently tried to bar Reform and Conservative converts from being accepted as citizens under the Law of Return. Israel's Supreme Court has repeatedly condemned his attempts.

In December 1989 Israel's Supreme Court rejected the petition of two Messianic Jews who wanted to become Israeli citizens under the Law of Return. The justices stated that Jews who believe in Jesus have withdrawn themselves from the Jewish people.

543. In 1949 Operation Magic Carpet saved the Jews of Yemen.

The primary aim of the State of Israel was to provide a homeland for all Jews. From its first day of existence, Israel focused its efforts on the ingathering of the exiles. In its first year, while fighting for her survival in the War of Independence, Israel succeeded in bringing more than 203,000 Jews home.

The most dramatic of these mass immigrations was from Yemen. The Jews of Yemen had been persecuted for hundreds of years. Since the late nineteenth century, some had been escaping to the Land of Israel, and by 1948 there were about 28,000 Yemenites living in Israel. In Yemen a huge number of Jews, caught up in a messianic excitement for the new Jewish state, wanted to emigrate. The Muslim authorities, after insisting that the Yemenite Jews sell their land and pay an exit tax, agreed to let them go.

Astonishingly, almost the entire Jewish population of the country left on foot and arrived in the British colony of Aden. From there, Israel organized an intensive large-scale airlift, unheard of before that time. Called Operation Magic Carpet, this airlift transported more than 47,000 Yemenite Jews who had never seen an airplane "on the wings of eagles" to Israel. There, in primitive camps called ma'abarot, they were slowly assimilated into modern Israeli society.

544. El Al is Israel's national airline.

El Al, literally "To-On," is traditionally translated "Skyward." It is Israel's national airline, founded in 1948 to transport Jewish immigrants from Yemen and Iraq (see fact 543). Consisting originally of surplus

World War II aircraft flown by volunteers, El Al was soon flying scheduled routes to Paris and Rome. In 1961 El Al began its first nonstop service between New York and Tel Aviv.

El Al is owned primarily by the Israeli government and therefore became the focus of several controversies between the secular and religious political parties. In order to get his first coalition government (see data to fact 540), Ben Gurion had to agree that El Al would serve only kosher food (see facts 589–597) on its flights and would not fly on Shabbat. Despite minor protests by secular Israelis over the years, El Al has continued to serve only kosher food.

In the mid 1970s, however, El Al began scheduling its flights around the world to leave airports on Shabbat as long as they arrived in Israel after Shabbat. The religious parties objected vehemently to this breaking of halachah and the original 1948 agreement. The subsequent controversy caused the Labor government to fall. New elections were held, and Menachem Begin became prime minister of Israel (see fact 535). In order to achieve a coalition government in 1981, Prime Minister Begin agreed to enforce the rule. The religious parties called on him to keep his word, and he did. Huge protests broke out among the secular Israelis, who objected to the power the religious parties had in the government. They argued that El Al would lose much-needed income, and they threatened to boycott El Al flights. In August 1982, angry El Al workers prevented Orthodox and Chasidic Jews from entering the airport building. It was an ugly scene.

El Al's flights have the best safety record of any airline in the world. Israel provides tremendous security for all El Al flights since the PLO (see fact 551) made it clear that the airline is one of its major targets. Since 1969, no El Al plane has been successfully attacked or hijacked.

545. Israel's population doubled in size during her first three years of existence.

From Israel's birth in May 1948, through December 1951, 684,201 new Jewish immigrants arrived, doubling the population of the new state in less than three years and creating an incredible economic crisis. Jews flooded into the country from Iraq, Iran, Morocco, and the displaced persons' camps of Europe. The Jewish Agency had the responsibility for inoculating, vaccinating, housing, and feeding that enormous mass of people. The new immigrants were at first placed in huge tent camps, then moved to one-room shacks called ma'abarot.

The new immigrants had to be taught Hebrew, introduced to

modern Western culture and society, trained for work, housed, and brought into the mainstream of Israel. It was an enormous challenge. Many of the new immigrants were hired by the Jewish National Fund to help with afforestation and road building. The land area farmed in Israel grew eight-fold between 1948 and 1951. All these activities required huge amounts of money. The United Jewish Appeal and Israel Bonds enabled world Jewry to help pay for the tremendous population growth in the new state, in the largest private fund-raising drive in human history.

In 1951 the Jewish National Fund began its most ambitious land reclamation. North of Lake Kinneret was a 5-square-mile lake called Lake Huleh. It was surrounded by 68 square miles of malaria-infested swamps. The Jewish National Fund decided to drain Lake Huleh and the swamp by rechanneling the water into carp ponds and blasting both the northern and southern ends of the lake, creating deep channels that allowed the water to run easily into the Jordan River. By 1958 the job was completed, and the newly created Huleh Valley yielded over 20,000 acres of extremely fertile land.

546. Israel created absorption cities to integrate immigrants.

The Jewish Agency experimented with different kinds of refugee absorption programs. The first consisted of sending new immigrants to ma'abarot (see data to fact 545) and encouraging them to build their own homes and develop new towns. Israel also planned and created regional clusters of new towns. Yerucham, Dimona, Kiryat Gat, and Beit Shemesh all began as development towns.

In order to assimilate the new settlers as quickly as possible into the society, the Jewish Agency encouraged Israelis also to live in the new towns. Thus Israeli children played with immigrant children and quickly taught them Hebrew and Israeli culture. These children in turn helped their parents learn.

547. Kiryat Shmoneh was built in memory of the settlers killed at Tel Chai.

One of the first development towns to be built from ma'abarot (see data to facts 545, 546) was on the northeast border of Israel. Located less than a mile from Tel Chai (see facts 521, 522), the town was named

Kiryat Shmoneh, the town of the eight. It became a living symbol of the bravery of the eight Jews who died defending Tel Chai.

Because of its border location, Kiryat Shmoneh has suffered more casualties from terrorist attacks than any other town in Israel. From 1973 to 1982 the PLO (see fact 551) periodically fired Katyushah rockets into the town.

548. Israel accepted reparations from Germany for the Holocaust atrocities.

In 1945 the Jewish Agency submitted a demand to the Allies that Germany make financial restitution to the Jewish people for the horrors of the Holocaust (see facts 458–463). In 1951 West Germany (the German Federal Republic) indicated its willingness to compensate Israel and the Jewish people for material damage and personal losses incurred during the Holocaust.

Israel's populace split sharply over the question of reparations. Menachem Begin and his Herut party were horrified at the thought of either communicating with or accepting money from the Germans as a way of "forgiving" them. They viewed any form of negotiations with Germany an abomination, and they held three days of stormy street demonstrations during which they stoned the Knesset's windows and were, in turn, tear-gassed.

David Ben Gurion succeeded, by a small majority, in getting a Knesset resolution passed to engage in direct negotiations with Germany. As a result, West Germany agreed to pay Israel, over a long period of time, $845 million in reparations, two-thirds of the amount Israel estimated it cost to absorb and rehabilitate the 500,000 survivors. In addition, West Germany paid $110 million to Diaspora Jewry and individuals who had suffered during the Holocaust.

East Germany, accepting no national responsibility for the Holocaust, refused to respond to Israel's demand for $500 million in reparations. In fact, it wasn't until 1990 that East Germany ever made a statement accepting any responsibility for the Holocaust. At that time, East Germany agreed to establish a reparations plan with Israel.

549. Israel defeated Egypt in the Sinai Campaign.

Despite the armistice agreements of 1949 (see data to fact 539), Israel continued to have serious problems with her Arab neighbors. The

Syrians looked down on Lake Kinneret (see fact 479) and the Huleh Valley (see data to fact 545) from the Golan Heights in southern Syria and periodically shelled the kibbutzim. The children of one kibbutz slept inside bunkers from 1948 to 1967. More serious were the Arab refugees, located in camps in the Gaza Strip and the West Bank. No Arab country would take them in, and they became the responsibility of the United Nations. These angry Arabs, called fedayeen (peasants), would make one-night raids against Israelis, killing one here, raping one there. They were encouraged by the Arab states to do so. In fact, Egypt's military recruited and trained them. Egypt even offered a fixed price for Jewish heads.

Israel's first defense was to build a line of settlements along the borders, putting a fence of people between the fedayeen and the interior settlements. Despite these measures, more than 1,300 civilian Israelis were murdered between 1951 and 1956.

In 1956 General Abdul Nasser, president of Egypt, expelled the British from the Suez Canal Zone. France and Britain began planning to retake the Suez Canal.

Russian-supplied troops and tanks began to collect along the Egypt–Israel border. Egypt built new airfields in Sinai. Fedayeen raids increased. In October 1956 Egypt's artillery at Sharm el-Sheikh prevented Israeli ships from going through the Straits of Tiran into the Gulf of Eilat. Israel attacked.

Between October 29 and November 1, 1956, Israel, using fast armored divisions, outflanked, surrounded, and routed the Egyptian forces in Sinai. Israel's air force neutralized more than ninety armored vehicles which vainly tried to shore up Egypt's defenses. Using paratroops, Israel took Egypt's airfields in the Sinai. On October 31 Britain and France issued an ultimatum ordering both forces to keep all fighting at least 10 miles from the Canal Zone. Israel complied. Egypt didn't. French and British paratroops attacked the Egyptians, thus "protecting" the Canal.

Israel, meanwhile, surrounded Gaza and wiped out the Egyptian fortifications there. The Egyptian garrison at Sharm el-Sheikh was overwhelmed on November 5, ending the Sinai Campaign. The Arab world was stunned. In eight days Israel had taken all of the Sinai Desert with its touted fortifications.

The United States and the Soviet Union both condemned the Israel attack and ordered Israel to return to its previous borders. After six months of extensive negotiations, Israel complied but only on condition that the United Nations Emergency Force (UNEF) would station troops at Sharm el-Sheikh, thus guaranteeing the free passage of Israel's ships through the Gulf of Aqaba. The United Nations also promised to take control of the Gaza Strip, limiting the terrorist activities of the fedayeen.

550. Israel executed Adolf Eichmann for crimes against humanity.

Simon Wiesenthal suffered as an inmate of various Nazi concentration camps including Mauthausen and Buchenwald. Following his liberation, he dedicated his life to identifying and hunting down Nazi war criminals. Despite obstacles placed in his way by almost every government, over the years he succeeded in bringing more than 1,100 Nazi war criminals to prosecution. His most famous success was in 1960, when his data led to the capture of Adolf Eichmann.

Eichmann was responsible for all transportation of Jews during the Holocaust. He created the efficient assembly-line system which enabled the death camps to slaughter huge numbers of Jews daily. He set up the original gas chambers and purchased the Zyklon B used in the mass murder of Jews. He was unquestionably devoted to his assignment of ridding the world of Jews.

At the end of the war Eichmann escaped to Argentina. He lived in Buenos Aires with his wife and three children. He underwent plastic surgery to change his facial features and became Ricardo Klement. Israel's Secret Service, following leads supplied by Simon Wiesenthal, found him and abducted him in 1960. He was tried in Israel.

Eichmann's trial shook Israel. With more than 100 witnesses and 1,600 documents, a generation of young Israelis was shown the Holocaust in all its stark horror. Until that time, they hadn't known a great deal about the Holocaust because the survivors didn't speak about it; it was too painful. The Eichmann trial was a revelation to them.

At the same time that Eichmann was being tried, a powerful short novel by Elie Wiesel, a Holocaust survivor, was translated into English. Originally written in Yiddish and then in French, *Night* described Weisel's experience in the camps. Powerful and stark, Weisel's subsequent three novels in four years burned an image of the Holocaust into the consciousness of the world, and he became the Holocaust's living voice.

Adolf Eichmann was found guilty of genocide and hanged in 1962.

551. The goal of the Palestine Liberation Organization (PLO) was to destroy Israel.

In 1964 an Arab summit meeting established a "Palestinian army," the Palestine Liberation Organization, known as the PLO. Its primary purpose was to create a Palestinian State by destroying Israel through terrorism. One of the PLO groups, Al Fatah, was founded in 1965 and led by Yasir Arafat.

Because of Al Fatah's terrorist successes, Arafat was made chairman of the PLO in 1968. In addition to Al Fatah, terrorist branches of the PLO such as Black September and the Popular Front for the Liberation of Palestine (the PFLP) sprang up to commit terrorist attacks in Israel and around the world. Since 1965, despite Israel's vigilance and the successful prevention of more than 2,000 attempts, the PLO has been responsible for more than 3,000 acts of terror against civilians. Some of these include:

May 1972: the hijacking of a Sabena airplane

September 1972: the slaughter of eleven Israeli athletes at the Munich Olympic Games

October 1972: the hijacking of a Lufthansa airplane, forcing the release of the terrorists responsible for the Munich massacre.

April 1973: the slaughter of sixteen women and children in Kiryat Shmoneh

May 1974: the killing of twenty-one children and the wounding of seventy others during an attack of a school at Ma'alot

July 1975: a bomb explosion in Zion Square in Jerusalem, killing fourteen

March 1978: the bombing of a public bus, killing thirty-seven and wounding eighty-two

Despite these terrorist actions, the United Nations voted on October 15, 1974, to seat the PLO as the "representative of the Palestine people." On November 13, 1974, Yasir Arafat, carrying a pistol in his belt, addressed the United Nations.

The Israeli government has vowed never to negotiate with the PLO because it is a terrorist organization bent on Israel's destruction. Despite world pressure, Israel has officially maintained that position, although by 1990 there were members of Israel's government who were urging negotiations with members of the PLO.

In 1991 when Iraq attacked Israel with Scud missiles (see data to fact 514), Palestinians stood on their roofs and cheered. The PLO supported Saddam Hussein and Iraq and thereby lost a great deal of world political sympathy.

552. Israel took the Sinai Desert, the West Bank, and the Golan Heights in the Six Day War.

From 1956 to 1967 Syria continued to shell Israel's Kinneret fishing boats and to harass the settlements in the Huleh Valley (see data to fact 545). In 1964 Jordan and Syria planned to divert the waters of the Jordan River so Israel would lose her water supply. Israel warned that this act would not be tolerated and, after a number of raids, the work of water diversion ceased.

In April 1967 Syria increased her shelling of Israel's border villages. Israel attacked with planes. Syria responded and, in the air battle, Syria lost six planes. Early in May the Soviet Union, which was actively supporting Syria, strongly urged Egypt to join Syria in a united war against Israel.

On May 17 Nasser ordered the United Nations Emergency Force to leave Sinai. U Thant, secretary-general of the UN, acceded without objection. This action was a complete betrayal of the conditions the UN had accepted in 1956, when Israel returned the Sinai to Egypt.

On May 20 Nasser concentrated almost 100,000 troops and 1,000 tanks at Israel's border. On May 22 he closed the Gulf of Eilat to Israeli ships. On May 30 King Hussein of Jordan signed a pact pledging his army's support to Egypt. Iraq signed a similar agreement. Israel faced an Arab force of 200,000 men, 2,000 tanks, and almost 700 fighter planes and bombers. The Western countries did nothing.

On June 5, 1967, Israel's air force flew in low under Arab radar screens and attacked the air forces of Egypt, Syria, Jordan, and the planes of Iraq. In less than three hours, Israel destroyed 391 Arab planes on the ground and wiped out another 60 planes in air combat. Israel lost 19 planes.

With the control of the skies, Israel attacked the Sinai with fast-moving tank troops. Egypt was again outflanked, surrounded, and routed. Bombed from the air, Egypt's tank forces were overwhelmed. In one of the biggest tank battles in history, Egypt lost more than 800 tanks. By June 8 Israel had control of the entire Sinai all the way to the Suez Canal.

Despite Israel's warnings, Jordan joined in the attack by shelling Jerusalem and the suburbs of Tel Aviv. On June 5 Israel responded by pushing the Jordanians back south of Jerusalem and along the main road leading to Jerusalem. On June 6 Latrun (see data to fact 539) was taken. Israel then attacked the major Jordanian fortifications northeast of Jerusalem. Despite heavy casualties, Israel took Ammunition Hill, Jordan's major defense post in the Jerusalem area. The rest of the West

Bank fell when Jordanian tanks on their way from Jericho were destroyed by Israel's air force.

On June 9 the Israel air force shelled Syria's gun positions on the Golan Heights. Suffering heavy losses, Israel's troops engaged in fierce hand-to-hand combat, eventually taking all of the Golan Heights on June 10. Their success was due largely to the heroic work of Eli Cohen, Israel's most famous spy.

Eli Cohen was born in Alexandria, Egypt, in 1924. In 1945 he was enlisted by the Haganah's intelligence service to help get Jews out of Egypt. Eli Cohen worked successfully as an undercover agent in Egypt until after the Sinai Campaign (see fact 549), when the Egyptians expelled him from the country.

From 1961 to 1964, Eli Cohen performed his most remarkable feat of espionage. Disguised as a Syrian businessman, he was able to infiltrate the Syrian government, becoming good friends with the highest echelons of the military. At the invitation of his good friend General Amin Al-Hafez, Eli Cohen toured the Syrian defense posts on the Golan Heights and sent detailed reports back to Israel pinpointing all gun placements and artillery. Eli Cohen was so respected in Syria that when Al-Hafez became Syria's president, he seriously considered making Eli Cohen minister of defense!

In 1965, however, Eli Cohen was discovered, tried, and hanged. Because of his bravery and resourcefulness, Israel knew the position of most Syrian bunkers, tanks, and artillery placements on the Golan and thus were able to take the Heights in 1967.

553. Jerusalem was united after the Six Day War.

June 7, 1967, was one of the most important days in Israel's history. Breaking through St. Stephen's Gate, Israeli troops entered the Old City of Jerusalem. Arabs used the al-Aqsa Mosque (see fact 496) as a sniping post. Israeli soldiers took great care not to fire at any religious shrine, and as a result there were high Israeli casualties. At 10:15 A.M. the Israeli flag was raised over the Temple Mount and the kotel (see fact 337). For the first time since 1948, Jews could touch the Western Wall. Jerusalem was reunited.

The consequences of the Six Day War were extraordinary. For the first time, Israel had defensible boundaries along every one of her borders. The West Bank now separated Israel and Jordan. The Golan Heights were in Israel's hands. The Sinai separated Israel and Egypt. Most important, Jerusalem, the soul of the Jewish people, was again in

Jewish hands. In addition, the brilliance and total success of the operation ignited world Jewry. Hundreds of thousands of American Jews became emotionally involved with Israel. Tourism escalated. Money poured in via UJA and Israel Bonds. Israel's accomplishment became a source of pride and Jewish identification for previously unaffiliated and apathetic Jews.

It is clear that Israel had planned a unified Jerusalm for a long time. In less than 72 hours the Old City was linked to the New City with water lines, electric lines, and bus lines. All streets had signs in both Arabic and Hebrew. On June 28 the final barriers were knocked down and a special "day of reunification" was celebrated.

Jordan had systematically destroyed every building in the Jewish Quarter including the RaMBaN synagogue (see fact 403). Israel began rebuilding, determined to make the Quarter look as similar to the original as possible. RaMBaN's synagogue was rebuilt, as were other synagogues from the eighteenth and nineteenth centuries.

Mayor Teddy Kollek did everything possible to minimize tension and frustration between Arabs and Jews in Jerusalem. All shrines were open to all peoples for the first time since 1948.

554. Moshe Dayan was Israel's defense minister during the Six Day War.

Moshe Dayan became a symbol of the new Jewish Warrior. He was born in 1915 on the first kibbutz, Degania (see fact 513). The physical conditions were terrible, and he became tough at a very young age. During the Arab riots of 1936 (see fact 530), he trained with Orde Wingate and became one of the group commanders. During World War II he served in the British army and was part of a Jewish advance unit sent to prevent the Vichy French from blowing up the bridges between Lebanon and Palestine, thus providing time for the British main force to take the offensive. It was during that campaign that he lost one eye; he was looking through binoculars when a bullet ricocheted off them.

During the War of Independence (see fact 539) Dayan was involved in stopping the Egyptians just south of Tel Aviv. In July 1948 he became the area commander of Jerusalem. He was chief of staff of Israel's forces during the brilliant Sinai Campaign in 1956 (see fact 549).

Having gotten involved in politics, he became a member of the Knesset (see fact 540) in 1959 and was made defense minister in 1967, thus gaining international recognition as the planner of the Six Day War.

After the war Dayan was responsible for establishing the military government on the West Bank, allowing Arabs to travel between Israel and Jordan and opening the borders to Arab trade. He was held responsible for Israel's lack of readiness in the Yom Kippur War (see fact 556), then was actively involved in the peace negotiations with Egypt (see fact 559) as Israel's foreign minister.

Flamboyant and frequently controversial, Moshe Dayan died in October 1981, having actively participated in all of Israel's military encounters since 1936.

555. Golda Meir was the first woman prime minister of Israel.

Golda Mabovitch was born in Kiev, Russia, in 1898. She and her family suffered through a pogrom (see fact 451), an experience that greatly influenced her life. Her family moved to Milwaukee in 1906, and Golda became involved in both the Zionist and socialist movements. She married Morris Meyerson and in 1921 they moved to Palestine, where they joined a kibbutz.

Kibbutz life was extremely hard, but Golda Meyerson persevered. Her political skills were recognized, and in 1928 she began working for the Yishuv in executive positions. In 1934 she joined the executive committee of the Histadrut (see data to fact 525).

When the British arrested the leaders of the Yishuv in June 1946 (Black Saturday; see data to fact 535), Golda Meyerson became the acting head of the Jewish Agency, thus becoming the representative in the discussions to free the Jewish leaders.

In 1947 Golda Meyerson was selected to the top executive committee of the Jewish Agency responsible for preparing Israel for statehood. At Ben Gurion's urging, Golda changed her last name to Meir, and in January 1948 she flew to the United States to raise money for arms. She was tremendously successful, collecting almost $50 million in her whirlwind tour. She met secretly with King Abdullah of Jordan to beg him not to join in the Arab war effort, but there she failed.

Golda Meir served as Israel's first ambassador to the Soviet Union. In 1949 she became minister of labor, responsible for huge housing and road-building programs needed for the mass of new refugees (see fact 545). In 1956 she became foreign minister of Israel and eloquently presented Israel's case at the UN after the Sinai Campaign (see fact 549).

In 1967 she succeeded in uniting Mapai (see data to fact 540) with two other political parties to create the Israel Labor Party. On February

26, 1969, she became prime minister of Israel. Golda Meir resigned on
April 11, 1974, after the Yom Kippur War (see fact 556). She died on
December 8, 1978.

556. Egypt attacked Israel on Yom Kippur, 1973.

After the Six Day War, the Arab world's response was a vow to
continue the fight against Israel. Egyptian President Nasser's forces
shelled Israel's positions on the east bank of the Gulf of Suez in what
was called a War of Attrition. Israel built a huge set of fortifications all
along that defense line, called the Bar Lev Line. These were so
sophisticated that Israel assumed Egypt would not be able to break
through them.

In September 1973, Israel received intelligence reports that there
were tank and troop build-ups on both the Syrian and Egyptian fronts.
Because of an effective Arab deception plan, Israel assumed that these
were just military exercises because it was believed the Arab states were
not yet prepared for another war.

October 5 was Erev (the Eve of) Yom Kippur. Intelligence reports
noted that heavy concentrations of Egyptian and Syrian troops indicated
a serious threat. Israel's cabinet cancelled all army leaves and ordered
the standing army to be ready. After much argument, it was decided not
to call up the active reserve (practically the entire country) because of the
holy day.

At 4:00 A.M. on Yom Kippur Day, Israel's cabinet received information indicating that the Arabs were going to attack at 6:00 that evening.
At 10:00 A.M., while most of Israel was at Yom Kippur services, the order
went out for total mobilization. As it turned out, it was very fortunate
that it was Yom Kippur, because, since everyone was gathered in
synagogues, the army was able quickly to notify the entire country of
the mobilization order. All vehicles were available for transportation of
the troops. Things could have been worse, but not much: Egypt and
Syria attacked at 2:00 P.M., long before Israel's reserve forces could get
into position.

Approximately 70,000 Egyptian troops crossed the Suez Canal and
attacked the 500 Israelis stationed along the Bar Lev Line. It was easily
taken. Israeli planes counterattacked and were overwhelmed by Soviet-
made anti-aircraft missiles. Israel's reserve troops, arriving at 4:00 that
afternoon, were repulsed but took up defensive positions and stopped
the Egyptian advance. For the next week Egyptian forces kept trying to

break through beyond their positions, which remained 6 miles east of the Suez Canal.

The situation was even more serious in the Golan Heights. On October 6 Syria attacked with more than 1,400 tanks against an Israeli defense of 180 tanks. Unbelievably, the Syrians were able to overwhelm only one Israeli fortification, Mount Hermon. However, Syrian tanks advanced steadily toward Lake Kinneret. On October 8, Israeli tanks launched a major counteroffensive and, after two days of bitter fighting, pushed Syria back to the 1967 cease-fire lines.

Israel's greatest problem during the war was trying to maintain arms supplies. The Soviet Union began resupplying Egypt on the day hostilities began. Golda Meir sent urgent requests to the United States for aid. It took several days, but President Nixon under great pressure, finally agreed to an airlift to resupply Israel.

With those arms, Israel went on the offensive. In a daring drive led by General Ariel Sharon (see data to facts 560, 562), Israeli troops crossed the Suez Canal into Egypt. Combined with a large force on the east side of the Canal, two armies pushed south, wiping out Egypt's anti-aircraft missile sites and giving Israel control of the skies. Egypt's Third army found itself totally cut off, surrounded and threatened with annihilation. It was only when it was clear that Egypt was going to lose that the United Nations did anything; a cease-fire was ordered for October 22. At that time, Israel held the entire western side of the Suez Canal, coming within 42 miles of Cairo.

In the north, Israel had pushed Syria back to within 40 miles of Damascus, having destroyed more than 1,100 tanks. The Yom Kippur War officially ended as a tremendous victory for Israel, demonstrating great resourcefulness and incredible individual bravery. However, the war stunned the country. Israel lost more than 2,500 soldiers, a devastating number. People were shocked at how close Egypt and Syria had come to overrunning the country in the first hours of the war. Israel had been taken by surprise, and Moshe Dayan (see fact 554), Golda Meir (see fact 555), and David Elazar, the chief of staff, were held responsible. Although she was reelected prime minister in December, Golda Meir resigned in April 1974.

For the first time, Israelis looked cynically at their leaders and their government. Corruption scandals were uncovered. Israel's self-confidence was badly shaken, and much of the idealism which had founded the country went into hibernation.

Israel's response to the scandals and the Yom Kippur War was similar to America's response to President John F. Kennedy's assassination and the Watergate scandal.

557. On July 4, 1976, Israel freed hostages in a daring raid on Entebbe.

On June 27, 1976, an Air France plane was hijacked by a group of Arab terrorists. The plane refueled in Libya and finally landed in Uganda, with the approval and protection of Uganda's dictator Idi Amin.

The terrorists threatened to kill the passengers if Israel did not release fifty-three Palestinian terrorists. To the world's shock, Israel indicated its willingness to negotiate.

This was a ruse. Israel secretly put together a daring rescue mission called Operation Thunderbolt. Flying more than 2,500 miles into hostile territory, an Israeli commando group surprised the Ugandans, killed the terrorists, and freed all but four of the hostages who were killed. The commander of the operation, Jonathan (Yoni) Netanyahu, was the only Israeli military casualty.

After the anger and anguish of the Yom Kippur War, the raid on Entebbe ignited tremendous enthusiasm in Israel and among world Jewry.

558. The Good Fence allows Arabs to enter Israel for medical help.

In 1976 Syria and the PLO systematically began to slaughter the Christians in Lebanon. More than 75,000 people were killed. Many fled to southern Lebanon near Israel's border. Israel supplied them with equipment to protect them from the Syrians. Beginning in June 1976 Israel permitted Lebanese to cross into Israel at Metullah to receive medical care. Considering the fact that Lebanon and Israel remained in an official state of war, this humane action was unprecedented. From June to October 1976 Israel treated more than 11,000 wounded Lebanese who crossed "The Good Fence" into Israel for medical care.

559. The Camp David Accord established peace between Israel and Egypt.

Because of Arab oil pressure, practically the entire world condemned Israel after the Yom Kippur War. The United States put tremendous pressure on Israel to come to a settlement with Egypt over the Sinai, with Jordan over the West Bank, and with Syria over the Golan. Israel refused to talk with any representatives of the PLO (see fact 551). Jordan and Syria refused to talk until Israel returned the Golan Heights and the West Bank.

Henry Kissinger spent much of 1974 traveling between Israel and Egypt, speaking with each side separately because Egypt refused to be in the same room with Israel's representatives. This procedure, called "shuttle diplomacy," succeeded in establishing cease-fire lines in the Sinai. Israel agreed to withdraw east of the important mountain passes of Mitla and Gidi provided that detection equipment could be placed to note any Egyptian troop movement which would indicate a breaking of the cease-fire agreement. However, it was clear to everyone that both sides were deeply entrenched in their policy positions, and there was little room for further compromise or negotiation.

When the right-wing Likud party won the elections in Israel in 1977, the United States feared that even these peace negotiations would grind to a halt. To the world's shock, on September 10, 1977, Anwar Sadat, president of Egypt, announced his willingness to visit Israel. It was the first time an Arab leader had shown readiness to recognize Israel. Menachem Begin immediately invited him, and Sadat arrived on November 19. In addressing the Knesset, Sadat acknowledged Israel was "an existing fact," thus giving formal recognition to Israel. As a result of the negotiations between Sadat and Begin, Israel agreed to evacuate the Sinai on condition that Egyptian troops would not cross the Mitla and Gidi Passes. Face-to-face negotiations had begun.

With the support, encouragement, and nudging of President Carter, the two sides slowly worked out the wording of a complex agreement which included Israel's evacuation of the Sinai and a framework for conducting negotiations for establishing autonomy for Gaza, and "Judea/Samaria" (the West Bank). This agreement, signed in September 1978, was called the Camp David Accord. It was followed by months of negotiations as the two nations struggled to write a mutually acceptable peace treaty. Concerning the issue of the Palestinians, the treaty remained purposely vague so each side could interpret it in the way it wanted. The treaty concentrated on the specifics of Israel's withdrawal from the Sinai. When Egypt insisted that the treaty include defined steps for the autonomy of the West Bank, Israel refused, and the talks appeared to be stalemated again. Cyrus Vance flew back and forth between Egypt and Israel trying to break the deadlock. President Carter also flew to Cairo and Jerusalem. Many people suspect that these negotiations involved some secret treaty provisions still not disclosed. Finally, on March 26, 1979, Israel and Egypt signed a peace treaty.

As a result of all these negotiations, in 1979 Menachem Begin and Anwar Sadat received the Nobel Peace Prize.

The peace treaty between Egypt and Israel had tremendous ramifications for the two countries. Although Egypt got back the Sinai with its rich oil fields, she was ostracized for almost a decade by the other Arab nations as a traitor. Anwar Sadat was assassinated on October 6, 1981, by Muslim fundamentalists. His successor Hosni Mubarak vowed to keep the peace treaty.

Israel lost its prime source of oil and had to return to a boundary that was less secure. Most significant, Israeli settlers had created a community in northern Sinai on the Mediterranean, Yammit. One of the terms of the peace treaty was Israel's returning that land to Egypt. Riots broke out as the settlers refused to leave, and the Israeli army had to be called in to force the evacuation. Yammit was totally bulldozed, leaving Egypt with desert sand, but tremendous bitterness was created among the settlers, who felt that they had been betrayed. The return of Yammit to Egypt provided Israel's right-wing groups with a rallying point (see fact 562).

560. In 1982 Israel initiated a war in Lebanon.

In 1970 the PLO (see fact 551) failed in their attempt to overthrow Jordan's King Hussein and he forcibly expelled them from Jordan. They moved to Lebanon, where they joined Syria in a protracted civil war against the Christian Lebanese (see data to fact 558). Despite Israel's support of the Christian Lebanese and their leader S'ad Haddad, the PLO's military might continued to build. By 1981 the PLO in Lebanon had become an army consisting of 20,000 troops with hundreds of Soviet-supplied tanks and artillery. Syria had brought the Soviet's most advanced anti-aircraft missiles into Lebanon, and there was tremendous tension on the northern border of Israel, resulting in artillery exchanges between Israel and the PLO. Phillip Habib, an American special envoy, achieved a cease-fire agreement between the two groups.

Israel and the United States understood the PLO to promise that they would cease all terrorist activities. The PLO understood the agreement to be that they would cease terrorist activities from the Lebanese border. As a result, the PLO escalated their terrorist activities in Europe and in Israel by crossing the border from Jordan. During this official cease-fire, the PLO committed 248 separate acts of terrorism, many of them aimed toward Kiryat Shmoneh (see fact 547). Israel condemned the PLO for breaking the cease-fire agreement. The PLO denied breaking the ceasefire.

In December 1981 Israel declared the Golan Heights to be officially part of Israel. Through the spring of 1982 the PLO staged a wide series of terrorist activities in southern Lebanon and in Europe. Israel retaliated by bombing PLO centers in Lebanon. During this time, tension was high within Israel because the government had forced the evacuation of Yammit in April 1982 (see data to fact 559).

On June 3 the terrorists shot Israel's ambassador to Britain. Israel's air force bombed PLO targets. The PLO retaliated by shelling Israel's northern settlements for two days. On June 6, 1982, Israel's army attacked the PLO in Lebanon. Called Operation Peace for Galilee, the initial fighting, which lasted five days, was a brilliant Israeli victory. Israel's goals, while unfortunately fuzzy, were said to be the establishment of a 25-mile-wide PLO-free area in southern Lebanon.

Israel wiped out the Syrian anti-aircraft batteries and, in aerial combat, destroyed more than 70 Syrian planes without losing any of her own. On the ground, Israel took the tremendously fortified PLO position of Beaufort after a bloody struggle. Israeli-made Merkavah tanks defeated the Soviet made T-72s in a number of battles. The Syrians were pushed back, and the PLO fled to Beirut. By June 11 Israel had achieved all of her original goals. She had captured more than 5,600 tons of PLO ammunition, 1,300 armored vehicles including several hundred tanks, and more than 1,300 anti-tank weapons. She had captured 9,000 PLO members and had cleared southern Lebanon of terrorists. Israel had lost only 130 soldiers. It was a stunning victory.

Unfortunately, Israel's defense minister, Ariel Sharon, didn't stop there. Maintaining that the goals of Operation Peace for Galilee included the destruction of the PLO command and infrastructure located in Beirut, he proceeded to encircle Lebanon's capital, intent on wiping out the 15,000 PLO remaining there. Since the PLO purposely made their headquarters in hospitals, schools, and civilian areas, the fierce fighting over Beirut resulted in huge civilian casualties. Hundreds of Israeli soldiers were killed and wounded in the subsequent two-month siege. Israelis and Jews around the world were horrified and outraged. For the first time, more than 20,000 people in Tel Aviv demonstrated against an Israeli war effort.

In August 1982, after long negotiations with U.S. special envoy Phillip Habib as the mediator, the PLO were evacuated from Lebanon, and thus officially ended Operation Peace for Galilee. By that time Israel had lost 345 soldiers, with 2,100 more wounded, testimony to the horrors of the two-month siege of Beirut.

On August 23 Bahir Jemayel, a Christian, was elected president of Lebanon. At the beginning of September he secretly met with Prime Minister Begin, and there was hope for some form of peace agreement with Lebanon. Jemayel was murdered on September 14. Israel went back into West Beirut, including the refugee camps of Sabra and Shatilla, to stop any terrorist outbreaks. Christian Lebanese joined the Israelis to help mop up PLO resistance. Angered at the murder of Bahir Jemayel, the Christian militia slaughtered hundreds of unarmed men, women, and children in the two refugee camps. Although not actively participating, Israel was held responsible. In Tel Aviv, 400,000 people gathered to call for a Commission of Inquiry and the resignations of Begin and Sharon.

In May 1983 Lebanon and Israel signed a peace and evacuation agreement. In September Israel exchanged 4,500 terrorist prisoners for 6 captured Israelis. Israel didn't complete its evacuation until January 1984.

The war in Lebanon affected Israelis long after its conclusion. There was bitterness over the loss of life, the senseless continuation beyond the stated 25-mile strip, and the atrocities at Sabra and Shatilla.

561. Israel's capital is Jerusalem.

The status of Jerusalem has always been a point of international conflict. In 1947 the United Nations Partition Plan provided that Jerusalem be an international city. During the War of Independence, Jordan captured the Old City of Jerusalem (see data to fact 539) while Israel held the New City.

Despite Jordan's systematic destruction of the Jewish Quarter and its refusal to allow any Jews to enter the Old City, the United Nations reiterated its plan that Jerusalem be an international city. Israel responded by moving the Knesset to Jerusalem in February 1949 and declaring it the eternal capital of the Jewish people. Most countries insisted that the 1947 United Nations internationalization scheme for Jerusalem was still in effect and refused to move their embassies from Tel Aviv to Jerusalem.

After the Six Day War (see fact 553) Israel reunified the Old City and the New City. By June 27, 1967, the Knesset had already voted that united Jerusalem was the capital of Israel. In July the United Nations condemned this act, denying the unification of Jerusalem and urging Israel to retract its resolution. Israel refused. Gradually, because of the inconvenience of having to travel daily from the Tel Aviv embassies to Israel's Foreign Ministry office in Jerusalem, twenty-two countries moved their embassies to Jerusalem.

In 1980 Israel reaffirmed that all of Jerusalem was its capital. In protest, thirteen of the twenty-two embassies moved back to Tel Aviv. The controversy was exacerbated by the Vatican, which in September 1980 again declared Jerusalem to be an international city. In 1981 the World Council of Churches also declared Jerusalem to be an international city.

Under Israel's auspices, the holy places of Jerusalem have been available to all religions. Despite this fact, protests over Jerusalem have continued to be an issue in the United Nations.

Ironically, Jerusalem, the Holy City, has become the site of violence between extremely pious Jews (called chareidim) and secular Jews. There have been battles over movie theaters being open on Shabbat, mixed bathing in public pools, posters at bus terminals with pictures of scantily clad women, and vehicular traffic on Shabbat. Originally, the chareidim ghettoed themselves into isolated areas of Jerusalem, specifically Mea Shearim. The city permitted them to block off the roads of their area on Shabbat to keep people from driving through their streets. Cars and "immodestly dressed" people were stoned. Through the 1980s the chareidim systematically bought apartment complexes with the goal of completely surrounding the roads into the city, hoping thereby to prevent any driving on Shabbat in Jerusalem. There have been instances of arson in apartment complexes near the areas now occupied by the chareidim. The secular Jews are responding with anger and occasional violence. The outcome of the struggle between chareidim and secular Jews is not yet determined.

562. Gush Emunim and Kach are right-wing Jewish groups.

In 1968 an angry Orthodox rabbi organized some Brooklyn Jewish youth into a vigilante group called the Jewish Defense League. Its original function was to protect the elderly Jews from delinquent blacks and Hispanics in the area. Soon, however, the JDL developed a confrontational style to disrupt cultural exchanges between the United States and the Soviet Union as a protest against the Soviet's anti-Semitic policies (see data to fact 573).

The founder of the JDL, Rabbi Meir Kahane, soon directed his attention to Israel. Taking a rigid Orthodox position, he condemned the Israeli government for "corrupting Jewish values." He maintained that it was impossible for a state to be both democratic and Jewish. Either Israel was a Jewish state or it was a "Hellenized" democracy.

According to Kahane, God had given all of the Land of Israel to the Jews, the Chosen People, as a divine inheritance. Any objection by the outside world or by Arabs had to be ignored. Any Arab who demonstrated against the Jewish authority should, by Jewish Law, be expelled from the Land of Israel. Quoting the TaNaCH, Kahane emphasized that God requires vengeance against the enemies of Israel and decried the "soft, humanist, Westernized" values shown by Israel's government.

In 1967, immediately after the Six Day War, the Israeli government had permitted the rebuilding of the Gush Etzion, the three settlements which Jordan had destroyed in May 1948 (see data to fact 537). A Jewish urban center, Kiryat Arba, was also built above Hebron (see fact 484). Israel's Labor government, however, strictly limited the number and site of new settlements. Ten settlements were permitted in the Golan, and Yammit was built in the Sinai, but that was it. In 1974 a group of Orthodox Israelis created their own movement, Gush Emunim, the Bloc of the Faithful. Its focus was on the religious imperative for Jews to own and settle the entire Land of Israel, which, according to the Torah, included the West Bank.

The Gush Emunim began to religiously oppose the government's attempts to limit Jewish settlements on the West Bank. Encouraged by General Ariel Sharon (see data to fact 560), they established small settlements near Nablus and Shomron (see fact 482). They tried to build settlements south of Jerusalem. Although the Labor Party ordered some of the Gush Emunim settlements to be destroyed, Menachem Begin and Likud supported the Gush Emunim.

In 1977 the Gush Emunim published its 25-year plan: it included building two cities on the West Bank, each with 60,000 inhabitants; establishing four towns with 20,000 people each; creating 25 small towns with populations of 10,000 each; and founding 125 settlements averaging 1,000 people each.

Israeli liberals were worried that such proposals would increase the tension and conflict already festering on the West Bank, and when Menachem Begin was elected prime minister, they feared the worst. However, it was during the time that Begin was prime minister that Israel agreed to return Yammit to Egypt (see data to fact 559). This action enraged Kahane and some of his followers, who viewed it as a betrayal.

Although labeled a racist, Kahane founded the Kach party in Israel. He encouraged Jews to challenge the government's authority to return Yammit to Egypt. Bitter fighting between army troops and Jewish settlers ensued.

When West Bank Arabs committed acts of aggression or terror, the West Bank Jewish settlers retaliated with violence. Gush Emunim members became more radical.

Since the intifada began (see fact 569), there has been tremendous pressure placed on the Israeli government by Gush Emunim and Kach to respond more harshly to the demonstrations and riots. Although horrified by Kahane's rigid extremism, many Israelis fear that he might be right: it might not be possible to have a Jewish state that retains its high democratic principles for all peoples. Secretly, many Israelis wish that the Arabs would just disappear. Kahane's Kach party continues to receive very little electoral support, but the intifada has lent impetus to rightist extremism in Israel's population. Palestinian support for Saddam Hussein has increased the levels of animosity (see data to facts 514, 551). Because of his rigid response to the intifada and his insistence on Israel's right to build settlements on the West Bank, Ariel Sharon resurfaced in the 1990s as a popular representative of Israel's right-wing political parties.

In 1990, Rabbi Meir Kahane was assassinated in New York City while on a speaking tour in the United States.

563. All buildings in Jerusalem must be covered with Jerusalem stone that looks golden in the sunlight.

The walls surrounding the Old City of Jerusalem were ordered by Suleiman the Magnificent (see fact 500). They were made from the local stone, a yellowish, durable limestone. When the Yishuv began to build the New City of Jerusalem during the British Mandate, the British decided to keep the beauty of the city by insisting that all buildings in Jerusalem had to be built of that same local stone.

In 1967, when Israel systematically began to restore the Jewish Quarter (see data to fact 553), the buildings were all made from the same Jerusalem stone. The law remains today. As a result, at sunrise and sunset the city takes on the golden hue of the stone, creating an actual Jerusalem of Gold.

564. Hadassah Hospital's synagogue contains Chagall's magnificent stained-glass windows.

Hadassah Hospital was originally built on Mount Scopus, northeast of the Temple Mount in Jerusalem. In 1948 Hebrew University and the hospital were cut off from the rest of Israel and Mount Scopus became an Israeli island surrounded by Jordan (see data to fact 539). Once every two weeks, a convoy of supplies was permitted to go through Jordanian territory to Mount Scopus.

Subsequently a magnificent new medial center was built on the outskirts of Jerusalem. Hadassah commissioned painter Marc Chagall to create a set of stained glass windows for the synagogue at the hospital.

Chagall was born in Russia in 1887 and was influenced all his life by his shtetl experience. He considered the stained glass windows one of his major challenges. Chagall took as his theme the Twelve Tribes of Israel (see fact 142) and based his images on the description of each son provided by Jacob on his deathbed.

Using unique techniques, Chagall created three windows for each wall of the synagogue. Each window is about 11 feet high and 8 feet wide. The colors are brilliant and vibrant and the created rainbows dominate the small room. They have been universally praised as one of the art wonders of Israel, and some critics have called them the finest examples of stained glass in the world. Chagall unveiled the windows in 1962.

565. Heichal Shlomo in Jerusalem is the office of Israel's Chief Rabbis.

Under the Ottoman Turks (see fact 499), the religious Jews in Palestine selected a leader in Jerusalem. He was called the chacham bashi. When the British took over (see fact 524), they got rid of the office of chacham bashi and instead established the Rabbinate of the Jewish Community in Jerusalem. It consisted of elected Sephardic and Ashkenazic (see fact 229) chief rabbis and a council of rabbis and laypeople.

The Rabbinate of the Jewish Community had complete jurisdiction over divorce, marriage, alimony, adoption, wills, and funerals for the entire Yishuv.

In 1953 the Knesset voted to continue the same rabbinical institution and structured the election procedures for the Chief Rabbinate of Israel. The Chief Rabbinical Council (as it is called) appoints chaplains for the army; oversees kashrut in all restaurants and hotels (see facts 589–597); designates who may officiate at weddings, divorces, and funerals; writes responsa on halachic matters (see fact 374); and oversees the work of sofrim (plural of sofer, see fact 231) to ensure that all parchments are correct. The Chief Rabbinical Council and all of its offices are located in Jerusalem in a building called Heichal Shlomo (the Hall of Solomon).

Because of the wide-ranging authority given the Chief Rabbinical Council, there have been numerous disputes between it, liberal Jewish institutions in Israel, and secular Jews. The Council does not recognize any Reform, Reconstructionist, or Conservative rabbis as being legal officiants at weddings or funerals in Israel. In order for a liberal rabbi to officiate at a marriage in Israel, he or she must have an Orthodox rabbi sign the ketubah (see fact 263).

On occasion, the Chief Rabbinical Council has used its authority to cancel kashrut licenses as political leverage to influence institutions to observe other halachic laws as well (see facts 589–597). The Council does not recognize the conversion of anyone under the auspices of a Reform, Reconstructionist, or Conservative rabbi (see data to fact 542), nor does it accept divorces issued by Conservative rabbis in the United States.

In the late 1980s the Council established halachic rules for worship at the kotel (see fact 337). These have led to conflicts both with women's prayer groups who have tried to lead their own religious services and with liberal Jewish groups who have tried to conduct services there.

566. Hebrew Union College has a campus in Jerusalem, where all Reform rabbinical and cantorial students study for a year.

In the nineteenth and early twentieth centuries, many of the leaders of Reform Judaism were opposed to the political Zionist movement. They viewed Judaism as embracing universal values, and philosophically they separated their religion from their nationalities. They were intent on professing deep loyalties to their individual countries and felt that any focus on a Jewish homeland might cast doubts on their national loyalties. They did, however, always favor aid to Jews living in Palestine.

Although individual Reform Jewish leaders were passionately involved in political Zionism from its inception, most Reform Jews were non-Zionist until after World War I.

By the 1930s, however, a group of Reform Jewish leaders had become ardent political Zionists. Led by Rabbis Abba Hillel Silver and Stephen S. Wise (see data to fact 448), they became America's Zionist spokesmen. Rabbi Stephen Wise was involved in the founding of the American Jewish Congress (see data to fact 458) and the World Jewish Congress.

The rise of Hitler caused a tremendous change in the Reform Movement, and in 1937 the Central Conference of American Rabbis (see data to fact 448) passed a resolution calling on all Jews to support a Jewish homeland. In 1939 The Leo Baeck School, a high school for Reform Jews, was founded in Haifa. Today it has more than 1,000 students from kindergarten through twelfth grade, a preschool program, and numerous community outreach programs.

In 1941 the Central Conference of American Rabbis passed a resolution supporting a Jewish army in Palestine. A group of dissenting members established the American Council for Judaism, which continued to oppose the founding of the State of Israel, arguing that Judaism is a religion of universal values and not a nationality. While still in existence today, the American Council for Judaism lost much of its membership after the Six Day War (see fact 552).

Although a Reform (called "Progressive") synagogue already existed in Haifa, in 1957 the Israel Committee of the Central Conference of American Rabbis helped found the first "Progressive" congregation in Jerusalem.

When Stephen S. Wise's Jewish Institute of Religion merged with Hebrew Union College, Rabbi Nelson Glueck became its president (see fact 448). He was an archaeologist and had strong personal ties with Israel, and he was determined to strengthen the Reform Jewish presence in Israel. In 1963 he succeeded in establishing the Hebrew Union College Biblical and Archaeological School in Jerusalem. This gradually became the center for Progressive Judaism in Israel and the headquarters of the World Union for Progressive Judaism (WUPJ; see fact 467). The campus now includes a nursery school, a youth hostel, and a tremendous new library.

In 1970 Hebrew Union College–Jewish Institute of Religion required all first-year rabbinical students to spend their first year at the Jerusalem campus as part of an intensive Hebrew program. In 1986 all first-year cantorial students began spending their first year of study at the Jerusalem campus.

In 1970 the Central Conference of American Rabbis was the first American rabbinical group to hold its convention in Jerusalem. It did so again in 1974, 1981, and 1988, emphasizing the movement's ongoing commitment to the State of Israel.

567. ARZA is the Reform Movement's Zionist Association.

In 1977 the Union of American Hebrew Congregations (see data to fact 447) voted to create a Reform Zionist organization. ARZA, the Association of Reform Zionists of America, is a member of the World Zionist Organization and one of the largest representative participants in the World Zionist Congress. Besides being the voice for Reform Zionists in the international Zionist community, ARZA fights for religious pluralism in Israel. The Canadian Reform Zionist organization is called Kadima.

In 1987 ARZA founded the Israel Religious Action Center, which initiates and finances legal actions against Orthodox discrimination in Israel and litigates other social justice cases. The Israel Religious Action Center has been responsible for pressuring the Ministry of Absorption to register converts by Reform and Conservative rabbis as Jews (See data to fact 542). It is also involved in the never-ending attempts by the Orthodox to amend the Law of Return.

Events from 1983 to 1991

568. Operation Moses was Israel's airlift of Ethiopian Jews from Sudan to Israel.

With the overthrow of Emperor Haile Selassie in 1974, Ethiopian Jews found themselves in terrible danger (see data to fact 468). Thousands of Ethiopian Jews risked their lives by crossing the desert to escape to the Sudan. Although more than 2,000 people died on the dangerous journey, by 1984 about 10,000 Ethiopian Jews had succeeded in reaching the Sudanese refugee camps (see fact 468). As conditions worsened in both Ethiopia and the refugee camps, Israel decided to create a massive airlift to transport the Ethiopian Jews to Israel. From November 1984 to January 1985, Israel flew almost 7,000 Beta Esrael to Israel. This project was called Operation Moses. It was an open secret. Israel, afraid that publicity would ruin the operation, ordered that no information be given to the press. However, the cost of Operation Moses was tremendous, and Israel needed support from wealthy world Jewry to finance it. Numerous people were quietly told about the plan, and on December 11 the *New York Times* reported the story. More details were revealed on January 5. The Ethiopian government angrily accused Israel of kidnapping its nationals. Sudan officially refused to allow more Beta Esrael to leave the refugee camps, and many of the stranded Ethiopian Jews died. By 1987 more than 16,000 Ethiopian Jews had immigrated to Israel.

The absorption process was slow. Most Beta Esrael children and adults adapted to their new Western culture. They learned the traditions of rabbinic Judaism while maintaining their own unique Jewish rituals. Some Ethiopian Jews began preparing to become rabbis. Israel encouraged the Ethiopian Jews to observe their own ceremonies as well, including their traditional holiday, the Segad, which commemorates their separation from the Land of Israel. Unfortunately, by 1990 the majority of Ethiopian Jews were still unemployed. More than 40 percent had not yet received permanent homes. And they continued to worry about their family members still trapped in Ethiopia in the middle of a civil war.

Controversy remained concerning the Jewish status of the Beta Esrael. Although declared halachically Jewish in 1974 (see fact 468), the new immigrants were required by the Chief Rabbinate (see fact 565) to immerse in the mikvah just to make sure (see facts 261, 587, 588). The Beta Esrael angrily refused, insisting on no ceremony. The Chief Rabbinate tried to enforce this rule by not allowing the Ethiopian Jews to marry without the immersion. Some rabbis in the absorption centers ignored the ruling and officiated at such weddings. It remained a heatedly argued point of conflict between the Chief Rabbinate and the Beta Esrael.

In 1990 the civil war in Ethiopia intensified. Ethiopia's government, receiving military support from Israel, began to quietly permit Ethiopian Jews to emigrate.

As the rebels, supported by the PLO, became more successful, the Beta Esrael fled from their homes and relocated in Addis Ababa, Ethiopia's capital. More than 26,000 Ethiopian Jews waited for permission to leave. After a tense summer during which Beta Esrael were refused exit visas, the Ethiopian government again permitted about 600 Jews a month to leave. Happily, thanks to World Jewry's support, most of them were saved and arrived in Israel to be reunited with their families (see data to fact 468).

569. In December 1987 the Arabs on the West Bank and in the Gaza Strip began the Intifada.

Despite better medical care, education, and lifestyle under the authority of Israel, the Arabs on the West Bank continued to protest the military rule (see data to facts 552, 562). They wanted an independent Palestinian state on the West Bank and Gaza, and they maintained that this was possible only under the auspices of the PLO (see fact 551). Israel refused to negotiate with anyone associated with the PLO. When moderate Arabs tried working with Israel, they were murdered by less moderate Arabs.

Stoning of Jewish West Bank settlers and acts of terrorism resulted in angry retribution by Gush Emunim and Kach members (see fact 562). The army became harsher in its responses to violent outbreaks.

In December 1987 the Arabs on the West Bank declared that they didn't care what anyone did to them, that they were going to revolt. They set up huge riots, throwing rocks and fire bombs and burning tires. They called this uprising the Intifada. Israel's army responded with mass arrests, shootings, and beatings, all shown on American television.

The rioting continued, the shootings continued, and world Jewry became split in its response. Many people were horrified at the brutality shown by some Israeli soldiers and police. Others viewed the rioting as a threat to Israel's own security and insisted that the Intifada be smashed before negotiations could take place.

Arabs willing to work with Israel continued to be murdered. Although Israel's military succeeded in suppressing the extent of the rioting, morale in the army was seriously affected. Young recruits, not much older than the rioting Arab youngsters, found themselves in impossible situations in which they had to shoot at young rioters. Groups such as Peace Now demonstrated with 40,000 people urging the government to talk with the PLO. Other groups such as Kach and the Gush Emunim insisted the government had to get tougher with the Arabs.

As the number of casualties on each side mounted, the political responses of the Israelis became more extreme. The peace groups continued to insist that Israel negotiate with the PLO. The majority of Israelis began maintaining that the Intifada had to be put down and the acts of terrorism stopped at any price. In 1990 the United States, under Secretary of State James Baker, put together a peace negotiation plan. The Likud government, under Prime Minister Shamir (see fact 571), rejected the proposal. For the first time in Israel's history, the Knesset returned a vote of no confidence, and the Shamir government fell. The Labor party, under the leadership of Shimon Peres, attempted to establish a coalition government and failed. Likud finally succeeded in creating a right-wing coalition. Yitzchak Shamir remained prime minister, but an important political role was given to Ariel Sharon (see data to facts 560, 562, 573). In the 1990s there continued to be tremendous pressure on Israel both internally and internationally to change the status quo. More than 70 percent of American Jewish leaders urged Israel to speak with "moderate" PLO members. By 1990 more than 600 Arabs had been killed; about 250 (more than one-third) of them were murdered by fellow Arabs who claimed that they were "collaborators." More than 50 Israelis had been killed.

In 1991, because the Palestinians supported Saddam Hussein and

Iraq in the Persian Gulf War (see data to facts 514, 551, 562), American Jewish leaders stopped pressuring Israel to moderate her policy. However, the American government continues to urge Israel to negotiate "land for peace."

570. When the Intifada began, Yitzchak Rabin was Israel's defense minister.

Yitzchak Rabin was born in Jerusalem in 1922. He joined the Palmach in 1940 (see fact 533) and helped fight against the Vichy French. He was arrested by the British in 1946 on "Black Saturday" (see data to fact 535). During the "Prewar War" (see data to fact 537) he was in charge of the troops who fought for the road to Jerusalem. He was chief of staff during the Six Day War and gained great popularity in Israel. From 1968 to 1973 he was Israel's ambassador to the United States, and he became prime minister of Israel in 1974. Revelations about the Yom Kippur War, corruption in the Labor party, and the fact that his wife had an illegal bank account in the United States forced him to resign in 1977. His resignation opened the way for Menachem Begin to gain a plurality in the elections and to become the prime minister (see fact 562). In 1984 the Labor Party and the Likud agreed to create a "National Unity Government." Rabin became minister of defense.

When the Intifada broke out (see fact 569), it became Yitzchak Rabin's responsibility to suppress the riots. His policies ranged from simple beatings, to using rubber bullets, to shooting fire-bomb throwers. In 1990, when the National Unity Government fell and the Likud party under Shamir regained the majority (see data to fact 571), Yitzchak Rabin was replaced as defense minister by Moshe Arens.

571. When the Intifada began, Yitzchak Shamir was Israel's prime minister.

Born in Poland in 1915, Yitzchak Shamir joined Betar (see data to fact 522). He emigrated to Israel in 1935 and joined the Irgun in 1937 (see fact 531). In 1941, however, angered by the Irgun's decision not to continue attacks against the British during World War II, he joined the LECHI (see data to fact 532) and was soon one of its commanders. In 1946 he was captured and imprisoned by the British. He miraculously escaped and fled the country. Shamir returned to Israel only after it became a state.

In 1970 he joined Menachem Begin's Herut party and was elected to the Knesset in 1973. In 1980 he became foreign minister. When Begin resigned as prime minister in 1983, Shamir was elected. In 1984 Likud and Labor combined in a National Unity Government, in which Shimon Peres agreed to be prime minister for two years, followed by Shamir for two years.

Shamir was supported by the right-wing political groups, although Kach continued to see him as being too liberal and "hellenized." He favored increased settlements on the West Bank and took a rigid stance against the Intifada. When discussing the mass immigration of Soviet Jews (see fact 573), Shamir emphasized that the Jewish people had to concentrate all its efforts to help absorb the Soviet Aliyah. He added that a big Israel was needed to settle Soviet Jews, a statement that created a controversy (see data to fact 573).

Shamir continued his government's refusal to negotiate with anyone representing the PLO (see fact 551), which Shamir called a terrorist organization. When Ezer Weizman, one of Israel's cabinet members, had contacts with a PLO representative, Shamir had him removed from the cabinet. When Shamir rejected the Baker peace proposal (see data to fact 569), his government fell. However, his major opponent, Shimon Peres, was unable to create a coalition government, and Shamir was again made prime minister. His coalition remained a fragile one, and he depended on the right-wing political parties and the chareidim (see data to fact 561) for support. Thus there was great pressure on him not to make many compromises concerning the Palestinians and the Intifada.

572. Israel's army is called Tzahal.

When the British mandate ended (see data to fact 537), the Yishuv had three independent defense forces: the Haganah (see fact 523), the Irgun (see fact 531), and the LECHI (see data to fact 532). Each of these forces viewed the others with contempt, anger, or disdain. David Ben Gurion felt that it was essential to have only one army, and he ordered the other groups to join forces under one leadership. Only after some ugly incidents, including the blowing up of the *Altalena* (see data to fact 538), did the Irgun agree. The LECHI remained somewhat independent, even murdering Swedish Count Folke Bernadotte, who headed the UN negotiating group. The Yishuv was horrified, and LECHI disappeared. Israel's united army was called Israel Defense Forces, Tzahal. Newspapers frequently refer to it as the IDF.

Constantly under the threat of attack, Israel became a civilian defense nation. Except for yeshivah students and Orthodox women, all Israelis serve in the army. Men go into the army at 18 for three years of active service. After that they are called up as reserve troops for at least one month every year. This reserve service continues (albeit with a decrease in the time per year) until the age of 55. Women go into the army at 18 for two years, and they remain part of the army reserve until age 38. Women do not serve in the reserve after they marry. At times of military emergency a large portion of the population can thus be called up for active duty. In addition to the reservists and the conscripted young Israelis, there is also a core of career soldiers.

The army is tremendously important in helping immigrants integrate into Israeli society. All new male immigrants under the age of 29 serve eighteen months on active duty. They study Hebrew, learn about the Land of Israel, and are accepted into the larger society. Like college relationships in the United States, the friendships created in the army are frequently the most long-lasting. Moreover, because everyone is in the army, Tzahal serves as a unifying force within society. Israelis are more politically aware and active because they are personally involved in the day-to-day defense of the country. It is an Israeli tradition that officers lead their soldiers into battle.

The potential military exemption for yeshivah students has resulted in added tension between Israelis who accept military service and those who choose, on religious grounds, not to be conscripted. There are, of course, many religious Jews who do serve in the army.

Israel's air force is considered one of the best in the world. The level of rigorous training in Israel's military forces remains high, and new recruits still take pride in getting into elite regiments.

573. Operation Exodus provided for the mass immigration of Soviet Jews to Israel.

Because the Czars treated the Jews so abominably (see facts 437, 438, 451, 457), Jews were in the forefront of the Bolshevik Revolution of 1917. They had founded and served in many of the leading Socialist and Bolshevik organizations. One of Lenin's closest advisors was a Jew.

At the same time, many Jews were deeply committed to Zionism. Inspired by the Balfour Declaration of that same year (see fact 520), thousands enthusiastically prepared to join their fellow Jews in Palestine. The majority of Russian Jews, however, remained focused on traditional Judaism and its practices.

In March 1917 the Provisional Government of the USSR abolished all laws that had been aimed at the persecution and restriction of Jews. It looked as though the Jews of Russia had finally attained their freedom and equality. Their joy was short-lived. From October 1917 to the beginning of 1921, Russia was plunged into a horrible civil war. Jews, caught in the middle, were slaughtered in huge numbers. Although the Red Army had established a policy against anti-Semitism, it didn't prevent individual troops from pillaging and murdering Jews. The Russian peasants' virulent anti-Semitism couldn't be halted by a Red Army edict, and the Jews suffered terribly.

When the Communist Party finally took over, one of its platforms was a prohibition against the persecution of Jews. Ironically, however, the new regime also had an anti-religious policy, and it included opposition to the Jewish religion, Zionism, and Hebrew. Jews were considered complete citizens, but they weren't allowed to be different from other Soviets. The government systematically closed yeshivot (plural of yeshivah), synagogues, and schools. They fined rabbis and Hebrew teachers. Zionists were sent to labor camps. Despite this persecution, underground yeshivot sprang up, and most of the Zionists successfully fled the country. The Soviet government did permit Yiddish to be taught and written, and Yiddish theater continued.

Jews suffered economically, frequently depending on money from the American Jewish Joint Distribution Committee and ORT (see data to facts 438, 580) to survive. The Soviets tried to resettle Jews into a single Russian territory, Birobidjan, and more than 300,000 Jews were transported there. At the same time, thousands of Jews assimilated into Soviet culture.

During World War II, Soviet Jews suffered tremendously, killed by the Nazis and imprisoned by the Soviets (see facts 460, 461). Latent Russian anti-Semitism rose to the surface; there were pogroms in areas far from the German front. Yiddish was suppressed. The Yiddish press and Yiddish schools were forced to close.

Under Stalin, the Jews continued to suffer. In 1953, with the arrest of a group of prominent doctors, most of whom were Jewish, a wave of anti-Semitism ran through the country. An inordinate number of Jews were arrested and either executed or sent to labor camps. Fortunately, with Stalin's death there was some relief from this persecution, but under Nikita Khrushchev's leadership there was a rise in anti-Semitism again. In 1963 more than 60 percent of all executions for black marketeering in the Soviet Union involved Jews.

With the rise of the State of Israel, Jewish nationalism was reawakened in Soviet Jews. When Golda Meir (see fact 555) visited Russia in 1957, she was met by mass demonstrations of enthusiastic

Jews. The Soviet Union responded by repressing all expressions of Jewish culture and affiliations with Israel. They forbade the study of Hebrew. In the late 1960s Jews requesting visas to leave the country were labeled traitors and parasites. They were arrested, sent to labor camps, or jailed as insane. World Jewry, in large mass demonstrations, angrily protested these barbarities toward "refuseniks," and "Prisoners of Zion." Anatoly Scharansky, Yosif Begun, and Ida Nudel became American symbols of Soviet repression. The Jewish Defense League disrupted cultural events involving Soviet artists (see data to fact 562). However, despite world pressure and strong support for the refuseniks from the U.S. government, from 1960 to 1989 Jewish emigration was severely limited. Only about 320,000 Jews managed to leave the Soviet Union, about 125,000 of them going to Israel. Refuseniks were sentenced to long jail terms. Some, accused of treason, were executed. It was a bitter, brutal period of repression. Some of the most famous refuseniks were eventually released, but the Soviet government seemed relentless in its determination to prosecute its Jews. Synagogues were closed; Hebrew teachers continued to be arrested. Yet there were hundreds of Soviet Jews willing to risk their freedom and their lives to continue to study Hebrew and their heritage. From 1980 to 1988 fewer than 7,000 Soviet Jewish immigrants arrived in Israel. In 1986 only 904 Jews were permitted to leave the Soviet Union.

In 1987, to the shock and wonder of the rest of the world, Mikhail Gorbachev initiated the Soviet policy of glasnost (openness) and perestroika (economic rebuilding), which he had been speaking about for several years. His new policies allowed greater freedom of speech in the Soviet Union and permitted mass Soviet Jewish emigration. Hundreds of thousands of Jews indicated their desire to leave the Soviet Union. The United States limited immigration, thus forcing the vast majority of the Soviet Jews to emigrate to Israel.

Israel prepared for the mass immigration of these Jews. Many were intellectuals or skilled in computer technology. Israel, already glutted with its own white collar workers, emphasized its willingness to accept what some estimated would be up to one million Soviet Jews. Israel begged for economic help from the United States and world Jewry. Operation Exodus, a special campaign of the United Jewish Appeal, was initiated in the hopes of raising $400 million to help Israel settle all of the Soviet Jewish immigrants.

In 1990 significant problems developed. Prime Minister Yitzchak Shamir spoke about a Greater Israel for the incoming refugees, implying settlement of the Soviet Jews on the West Bank (see data to facts 562, 569). The Arab world raised a storm of protest against this. In response, the Soviet Union forbade direct flights to Israel, maintaining that the Jews would be settled on the West Bank.

This situation became serious when Soviet Jews were threatened with violence. One of the consequences of the new Soviet policy of freedom of speech was an outbreak of rabid anti-Semitism. Especially vocal was Pamyat, a nationalist Russian group, which viewed Jews as the source of all of Russia's problems. Pamyat threatened to initiate major pogroms against the Soviet Jews. The Soviet authorities denied that this was a serious threat and refused to respond.

Israel tried escalating the number of flights to enable more Jews to get out quickly, but there were few countries willing to risk Arab wrath by increasing direct flights to Israel. One of the exceptions was Hungary, which allowed two direct flights each day. Poland also agreed to allow direct flights, and Finland responded positively as well.

Trying to pressure Israel into changing its policy concerning the West Bank and the Intifada (see fact 569), the United States threatened to rescind funds to Israel if Soviet Jews were settled on the West Bank. President Bush then included East Jerusalem as one of the areas where Soviet Jews were not to be settled. This stand created an angry outcry in Israel, which considered all of Jerusalem to be its capital (see fact 561).

Internal arguments also developed in Israel over the identity of Soviet Jews. Many of them were uncircumcised. Moreover, Jewish identity in Russia was not determined according to Jewish tradition (see fact 273). In Russia, anyone who claimed that he or she was a Jew received an identity card indicating Jewish nationality. As a result, the Israeli ministers of absorption and interior were concerned that the incoming Soviet Jews undergo either careful family examination to determine their Jewish identity or a conversion ceremony. This led to an even greater uproar.

From January to December 1990, more than 180,000 Soviet Jews arrived in Israel. In April alone, more than 10,000 Soviet Jews emigrated. The vast majority of Israelis indicated their willingness to undergo personal financial difficulties in order to absorb more Soviet Jews. They provided family hospitality for 20,000 new Soviet immigrants at Pesach seders (see fact 73). Suburbs of Tel Aviv, such as Rishon L'Tzion and Ra'anana, agreed to absorb large numbers of Soviet Jews. The huge influx began changing Israel's culture as well. Among the immigrants were more than 2,000 professional musicians. Israel's budget for art and culture couldn't provide for such an enormous number of new professionals. Israel created new music programs for the public school curriculum, utilizing many of the talented Soviet Jews, thereby doubling the number of music teachers in the school system and promising a more culturally attuned generation of Israeli children.

Soviet Jews continued to flood into Israel at a rate of 1,400 per week during the early 1990s. During one weekend in December 1990 more than 7,000 Soviet Jews arrived! Israel suffered from a severe housing shortage. Ariel Sharon (see data to facts 560, 562) was given the responsibility to solve the housing crisis. Apartment rents skyrocketed, forcing some Israelis out of their homes to create tent villages. Many found themselves unemployed. World Jewry provided large sums of money via Operation Exodus to help Soviet Jews emigrate, and the challenge to Israel to absorb Soviet Jews into its society remained the top priority issue of the 1990s. The costs connected with this enormous immigration soared into the billions of dollars.

Because of the more open policy in the Soviet Union, the World Union for Progressive Judaism (see fact 467) succeeded in establishing a Reform synagogue in Moscow in 1990. In addition, the National Yiddish Book Center began to send Yiddish books to Soviet Jews, reintroducing Yiddish literature and culture to the Soviet Union (see data to fact 415). Thus American Jewry focused its efforts on helping all Jews who wanted to do so to emigrate, and on providing Jewish enrichment for those Jews who wanted to remain in the Soviet Union.

Jewish Thought and Values

Modern Jewish Thinkers

574. Hermann Cohen introduced the concept of "ethical monotheism" to describe Judaism.

Hermann Cohen (1842–1919) was probably the most important Jewish philosopher of the nineteenth century. His major works, ironically, were purely secular, as he advanced the basic ideas of Immanuel Kant.

Kant maintained that the most that humans can know about the world is how we systematically view it and behave in it. What we view and how we view it is our idea of reality. It doesn't mean that the world is actually the way we see it. That certainty of actuality transcends us.

If we know, however, how a reasonable person should view the world and behave in the world, then we, being reasonable, must behave accordingly. Thus we are obligated to live our lives by a set of universal imperatives which are clear and understandable to every reasonable human.

Cohen agreed with Kant that ethics had to be universal. Moreover, every ethical act had to, in the end, aim toward the entire society. We cannot rationally be content until there is complete social justice in our world. Therefore striving for the ethical is an infinite process. In addition, every time we use our minds to learn something, we are rationally aware of what we still do not know. The search for ideas (knowledge) is equally infinite.

Cohen noted an apparent conflict between the viewed natural world and the viewed ethical challenge. In the physical world, things are apparently ordered without the option for change. The sun comes up in the east; the seasons alternate. Yet the apprehended moral imperatives remain our choice to do or to discard. It would appear irrational for one part of an apprehended world to be voluntary (ethics) and another part involuntary (science), so there must be an idea that will allow two different kinds of rationality to exist at the same time and also be connected. The idea that enables us to view a physical world that is ordered and involuntary, while living a life of ethics that is our personal voluntary option, is *God*.

Moreover, since the goal of ethics is to achieve universal global justice, we must have some hope of achieving that goal; if we felt the goal were impossible, we would just give up. Yet the world empirically threatens to fall into further physical randomness. Therefore the idea of God as the guarantor of an eternal world and our ability eventually to achieve ethical justice is necessary. Cohen called this world-view of ordered world and voluntary ethics integrated with the idea of God "religion of reason."

He then pointed to Judaism's belief in the uniqueness of God. In the Torah, God is not part of the world (that idea would be idolatry); God transcends the physical world. Yet at the same time, this idea of an eternal God provides us with the imperative to act ethically. Thus, for Hermann Cohen, Judaism provides the source for "religion of reason," namely ethical monotheism.

Hermann Cohen's influence on modern nineteenth-century Jews was tremendous. His emphasis on Judaism's universal ethics to better the entire world encouraged Jews to integrate into the secular cultures around them as an aspect of their religion. It was legitimately Jewish to assimilate into society so long as the individual's goals focused on social justice. If a Jewish ritual enhanced that ethical imperative, it was important to retain it. If it appeared to contradict the high ethics of religion of reason, it was to be dropped.

Moreover, Hermann Cohen's description of Judaism emphasized that it was a much better religion of reason than Christianity. Judaism focused on acts, ethics; Christianity was involved in faith. Judaism was much more clearly a religion that found its source in ethical monotheism; Christianity's involvement with the Trinity and saints and a variety of other beliefs got in the way of a religion of reason.

The term "ethical monotheism" has become a Jewish household word synonymous with Judaism. The systematizer of that concept was Hermann Cohen.

575. Rabbi Leo Baeck wrote *The Essence of Judaism.*

Rabbi Leo Baeck (1873–1956) accepted Hermann Cohen's idea of ethical monotheism as the essence of Judaism but added mystery, a sense of the holy, as a second Jewish essence. Unlike Cohen, who found the *idea* of God sufficient, Leo Baeck wrote about our emotional awareness, our *experiencing* the Divine. This awareness naturally leads to ethical acts, what Baeck called the commandments. At the same time, we can also maintain peoplehood, a sense of our role in history, through ritual acts which give expression to our sense of mystery.

Baeck, a liberal, modern Jew, was not prepared to assign authority to the ritual acts, only to the ethical imperatives. Unlike Cohen, however, he was not willing to give up the reality of God for Cohen's "idea." God is both transcendent and immanent. For Baeck, God is real. Therefore, being Jewish consisted of being ethical and striving for universal good, experiencing the mystery of the Divine, and maintaining the survival of Jews throughout history.

By emphasizing experience and mystery as part of the essence of Judaism, Baeck moved radically away from Cohen's "religion of reason." However, Baeck's emphasis on universal ethics and ethical monotheism made him a bridge between the rationalists and the modern Jewish existentialists.

Baeck's personal life deserves some mention because he lived by the values described in his writings. As president of the representative body of Jews in Germany after 1933, he was given many opportunities to escape. He refused, insisting that he would stay so long as there was a minyan (see fact 289) in Germany. In 1943 he was sent to the Theresienstadt concentration camp. He survived the horrors by helping others, teaching, and refusing to lose his sense of self or dignity. His philosophical beliefs were not swayed by the Holocaust. He always maintained that evil was the result of humans using their free will to not do the ethical. The enormity of the Nazi atrocities did not shake that belief.

576. Franz Rosenzweig wrote *The Star of Redemption.*

Franz Rosenzweig was the first of the Jewish existentialist philosophers. Unlike the philosophy of Cohen or Baeck, who concentrated on universal ethics and values, Rosenzweig's philosophy begins with the individual. He wrote his major book, *The Star of Redemption,* while a soldier during World War I.

Rosenzweig begins his philosophical search by noting a major insufficiency in the rational philosophical systems: they fail to console a person who is afraid to die. Through our fear of death, we demonstrate an awareness about the self which is real and not just an abstract idea; otherwise, universal ideas would suffice. The individual exists, and that fact, not reason, must be the starting point for a philosophical system. As real, separate selves, each of us experiences the world differently. Therefore the world is also real and not just an abstract idea. For Rosenzweig, there is a third reality which transcends both the individual and the world and at the same time connects them. That third reality is God.

Rosenzweig then demonstrates how these three realities—God, the world, and the individual—interact. God relates to the world by creating it. The world is not independent of God. This process of creation, while at some level ongoing, occurred primarily in the past.

God's moment-to-moment relationship with humans is called revelation. It is immediate. Humans respond to God by doing what God commands in this moment-to-moment relationship. The commands are not words but rather consist of the individual's response to God's identification and love. What was felt at Sinai can be felt today because revelation continues.

When experiencing revelation from God, the individual has a need to transcend, to join with people and respond, like God, with love. When such a community of individuals is built, it will reach out to touch all humanity and perfect the world, a state we call redemption.

By creating a triangle of God, People, and the World, and superimposing over it a reverse triangle of Creation, Revelation, and Redemption, Rosenzweig encapsulated his philosophy into a Magen David (see fact 257), the Star of Redemption.

Ironically, Rosenzweig then demonstrates that two religions share all of these elements and thus merit being called true religion: Christianity and Judaism. In Judaism, the Jew is born into the entire pattern of being in the revelation experience with God. The Christian has to be initiated into the relationship through baptism. Rosenzweig calls Judaism the "fire of the Star," and Christianity he calls "the rays of the Star." Neither religion is complete yet because redemption is not yet complete.

The major controversy for Rosenzweig focused on what a Jew has to do. Since revelation is continuous, what God demanded in the past might not be God's commandment at this moment. Unlike the rationalists, Rosenzweig refused to limit Jewish observance to universal ethics. Instead, he maintained that the individual's observance of a traditional ritual creates a sense of commandment in the individual. In following Jewish law, the individual senses the divine demand in those actions. However, should a Jew feel "unable" to do a specific commandment, he need not do it. For Rosenzweig there were "not-yet-fulfilled" commandments. This is the weakest spot in his philosophical system, since many people have personally noted that doing a traditional action does not necessarily lead them to a sense of its being commanded.

However, Rosenzweig's schema of Creation, Revelation, Redemption, God, People, and World became an accepted vocabulary in contemporary discussions of modern Jewish thought.

577. Martin Buber wrote *I and Thou*.

Martin Buber (1878–1965) wrote his most famous book, *I and Thou*, in 1923. It focuses on the way humans relate to their world. Frequently we view both objects and people by their functions. Doing this is sometimes good: when doctors examine us for specific maladies, it's best if they view us as organisms, not as individuals. Scientists can learn a great deal about our world by observing, measuring, and examining. For Buber, all such processes are I–It relationships. Unfortunately, we frequently view people in the same way. Rather than truly making ourselves completely available to them, understanding them, sharing totally with them, really talking with them, we observe them or keep part of ourselves outside the moment of relationship. We do so either to protect our vulnerabilities or to get them to respond in some preconceived way, to get something from them. Buber calls such an interaction I–It.

It is possible, notes Buber, to place ourselves completely into a relationship, to truly understand and "be there" with another person, without masks, pretenses, even without words. Such a moment of relating is called "I–Thou." Each person comes to such a relationship without preconditions. The bond thus created enlarges each person, and each person responds by trying to enhance the other person. The result is true dialogue, true sharing.

Such I–Thou relationships are not constant or static. People move in and out of I–It moments to I–Thou moments. Ironically, attempts to achieve an I–Thou moment will fail because the process of trying to create an I–Thou relationship objectifies it and makes it I–It. Even describing the moment objectifies it and makes it I–It. The most Buber can do in describing this process is to encourage us to be available to the possibility of I–Thou moments, to achieve real dialogue. It can't be described. When you have it, you know it. Buber maintains that it is possible to have an I-Thou relationship with the world and the objects in it as well. Art, music, poetry are all possible media for such responses in which true dialogue can take place.

Buber then moves from this existential description of personal relating to the religious experience. For Buber, God is the Eternal Thou. By trying to prove God's existence or define God, the rationalist philosophers automatically established an I–It relationship. Like a person we love, we can't define God; we can't set up preconditions for the relationship. We simply have to be available, open to the relationship with the Eternal Thou. And when we experience such an I–Thou moment, we respond, just as we do with a love. Like an I-Thou love relationship, the moment doesn't need words. In fact, the most intense moments we experience with another person take place without words. Nor is the intensity of the experience significant. Buber wasn't encouraging mystical moments. The I–Thou relationship changed the sharers, but it did so naturally, sometimes almost imperceptibly. For Buber, it is possible to have an I–Thou relationship with God through I–Thou moments with people, nature, art, the world.

Finally, Buber offers us a Jewish insight into the I–Thou relationship. After our redemption from Egypt (see facts 156, 157), we as a people encountered God. We were available and open, and the Sinai moment was an I–Thou relationship for an entire people and for each individual. The Torah, the prophets, and our rabbinic texts were all written by humans expressing the I–Thou relationship with the Eternal Thou. By reading those texts and being available to the relationship inherent in them, it is also possible for us to make ourselves available for the I-Thou experience with the Eternal Thou. We must come without precondition, without expectation because that would already attempt to limit our relationship partner, God, and thus create an I–It moment. If we try to analyze the text, we again create an I-It relationship because analysis places ourselves outside of the dialogue, as an observer and not a total participant.

For Buber, to do an action because it has been previously legislated is meaningless. Only our response at the moment of I–Thou can have meaning. Because of that premise, Buber disagreed with Rosenzweig over the importance of traditional practices in daily life. It was enough to respond to the I–Thou encounter in whatever individualized way the moment created.

578. Abraham Joshua Heschel wrote evocative books encouraging traditional Jewish practice.

Just as Judah HaLevi used the vocabulary and logic of Greek philosophy to "prove" that Judaism was the best religion (see fact 393), Abraham Joshua Heschel (1907–1972) used the vocabulary of modern, liberal Jews to try to bring them to traditional Jewish faith.

Heschel believed that the modern Jew needed more than an intellectual, philosophical foundation for being a Jew. The modern Jew was separated from his natural sense of wonder and awe which were the true underpinnings of being human. Our modern scientific skepticism had dulled our senses and reversed our perspective. By writing in beautiful, almost poetic paragraphs about humans viewing the miracles of nature, Heschel evoked in the reader a sense of "radical amazement," awe at our total dependence on God. Rather than allowing the reader to analyze, Heschel's words pull the reader into feeling our fundamental need for God in every aspect of our lives. Through radical amazement, we realize that our existence is made meaningful only because of the Divine Presence.

After evoking the moment-to-moment wonder which every human feels when looking freshly at the natural world as God's creation, Heschel introduced the second mainstay of his philosophy: revelation. For Heschel, the descriptions of the prophets are magnificent examples of people experiencing radical amazement and realizing insights about the Divine. Most significant, Heschel emphasizes that the prophets describe God as having feelings. God cares, God desires. For Heschel, the prophetic image of a feeling God is not anthropomorphic; it actually describes the Divine. The TaNaCH (see fact 104) is a living book describing God's search for humanity, inspired by the Divine. Judaism, rather than being the modern man's quest for religious understanding, is really the history of God searching for the convenant people.

These two elements of radical amazement and TaNaCH revelation lead to the third part of Heschel's Judaism: action. As humans, we must respond in wonder to the Divine's revelation by Doing. The prophetic imperative for social justice describes the Divine Will, and it is our duty as awed humans to respond. For Heschel, rabbinic Judaism is the authentic way of doing what the Divine wants; therefore, it is our obligation (mitzvah) to live our lives according to Jewish tradition, doing the Divine will especially as described by the prophets.

Through evocative, poetic language, Heschel thus leads the modern reader to a sophisticated, fundamentalist Jewish faith.

Tzedakah and Gemilut Chasadim

579. Tzedakah is the mitzvah of giving money to the needy.

Tzedakah means righteousness. It refers to the mitzvah (see fact 162) of giving to the needy. As Jews, we do not give out of the goodness of our hearts; we give because it is a mitzvah. It is thus different from the Christian term *charity*, which implies giving through personal generosity. Our tradition views the rich as having been given a major loan by God. It is the wealthy person's obligation to take care of the poor. Failure to provide for the poor is tantamount to stealing from them, since the money originally had been given to them by God. It is considered so important that our rabbis declared that it is one of the ways to avert God's stern decree on the Yamim Nora'im (see fact 9). The Torah legislates tzedakah in numerous places.

Farmers are forbidden to harvest the corners of their fields; they must leave the grain for the poor and the stranger. Similarly, a farmer may not go over a harvested field, for the gleanings belong to the poor (Leviticus 19:9).

Deuteronomy 14:28–29 also commands that in the third and sixth years of the Sabbatical year cycle (see fact 174), a tenth of the farmer's produce go to the poor, the stranger, and the widow. The prophets (see facts 206–214) stressed repeatedly that caring for the poor and the needy was more important to the Divine than sacrifices.

Our rabbis continued to legislate rules about tzedakah. Even the poor person receiving tzedakah is required to give tzedakah to a person even poorer. Giving a twentieth of one's earnings was considered stingy. On the other hand, the Tanna'im (see fact 329) legislated that a person may not give more than a fifth lest he impoverish himself. Most rabbis agreed that giving a tenth of one's earnings to tzedakah was legitimately fulfilling the mitzvah. Courts had the right to assess a person's earnings and force him to give the minimum amount to tzedakah. RaMBaM established eight steps of tzedakah (see fact 400).

There are numerous stories about Jews being generous to the poor and receiving divine rewards for their goodness. It is a recurring theme in Jewish literature. The protector of the poor is Elijah the Prophet (see data to fact 208), and he returns to test the goodness of Jews to see if they give tzedakah generously. Jews felt a financial responsibility to extended family members and tried to ensure that even distant relatives were taken care of.

Early on, Jewish communities established both charity institutions and soup kitchens to meet the needs of their poor. If a needy person still knocked on doors to receive tzedakah, it was a mitzvah to give him something, but major contributions were reserved for the organized tzedakah funds, run by a charity warden, a community leader held in the highest respect. Even so, the rabbis legislated that the wardens had to go in pairs to collect tzedakah lest the community suspect a leader of impropriety.

In the nineteenth and twentieth centuries tzedakah has been channeled into an incredible number of organizations which have been established to meet the needs of the poor. Homes for the blind, hospitals, and religious schools for the poor were created. In America, neighborhood settlement houses were established to help the immigrants learn American customs, language, and culture.

Many of the early tzedakah institutions were created to aid the great numbers of immigrants from 1881 to 1920 (see facts 452, 454). Because coordination and planning were vital, the community set up the Council of Jewish Federations and Welfare Funds, which has 222 affiliates in the United States and Canada.

Today, in addition to the United Hebrew Immigrant Aid Society, the American Jewish Joint Distribution Committee, the United Jewish Appeal, the Federations, and innumerable small schools and programs for the poor, the American Jewish community provides large tzedakah funds for Soviet Jews (see fact 573), Ethiopian Jews (see facts 468, 568), Cambodian boat people, and all other groups in need.

Mazon, an institution aimed at ending world hunger, has established a unique form of tzedakah fund raising: it asks that every Jew send a check for 3 percent of the cost of any social event or celebration. This endeavor has enabled Mazon to work with a budget of over $3 million with very little overhead.

580. Gemilut chasadim is the mitzvah of caring for others through special deeds.

Gemilut chasadim means undertaking deeds of loving kindness. It refers to the mitzvah of sharing with fellow Jews at times of crisis and need, and it is considered one of the most important mitzvot. Unlike tzedakah, which involves material gifts, gemilut chasadim demands time and personal commitment. In today's society, these two types of mitzvot, once distinct, have frequently become combined. For example, ORT, an institution which provides vocational training to people around the world, began as gemilut chasadim, the mitzvah of personally helping people (see data to fact 438). Today most people support ORT by sending money for the maintenance of the gemilut chasadim programs. The same is true for Hadassah's Youth Aliyah program (see fact 526). Whether we call these programs tzedakah or gemilut chasadim, they still provide Jews with needed community services to help enrich their lives.

The mitzvah of gemilut chasadim can be done toward anyone, wealthy or poor. The primary example is the community's obligation to prepare a corpse for burial and perform the burial rites. By the eleventh century there were already special societies in each town which took the responsibility for burying their own members. These societies were called chevrah kaddisha, holy friendship groups. Yehudah Loew of Prague (see fact 418) was the first to institutionalize the chevrah kaddisha in his community. Until recent times, every Jewish community had its own chevrah kaddisha, and it was considered a great honor to be a member. A chevrah kaddisha was a necessity because, according to halachah, no one may make money from a person's death. The irony of today's funeral homes is obvious.

Sephardic communities called the members of the chevrah kaddisha *lavadores* (the washers) because the principal preparation for burial is the careful washing of the body. Sir Moses Montefiore took pride in the fact that he was a lavadore (see fact 501).

Other forms of gemilut chasadim include showing hospitality to strangers (see fact 581), visiting the sick (see fact 582), comforting the bereaved, honoring parents, bringing arguing friends back together, taking care of animals, and being a mensch, a gentle caring person (see fact 584).

581. Hachnasat orchim is the mitzvah of inviting strangers into our homes.

Showing hospitality to the stranger is one of the major mitzvot of gemilut chasadim (see fact 580). There are numerous examples of our ancestors fulfilling the mitzvah of hachnasat orchim. Abraham ran to the three strangers when he saw them and offered them a meal (Genesis 18:2). Leban offered his hospitality to Eliezer, Abraham's servant (Genesis 24:30–32; see fact 132). Job maintained his righteousness by claiming, "The stranger didn't sleep in the street because I opened my doors to the traveler" (Job 31:32; see fact 223).

Hachnasat orchim was a great mitzvah for our rabbis. They maintained that it involved a higher level of holiness than seeing the Divine Presence. A midrash (see fact 333) describes Abraham's and Job's tents as being open on all four sides so any stranger could enter directly.

It was considered a wicked act to eat without inviting the poor to join, and, we are told, people in Jerusalem would set up a flag to notify the needy that a meal was in progress.

It became the custom throughout our history to invite a stranger home for Shabbat, and frequently people vied for the mitzvah.

Most yeshivot couldn't provide their students with meals, so in the 1400s student hostels were established to feed them. In addition, families living in the community would often establish specific days on which they would feed a student. These were called *essentagen* (eating days) (see data to fact 427).

Hachnasat orchim, opening our homes to the stranger and the needy, remains a primary mitzvah. It is ritualized on Pesach during the seder (see fact 73) when we say, "Let all who are hungry come and eat."

582. Bikkur cholim is the mitzvah of visiting and helping sick people.

Bikkur cholim is one of the most important mitzvot of gemilut chasadim (see fact 580). According to a midrash (see fact 333) after Abraham circumcized himself (see fact 126), God came to fulfill the mitzvah of bikkur cholim during Abraham's discomfort. The Talmud states that a person who visits the sick removes a sixtieth of his illness.

Friends are supposed to visit the sick after the third day of illness. The Talmud includes much advice about how long to visit and what to say, including a prayer for the sick and the recitation of psalms. It was considered a mitzvah to visit the sick after Shabbat morning services.

Caring for the sick became institutionalized in the Jewish community by the fourteenth century. Many communities had special societies which took responsibility for providing health care for the needy. These bikkur cholim societies were available to any community member or stranger who needed help.

By the eighteenth century, bikkur cholim societies received dues from community members (an early Major Medical program). The societies not only provided beds for strangers and the needy, they paid for doctors and medicine, and on occasion they provided loans so the family could live while the person was ill.

583. Tza'ar baalei chayim is the mitzvah of not being cruel to animals.

We are forbidden to be cruel to animals, tza'ar baalei chayim, because they are God's creation. The Torah includes a remarkable list of mitzvot which focus on this commandment:

1. You may not muzzle an animal while it threshes grain; the animal must be permitted to eat while it works (Deuteronomy 25:4).
2. If you see the donkey of your enemy foundering under a load, you must stop to help the animal (Exodus 23:5).
3. Animals rest on Shabbat (Exodus 23:12; Deuteronomy 5:14).
4. If you see your neighbor's animal wandering, you must return it him. If you don't know who the owner is, you must care for the animal until the owner claims it (Deuteronomy 22:1–3).
5. You may not yoke an ox and a donkey together; the ox is too big and will hurt the donkey (Deuteronomy 22:10).
6. You may not take a mother bird and her eggs at the same time (Deuteronomy 22:6).
7. You must frighten the mother bird away before you take her young (Deuteronomy 22:7).
8. You may not slaughter an animal and its young on the same day (Leviticus 22:28).

Deuteronomy 11:15 states, "I will provide grass in your fields for your cattle, and you will eat and be satisfied." Noting that grass for cattle is mentioned before our eating, the rabbis ordered that animals must be fed before we are permitted to eat. They also legislated that cows must be milked on Shabbat and the festivals to save them from discomfort. There are midrashim (see fact 333) that emphasize that Moses and David were selected by God only after they showed gentleness to their flocks when they worked as shepherds.

There were numerous arguments about the morality of eating meat at all. Genesis 9:3 notes that after the flood, Noah was permitted to eat meat (see fact 119), but some rabbis maintained that it would have been better to retain the vegetarian diet of the Garden of Eden.

It should be noted, however, that there are limits to the extent that our tradition was concerned about animals. Even the lowest criminal was considered more important than the finest animal. Halachah is quite clear: if both your champion dog and a murderer are drowning, it is your obligation to save the murderer, because every human (even a rotten one) has a soul, and animals, according to our tradition, do not.

584. Being a mensch means being a good, caring person.

Judaism has always emphasized the mitzvah of caring about other Jews. Each of us has a spark of the Divine within us, and it is our obligation to support and recognize the worth of every other person. Rabbi Akiva (see fact 347) said, "How greatly must humans be loved to be created in (God's) image; yet even greater love (is shown) by making it known to him that he is created in (God's) image." For that reason, being a mensch is one of the highest values within Judaism. It is the personal characteristic that enables us to meet someone in an I–Thou relationship (see fact 577). In *Pirkei Avot* (see fact 359) Hillel (see fact 331) said, "In a place where no one behaves like a human being (a mensch), you must strive to be human." Rabbi Meir added: "Every person who studies Torah for its sake acquires many merits. Not only that, but the whole world is indebted to him. He will be called a friend, cherished, a lover of God, a lover of humanity. It clothes him with humility and reverence. It gives him the ability to be righteous and pious, upright and trustworthy. It keeps him far from sin and brings him near to merit. Humanity benefits from him with counsel and knowledge, wisdom, and strength. It gives him the ability to govern and the skill to judge. It reveals to him the secrets of Torah and makes him like a gushing and continuous fountain, like a never-ending river. He is modest and slow to anger, he forgives insults, and it magnifies and exalts him above all things."

585. Pikuach nefesh is the concept that preservation of human life transcends all other mitzvot.

Our rabbis declared that the saving of human life transcends all other commandments, deriving this rule from two separate Torah commandments.

Leviticus 18:5 says, "You will keep my laws and my statutes for if (you do), (you) shall live by them." Mitzvot are there as a source of life, not a cause of death. Our rabbis ruled that if a person is gravely ill or suffering from a condition that might deteriorate, then all other commandments are postponed, including breaking Shabbat and the festivals, so that we might live by Torah. Moreover, Leviticus 19:16 states, "You shall not stand idle while your neighbor bleeds." From this, our rabbis decreed that it is a mitzvah (commandment) to help the person in need even if doing so means breaking the commandments ourselves. Thus food must be prepared for a gravely ill person on Yom Kippur, and a Jew may cook it and transport it to the sick person. For this reason, Jewish doctors frequently work on Shabbat *as a mitzvah, a commandment*.

The Talmud (see fact 363) also addressed the problem of a person faced with the dilemma of saving someone else's life at the risk of his own. The ultimate ruling was that he should save his own life and not jeopardize it. If a man has water enough only for himself and meets someone without water, he must save himself.

The question of smoking has caused some controversy among Orthodox rabbis. Some of them have taken the position that because smoking is clearly a danger to personal health, it is forbidden to smoke on the grounds of pikuach nefesh, regard for human life. Other Orthodox rabbis disagree.

Conversion

586. A ger is a convert to Judaism.

In the Torah (see fact 105) there is no mention of conversion; it wasn't possible. The Hebrews viewed themselves as a tribe, descended from Abraham (patrilineally; see fact 275). Strangers were permitted to co-exist with the Hebrews so long as they weren't members of the native Canaanite tribes, whom the Torah ordered to be exterminated.

Sometime between the Babylonian Exile and the Roman period (we don't know exactly when) it became possible for a non-Jew to convert to Judaism. The Tanna'im (see fact 329) established quite specific rules for this procedure and apparently worked hard at bringing non-Jews to Judaism. They also retrojected their proselytizing onto Abraham and Sarah, who were said to have converted their entire entourage to Judaism. Conversion was fairly extensive. However, feelings about the convert—called a ger (stranger), were mixed. Many rabbis welcomed them with open arms; others were less hospitable. A proselyte who became a Jew in order to marry a Jew was still recognized as a Jew, although this practice was frowned upon.

When Christianity came to power in 325 B.C.E. (see fact 370), Jews were forbidden to proselytize on pain of death. This ruling put a 1,600-year damper on the proselytizing process in Judaism. However, if a non-Jew approached a beit din (see fact 425) and insisted on becoming a Jew, after three attempts to dissuade the person, the beit din had to officiate at the conversion ritual even during the darkest periods of persecution.

Today, because of the large number of non-Jewish spouses in intermarriages, the Reform and Reconstructionist Movements are again reaching out to non-Jews, welcoming them into synagogue programs and Basic Judaism classes. The children of intermarried couples are welcomed into Reform synagogues and religious schools because of the Central Conference of American Rabbis' resolution on who is a Jew (see fact 274). The Orthodox rabbinate continues to frown on someone wishing to convert in order to marry a Jew. Many Orthodox rabbis will refuse to accept such a ger.

It was understood that the ritual of conversion radically changed the person. Originally, the convert's former family was no longer considered to be related to him or her. Theoretically (although it was frowned upon and probably never done), a convert could marry his converted sister since they were no longer related! This idea led to the belief that, at the moment of conversion, the convert received a different soul, a Jewish soul—but only if the conversion ceremony was done "correctly." Gradually, halachah (see fact 342) became more lenient toward the ger. For example, today a convert is required to say Kaddish for a dead parent, emphasizing the ongoing relationship. However, for traditional Jews, becoming a Jew meant much more than accepting precepts, beliefs, and a Jewish lifestyle; it meant the physical/spiritual changing of a person. This is one of the reasons (politics aside) that Orthodox authorities will not recognize a conversion under the auspices of Reform or Conservative rabbis, fearing that it wasn't done "right." Because this issue affects the definition of who is a Jew (see facts 273–275, 542), the Orthodox, Conservative, and Reform Movements are trying to arrive at some agreeable compromise so that all converts will be recognized as Jews.

Our tradition tells us that a convert, being a fully souled Jew, is at the same—if not a higher—level of spirituality than the born Jew. Unfortunately, sociologically there have been many instances of Jews' treating the Jew by choice (the ger) as an inferior. The Reform Movement's Outreach programs work to counter this prejudice.

587. The traditional way for a woman to convert to Judaism is to immerse in a mikvah.

Moving from ritual impurity to ritual purity is a change in personal status, and it is effected by immersion in the mikvah (see fact 261). Since, the process of becoming a Jew by choice is a change in status, our rabbis instituted the same source, water, for its concretization. The conversion process requires a beit din (see fact 425).

Many Reform and Reconstructionist rabbis do not agree with the traditional assumption that the conversion ceremony radically changes the convert. They see conversion as a statement of faith, of a person's religious declaration. A Jew by choice, through conversion, is accepting the religious lifestyle of a Jew. The person is the same; the person's non-Jewish family remains family. Many liberal rabbis deny that being Jewish has a biological component. Therefore, the primary focus among many Reform rabbis is the study aspect of conversion. They insist that the potential convert learn about our tradition, understand its development, its history, its significance. The conversion ritual is viewed as secondary. Many liberal rabbis do not insist that a woman convert go to the mikvah. Others, striving for continuity with Jewish tradition, do require this immersion.

Ironically, Orthodox rabbis require much less study on the part of a convert. They assume that the new Jew will learn after conversion as part of a Jewish lifestyle. Knowledge of Judaism prior to conversion is therefore less important. Many Orthodox rabbis do, however, require a statement promising to follow the mitzvot (commandments; see fact 162) from the convert.

588. The traditional way for a man to convert to Judaism is to undergo circumcision and to immerse in a mikvah.

From the time of Abraham, circumcision has been the primary sign of our covenant with the Divine (see facts 126, 270). Therefore, traditionally, part of the conversion ceremony for men requires circumcision followed by immersion in the mikvah. If a man is already circumcised, a drop of blood is ritually taken as a sign of his new contract with God. The School of Hillel and the School of Shammai (see fact 332) argued this issue, and it is one of the few occasions when the more stringent position of Shammai is accepted.

Reform rabbis have not yet standardized the conversion ritual.

Some rabbis require circumcision and traditional immersion. If the potential convert is already circumcised, some rabbis forgo taking a drop of blood. Some rabbis do not require immersion. As they do with women converts, the vast majority of Reform rabbis concentrate on the amount of learning a potential male convert has done prior to their officiating at a conversion ceremony.

Dietary Rules

589. Kashrut is the discipline of Jewish dietary laws.

Every culture makes rules which limit what the members of that society may or may not eat. The Torah (see fact 105) lists a number of specific empirical rules for determining whether an animal is permitted for sacrificial purposes. The Torah describes an edible animal as *tahor* (ritually pure). A forbidden food is called *tamei* (ritually impure). Since a major part of most sacrifices involved sharing the food with the Divine by eating part of the meat, the rules described in Leviticus 11 and Deuteronomy 14 determined what foods Hebrews could consume.

With the destruction of the Temple in 70 c.e. (see fact 336), our rabbis instituted a number of daily reminders of the Temple and the sacrifices. One was establishing prayer services at the times when the sacrifices would have taken place (see facts 295, 346). An equally encompassing reminder was their declaration that, with the destruction of the Temple, every family's table was to become a "mini-altar." All meals were to be viewed as personal sacrifices to the Divine. It is for that reason that traditional Jews ritually wash their hands before eating; this act is a reenactment of the purification process done by the priest. In addition, they traditionally placed salt on bread as a reminder of the meal offering in the Temple.

Most important, the rabbis transferred the Torah-ordained regulations concerning the foods permissible for sacrifices and applied them to all Jewish eating. The term for this discipline of dietary laws is *Kashrut*, derived from the word *kasher*, fit. Ironically the TaNaCH (see fact 104) never uses the term *kosher* to describe acceptable food; it is a post-biblical term.

According to halachah (see fact 342), all fruits and vegetables are permitted to be eaten. The Torah even states in Genesis 1:29, "I have given you every variety of vegetable which is on the face of the earth and every fruit-yielding tree—to you it shall be for food." The laws of kashrut concentrate on meat, fowl, fish, and the mixing of meat and milk foods.

One of the early principles of Reform Judaism was the Jew's responsibility to fit into the modern world and be a light to the other nations through high ethical conduct (see fact 442). It viewed all rituals that separated us from the modern, non-Jewish world as being ethically wrong. Obviously, the dietary laws were meant to set us apart, and therefore the early Reformers denied their religious legitimacy for modern Jews.

In recent decades, as ethnic identity became an important value, more and more modern Jews have returned to the discipline of the dietary laws in some form.

590. An animal is potentially kosher if it both chews its cud and has completely split hooves.

The Torah regulations concerning the ritual acceptability of four-footed animals are empirical: it must have totally split hooves and it must chew its cud. The Torah notes that three animals chew their cud but do not have split hooves, so they are not ritually pure and are not permitted for consumption: the camel, hare, and rock badger.

Biologically, the hare does not fit into the above category; having only one stomach, it does not chew its cud. Rabbis have shrugged off this apparent Toraitic mistake by stating that the hare looks as if it's chewing its cud and therefore had to be specifically noted.

The Torah notes that the pig is the only animal that has a split hoof but doesn't chew its cud, thus making it tamei, ritually impure, and unfit for consumption. Because the Greeks ordered that Jews eat a sacrifice of pig or die (see data to fact 38), the pig, for the rabbis, became the most odious of the forbidden foods. The Book of Maccabees describes how Antiochus ordered the seven sons of a Jewess (Hannah) to commit idolatry by eating pork. Each refused, and all were put to death.

There is a midrash (see fact 333) that the pig itself tries to get Jews to sin by holding out its cloven hoof to convince Jews that it is kosher.

By these empirical regulations, the following animals are potentially edible according to the laws of kashrut: buffalo, giraffe, deer, sheep, goat, ibex, gazelle, cow, and antelope: they all chew their cud, and they all have totally split hooves.

There is one part of a kosher animal that the Torah forbids us to eat: because Jacob's hip was injured while struggling with the angel (see fact

141), Jews are forbidden to eat the sciatic nerve, *gid hanasheh*. The process of removing this from the hindquarters is very time-consuming so most kosher slaughterhouses in the United States don't bother; they simply sell the hindquarters to nonkosher stores. As a result, it is impossible to find a kosher porterhouse steak in the United States. In Israel, where they import much of their meat from Argentina, it is possible to find butchers who take the time to remove the entire sciatic nerve, thus rendering the hindquarters of animals kosher.

The Torah also lists forbidden birds. Here it does not give any empirical descriptions as it does for four-legged beasts. The forbidden birds include all hawks, falcons, vultures, night birds of prey, water and marsh birds with the exception of ducks and geese, and other carrion-eating fowl such as the crow and the ostrich.

No reasons are given for any of the prohibitions against animal or bird. Rabbis have speculated about them for the past 2,000 years. Almost all of them note that the dietary laws serve as a discipline to separate the Jews from the cultures surrounding them. RaMBaM (see fact 396) even suggests that the other peoples probably had sacrifices that used the forbidden animals, and the divine provided the laws as an anti-assimilation measure.

RaMBaM also notes that the pig is a markedly unclean animal and the laws were provided for hygienic purposes. Other rabbis add that by prohibiting all carnivores, the Torah guaranteed that the Jews would be a gentle, mild people.

Rabbi Samson Raphael Hirsch (see fact 443) adds that the discipline of keeping kashrut keeps Jews from becoming like animals, controlling their baser urges by providing strict limits.

591. A sea creature is kosher if it has both fins and scales.

Leviticus 11:9 regulates empirically the permitted sea creatures as well. For a sea creature to be ritually pure, it must have fins and scales. This requirement automatically excludes all shellfish from ever being tahor (ritually pure). A number of arguments have developed over fish that are born without scales but then grow them and fish that are born with scales but then lose them. They are both considered ritually pure.

Reptiles and amphibians and all other creatures that crawl on the earth are totally forbidden for consumption. Also, with the exception of eight specified species of locusts, the Torah forbids the eating of all insects and other invertebrates.

592. Halachah forbids mixing milk and meat products.

The Torah commands us three times not to "boil a baby goat in the milk of its mother" (Exodus 23:19, 34:26; Deuteronomy 14:21). Our rabbis determined that this regulation meant that we could eat no milk products (milchig in Yiddish) and meat products (fleishig) together. They then applied further rules concerning this prohibition: we are not permitted to eat fowl and milchig products together even though there is objectively no worry about cooking a chicken in the milk of its mother. For the separation of milk and meat, chicken, ducks, geese, and turkeys are considered meat. However, we may eat fish and milk together.

We must separate milchig products and fleishig products further by keeping two sets of dishes, pots, and utensils. Because glass is not porous, we are permitted to use glass plates for a milchig meal, wash them, and then use them for a fleishig meal. Different communities disagreed about the length of time permitted between eating milk and meat. Most Western European communities ordained that one must wait three hours after eating meat before eating a milchig product. Other communities insist on a six-hour wait. The Talmud simply states that one may not eat milk and meat at the same meal.

Many communities permit a person to eat meat immediately after having milk, provided the person wash his or her mouth and eat a piece of bread (thus legally making a new meal). However, it became the custom to wait three hours after eating hard cheese before eating meat.

RaMBaM (see fact 396) suggested that the prohibition against boiling a baby goat in the milk of its mother served as an anti-assimilation regulation. He was probably correct. Other rabbis emphasized that this rule shows a consideration for animals (see fact 583); it would be inhumane to cook a baby goat in its mother's milk.

593. Parve refers to any food that contains neither milk nor meat.

Fruit, vegetables, eggs, and fish may be consumed at any meal. Breads and desserts that contain neither milchig nor fleishig (see data to fact 592) ingredients may be served at any meal. With modern chemistry, nondairy creamers and whipped desserts are halachically acceptable at meals, provided it is made clear to the eaters that the products are parve. However, the determination of which chemicals found in milk make a product milchig or parve continues to be a subject of debate among Orthodox rabbis.

When babies are beginning to eat solid food, their mother's milk is considered parve.

594. Halachah forbids the consumption of blood.

Leviticus 17:10–14 explicitly prohibits the consumption of any blood because it is the essence of life and therefore should not be eaten. In order to avoid consuming any blood, our rabbis ordered that meat be covered with salt which draws all blood out of the meat. The salt is then washed off and the meat is cooked. This process is called *kashering*. The only food for which it is impossible to get rid of all the blood through salting is liver. Liver must be split and broiled directly over a fire. The resultant dish tends to be almost inedibly tough. Jewish ingenuity solved that problem. By chopping the leatherlike liver with schmaltz (chicken fat), onions, and hard-boiled eggs, we were able to make it kosher and palatable. That's how chopped liver was created.

595. A shochet is a ritual slaughterer.

Although they are not found in the Torah, strict rules were established by our rabbis about the slaughter of animals that are tahor (potentially fit for consumption). In order for an animal to be kasher (fit for eating), it must be killed correctly. Our rabbis quote Deuteronomy 12:21 as their proof text, "Then you will kill of your herd and your flock as I have commanded you." They stated that Moses had received the specific details from the Divine and had passed them on orally to the people.

The process of ritual slaughter, sh'chitah, includes using a spotlessly clean and very sharp knife (called a chalaf) entirely void of nicks. The knife cuts horizontally across the throat one or more times, severing the carotid artery, the jugular vein, and the esophagus. If there is a pause during the strokes, the animal becomes unfit for eating. If the knife causes a nick or a puncture in the process, the animal also becomes unfit for eating.

Our rabbis viewed sh'chitah to be the swiftest and least painful slaughtering process for the animal. They therefore considered sh'chitah to fulfill the mitzvah of tza'ar baalei chayim (see fact 583).

Originally, anyone who knew the halachah was permitted to slaughter animals. Gradually, however, sh'chitah became such a highly specialized skill that by the thirteenth century it was declared that only professionals could perform this ritual. The professional was called a shochet.

Prior to killing any animal, the shochet is required to check the chalaf carefully for any nicks. If there are none, the shochet recites a brachah (see fact 287) recognizing that he is performing the mitzvah of ritual slaughter and then, in one uninterrupted stroke, kills the animal.

Some humane societies object to this traditional way of slaughtering, maintaining that the animal suffers. They recommend that the animal be stunned prior to killing, so that it is rendered unconscious. The halachah forbids stunning because it causes blood clots in the animal, which would make the meat unfit (see fact 594), and sometimes injure the brain and organs, which would also render the animal unfit for eating (see fact 597).

596. Traif is the Yiddish term to indicate that a food is not permitted to be consumed.

Leviticus 22:8 forbids any priest to eat an animal that has died of natural causes. Such an animal is called a neveilah. Our rabbis also prohibited him from eating an animal killed by another or wounded in such a way that, within a year, it might die. The Yiddish word for such a torn animals is "traif." Because the Tanna'im (see fact 329) associated our table with the sacrificial cult, calling it a mini-altar (see data to fact 589), they prohibited all Jews from eating an animal that was traif.

One of the important jobs of a shochet is to examine the organs of the animals after it has been correctly slaughtered. If the animal was healthy and without broken bones, the shochet declares the animal kasher (fit for eating). If the organs indicate that the animal was diseased or injured, the shochet must declare the animal *traif* (torn) and therefore unfit for consumption. The word *traif* is frequently (albeit incorrectly) used to refer to any food that is not permitted. For example, shrimp is called traif. It really isn't; it's tamei, ritually impure.

Many diseases attack an animal's lungs. Sometimes thorns eaten by animals puncture their lungs. As a result, the lungs frequently contain scar tissue, ridges, pits, and the like. Some of these make the animal traif; many do not. Some Jews, not wishing to take the chance of making a mistake, will eat only meat that comes from animals with completely smooth lungs. The Yiddish word for smooth is *glatt*. Stores that offer glatt kosher meat promise that the meat sold there comes only from animals with totally unblemished lungs.

Today the word *glatt* means super-kosher, and stores even offer glatt kosher toothpaste.

597. A mashgiach makes sure that the laws of kashrut are maintained.

Because the regulations concerning ritual slaughter and the determination of the fitness of an animal for eating were so complicated, communities hired a respected scholar to oversee the ritual slaughtering process. This function became even more important when canning and industrialized food processing became prevalent. The overseer was called a *mashgiach*. In order for a food to be considered kosher, fit, it has to be marked by an accepted authority, a mashgiach.

In addition, kosher butcher shops, restaurants, and catering halls are required to hire an overseer, a mashgiach, who makes sure that the laws of separation of milk and meat are scrupulously maintained. There have been scandals, of course, when it is discovered that nonkosher food has been labeled kosher, but the Orthodox community seriously tries to maintain the laws of kashrut even on the mass scale now necessary in the United States.

Jewish Concepts and Beliefs

598. Middah k'neged middah is the traditional belief that God provides specific consequences for our actions.

Translated "measure for measure," middah k'neged middah is a fundamental principle of traditional Judaism. Humans have free will (see fact 602), and their actions initiate divine consequences. According to a midrash, because Jacob fooled his father into thinking that he was Esau so he could receive the special blessing (see fact 136), God allowed Laban to fool him into thinking that Leah was Rachel so he would marry the wrong woman (see fact 138). Similarly, because Jacob didn't let his parents know where or how he was for twenty-two years, God punished him by making him believe that Joseph was dead for twenty-two years. In the same way, Samson followed his eyes when he was seduced by Delilah, so the Philistines put out his eyes (see fact 190).

For modern liberal Jews, there are philosophical problems with the principle of divine consequence for all of our actions. Measure for measure seems to take away part of our free will. When King David committed adultery with Bathsheba, Nathan the Prophet came to him and declared that King David would be punished for his adulterous relationship when his son slept with his own concubines. Was not the son's free will compromised in making his action a punishment for David's sin? The tension between divinely decreed consequences for each of our actions and the principle of free will is clear. Our rabbis never bothered to resolve that tension; they applied each principle separately.

599. Zechut avot is the belief that because our ancestors were worthy, we get credit with God.

Zechut avot means literally "the merit of the ancestors." It begins with the principle that there are rewards and punishments for our actions. The righteousness of our ancestors provides us with some credit with the Divine. Thus Deuteronomy 4:37 states, "And because He loved your fathers . . . He Himself in his great might led you out of Egypt." Redemption was provided not because of our deeds, then, but rather as a result of God's relationship with our ancestors.

When Moses pleads for God's forgiveness concerning the Golden Calf incident (see fact 163), he begs, "Remember your servants, Abraham, Isaac, and Jacob."

We repeat three times daily in the Amidah (see fact 302) "(You) remember the deeds of lovingkindness of the Patriarchs, and bring redemption to their children's children for your name's sake with love."

Our rabbis emphasized, however, that ancestral merit has its definite limits. Rabbi Kahana taught, "Don't let a man say for the sake of my righteous brother or father I shall be saved, for Abraham could not save his son Ishmael, nor Jacob save his brother Esau . . . as it is written, 'no person can by any means redeem a relative' (Psalm 49:8)."

The Torah also provides us with an apparent contradiction about the consequences of wicked parents. Exodus 20 states, "(God will) visit the guilt of the parents onto the children, upon the third and fourth generations." Deuteronomy 24:16 states, "Parents shall not be put to death for children, nor children be put to death for parents." Our rabbis resolved this apparent contradiction by explaining that children suffer for the sins of their parents only when they commit the same sin; if they are guiltless, there is no punishment.

600. Musar is Jewish ethics.

The TaNaCH and the Talmud (see fact 363) never made a distinction between halachah, Jewish law, and musar, ethics. They were one integrated whole. However, influenced by the Muslim world and its concentration on Greek philosophy, Jewish writers created a specific literature which concentrated on moral virtues and actions. These books utilized midrash (see fact 333) and Talmudic references to focus on living morally.

One of these literary genres was the ethical will. This was a brief moralistic instruction directed toward the scholar's children and students. By writing the ethical will supposedly on his deathbed, the scholar imbued the brief ethical treatise with more authority than his other works might be accorded. It is not clear whether or not they were actually written at the time of death.

Beginning in the eleventh century many Jews in Spain actually began to write ethical rules for their family just prior to dying. These included instructions concerning marital partners, personal neatness, and studiousness. They were not intended to be read by anyone other than the family members involved. Gradually, the practice became more widespread, and even nonscholars wrote ethical wills instructing their family in personal moral actions.

The custom is gaining popularity among modern liberal Jews today. Besides leaving property and objects, a Jew wants to share with his family some important values and thoughts which will transcend death. Families are most attentive at the time of a death, so writing an ethical will for family members can be a powerful and meaningful act of love, intimacy, and sharing.

In the early nineteenth century the leaders of Lithuania's mitnagdim (see fact 430) were worried. They saw their communities being corrupted by the Haskalah (see fact 436), the Chasidim (see facts 428, 429), and the new Reformers (see fact 442). Jews were not concentrating on following halachah diligently enough. Yeshivah students were getting lax in their Talmud studies and were even secretly reading secular books. The poverty of the shtetl (see fact 438) was threatening to break the Jewish spirit.

One of the mitnagid leaders, Israel Salanter, devised a discipline to counteract these corroding influences. He instituted daily half-hour contemplation sessions during which all yeshivah students would quietly chant musar literature. It didn't matter which text a student chanted; the melody remained the same; the students sang together from different texts. On a weekly basis, the ethics mashgiach (see fact

597) would speak privately with each student on ethical matters. In addition, the students established their own private support groups to focus on musar (ethics). This Musar Movement succeeded in retaining a generation of yeshivah students in a spiritual cocoon of self-support groups which provided religious leadership in Lithuania into the twentieth century.

601. Mazal tov means literally "good planet."

The most common Yiddish shout at celebrations is "Mazal tov," usually understood to mean "Congratulations!" Actually, the origin of the phrase is quite complicated. *Mazal* is the Hebrew word for planet and originally referred to the personal astrological star which affected a person's life. Rabbinic Judaism is full of astrology.

Although a few Tanna'im (see fact 329), including Rabbi Akiva (see fact 347), believed that the stars did not affect the People of Israel, the vast majority of Tanna'im and Amora'im (see fact 361) believed that the position of the planets and stars determined a person's personality, profession, and length of life. Almost all of them agreed, however, that a person who concentrates on righteousness and virtue can change the decrees of the astral configurations; we *do* have free will (see fact 602).

Most important, many rabbis spoke out against using astrology to foresee the future because they maintained that astrologers inevitably made mistakes in their calculations. The rabbinic warning was thus focused against astrologers, not astrology, and there are numerous midrashim (see fact 333) which demonstrate how astrologers misunderstood the future by misreading the stars. One of these involved the story of Moses.

According to the midrash, Pharaoh was informed by his astrologers that a savior of the Jews was coming who would be his downfall. This savior could be killed by water. Thereupon, Pharaoh ordered all male Hebrews to be thrown into the Nile River to try to avert the astrological decree. It didn't work. Moses saved the Hebrews, and Pharaoh was destroyed at the Sea of Reeds (see facts 154–157). The astrologers' prediction, however, was correct. Moses, the savior of the Hebrews, did destroy Pharaoh and was killed by water: by striking the rock at Merribah (see fact 179), Moses effected his death through that water. The astrologers had seen the future in the stars, *but they had misunderstood the details and thus failed to save Pharaoh.*

RaMBaM (see facts 395–401) was the only major medieval Jewish philosopher to reject astrology completely, but most philosophers after him continued to assume the important influence of the stars and planets on the events in this world.

Needless to say, astrology played an important role in kabbalah (see fact 417), and the followers of kabbalah applied astrological connections to the letters of Torah (see fact 105).

Besides the phrase "mazel tov," Judaism's association with astrology produced another commonly used Yiddish word. A shlimmazel is someone who never has anything go right for him. The word is really two words: shlim (bad) and mazel (star).

602. Judaism emphasizes that humans have free will.

Belief in free will is an essential principle of Judaism. Without human free will, the rabbinic understanding of divine judgment (see data to fact 9) and reward and punishment (see data to fact 607) would make no sense at all. Humans can be held accountable only for what they can personally control. On the other hand, the Tanna'im (see fact 329) and Amora'im (see fact 361) also emphasized that God rewards and punishes every action of humans in this life as well as in the Olam HaBa (see fact 320). Nothing happens except as part of the divine will and plan. There is an obvious tension between these two beliefs. Rabbi Akiva (see fact 347) succinctly described the problem when he said, "Everything is foreseen, and freedom of choice is given." Our Talmudic rabbis never did try to systematize these two apparently conflicting beliefs; they simply maintained both of them.

Philosophers did try to reconcile these two positions. Saadia Gaon (see fact 377) emphasized that humans had free will and this free will, felt from within each person, is not affected by God's transcendent foreknowledge. God, being timeless, knows what will take place in ways that we humans can't even comprehend. Therefore, at the moment of our choosing we have free will.

Our rabbis also noted that God encourages within us our own basic tendencies. In every person there are two conflicting inclinations: the yetzer hatov, the inclination to do good, and the yetzer hara, the inclination to do evil.

There are midrashim (see fact 333) which emphasize that the yetzer hara is not really evil; it just concentrates on physical gratification, a Talmudic id. If it were not for the yetzer hara, humans would never procreate, build, or invent. However, in order to be a good person, we must control our yetzer hara with our yetzer hatov, our good inclination which desires to follow God's commands. If we allow our yetzer hatov to govern the yetzer hara, God supports us; if we allow our yetzer hara to ignore our yetzer hatov, again, God will support us.

Thus Pharaoh, because of his character, was prepared to behave cruelly. His yetzer hara was dominant. God, in hardening Pharaoh's heart, simply allowed Pharaoh to respond naturally to the situation. Similarly, God would provide a righteous person with the strength and commitment to act according to his basic nature, righteously.

Liberal Jews argue that the traditional Jewish position against homosexuality should be changed. They feel that homosexuality is an inborn tendency that cannot be changed, and therefore a person has no choice about his or her sexual preference. Since there is no choice, there can be no stigma attached to being homosexual. There is disagreement about the matter (see fact 605).

603. "Bis hundert und tzvantzig" is the appropriate greeting on someone's birthday.

In Genesis 6:3 God declares that humans will live only 120 years. According to the Torah, Moses died at the age of 120. Because long life was viewed as a reward for righteous behavior, living to 120 became an idealized goal, a sign of righteousness and divine protection. It therefore became a tradition to greet someone on his or her birthday by saying, "Bis hundert und tzvantzig," "Until 120!" Not only are we wishing them long life; we are hoping that they will be, in some way at least, like Moses.

This greeting is clearly a formula and not a real expectation. Psalm 90:10 (see fact 200) more realistically notes that "the days of our years are 70 years, and if by reason of strength, 80 years." In some communities, because a person's full life was viewed as 70 years, on his eighty-third birthday the community would celebrate his becoming a Bar Mitzvah again (see fact 277).

Although the TaNaCH (see fact 104) frequently combines old age with wisdom, and Leviticus 19:32 commands us to respect old age, there are also realistic passages that describe the difficulties inherent in getting old. Ecclesiastes 12:1–8 (see fact 34) describes aging as follows:

So appreciate your vigor in the days of your youth, before those days of sorrow come and those years arrive of which you will say, 'I have no pleasure in them. . . . When the arms become shaky; and the legs are bent; and the teeth,

grown few, are idle; and the eyes grow dim; and the ears are
shut, with the noise of the handmill growing fainter . . .
when one is afraid of heights and there is terror on the
road . . . and the dust returns to the ground as it was, and
the lifebreath returns to God who bestowed it.' Utter futility,
said Kohelet, all is futile.

Gematriya

604. Gematriya is Hebrew numerology.

Every Hebrew letter has a numerical equivalent. Gematriya is the
skill of finding relationships between different Hebrew words and
phrases through their numerical values. The Tanna'im (see fact 329)
never used gematriya as a proof of the relationship between words; it
served as a sermonic lesson, a way for people to remember relationships.

The simplest form of gematria is direct numerical relationship. The
Hebrew word for ladder, סולם (sulam), has the same numerical value as
the Hebrew word for Sinai (סיני), 130, thus reminding people that
Jacob's dream of a ladder (see fact 137) actually took place at Mount
Sinai.

The name Eliezer, אליעזר , has the numerical value of 318. In
Genesis 14:14, Abraham is described as having a force of 318 men to
fight in a battle. The Tanna'im created the midrash (see fact 333) that the
only help Abraham really had in the battle was his servant Eliezer (see
fact 132), whose name equalled 318.

A more complicated form of gematriya was created by reversing
the numerical value of Hebrew letters. Tav, the last letter of the
alphabet, was given the numerical value of 1, while aleph, the first letter
of the alphabet, was given the numerical value of 400. By this system,
different relationships between words in the TaNaCH (see fact 104)
could be derived.

Gematriya became important in Lurianic Kabbalah (see fact 417)
and the followers of Isaac Ben Solomon Luria frequently used numerology to derive mystical truths from the TaNaCH. Over the centuries,
more than seventy different methods of gematriya were developed.
These included finding the relationship between each numerical value
of the letters in a word squared and another word (God's name יהוה
$= 10^2 + 5^2 + 6^2 + 5^2 = 186 =$ God's name מקום).

Gematriya is another example of how important Torah study is to Jews. The desire to learn every possible insight, nuance, and fact about the Torah has been a challenge to us for over 2,000 years, and gematriya shows how devoted Jews have been to this search. We have gone to great extremes to find these Torah truths. Today, traditional Jews are using computer technology to help them in their continuing search for hidden relationships in the TaNaCH.

Homosexuality

605. Traditional Judaism has always considered male homosexuality to be an abomination.

The Torah calls a variety of human actions abominations *to'ayvah*. These include unethical use of weights and measures (Deuteronomy 25:16), the foods forbidden to be eaten (see facts 590–594), idolatry (Deuteronomy 12:31), incest (Leviticus 18:17), bestiality (Leviticus 18:23), magic (Deuteronomy 18:10–12), wearing the clothes of the opposite sex (for both men and women; Deuteronomy 22:5), and homosexuality (Leviticus 18:22).

Although the Torah refers to only male homosexuality, our rabbis declared female homosexuality to be forbidden as well. It then became almost a dead issue. Rabbi Judah HaNasi (see fact 356) instituted a rule that bachelors must not share the same blanket to avoid even the possibility of homosexuality, but the Amora'im (see fact 361) responded that such a fence around the law was unnecessary since no Jews were involved in the practice.

Homosexuality did not become a burning issue within Judaism until the rise of Gay Rights advocacy in the 1960s and 1970s. As more homosexuals came "out of the closet," the Reform Movement responded to the reality that possibily 10 percent of the Jews in the United States were homosexual. The justification for the change in attitude toward homosexuality includes the following arguments:

1. Many doctors no longer believe that homosexuality is an illness. They maintain that homosexuality is not a matter of choice or preference, it is a natural trait that one is born with. Since one of the fundamental beliefs in Judaism is that you can be held responsible for an action only if you have free will (see fact 602),

then homosexuality cannot legitimately be condemned. If it is a natural phenomenon in a group of people, it should be accepted as a legitimate sexual lifestyle.

2. Some of the actions called "abomination" in the Torah are routinely done by most modern, liberal Jews (eating nonkosher food, women wearing men's clothing, etc). Autonomy has always been a fundamental tenet of Reform Judaism. Therefore, to suddenly quote Torah text on homosexuality maintaining that it is an abomination is inappropriate and simply shows an ongoing societal tendency toward homophobia.

3. As a movement, we had no problem ignoring Torah limitations when it came to recognizing full equality between men and women (see fact 466) or creating a liberal position toward abortion (see fact 610). When a modern value conflicts with Torah, we are dedicated to reforming Judaism to meet modern values and needs. We consider it a mitzvah, a commandment, to do so. Our reluctance to apply the same standard on the issue of homosexuality merely shows the ongoing tendency toward homophobia within our society.

Responding to these arguments, the Union of American Hebrew Congregations (see data to fact 447) recognized a number of "outreach" congregations which had formed with the goal of welcoming homosexuals as members. The Union of American Hebrew Congregations also passed resolutions urging congregations to grant homosexuals full membership rights and privileges. The resolutions urged congregations not to discriminate against homosexuals in any way.

In 1986 an ad hoc committee of the Central Conference of American Rabbis was formed to make recommendations concerning the Reform rabbinate's position on homosexuality. The questions being considered included the following: Should the CCAR recognize homosexuality as a legitimate sexual lifestyle? Can/Should homosexual monogomous relationships be sacralized? Should the CCAR urge the faculty of Hebrew Union College–Jewish Institute of Religion (see fact 448) to ordain rabbis without regard for their sexual focus?

In 1990 the CCAR voted to accept the committee's report. It included the following points:

1. The Hebrew Union College–Jewish Institute of Religion would not preclude a qualified rabbinic student because he or she was

a homosexual (the president of HUC–JIR had announced this policy in 1988).

2. The Central Conference of American Rabbis endorsed the position of the college and agreed to accept qualified gay and lesbian rabbis.

3. The majority of the committee maintained that the ideal Jewish relationship was still a monogamous heterosexual one. The Central Conference of American Rabbis endorsed that position.

4. The Central Conference of American Rabbis approved the resolution that homosexuals should have full civil rights and freedoms.

5. The committee and the Conference noted the indecision on the part of the medical community concerning the nature of homosexuality.

6. Although a minority of the committee felt that monogamous homosexual relationships merited sacralization, the Conference did not endorse that position.

Tikkun Olam

606. Tikkun olam means repairing the world.

Although mentioned occasionally in the Talmud (see fact 363), the concept of tikkun olam wasn't amplified until the founding of Lurianic Kabbalah (see fact 417). According to that philosophy, the world is not complete; there are shards of evil from earlier attempts at creation which failed: too much of the divine emanation was used, and the worlds exploded.

It is the job of Jews to repair the world, to raise it to perfection, and doing so will bring the Messiah. This concept of participation in perfecting the world had great influence on the followers of Shabbetai Tzvi (see fact 423). Ironically, it also became one of the cornerstones of the Reform Movement in the United States after World War II. With our concentration on ethical monotheism (see fact 574), tikkun olam became a rallying code word for achieving social justice and universal peace.

Inspired by the value of tikkun olam, the Reform Movement was actively involved in the civil rights movement (see fact 464) and has become a leading representative of liberal American politics. In 1962 the Union of American Hebrew Congregations (see data to fact 447) founded the Religious Action Center in Washington, D.C. The Religious Action

Center serves as an advocacy group for social action issues in Washington. Through its monthly bulletin, *Chai/Impact*, it provides information to its membership on social action issues, keeping them informed about what bills are coming up in Congress and how senators and representatives are voting; it invites congregational groups to Washington to learn about specific social action issues and to meet with the congregants' representatives and senators as advocates; it sponsors the biennial Consultation on Conscience, a 2- to 3-day meeting of hundreds of people concerned with the social action problems in our world; and it provides guidance to help congregations set up social action programs. Thus tikkun olam, repair of the world, continues to be a fundamental value within Reform Judaism today.

Resurrection

607. Techiyat hamaytim is belief in resurrection of the dead.

The Torah (see fact 105) offers no concrete description of what happens when we die. There was a murky place called Sheol where all the dead descended. Reward in the Torah meant long life, not reward after this life. Mention of immortality and resurrection of the dead was first made in the book of Daniel (see fact 224), and our rabbis developed the belief of the Olam HaBa, the World to Come (see fact 320).

During the Roman period the Pharisees emphasized that belief in their political struggle against the Sadducees (see facts 318, 319, and data to fact 320), and Olam HaBa became an important part of the rabbinic belief in reward and punishment. Righteous following of the mitzvot would result in reward in the Olam HaBa.

However, the Tanna'im (see fact 329) were not systematic in their descriptions of resurrection and the Olam HaBa. It is not clear whether they believed that when a person dies, he or she goes first to Olam HaBa and waits for the final resurrection, when all righteous receive physical bodies again, or whether Olam HaBa actually refers to the time when resurrection takes place. Nor is there agreement about the nature of resurrection. Some Tanna'im maintained that resurrection will result in totally new bodies; others were concerned that the resurrected will have all of their previous physical problems.

Such questions could remain unanswered within our tradition, because Judaism never focused on faith or what happens to us after we die. Our concentration has always been on doing mitzvot, meeting our living contract with the Divine. However, resurrection of the dead, whether before or after final judgment, entailed the literal return of the righteous to physical bodies, and it was a fundamental belief for our rabbis. Belief in physical resurrection of the righteous is one of RaMBaM's thirteen articles of faith (see fact 397), but even he gave contradictory positions about the actual nature of resurrection.

One of the pragmatic consequences of the belief in physical resurrection has been the traditional Jew's reluctance to permit autopsies. If the "come back as you are" belief is correct, then Jews want to retain their organs and their limbs. On the other hand, for the sake of saving a life (pikuach nefesh; see fact 585), halachah does permit amputations and organ donation.

Early on, the Reform Movement dismissed resurrection of the dead and the Olam HaBa as "beliefs not rooted in Judaism." In the second prayer of the Amidah (see fact 302), they removed all references to "giving life to the dead" and replaced them with "giving life to all" (see data to fact 302).

Intermarriage

608. Intermarriage is forbidden in halachah.

Deuteronomy 7:1–3 forbids a Hebrew from marrying anyone from the seven Canaanite nations. Our rabbis interpreted that prohibition to include all non-Jews. Upon their return from the Babylonian Exile (see fact 218), Ezra and Nehemiah forced the Jewish population to give up their non-Jewish spouses (see facts 220, 221).

The Talmud (see fact 363) took the prohibition against intermarriage a step further. The Amora'im (see fact 361) stated that an intermarriage is no marriage, that is, it does not change the status of the Jew. It requires no get (see fact 268), and it does not affect the line of inheritance; it does not exist.

Feelings ran so high in some Jewish communities against intermarriage that frequently the parents of someone marrying a non-Jew would say Kaddish (see fact 279) and sit Shivah for them (see fact 280), indicating that their child was dead.

As American society became more secularized and barriers between Jews and non-Jews disappeared, there was a dramatic increase in intermarriage. Statistics differ widely, but estimates as high as 38 percent have been offered by sociologists. The Jewish community has responded in a variety of ways. The Orthodox not only continue to forbid intermarriage; they tend to ostracize the interfaith couple. The vast majority of Conservative rabbis refuse to officiate at a ceremony between a Jew and a non-Jew. However, many will encourage the non-Jewish member of the couple to convert, and conversion courses have been set up for this purpose. Within many Conservative congregations, there is still a noted stigma attached to an intermarried couple.

The Central Conference of American Rabbis continues its position opposing intermarriage and the officiating of Reform rabbis at such marriages. However, there is tremendous pressure from Reform Jews to have their rabbis officiate, thus lending some Jewish "legitimacy" to the marriage ritual. Some rabbis officiate after establishing that the children of the marriage will be raised as Jews. They see their participation as a way of bringing the couple into the Jewish fold, hoping eventually to encourage the non-Jewish spouse to convert. Some rabbis officiate because their congregations have placed pressure on them to do so. Some honestly believe that meeting the personal needs of a Jewish family transcends the traditional prohibition against such a union. An estimated 40 percent of Reform rabbis officiate at intermarriages.

Unlike the Orthodox and Conservative communities, once a couple has intermarried, the vast majority of Reform congregations welcome such a couple with open arms. The UAHC Outreach Commission (see data to fact 586) has created educational workshops, support groups, and congregational programs to encourage interfaith couples to participate in the life of the congregation.

Gambling

609. Our rabbis struggled against gambling.

Our sages viewed professional gambling as larceny. They declared that the gambler was a parasite in society and could not be trusted. Gamblers caused distress and financial crisis in families. Therefore the Talmud forbids a gambler from serving as a witness in court.

Many medieval rabbis refused to call a gambler to the Torah. The batei din (plural of beit din; see fact 425) refused to force the payment of gambling debts. In some communities, gamblers were flogged or placed in cherem (excommunicated; see data to fact 425). Although the Talmud made a distinction between professional and occasional gamblers, many rabbis viewed any form of gambling as criminal.

Despite 2,000 years of rabbinic legislation and condemnation, Jews continued to gamble. They played dice and cards; some played tennis and chess for high stakes. Some community leaders, seeing that the prohibitions and bans were failing to influence their people, tried compromising. They declared that, although gambling was destructive (the gematriya [see fact 604] of *Karten*, Yiddish for cards, is the same as the word for Satan), Jews were permitted to gamble on Chanukkah and Purim. In some towns, Simchat Torah (see facts 35–37), the intermediate days of Passover and Sukkot, and Rosh Chodesh (see fact 1) also became gambling days. Some rabbis thus made a distinction between compulsive, frequent, professional gambling and periodic, casual gambling as a form of entertainment.

In addition, some medieval rabbis permitted institutionalized gambling as long as the winnings went to the community tzedakah organizations (see fact 579). Their responsa on the subject were viewed by some Reform congregations as justification for legitimizing Bingo as a Temple fund-raiser. Many congregations still consider gambling to be an inappropriate synagogue function, and the conflict continues.

Abortion

610. The Reform Movement maintains that abortion should be the personal choice of the pregnant woman.

Exodus 21:22 states, "If men fight and hurt a woman with child, so that her fruit departs, and yet no harm follows (to the woman), he shall surely be fined. . . ." This has always been the proof-text quoted by the rabbis in the Talmud to show that the fetus is not considered legally a life. Otherwise, they argue, the punishment would have been death of the offender, not a fine. First and foremost, therefore, is the legal position that the fetus does not have full legal rights as a living human being until birth.

This position is emphasized further in a case where the mother's life is endangered by her pregnancy. Our rabbis insist that should the fetus threaten the mother's life, she must abort it. Even if it is during labor, the mother's life is to be protected at all costs until the shoulders of the baby exit her body. From that point on, insists our tradition, the baby has equal rights with the mother even if her life is threatened.

Thus it is clear that in our tradition the fetus is not viewed as a life until it exits the mother's body. From that moment on, the newborn has complete legal rights as a living human.

Having begun with this long introduction, it is now necessary to note that, traditionally, our rabbis were strongly opposed to abortion, viewing it as a desecration of God's craftsmanship. The vast majority of our rabbis forbade abortion even if the offspring was conceived through an illegitimate union, thus creating a bastard. In modern Jewish legal cases involving children who would be born with serious birth defects and illnesses, most Orthodox rabbis continue to prohibit abortion on the grounds that a potential soul is not to be destroyed.

There have, of course, been some minority opinions among the Orthodox which are much more lenient, but, if we are to present our tradition with integrity, we must emphasize that the vast majority of rabbis prohibit abortion unless the mother's life is endangered by the pregnancy or by the labor prior to the emergence of the fetus's shoulders.

This is one of those sensitive issues where modern liberal Jews quote half of our tradition and ignore the other half. We emphasize that our rabbis and traditional texts do not view the fetus as having full legal rights, and so we can then emphasize that abortion is not murder within the context of Jewish tradition. We then ignore the large number of rabbinic statements prohibiting almost all abortions and support the modern principle that women should have final moral say over their bodies. We argue that there is a morality that transcends our tradition, and we push for a much more liberal position than our tradition actually warrants. That's an important part of being Reform Jews; we wrestle with our 2,000 years of tradition and create new values and principles that meet our modern world.

Jewish Value Terms

611. Klal Yisrael is the unity of all Jews.

Although the term "Klal Yisrael" is found in the Talmud, the term did not become popular until modern times. This principle, however, has a been an important mainstay of Judaism for at least the last 2,000 years. We frequently find the phrase, "All Israel are responsible each for the other." For example, it was a fundamental mitzvah for the Jewish community to pay the ransom for a captive. Also, our recitation of sins on Yom Kippur is always done in the plural (see fact 26).

Rabbi Solomon Schechter (see fact 449) used the term "Klal Yisrael" to mean the collective conscience of the Jewish people. Klal Yisrael served as Rabbi Schechter's guide for determining what ritual actions a modern Jew is required to maintain in the modern world. As a result, he recommended the performance of many traditional practices for the sake of Klal Yisrael.

This concept became a source of tension in the late twentieth century: Orthodox Jews regularly called upon liberal Jews to maintain the traditional status quo for the sake of Klal Yisrael, but liberal Jews responded that they had the moral obligation to change rules they viewed as immoral. Reform didn't take place out of a need for passive convenience; Reform changes were a result of religious, moral choices.

Because of these conflicts, Rabbi Irving "Yitz" Greenberg, an Orthodox rabbi, became concerned that the Jewish people would not remain a unified group into the twenty-first century. He cited points of conflict among the different streams of Judaism concerning major personal issues: who is a Jew (see facts 273–275, 542); the rules for divorce (see fact 268); and the rules for conversion (see facts 586–588).

In 1974, as an attempt to bridge the gap between the different streams of Judaism, Rabbi Greenberg created the organization CLAL (The National Jewish Center For Learning and Leadership). The purpose of CLAL was to provide a forum for dialogue between Jews, to increase understanding between the different streams of Judaism, and to try to find compromises among the different positions which Jews maintain.

In addition, CLAL became actively involved in Operation Exodus, helping large masses of Soviet Jews to emigrate (see fact 573).

612. Emet is the Hebrew word for truth.

Our tradition has always emphasized the importance of truth because it is a divine attribute. The Psalms refer to the Divine as "the God of Truth." Our sages stated, "The Seal of God is Truth." *Pirkei Avot* says that truth is one of the pillars of the world (see fact 359), and Proverbs exhorts, "Remove falsehood and lying far from me."

It is a basic Jewish belief that God created the universe with integrity. When someone dies, the mourning family responds by saying, "Blessed is Adonai, the Judge of Truth, Dayan HaEmet" (see data to fact 278). This statement reaffirms that the world is ordered, just, and true.

613. Shalom means hello, goodbye, and peace.

The Hebrew root SH, L, M connotes wholeness, completion, contentment. When we attain the state of SH L M, we have peace. It is one of our highest goals. Hillel said, "Love peace and strive for peace." One sage added: "The whole Torah exists only for the sake of peace. For the sake of peace, truth may be sacrificed."

A traditional greeting on Shabbat (see facts 95–101) is "Shabbat Shalom," "a Sabbath of contentment, of wholeness."

We greet each other with this wish for wholeness and peace. "Shalom Aleichem" means "Peace, contentment to you." The appropriate response back is "Aleichem Shalom," "To you peace." It is also the proper farewell. Shalom, Peace to you!

Part III

TWO
SELF-TESTS

We can attain basic Jewish literacy at two different levels. The first and more important level of fact retention is passive. It consists of remembering a fact association when we see or hear a word. If we hear the word *get* and the association "a Jewish divorce document" pops into our heads, then we have achieved passive retention of that fact. The primary purpose of this book is to help the reader attain passive retention.

However, there is another level of fact recognition. It is called applicative or active retention. When we hear the association "a Jewish divorce document" and the term *get* pops into our minds, then we are applying the fact actively. We are able to use the term ourselves.

When we read a resource book, we're not always sure what we *really* know and what we only *think* we know. Having the information in front of us sometimes fools us into thinking we know facts when we really don't. To help you determine what you really know, this section consists of two self-tests whose numbers correspond to the 613 facts and data in the book.

The first self-test lets you check your passive retention of the facts in this book. If you can answer the questions in this test, then you have achieved an important goal. You have successfully created the necessary data associations in your mind to understand the basic terms, words, and events that are the essence of our tradition. You now have the passive background you need to succeed in any Adult Education class. However, you will not necessarily be able to apply the Hebrew terms, names, and events as part of your Jewish vocabulary. They may be on the tip of your tongue, but they won't necessarily come popping out correctly. That is a different learning skill, applicative retention.

The second self-test lets you check your *active* knowledge of the terms, names, and events cited in this book. That's a much more difficult skill. If you can answer the second self-test questions, then you have acquired a solid basic literacy background. You'll be able to converse confidently on any Jewish topic. You'll be able not only to catch references, but to make them yourself. You will have achieved your goal in reading this book: you will be a literate Jew. Mazal tov!

Self-Test Questions: Passive Retention

1. What is Rosh Chodesh?
3. What is the month of Adar II?
7. What is the Hallel?
11. What does teshuvah mean?
11. What is the goal of the Yamim Nora'im?
12. What do we do during the month of Elul?
13. What are Selichot?
13. When do we recite Selichot?
15. What sweet foods do we eat on Rosh HaShanah?
16. What shape of challah do we eat on Rosh HaShanah?
18. What holiday is called Yom HaZikaron?
19. What does Avinu Malkaynu mean?
20. How many times do we blow the shofar?
21. What is Tashlich?
23. When is Shabbat Shuvah?
25. When is Kol Nidrei chanted?
26. What do we ask of God on the Yamim Nora'im?
27. When we had a Temple, what did we do on Pesach, Sukkot, and Shavuot?
28. What is Sukkot?
30. What do willow, palm, and myrtle make?
31. When are the lulav and etrog waved?
33. What are Ushpizin?
34. What is Kohelet?
36. What do we do when we finish reading the Torah?
36. What does Simchat Torah celebrate?
37. What are Hakafot?
38. What does Chanukkah celebrate?
39. Who were the Hasmoneans?
40. Who was Mattathias?
41. Who was Judah the Maccabee?
42. How long does Chanukkah last?

45. What is a chanukkiyah?
46. What does the shamash do?
49. What is Tu BiShvat?
50. How do we celebrate Tu BiShvat?
52. What is a megillah?
52. What do we read on Purim?
54. Who was Ahasuerus?
55. Who was Vashti?
56. Who was Esther?
60. What is Adloyada?
62. What is a gragger used for?
63. When are hamentaschen eaten?
66. What are we forbidden to eat on Pesach?
67. What is Shabbat HaGadol?
68. What does Pesach celebrate?
69. What harvest did Pesach begin?
71. What does the lamb bone signify?
72. What is maror?
73. What is a seder?
74. What is charoset?
75. What is the afikoman?
79. What is the Haggadah?
80. Which harvest did Shavuot begin?
82. When is Lag BaOmer?
84. On Shavuot what did we receive?
86. What do we read on Shavuot?
90. What does Yom HaShoah commemorate?
91. What is Yom HaAtzmaut?
92. What is the primary ritual on Tisha B'Av?
93. What does Tisha B'Av commemorate?
96. What is the meaning of two challot?
97. What is the primary way of celebrating Shabbat?
98. What is an eruv?
99. What is Kabbalat Shabbat?
100. What is the theme of L'Cha Dodi?
101. What is cholent?
102. What is Havdalah?

104.   Into how many parts is the TaNaCH divided?
106.   What is Genesis?
107.   What does the book of Exodus contain?
108.   What does Leviticus describe?
109.   What does the book of Numbers tell about?
110.   What is the content of Deuteronomy?
111.   What did God create on the first day?
112.   In how many days did God create the world?
113.   When did God create Shabbat?
114.   Who was Adam?
115.   Who was Eve?
116.   What did Cain do?
116.   What happened to Abel?
117.   What did God command Noah to build?
120.   What was the rainbow?
121.   What happened because of the Tower of Babel?
122.   Who was Abraham?
123.   Who was Sarah?
124.   Who was Lot?
125.   Who was Hagar?
125.   Who was Ishmael?
128.   What happened to Lot's wife?
130.   What was the Akedah?
133.   Who was Rebecca?
134.   Who were Esau and Jacob?
135.   What did Jacob cheat Esau out of?
137.   About what did Jacob dream?
138.   Who were Rachel and Leah?
139.   How many children did Jacob have?
140.   Who were Joseph and Benjamin?
143.   What clothing did Joseph have?
146.   Who were Ephraim and Menasseh?
150.   Who was Amram?
150.   Who was Yocheved?
151.   Who was Aaron?
152.   Who was Miriam?
153.   Who was Tzipporah?

156.   Why did God bring Ten Plagues on Egypt?

157.   When did we first sing "Mi Chamocha"?

157.   What does "Mi Chamocha" mean?

158.   What terrible thing did Amalek do?

159.   What did we receive on Mount Sinai?

159.   Where did we receive the Torah?

160.   What is in Exodus 20 and Deuteronomy 5?

162.   How many mitzvot are there in the Torah?

162.   What does the word *mitzvot* mean?

162.   What is the significance of the number 613?

163.   What did Moses do when he saw the people worshiping the Golden Calf?

164.   What was the Mishkan?

165.   How many branches did the Temple menorah have?

166.   Who was Bezalel?

167.   What was the priests' primary duty?

168.   Who came from the tribe of Levi?

169.   Who were the Kohanim?

170.   What was Aaron's function?

174.   How often does Sh'mittah occur?

174.   What is the law of Sh'mittah?

175.   What happened to Nadav and Avihu?

176.   How many scouts did Moses send to check out the Land of Canaan?

177.   Who was Caleb ben Yefuneh?

178.   What did Korach do?

179.   What happened at Merribah?

180.   What special decision involved Zelophechad's daughters?

181.   What was a City of Refuge?

182.   Who died at the end of Deuteronomy?

183.   What did Joshua ben Nun do?

184.   Who were the Judges?

185.   What did Deborah and Barak do?

186.   Who was Deborah?

187.   What did Gideon do?

188.   What was the source of Samson's strength?

189.   Who were the Philistines?

190.   Who was Delilah?
191.   Who was Hannah?
192.   Who was Saul?
194.   Who was Goliath?
196.   What happened on Mount Gilboah?
197.   Who was David?
198.   What city did David make the capital of Israel?
199.   What did David bring to Jerusalem?
200.   What are the Psalms?
201.   Who was Batsheva?
202.   From what tribe did King David come?
204.   What did King Solomon build?
205.   What happened after Solomon died?
205.   What was the kingdom of Judah?
205.   What was the kingdom of Israel?
205.   When did Israel and Judah split into two separate nations?
207.   What was a prophet?
208.   What did Elijah do?
214.   What was Jonah's message to Nineveh?
215.   Whom did Assyria conquer?
216.   Why did King Hezekiah build a water tunnel?
217.   What did Nebuchadnezzar do on the Ninth of Av in 586, B.C.E.?
218.   What was the Babylonian Exile?
219.   What was one of Ezekiel's visions?
220.   What was Nehemiah's official position?
221.   What did Ezra the scribe do?
223.   What happened to Job?
224.   What happened to Daniel?
225.   Where can the Book of Esther be found in the TaNaCH?
226.   What relationship did Ruth have to King David?
227.   What is the Apocrypha?
229.   Where do Sephardic customs come from?
229.   Where do Ashkenazic customs come from?
230.   What is an Aron HaKodesh?
231.   What does a sofer do?
231.   On what are Torah scrolls written?
231.   With what does a sofer write?

233. The Torah is dressed to symbolize whom?
234. What are atzei chayim?
235. What is a yad?
236. What is a menorah?
237. What is the ner tamid?
238. What is a mechitzah?
239. What is a mizrach?
240. What is a sheliach tzibbur?
241. What is a bimah?
242. What is a chazzan?
243. What is the Septuagint?
244. What is the Targum?
245. What is a Chumash?
246. What is the Haftarah?
247. What does *mezuzah* mean?
249. What are tefillin?
250. What are tzitzit?
251. What is a tallit?
252. What is a yarmulke?
252. What is a kippah?
253. What is a shtreimel?
254. What is a kittel?
255. What is sha'atnez?
256. What are payot?
257. What is a Magen David?
258. What is a chamsa?
260. What is a genizah?
261. What is a mikvah?
262. What is kiddushin?
263. What is a ketubah?
264. What is a chuppah?
265. What are the Sheva Brachot?
265. When are the Sheva Brachot recited?
266. What is a mamzer?
267. What is chalitzah?
268. What is a get?
269. What is an agunah?

270.   What is a brit milah?

271.   What is a mohel?

272.   What is a sandak?

276.   What is a brit banot?

277.   What is a Bar/Bat Mitzvah?

278.   What is k'riyah?

278.   What purpose does k'riyah serve?

279.   What is the Kaddish?

280.   What is Shivah?

282.   What is Sh'loshim?

283.   What is a Yahrzeit candle?

284.   What is Yizkor?

285.   How many blessings does a Jew traditionally say?

286.   What is Birkat HaMazon?

287.   Before we do almost any mitzvah, what do we say?

288.   What is kavannah?

289.   What is a minyan?

289.   How many Jews do you need to recite communal prayers?

290.   What is a Siddur?

291.   What are piyyutim?

292.   What is a Machzor?

293.   What is davvening?

294.   What is shuckling?

295.   How many daily prayer services are there?

296.   What is Shacharit?

297.   What is Minchah?

298.   What is Maariv?

299.   What is Musaf?

301.   Of what event does the Mi Chamocha remind us?

302.   What is the Amidah?

303.   What is the main quote in the Kedushah?

304.   What is duchenen?

305.   What is the Alaynu?

307.   What are trop?

308.   What is an aliyah (connected with the prayer service)?

309.   What is a baal koray?

310.   What is hagbahah?

310. What is gelilah?
311. Who was Josephus?
313. Who made Herod king of Judea?
317. Where is Masada?
318. Who were the Sadducees?
319. Who were the Pharisees?
320. What is Olam HaBa?
321. Who were the Essenes?
325. What is the Holy Sepulchre?
327. What was the Sanhedrin?
328. The Sanhedrin consisted of how many rabbis?
329. Who were the Tanna'im?
330. What did the Tanna'im do for 200 years?
332. What was the School of Hillel?
332. What was the School of Shammai?
333. What is midrash?
334. What is aggadah?
335. Who was Philo?
336. What did Titus do?
337. What is the kotel?
339. What happened to the Jews on top of Masada?
340. What did Rabbi Yochanan ben Zakkai do?
342. What is halachah?
343. When did the rabbis take over authority in Judaism?
344. What is s'michah?
351. What happened to Rabbi Akiva after the Bar Kochba Revolt?
352. What did Shimon Bar Yochai say about non-Jews?
354. What is the *Zohar*?
355. What is Kabbalah?
356. What did Judah HaNasi edit?
357. What is the Mishnah?
358. What are B'raitot?
359. What is *Pirkei Avot*?
360. What did Rav take to Babylonia?
361. Who were the Amora'im?
362. What is the Gemara?
363. What is the Talmud?

367.   What role does the Talmud play in Jewish law?

368.   What was the exilarch?

372.   What was a gaon?

373.   What was the gaon's primary duty?

374.   What are responsa?

375.   What did Gaon Amram write?

376.   What was one of the outcomes of responsa?

378.   Who were the Karaites?

380.   When was the Golden Age of Spain?

381.   Who were the Almohads?

382.   What happened to Jews during the First Crusade?

383.   What is Kiddush HaShem?

384.   What was one of the rules that Rabbenu Gershom made?

385.   Who was Samuel HaNagid?

386.   Who was Rashi?

387.   Who was Ibn Ezra?

390.   Where are the Tosafot found?

391.   Who was Meir of Rothenberg?

392/393.   What did Judah HaLevi write?

394.   Who was Benjamin MiTudelo?

395.   Who was Maimonides?

396.   Who was RaMBaM?

399.   What is the *Mishnah Torah*?

402/403.   Who was RaMBaN?

403.   What did RaMBaN create in Jerusalem?

404.   What were Blood Accusations?

405.   What did England do first, in 1290?

406.   What was the "badge of shame"?

408.   Who were accused of causing the Black Plague?

410.   What does Marrano mean?

410.   Who were the Marranos?

411.   What was the Inquisition?

412.   Who was Torquemada?

412.   As head of the Inquisition, what did Torquemada do?

414.   What is Ladino?

415.   What is Yiddish?

416.   What did Venice do first to Jews?

418.   What was Yehudah Loew of Prague said to have built?

419.   Who was Joseph Caro?

420.   What is the *Shulchan Aruch*?

421.   What is the *Mappah*?

421.   What did Moses Isserles write?

422.   Who was Chmielnitzky?

423.   Who was Shabbetai Tzvi?

424.   What was pilpul?

425.   What is a beit din?

426.   What is a posek?

427.   What did the Baal Shem Tov do?

428.   What do Chasidic Jews believe about themselves and God?

429.   What is a Rebbe?

430.   What were mitnagdim?

433.   Who was Baruch Spinoza?

434.   Who were the Rothschilds?

435.   What did Moses Mendelssohn do?

436.   What was the Haskalah?

437.   What was the Pale of Settlement?

438.   What was a shtetl?

439.   Who was Sholom Aleichem?

440.   What were chappers?

441.   What did Napoleon do for the Jews?

442.   What was the original goal of Reform Judaism?

443.   What did Rabbi Samson Raphael Hirsch do?

445.   What is B'nai B'rith?

446.   What is the Jewish Chautauqua Society?

447.   Who was Rabbi Isaac Mayer Wise?

448.   What is the Hebrew Union College?

449.   Who was Rabbi Solomon Schechter?

450.   Who was Rabbi Mordechai Kaplan?

451.   What were pogroms?

452.   How many Jews came to the United States between 1880 and 1920?

453.   Who was Emma Lazarus?

454.   Why is the Lower East Side of New York important for Jews?

457.   Who was Mendel Beilis?

458.   What was the Holocaust?

459.   What was Kristallnacht?

460.   What was the Nazi plan for the Jews?

461.   How were 6 million Jews slaughtered?

462.   What happened in the Warsaw Ghetto during the Holocaust?

465.   What are havurot?

466.   Who is Sally Priesand?

467.   What is WUPJ?

468.   Who are the Falashas?

469.   What is the Conference of Presidents of Major American Jewish Organizations?

470.   Israel connects which two continents?

471.   In ancient times, why was the Yizrael Valley important?

472.   Why were Hatzor, Megiddo, and Beit Shean important?

473.   What is a tel?

474.   What primary function did Jaffa serve?

475.   What primary function does Haifa serve?

476.   What happened frequently on Israel's coastal plain?

477.   What is the Galilee?

478.   What was Tzfat famous for in the sixteenth century?

479.   What function does Lake Kinneret have in Israel?

480.   What was Tiberias?

481.   What was found at Beit Alfa?

482.   What is Nablus?

483.   What is Bab El Wad?

484.   What is the Cave of Machpelah?

485.   Of what importance is the Jordan River?

486.   For what is Jericho famous?

487.   What is special about The Dead Sea?

488.   What is the Negev?

489.   What is Be'er Sheva?

490.   Where do the Bedouin live?

491.   What are Yahel and Lotan?

492.   What is Eilat?

493.   What major structures did the Crusaders build in Israel?

494.   To whom is Jerusalem holy?

495.   Where is the Dome of the Rock located?

496. What is the Mosque of al-Aqsa?
496. Where is the Mosque of al-Aqsa located?
497. What is on the Mount of Olives?
498. What is Zion another name for?
499. Who were the Ottoman Turks?
500. What surrounds the Old City of Jerusalem?
501. Who was Sir Moses Montefiore?
502. What did the BILU do?
503. What did Baron Edmund de Rothschild do?
504. What did Eliezer Ben Yehuda do?
505. Who was Alfred Dreyfus?
508. Who was Theodor Herzl?
509. What is the Jewish National Fund?
510. What was the Second Aliyah group?
511. What did A. D. Gordon believe?
512. What was HaShomer?
513. What was Degania?
515. What was the Yishuv?
517. What organization was founded by Josef Trumpeldor?
518. What was the Jewish Legion?
519. What was the NILI?
520. What did the Balfour Declaration promise?
521. What happened to Tel Chai?
525. Who were the chalutzim?
526. What did Henrietta Szold found?
528. What did the Youth Aliyah accomplish?
529. What did Aliyah Bet do?
530. What was the purpose of tower and stockade settlements?
533. What was the Palmach?
534. What did Hannah Senesh write?
538. Who was David Ben Gurion?
540. What is the Knesset?
541. Who was Chaim Weizmann?
542. What is the Law of Return?
543. What was Operation Magic Carpet?
544. What is El Al?
546. What are absorption cities?

547.   What is Kiryat Shmoneh?

548.   From which country did Israel accept reparations for the Holocaust?

549.   What happened in the Sinai Campaign?

550.   What happened to Adolf Eichmann?

551.   What was the goal of the PLO?

553.   When was Jerusalem finally united?

554.   Who was Moshe Dayan?

555.   Who was Golda Meir?

557.   What happened at Entebbe?

558.   What is the Good Fence?

559.   What was the Camp David Accord?

561.   What is the modern political significance of Jerusalem?

562.   What is Gush Emunim?

562.   What is Kach?

563.   Why does Jerusalem look gold at sunset?

564.   What did Chagall design at Hadassah Hospital?

565.   What is Heichal Shlomo?

567.   What is ARZA?

568.   What was Operation Moses?

569.   What is the Intifada?

570.   What role did Yitzchak Rabin play during the Intifada?

571.   In what capacity did Yitzchak Shamir serve Israel?

572.   What is Tzahal?

573.   What was Operation Exodus?

574.   Who was Hermann Cohen?

575.   Who was Rabbi Leo Baeck?

576.   Who was Franz Rosenzweig?

577.   Who was Martin Buber?

578.   Who was Abraham Joshua Heschel?

579.   What is tzedakah?

580.   What is gemilut chasadim?

581.   What is hachnasat orchim?

582.   What is bikkur cholim?

583.   What is tza'ar baalei chayim?

584.   What is a mensch?

585.   What is pikuach nefesh?

586.   What is a ger?

589.   What is kashrut?

593.   What does parve mean?

594.   What does halachah say about consuming blood?

595.   What is a shochet?

596.   What does traif mean?

597.   What is a mashgiach?

598.   What is middah k'neged middah?

599.   What is zechut avot?

600.   What is musar?

601.   What does *mazal tov* mean?

603.   When do you say, "Bis hundert und tzvantzig"?

604.   What is gematriya?

605.   What is the traditional view on homosexuality?

606.   What does tikkun olam mean?

607.   What is Techiyat HaMaytim?

608.   What is the halachic position on intermarriage?

609.   What is the rabbinic position on gambling?

610.   What is the Reform Movement's position on abortion?

611.   What is Klal Yisrael?

612.   What is emet?

613.   What is shalom?

Self-Test Questions: Active Knowledge

1.   What is the celebration of the New Moon called?

2.   How many days are there in a normal Jewish year?

3.   What month do we add to make a Jewish leap year?

4.   When does a Jewish day start?

5.   What ritual action begins each holiday?

6.   What ritual action makes a day holy?

7.   What special psalms do we recite on holidays?

8.   What four holidays occur in the month of Tishri?

9.   What are Rosh HaShanah and Yom Kippur called?

10.   What is the greeting on Rosh HaShanah?

11.   What is the goal of the Yamim Nora'im?

11.   What is the Hebrew word for returning?

12.   During what month do we prepare for the Yamim Nora'im?

13.   Name the prayers asking for forgiveness.

13.   When do we begin praying for forgiveness?

14.   What holiday celebrates the creation of the world?

15.   On what holiday do we eat apples and honey?

16.   On what holiday do we eat a round challah?

17.   Who were supposedly born on Rosh HaShanah?

18.   How do we say Day of Remembrance in Hebrew?

18.   What holiday is called the Day of Remembrance?

19.   How do we say "Our Father Our King" in Hebrew?

20.   On what holiday do we blow the shofar?

21.   What ritual is called the Tossing?

22.   How many days are there between Rosh HaShanah and Yom Kippur?

23.   What is the Shabbat between Rosh HaShanah and Yom Kippur?

24.   What is the primary ritual on Yom Kippur?

25.   What is the best-known prayer on Yom Kippur?

26.   When do we ask God to forgive us for our sins?

27.   What are the three festivals when we used to bring offerings to the Temple?

28.   What is the fruit harvest?

29.   How many days are there between Yom Kippur and Sukkot?

30.   What are the three parts of a lulav?

31.   What do we wave on Sukkot?

32.   What do we build on Sukkot?

33.   What are special Sukkot guests called?

34.   What is the Hebrew word for Ecclesiastes?

35.   What holiday do Reform Jews combine with Atzeret?

36.   What holiday celebrates our finishing the reading of the Torah?

37.   What are the processions around the synagogue called?

38.   Who was the king in the Chanukkah story who made Judaism illegal?

39.   What priestly family led the revolt against the Greeks?
40.   Name the priest who began the revolt against the Greeks.
41.   Who was the Jewish general who led the Hasmonean Revolt?
42.   The first Chanukkah substituted for what holiday?
43.   When does Chanukkah begin?
44.   How long did the oil last in the Chanukkah legend?
45.   On what holiday do we light a nine-branched candelabrum?
45.   What is a nine-branched candelabrum called?
46.   What do we call the candle that lights all the other Chanukkah candles?
47.   On what holiday do we eat latkes?
48.   On what holiday do we play with a dreidl?
49.   What is the New Year of the Trees?
50.   On what holiday do we plant trees in Israel and eat fruit?
51.   What is the last month of the Jewish calendar?
52.   On what holiday do we read the Book of Esther?
52.   What is the Hebrew word for "scroll"?
53.   What book of the TaNaCH doesn't mention God?
54.   Who was the foolish king in the Purim story?
55.   Who was the first queen in the Purim story?
56.   Who was the second queen in the Purim story?
57.   How did Haman decide when to get rid of the Jews?
57.   What is the Hebrew word for dice?
58.   When is Purim?
60.   What is the zany Purim parade in Israel called?
61.   When do we read the commandment to wipe out the memory of Amalek?
62.   With what do we wipe out Haman's name?
63.   What do we eat on Purim?
64.   When does Pesach begin?
65.   How long does Pesach last?
66.   On what holiday don't we eat leaven or yeast products?
67.   What is the Shabbat before Pesach called?
68.   What holiday celebrates our redemption from Egypt?
69.   What holiday began the barley harvest in Israel?
70.   What grain product do we eat on Pesach?
70.   On what holiday do we eat matzah?

71.   What reminds us of the Divine passing over the Hebrew homes in Egypt?

72.   What do we call the bitter herbs for Pesach?

73.   What is the Pesach ritual meal called?

74.   What reminds us of the mortar we used as slaves?

75.   What is the Pesach dessert?

76.   On Pesach whom do we invite into our homes?

77.   How do we end the seder?

78.   Which megillah do we read on Pesach?

79.   How do we say the Telling in Hebrew?

80.   What holiday began the wheat harvest?

81.   How many weeks are there between Pesach and Shavuot?

82.   What holiday is on the thirty-third day between Pesach and Shavuot?

83.   In Temple times what did the people do on Shavuot?

84.   On what holiday did we receive the Torah?

85.   What do many Jews do on the night of Shavuot?

86.   On what holiday do we read the Ten Commandments?

87.   Which megillah do we read on Shavuot?

88.   What do we eat on Shavuot?

89.   What ceremony takes place on Shavuot?

90.   What day commemorates the Holocaust?

91.   What holiday celebrates Israel's Independence Day?

92.   What is the second most important fast day?

93.   What day is the anniversary of the destruction of the two Temples?

94.   Which megillah do we read on Tisha B'Av?

95.   What two things does Shabbat remind us of?

96.   On what holiday do we eat two challot?

97.   What is the primary way of celebrating Shabbat?

98.   What is a special fence which enables traditional Jews to carry things on Shabbat called?

99.   What ritual welcomes Shabbat?

100.   What song welcomes Shabbat as a bride?

101.   Name the meat, bean, and potato stew eaten on Shabbat.

102.   What ceremony ends Shabbat?

103.   What are the three objects used for Havdalah?

104.   What are the three parts of the TaNaCH?

105.   How many books are in the Torah?

106.   What is the first book of the Torah?

107.   Which book of the Torah describes how we were freed from Egypt?

108.   Which Torah book tells about holidays and sacrifices?

109.   Which Torah book describes our wanderings in the desert?

110.   Which book consists of three long speeches by Moses?

111.   What did God create on the first day?

112.   In how many days did God create the world?

113.   What did God create on the seventh day?

114.   Who was the first man?

115.   Who was the first woman?

116.   Who was the first murderer?

116.   Who was the first murder victim?

117.   Whom did God command to build an ark to save him and his family from a flood?

118.   What proof was there of dry land after the flood?

119.   What agreement did God make with Noah?

120.   What was the sign of God's agreement with Noah?

121.   What motivated God to create numerous languages?

122.   Who was the first Hebrew?

123.   Who was Abraham's wife?

124.   Who was Abraham's nephew?

125.   Who was Ishmael's mother?

125.   Who was Abraham's oldest son?

126.   What physical act, the sign of our covenant, did God command Abraham to perform?

127.   Abraham pleaded with God not to destroy which city?

128.   Who turned into a pillar of salt?

129.   Who was Sarah's son?

129.   Who was Isaac's father?

129.   Who was Isaac's mother?

129/125. Who was Isaac's brother?

130.   What do we call the incident of Abraham's sacrificing a ram instead of Isaac?

131.   Where did Abraham bury Sarah?

132.   Who was Abraham's servant?

132.   For whom did Eliezer find a wife?

133.   Who was Isaac's wife?

134.   Who were Isaac's sons?

134.   Who were Rebecca's sons?

134.   Who was Jacob's father?

134.   Who was Esau's father?

134.   Who was Esau's mother?

134.   Who was Jacob's mother?

134.   Who was Jacob's grandfather? (See also 129.)

134.   Who was Jacob's grandmother? (See also 129.)

135.   Who cheated Esau out of his birthright?

136.   Who cheated Esau out of his special blessing?

137.   Who dreamed about a ladder and angels?

138.   Whom did Jacob marry?

139.   How many children did Jacob have?

140.   Who were Jacob's two youngest sons?

140.   Who was Joseph's grandfather? (See also 134.)

141.   Who wrestled with an angel?

141.   What was Jacob's new name?

142.   Who became the twelve tribes of Israel?

143.   Who had a special coat of many colors?

144.   Who was sold into slavery?

144.   Who sold Joseph into slavery?

145.   Who became second in command to Pharaoh?

146.   Who were Joseph's two children?

146.   Who was Ephraim and Menasseh's grandfather? (See also 140.)

147.   Where did Jacob and his family move because of Joseph?

149.   What status did the Hebrews have in Egypt?

150.   Who were Moses' parents?

151.   Who was Moses' brother?

152.   Who was Moses' sister?

153.   Who was Moses' wife?

154.   Who saw a burning bush that wasn't consumed?

155.   What was God's message to Pharaoh?

155.   Through whom did God speak to Pharaoh?

156.   How did God force the Egyptians to let the Hebrews go?

157.   What did we sing when God parted the Sea of Reeds?

157.   How do you say "Who is like you?" in Hebrew?

158.   Who first attacked the Hebrews in the desert?

159.   What did we receive on Mount Sinai?

160.   Where are the Ten Commandments found in the Torah?

161.   What are the Ten Commandments?

162.   How do we say *commandments* in Hebrew?

162.   What is the significance of the number 613?

163.   When did Moses smash the stones that held the commandments?

164.   What was the portable Temple in the desert called?

165.   What do we call a candelabrum with seven branches?

166.   What artist made the Ark and the Mishkan?

167.   Who were responsible for the sacrificial cult?

168.   From what tribe did the priests come?

169.   What is the Hebrew word for our priests?

170.   Who was the first High Priest?

171.   What did the High Priest wear?

172.   Where is the commandment "You shall be holy" found?

173.   Where is the commandment "Love your neighbor as yourself" found?

174.   When must we not use the land of Israel?

175.   Who were struck down by fire?

176.   Whom did Moses send to scout the Land of Canaan?

177.   How many scouts frightened the people with their report on Canaan?

177.   Who reassured the people after the scouts frightened them?

178.   Who attempted a revolution against Moses and Aaron?

179.   Where did Moses strike a rock to get water?

179.   Where did Moses disobey God?

180.   Whose daughters were allowed to own land?

181.   Where could an accidental murderer flee?

182.   Who died at the end of Deuteronomy?

183.   Who led the Hebrews into the Land of Canaan?

184.   What did we call charismatic fighting leaders?

185.   Who defeated Sisera's army?

185.   Where was Sisera's army defeated?

186.   Who was a female prophet and judge?

187.   Who defeated the Midianites?

188.   Who got strength from his hair?

189.   In the TaNaCH, what group was the Hebrews' worst enemy?

190.   Who tricked Samson and had his hair cut?

191.   Who was Samuel's mother?

192.   Who was the first king of Israel?

193.   Who declared Saul king?

193.   Who anointed David king?

194.   Who killed the Philistine giant named Goliath?

195.   Who was Saul's son?

195.   Who was Jonathan's friend?

196.   Who died on Mount Gilboah?

197.   Who was the second king of Israel?

198.   Who made Jerusalem the capital of Israel?

199.   Who brought the Ark to Jerusalem?

200.   What is the name of the 150 poems found in the TaNaCH?

201.   Who was Solomon's mother?

202.   From what tribe did King David come?

203.   Who was Solomon's father?

203.   Who was the third king of Israel?

203.   From what tribe did King Solomon come? (See also 202).

204.   Who built the Temple in Jerusalem?

205.   What was the northern kingdom called?

205.   What was the southern kingdom called?

205.   When did Israel and Judah split into two separate nations?

206.   Which group thundered for social justice during the period of the divided kingdom?

207.   Who spoke the words of God?

208.   Who defeated the priests of Baal?

208.   Where were the priests of Baal defeated?

209.   Who said, "Let justice well up as waters and righteousness like a mighty stream"?

210.   Who equated idolatry with adultery?

211.   Who said, "They shall beat their swords into ploughshares and their spears into pruning hooks"?

212.   Who was thrown into a pit for being a prophet?

213. Who fled from being a prophet?

213. Who was forced to prophesy after being swallowed by a fish?

214. Who warned Nineveh that they would be destroyed unless they changed their evil ways?

215. Who conquered Israel?

216. Who built a water tunnel that saved Jerusalem?

217. What nation destroyed our Temple and Jerusalem in 586 B.C.E.?

217. When was the First Temple destroyed (day, month, year)?

218. How do we refer to our having been expelled from the Land of Israel in 586 B.C.E.?

219. Who had a vision of a field of dry bones that came to life?

220. Who became governor of Judea after the exile?

221. Who brought the Torah back from Babylonia?

221. To what profession did Ezra belong?

222. What book of the TaNaCH praises the woman of valor?

223. Who suffered greatly for no apparent reason?

224. Who was thrown into a den of lions and survived?

225. Where can the Book of Esther be found in the TaNaCH?

226. Who was the great-grandmother of King David?

227. What are the books not accepted into the TaNaCH called?

229. What do we call customs coming from Spain and the Middle East?

229. What do we call customs coming from Northern Europe?

230. What do we call the ark where we keep the Torah?

231. Who writes a Torah scroll?

231. On what are Torah scrolls written?

231. With what does a sofer write?

232. What is the difference between a Sephardic and an Ashkenazic Torah?

233. The Torah is decorated to symbolize whom?

234. What are the wooden poles that hold a Torah scroll called?

235. What is a Torah pointer called?

236. What seven-branched candelabrum do many synagogues have?

237. What is the eternal light called?

238. Name the wall that separates men and women in an Orthodox synagogue.

239. What is the sign telling you which way is east called?

240.   What do we call the leader of a service?

241.   Name the raised area from which the sheliach tzibbur leads services.

242.   What is the Hebrew word for cantor?

243.   What is the Greek translation of the TaNaCH called?

244.   What is the Aramaic translation of the TaNaCH called?

245.   What is the printed book that contains the Torah called?

246.   What do we call the set portion from the Prophets that is read after the Torah portion?

247.   What is the Hebrew word for doorpost?

248.   What does the mezuzah contain?

248.   Who writes a mezuzah?

249.   What do we call the leather boxes that contain Torah passages commanding us to bind the mitzvot on our hand and have them between our eyes?

250.   What is the Hebrew word for fringes?

251.   What is a shawl with tzitzit on the four corners called?

252.   What is the Hebrew word for skullcap?

252.   What is the Yiddish word for skullcap?

253.   What is a round fur hat worn by Chasidic Jews called?

254.   What is a white robe worn on the Yamim Nora'im, on Pesach, and at a wedding called?

255.   What word means the mixing of wool and linen together?

256.   What are side curls called?

257.   What is the Jewish star called?

258.   What is the hand-shaped charm called?

259.   What is the rule about God's name once it has been written?

260.   Name the room where damaged scrolls and books are stored.

261.   What is a ritual bath called?

262.   What is the marriage ceremony called?

263.   What is a marriage contract called?

264.   What is a wedding canopy called?

265.   What are the seven blessings recited at a wedding?

266.   What is the offspring from a forbidden union called?

267.   Name the ceremony that annuls a man's responsibility to marry his childless brother's widow.

268.   What is a divorce document?

268. Who writes the divorce document?
269. What is a woman called whose husband has left without giving her a get?
270. What is the circumcision ceremony called?
271. Who performs the circumcision?
272. Who holds the baby during the circumcision?
273. According to the rabbis, who is a Jew?
274. According to the Reform Movement, who is a Jew?
275. According to the Torah text, who is a Jew?
276. What do we call the covenant ceremony for girls?
277. What is a Jew responsible for his or her actions called?
278. What is the ritual tearing of clothes called?
279. What is the liturgical statement that God is all-powerful?
280. What is the seven-day period of deep mourning called?
281. What is the mitzvah connected to a house of mourning?
282. What are the first thirty days of mourning called?
283. What is lit on the anniversary of a death?
284. What is the memorial service called?
285. How many blessings does a Jew traditionally say?
286. What is the blessing after eating called?
287. When do we say a blessing?
288. What is focusing on prayers called?
289. What is a quorum of ten Jews called?
290. What is a Shabbat/daily prayerbook called?
291. What are liturgical poems called?
292. What is the festival prayerbook called?
293. What is the traditional way of praying called?
294. What is swaying rhythmically while praying called?
295. How many daily prayer services are there?
296. What is the morning service called?
297. What is the afternoon service called?
298. What is the evening service called?
299. What is the Shabbat and festival additional service called?
300. How often are the Shema and its blessings recited each day?
301. What prayer reminds us of being saved at the Sea of Reeds?
302. What is the Standing Prayer?
302. What prayer on weekdays consists of nineteen prayers?

303.   What prayer quotes, "Holy, holy, holy"?

303.   From what prophet does the central sentence of the Kedushah come?

304.   What is the giving of the Priestly Blessing called?

305.   What is the statement of God's majesty called?

306.   At what times is Torah read?

307.   What are the cantillation notes for chanting Torah and Haftarah called?

308.   What is the honor of being called to the Torah called?

309.   Who chants the Torah?

310.   What is the honor of lifting the Torah called?

310.   What is the honor of rolling the Torah called?

311.   Who was the Jewish historian who lived during the Roman period?

312.   Who took over Judea after the Hasmoneans?

313.   Who made Herod king of Judea?

314.   Who was responsible for an enormous number of building projects in Roman Judea?

315.   Who enlarged the Temple Mount in order to make the Second Temple larger?

315.   Who enlarged the Second Temple?

316.   How did Herod make so many enormous buildings?

317.   Who build Masada?

317.   Where is Masada?

318.   What was the political party of the priests?

319.   What was the political party of the rabbis?

320.   What is the Hebrew term for life after earthly life?

321.   What group dropped out of normal Jewish society and wrote the Dead Sea Scrolls?

322.   Where were the Dead Sea Scrolls found?

323.   What happened when Herod died?

324.   During what period did Jesus live?

325.   What is the name of the place where many Christians believe Jesus was killed, buried, and rose on the third day?

326.   What is the difference in belief between Christians and Jews concerning Jesus?

327.   What was the Jewish Supreme Court called?

328.   The Sanhedrin consisted of how many rabbis?

329.   What were the sages of the Roman period called?

330.   For how long did the Tanna'im make Oral Law?

331.   Who said, "What is hateful to you, don't do to anyone else"?

332.   What were the two most famous law schools of the Pharisees?

333.   What are TaNaCH-based stories called?

334.   What are rabbinic stories not based on TaNaCH called?

335.   Name a Jewish philosopher of the Roman period.

336.   Who destroyed the Second Temple?

336.   When was the Second Temple destroyed?

337.   What is the Western Wall called?

338.   What did the Romans build to conquer Masada?

339.   Where did more than 900 Jews decide to die rather than become prisoners of the Romans?

340.   Who established a law school at Yavneh?

341.   Who gave Yochanan ben Zakkai permission to establish a law school at Yavneh?

342.   What is the Hebrew word for Jewish law?

343.   Who became the authority in Judaism when the Temple was destroyed?

343.   Who lost authority when the Temple was destroyed?

344.   What is the ceremony ordaining a rabbi called?

345.   What is the first assumption of rabbinic Judaism?

345.   According to rabbinic Judaism, what was given at Mount Sinai?

345.   According to rabbinic Judaism, who has the authority to explain halachah?

346.   What serves as a substitute for the sacrifices?

347.   Which great rabbi began studying when he was 40?

348.   What rabbi supported the Bar Kochba Revolt?

350.   Which Roman emperor made Judaism illegal?

351.   What did the Romans do to ten rabbis after the Bar Kochba Revolt?

352.   Who said, "Kill the best of the non-Jews."

353.   According to tradition, who wrote the *Zohar*?

354.   What is the central book of Kabbalah?

355.   What is Jewish mysticism?

356.   Who edited the Mishnah?

357.   What is the Written Law called?

358.   What do we call laws of the Tanna'im that didn't get into the Mishnah?

359.   Name the six chapters of wisdom in the Mishnah about how to live.

360.   Who took the Mishnah to Babylonia?

361.   What do we call the law students who argued about the laws in the Mishnah?

362.   What do we call the discussions of the Amora'im?

363.   Mishnah + Gemara = ?

364.   According to tradition, who wrote the Talmud?

364.   According to tradition, when was the Talmud written?

365.   What did the Jewish law school in Tiberias write?

366.   In what language is most of the Gemara?

367.   What is the beginning resource book for Jewish law?

368.   Who represented Babylonian Jews to the non-Jewish authorities?

369.   From 200 to 1000 c.e. where were the greatest Jewish cultural centers?

370.   How did the Jews fare under Byzantine rule?

371.   Who were the great conquerers of the seventh century?

372.   What was the head of the Babylonian law schools called?

373.   Who was responsible for disseminating Talmud?

374.   What are answers to questions about halachah called?

375.   Who wrote the first Siddur?

376.   Which Jewish texts helped unify world Jewry for a while?

377.   Who wrote the first medieval book of Jewish philosophy?

378.   Which group of Jews didn't accept Rabbinic authority?

378.   Which group of Jews accepted Torah but not the Talmud?

379.   Who opposed the Karaites?

380.   What famous period lasted from 900 to 1300 c.e.?

381.   Who were the Muslims who slaughtered Jews in the 1100s?

382.   What happened to Jews during the First Crusade?

383.   What is dying as a Jewish martyr called?

384.   Who limited Ashkenazic Jewish men to one wife?

385.   Who was a Jewish general for the Muslims in Spain?

386.   Who wrote the most important TaNaCH commentary?

388. What two commentaries are found surrounding the text on every page of the TaNaCH?

389. Who wrote the most widely read commentary to the Talmud?

390. What two commentaries are found on every page of the Talmud?

391. Who was one of the great Tosafists?

392. Who wrote poems about Zion?

393. Who wrote *The Kuzari*?

394. Who traveled around the world describing different Jewish communities?

395. Who was the greatest medieval Jewish philosopher?

396. What is Maimonides' name in Hebrew?

397. Who wrote thirteen statements of Jewish faith?

398. Who wrote the *Mishneh Torah*?

399. What was RaMBaM's fourteen-volume code of law?

400. Who described eight steps of tzedakah?

400/401. What did RaMBaM write? (See also 397, 398.)

401. Who wrote the *Guide of the Perplexed*?

402. What was Nachmanides called in Hebrew?

403. What great TaNaCH commentator created a synagogue in Jerusalem?

404. What were false accusations of killing non-Jewish children for Jewish ritual called?

405. What was the first country to expel all Jews?

406. What were Jews forced to wear in Christian countries?

407. What text did the Christians burn by the cartload?

408. What were Jews accused of in 1348 in Europe?

409. What happened in the fourteenth-century to Jews in France?

410. What did Spanish Christians call the Jews who had been forced to convert to Christianity?

411. What was set up to catch heretical Christians?

412. Who was head of the Inquisition in Spain?

413. When did Spain expel all Jews?

414. What is the language of Sephardic Jews?

414. What language is a combination of Spanish and Hebrew?

415. What language is a combination of German mixed with Hebrew and Slavic words?

416. Where was the first ghetto?

417.   Where did Lurianic Kabbalah flourish?

417.   When did Lurianic Kabbalah flourish?

418.   Who was said to have built a golem?

419.   Who wrote the *Shulchan Aruch*?

421.   What are the Ashkenazic additions to the *Shulchan Aruch* called?

421.   Who wrote the Ashkenazic additions to the *Shulchan Aruch*?

422.   Who led the Cossacks in riots against the Jews?

423.   Who was the false Messiah in the 1600s?

424.   What was the skill of resolving Talmudic problems called?

425.   What is a court of three rabbis called?

426.   What is someone called who is a Jewish legal authority?

427.   Who founded the Chasidic movement?

428.   What group believes that they can connect with God through joy?

429.   What do Chasidic Jews call their leader?

429.   What do Chasidic Jews believe about their leader?

430.   Who were the Jews opposed to the Chasidic Movement?

431.   Who were the first Jews to come to North America?

431.   Where did the first Jews in North America settle?

431.   From where did the first Jews to North American come?

431.   When did the first Jews come in North America?

433.   Who was excommunicated because of his beliefs?

434.   Who were the richest Jewish bankers in Europe?

435.   Who introduced European culture into the ghetto?

436.   What was the Enlightenment movement called?

437.   Where were Jews forced to live in Russia?

438.   What were little Russian villages called?

439.   Who wrote funny and sad Yiddish stories about the shtetl?

440.   What did we call Jews who stole children to meet the Russian army quota?

441.   Who gave Jews full French civil rights?

442.   What movement began as an attempt to keep Jews from converting?

443.   Who showed Jews how they could be both Orthodox and modern?

444. Why did large numbers of German Jews come to America in the 1840s?

445. What was the first and largest Jewish service organization?

446. What organization was founded to create better understanding between Christians and Jews on college campuses?

447. Who was one of the great pioneers of American Reform Judaism?

448. What was the first rabbinical seminary in the United States?

449. Who was one of the founders of the Conservative Movement?

450. Who founded the Reconstructionist Movement?

451. What were government-organized riots in Russia called?

452. How many Jews came to the United States between 1880 and 1920?

453. Who wrote the poem inscribed on the Statue of Liberty?

454. Where did new Jewish immigrants settle in New York?

455. What were Jews actively creating to help workers in early twentieth-century United States?

456. Which women's organizations support the Reform and Conservative Movements?

457. Which Russian Jew was the victim in 1911 of a Blood Accusation?

458. What happened in Europe from 1933 to 1945?

459. What was the enormous Nazi pogrom in November 1938 called?

460. What was the Nazi plan for the Jews?

461. How many Jews were slaughtered during the Holocaust?

462. Where did the Jews fight the Nazis?

463. Until the Holocaust, where were the greatest yeshivot and Jewish cultural centers?

464. In the 1950s and 1960s Jews were prominent in what major American social action movement?

465. What are small groups of Jews who study and celebrate Judaism together called?

466. Who was the first woman rabbi?

466. When was the first woman rabbi ordained?

467. What is WUPJ?

468. Who are the black Jews from Ethiopia?

469. What is the umbrella organization for forty-six Jewish institutions?

470.   Israel connects which two continents?

471.   What valley did merchants in ancient times have to go through to get from Mesopotamia to Egypt?

472.   What three ancient cities guarded the Yizrael Valley?

473.   What is a hill consisting of layers of old cities called?

474.   Name the 4,000-year-old port in Israel.

475.   Name the main port of Israel.

476.   What has happened frequently on Israel's coastal plain?

477.   What is the north of Israel called?

478.   What is the city of Kabbalah?

479.   What is the only fresh-water lake in Israel?

480.   What was the Roman capital of the Galilee?

481.   Where is there a beautiful synagogue mosaic floor?

482.   Name the city of the Samaritans.

483.   Name the mountain pass between Tel Aviv and Jerusalem.

484.   What cave in Hebron is holy to Muslims and Jews?

485.   What is the largest river in Israel?

486.   Name the world's oldest occupied city.

487.   What place on earth is the furthest below sea level?

488.   What is the large desert in the south of Israel?

489.   Name the modern city in the middle of the Negev.

490.   What Arab group lives in the Negev?

491.   What are the two Reform kibbutzim in Israel?

491.   Where are Yahel and Lotan located?

492.   Name the southernmost city in Israel.

493.   Who built more than 250 forts in the Land of Israel?

494.   What city is holy to Christians, Muslims, and Jews?

495.   What now stands on the Temple Mount?

496.   What is the third holiest spot in the world for Muslims?

496.   Where is the Mosque of al-Aqsa located?

497.   Where is Jerusalem's huge ancient cemetery?

497.   What is opposite the Mount of Olives?

498.   What is another name for all of Israel?

499.   Who ruled Palestine from 1520 to 1920?

500.   What ancient city in Israel in surrounded by a wall?

501.   Who built the first set of houses outside the Old City of Jerusalem?

501. Who built a windmill outside the Old City of Jerusalem?

502. When was the First Aliyah?

502. Who led the First Aliyah?

503. Who helped the Jews of the First Aliyah?

504. Who created the modern language of Hebrew?

505. Name the captain framed by the French army because he was a Jew.

506. Name the book written by Theodor Herzl in reaction to the Dreyfus trial.

507. What Jewish organization first met in 1897?

508. Who was the father of political Zionism?

509. What organization plants trees in Israel?

510. Who were the young idealists hoping to create a new world in Palestine?

511. Who believed that making the Land of Israel fertile was the highest imperative for a Jew?

512. What was the first Jewish defense group in Palestine?

513. Name the first kibbutz.

513. What group founded the first kibbutz?

514. When was Tel Aviv founded?

514. Where was Tel Aviv founded?

515. What was the Jewish community in Palestine called?

516. What army did the Jews support in World War I?

516. Whom did the Jews of Palestine fight in World War I?

517. Who founded the Zion Mule Corps?

518. What Jewish military group fought for the British in World War I?

518. Who helped found the Jewish military group that fought for the British in World War I?

519. What was the Jewish spy ring working for the British in World War I called?

520. What document promised the Jews a homeland in Palestine?

521. What settlement did the Arabs destroy?

522. Who said, "No matter. It is good to die for our country"?

523. Who first founded the Haganah?

524. Who was in charge of the Land of Israel from 1920 to 1948?

525. Who were the Pioneers?

525. Who comprised the Third Aliyah?

526.   Who founded Hadassah?

527.   Although European Jews were desperate to escape from Hitler, what did the British do?

528.   What organization saved thousands of children from the Nazis?

529.   What organization smuggled Jews into Palestine despite the British?

530.   What did the Jews build to protect themselves from marauding Arabs?

531.   Who founded the Irgun?

532.   Whom did the Jews join in World War II to fight the Nazis?

533.   Who trained the Palmach?

533.   What group comprised the top Jewish troops under the British?

534.   Who wrote, "Blessed is the match"?

535.   In what underground organization did Menachem Begin become the leader?

536.   When did the United Nations vote to partition Palestine?

537.   When was the State of Israel born?

538.   Who was the first prime minister of Israel?

539.   When did seven Arab armies attack Israel?

540.   What is Israel's parliament called?

541.   Who became the first president of Israel?

542.   Which law states that any Jew who comes to Israel can become a citizen of Israel?

543.   What action saved the Jews of Yemen in 1949?

544.   Name Israel's airline.

545.   How much did Israel's population change in the first three years of the state's existence?

546.   How did Israel integrate immigrants?

547.   What city was built in memory of the settlers killed at Tel Chai?

548.   What did Israel accept from Germany because of the Holocaust?

549.   Whom did Israel defeat in the Sinai Campaign?

550.   Whom did Israel execute for war crimes?

551.   What Arab organization's goal was to wipe out Israel?

552.   When did Israel take the Sinai Desert, the West Bank, and the Golan Heights?

553.   What city was united after the Six Day War?

554.   Who was Israel's defense minister during the Six Day War?

555.   Name Israel's only woman prime minister.

556.   When did Egypt attack Israel?

558.   What border crossing allows Arabs to enter into Israel for medical help?

559.   What document created peace between Israel and Egypt?

560.   Against whom did Israel initiate a war in 1982?

561.   Name Israel's capital.

562.   Name Israeli right-wing Jewish groups.

563.   What are all buildings in Jerusalem covered with?

564.   Where are Chagall's stained glass windows?

565.   Where are the offices of Israel's Chief Rabbis?

566.   Where do all Reform rabbinical and cantorial students spend their first year of study?

567.   What is the Reform Movement's Zionist Association?

568.   What was Israel's airlift of Ethiopian Jews called?

569.   When did the Intifada begin?

569.   Who began the Intifada?

570.   Who was defense minister at the time of the Intifada?

571.   Who was prime minister at the time of the Intifada?

572.   What is Israel's army called?

573.   What plan provided for the mass immigration of Soviet Jews to Israel?

574.   Who introduced the concept of ethical monotheism?

575.   Who wrote *The Essence of Judaism*?

576.   Who wrote *The Star of Redemption*?

577.   Who wrote *I and Thou*?

578.   Who wrote evocative books encouraging traditional Jewish practice?

579.   What is the mitzvah of giving money to the needy?

580.   What is the mitzvah of caring for others through special deeds?

581.   What is the mitzvah of providing hospitality to strangers?

582.   What is the mitzvah of visiting the sick?

583.   What is the mitzvah of caring for animals?

584.   What is a caring, good person called?

585. What is the value that preservation of human life transcends all other mitzvot?

586. What is the Hebrew word for a convert to Judaism?

587. What is the traditional way for a woman to convert to Judaism?

588. What are the two traditional actions involved in a man's converting to Judaism?

589. What is the discipline of the dietary laws called?

590. What makes an animal potentially kosher?

591. What makes a sea creature potentially kosher?

592. What two foods may not be mixed together?

593. What is a food that contains neither milk nor meat called?

594. What natural substance is forbidden to be consumed?

595. What is the name for a ritual slaughterer?

596. What is the term that indicates a food is forbidden for consumption?

597. Who makes sure that the laws of kashrut are maintained?

598. What is the traditional belief that God provides specific consequences for our actions?

599. What is the belief that because our ancestors were good, we get credit with God?

600. What is the Hebrew word for ethics?

601. What are the Hebrew words for good planet?

602. What is the Jewish position concerning free will?

603. What is an appropriate greeting on someone's birthday?

604. What is Hebrew numerology?

605. What is the traditional view on homosexuality?

606. What is the phrase for repairing the world?

607. What is the belief in resurrection called?

608. What is the halachic position on intermarriage?

609. What is the rabbinic position on gambling?

610. What is the Reform Movement's position on abortion?

611. What is the unity of the Jewish people?

612. What is the Hebrew word for truth?

613. What is the Hebrew word for hello, goodbye, and peace?

Index

About the Author

Rabbi David E. Cahn-Lipman was ordained in 1978 from Hebrew Union College-Jewish Institute of Religion, New York. He is Rabbi of Sinai Temple in Mount Vernon, New York, where he developed the Diad Learning Center and the Family Jewish Literacy Program. He is a member of The Central Conference of American Rabbis' Committee on Reform Jewish Practices, The Central Conference of American Rabbis' Committee on the Aging, and the Jewish Community Council of Mount Vernon. Rabbi Cahn-Lipman lives in Mount Vernon, New York, with his wife and two children.